BRITISH ENTREPRENEURSHIP IN POLAND

Modern Economic and Social History Series

General Editor: Derek H. Aldcroft

Titles in this series include:

Land, Proto-Industry and Population in Catalonia, c. 1680–1829
An Alternative Transition to Capitalism?
Julie Marfany

The Making of a World Trading Power
The European Economic Community (EEC) in the GATT Kennedy Round Negotiations (1963–67)
Lucia Coppolaro

Eastern European Railways in Transition
Nineteenth to Twenty-first Centuries
Edited by Ralf Roth and Henry Jacolin

Vicarious Consumers
Trans-National Meetings between the West and East in the Mediterranean World (1730–1808)
Manuel Pérez-García

National Identity and the Agrarian Republic
The Transatlantic Commerce of Ideas between America and France (1750–1830)
Manuela Albertone

The River Pollution Dilemma in Victorian England
Nuisance Law versus Economic Efficiency
Leslie Rosenthal

British Mail Steamers to South America, 1851–1965
A History of the Royal Mail Steam Packet Company and Royal Mail Lines
Robert E. Forrester

Money Pits: British Mining Companies in the Californian and Australian Gold Rushes of the 1850s
John Woodland

From Rail to Road and Back Again?
A Century of Transport Competition and Interdependency
Edited by Ralf Roth and Colin Divall

British Entrepreneurship in Poland

A Case Study of Bradford Mills at Marki near Warsaw, 1883–1939

SARAH DIETZ

Routledge
Taylor & Francis Group
LONDON AND NEW YORK

First published in paperback 2024

First published 2015 by Ashgate Publishing

Published 2016
by Routledge
4 Park Square, Milton Park, Abingdon, Oxon OX14 4RN

and by Routledge
605 Third Avenue, New York, NY 10158

Routledge is an imprint of the Taylor & Francis Group, an informa business

Publisher's Note
The publisher has gone to great lengths to ensure the quality of this reprint but points out that some imperfections in the original copies may be apparent.

British Library Cataloguing in Publication Data
A catalogue record for this book is available from the British Library

The Library of Congress has cataloged the printed edition as follows:
Dietz, Sarah.
British entrepreneurship in Poland : a case study of Bradford Mills at Marki near Warsaw, 1883–1939 / by Sarah Dietz.
pages cm.—(Modern economic and social history)
Includes bibliographical references and index.
ISBN 978-1-4724-4138-6 (hardcover)
1. Investments, British—Poland—History—19th century. 2. Investments, British—Poland—History—20th century. 3. Industrial policy—Poland—History. I. Title.
HG5587.D54 2015
338.8'8777310943841—dc23

2014048293

ISBN: 978-1-4724-4138-6 (hbk)
ISBN: 978-1-03-292234-8 (pbk)
ISBN: 978-1-315-57010-5 (ebk)

DOI: 10.4324/9781315570105

Contents

List of Figures

Acknowledgements

This book is dedicated to my late husband, John Haigh, who first showed me the Marki memoir of his great-grandfather John Hinchcliffe in the early 1990s. At that time I was working at Briggella Mills in Bradford and the story of the firm's Polish sister company, Bradford Mills at Marki, was largely forgotten. Hinchcliffe's unpublished memoir began with his first train journey across Europe in 1910 and ended with his dramatic escape into Russia as the Germans advanced on Warsaw in the summer of 1915. It is full of affectionate descriptions of afternoon teas in Warsaw's luxurious Hotel Bristol, riotous nights of drinking in the Marki social club and more than one dramatic report of being threatened at gunpoint in the lawless suburbs of Warsaw, but provides very little information about factory life in Poland. Nevertheless, it inspired my interest in the subject and a trove of family letters and postcards exchanged between Marki and Bradford from 1910 to 1924 provided a more intimate portrait of expatriate life in the remote factory settlement. Thus my connection with this subject is both personal and professional: my career in Bradford's textile industry and our family history in Marki have encouraged almost a decade's research into why and how Bradford's Briggs-Posselt partnership built a factory and town in Poland in 1883 and what became of it.

I consider myself privileged to have had the guidance of Dr James Gregory of the University of Plymouth, Dr Gábor Bátonyi of the University of Bradford and Professor Derek Aldcroft of the University of Leicester. I am enormously grateful to Anna Wawrzyniak, née Ptasinska, for her assistance throughout this project: for facilitating my interviews with the mayor of Marki, Janusz Werczyński, local historian Zbigniew Paciorek, residents of Briggs' factory housing at Marki and with Dr Piotr Jaworski, senior curator of the *Centralne Muzeum Włókiennictwa* in Łódź. In the interests of historical research we have also enjoyed many leisurely afternoon teas in the Hotel Bristol! I offer heartfelt thanks to Anna Draniewicz for her patience and dedication in teaching me the Polish language and involving me in Polish cultural events in Bradford. I am indebted to both Olga Lawler and Alexander Magen for translations of the Russian sources and would like to thank Ghislaine Young for her assistance with the nineteenth-century French texts, as well as a great deal of general encouragement.

Dr Jochen Ostermeyer, great-grandson of Ernst Posselt, generously shared his recollections with me and I thank Dr Annette Frese, curator of Posselt's art collection at the *Kurpfälzische Museum*, for her hospitality in Heidelberg. I am grateful for the interest and advice of Professor Andrew Popp of the University of Liverpool Management School, Colum Giles of English Heritage, Ewa Wartalska at the *Muzeum Wojska Polskiego*, Dr Marcin Górski at the Faculty of Architecture for Warsaw University of Technology and Dr Mary Blewett of the University of Massachusetts, Mark Keighley, the author of *Wool City*, and Dr Andrzej Suchcitz of the Sikorski Institute in London. My particular thanks go to the Saltaire Historians, David King and David Shaw, who provided the answers to so many of my questions about Bradford, Saltaire and the Salt's foreign direct investments in the USA.

The assistance of residents of the Briggs brothers' former homes in Ilkley: Tim Edwards at Westwood Lodge, David Wiley at Hebers Mount and also Dairine Nethercott at Briggella Mills in Bradford has been much appreciated. I would like to acknowledge the research of a community of amateur genealogists with connections to Marki: particularly Nancy Peel, Teresa Baron, née Lilpop, and my own father-in-law Ralph Haigh who preserved the Hinchcliffe letters and memoir which have provided so much useful insight for this case study. Finally, I would like to thank my friends and family, making special mention of Anita Southwell and Fionna and Peter Harnett who all told me to write this book, and especially my late parents, Doreen and David Dietz, for all their support and encouragement.

Sarah Dietz

List of Translations and Abbreviations

Polish Periodicals and Newspapers

Czas	Time
Czerwony Sztandar	Red Flag
Dziennik Łódźki	Łódź Daily Journal
Dziennik Warszawski	Warsaw Daily Journal
Gazeta Bankowa	Banking Gazette
Gazeta Handlowa	Commercial Gazette
Gazeta Losowań Papierów Publicznych	Public Securities Gazette
Gazeta.pl	Warsaw Gazette online
Gazeta Robotnicza	Workers' Gazette
Gazeta Rzemieślnicza	Craftsman's Gazette
Gazeta Sądowa Warszawska	Warsaw Judicial Gazette
Gazeta Warszawska	Warsaw Gazette
Głos: dziennik polityczny	The Voice: a political journal
Kurjer Asekuracyjny	Assurance Courier
Kurjer Codzienna	Daily Courier
Kurjer Kolejowy	Rail Courier
Kurjer Warszawski	Warsaw Courier
Kwartalnik Architektury i Urbanistyki	Architecture and Urban Planning Quarterly
Kwartalnik Historii Kultury Materialnej	History and Material Culture Quarterly
Nowinny Codzienne	Daily News
Polski Słownik Biograficzny	Polish Dictionary of National Biography
Prawda	Truth: Political, Social and Literary Weekly
Przegląd Katolicki	Catholic Review
Przegląd Techniczny	Technical Review
Przegląd Tygodniowy	Weekly Review
Rozwój	Development
Tygodnik Illustrowany	Weekly Illustrated

Archives

AGAD	*Archiwum Główne Akt Dawnych* [Central Archive of Historical Records in Warsaw]
APW	*Archiwum Państwowe w Warszawie* [National Archives in Warsaw]
FO	British Foreign Office documents accessed at the National Archives at Kew
HC	House of Commons records accessed via Hansard
PBN	*Państwowe Biuro Notarialne w Warszawie Archiwum* [Archive of the National Notaries Office in Warsaw]
WYAS	West Yorkshire Archive Service, Bradford and Wakefield

The Russian and European calendars were used simultaneously in nineteenth-century Poland, thus most official documents quoted in this book show both. For this reason, although most of the Polish press references are dated, the issue number identifies the source more reliably.

The abbreviated title *Textile World* has been used for the Bradford trade journal *Textile World Included with the Yorkshire Inventor.* The misspelling of Łódź and Białystok which appears in most nineteenth-century British press reports and much British-language correspondence of the period as Lodz and Bialystok has been corrected.

Modern Economic and Social History Series General Editor's Preface

Economic and social history has been a flourishing subject of scholarly study during recent decades. Not only has the volume of literature increased enormously but the range of interest in time, space and subject matter has broadened considerably so that today there are many sub-branches of the subject which have developed considerable status in their own right.

One of the aims of this series is to encourage the publication of scholarly monographs on any aspect of modern economic and social history. The geographical coverage is world-wide and contributions on the non-British themes will be especially welcome. While emphasis will be placed on works embodying original research, it is also intended that the series should provide the opportunity to publish studies of a more general thematic nature which offer a reappraisal or critical analysis of major issues of debate.

Derek H. Aldcroft
University of Leicester

Introduction

In December 1882 Edward Briggs, a Bradford worsted manufacturer, wrote to the British consul at Warsaw announcing his intention to build a factory in Russian Poland. By the end of the following month, the industrialist and his partners had purchased a 75-acre estate of undeveloped land at Marki outside Warsaw where they laid the foundations of a business which would endure for generations. With blueprints drawn up in Bradford, under the supervision of a Polish architect, the venture capitalists built a state-of-the-art worsted-manufacturing plant and British-style model industrial village. While construction was underway they recruited 100 Polish girls from the surrounding countryside and, provided with decent clothes and shoes, dispatched them to England to learn factory skills.[1]

From family politics, economic depression and rising foreign protectionism, to the significant attractions of unexploited resources and burgeoning markets in the Russian empire, this book explores the complex rationale which led the already wealthy and successful businessmen Edward Briggs, his younger brother John and Bradford-based German merchant-industrialist Ernst Posselt to embark on a visionary foreign enterprise in the Polish lands. The formation and organisation of the partnership is considered against the backdrop of Bradford's industrial history and the socio-economic and political factors which encouraged the venture capitalists to target Poland are described. The various facets of the entrepreneurs' strategy for the foreign enterprise are explored, including their methods to engender the cooperation of Warsaw's commercial elite, their utilisation of state-of-the-art technology, their highly selective employment policy and recruitment of skilled staff from Bradford. The latter part of the book charts the firm's fortunes: from its meteoric rise and huge expansion within its first decade to the tactics employed by the Bradford men to negotiate local socio-political turbulence, war and economic uncertainty in the twentieth century.

Throughout this book the influence of British industrial experience on numerous aspects of this foreign enterprise will be explored. Nevertheless, in its organisational structure and mode of operation Briggs, Posselt and Co., Marki is identified not as a branch of the founders' Bradford businesses or a facility for cheap off-shore processing, but as an independent company with a carefully tailored strategy for the commercial environment of the host nation. In a period of extraordinary economic dynamism for Warsaw, through membership of the city's influential Evangelical-Augsburg church and local intermarriage, the Bradford

1 'Polskie dzieci w Anglji' ['Polish children in England'], *Kurjer Warszawski*, No. 166b, 22 June/4 July 1883, p. 3.

men integrated their interests with those of the local cosmopolitan elite. Through collaboration with the city's wealthiest industrialists and financiers, as well as with the Tsarist president Sokrates Starynkiewicz,[2] they extended their activities into other branches of textile manufacture, as well as railway building, tanning and dairy farming.

Marki was described in the British press as 'a second edition of Saltaire' and by the author Coningsby Dawson as 'the Polish Bournville or Port Sunlight'.[3] Such comparisons convey the founders' ambitions rather than evidence that their foreign enterprise was a direct emulation of the model communities built by their industrialist peers Salt, Cadbury or Lever. Nevertheless, this study will reveal the socio-political circumstances resulting from the complicated historiography of the Polish lands, which led British-style industrial paternalism to be particularly appropriate for Marki. Further to this, the regional influence of the partnership's program of social-overhead investment for mass-workforce management on both their Warsaw circle and on developing Russian factory legislation is shown.

It is worth mentioning here that the chapter titles used in this book reflect some popular contemporary attitudes to the subject matter. For example, the outspoken Polish newspaper editor Aleksander Świętochowski famously decried what he viewed as the exploitative foreign ownership of Polish industry as 'goods to the east and profits to the west' which is the title of Chapter 4.[4] He argued that foreign industrial investment did nothing to enrich the region's economy because both its products and profits were exported. Conversely, this study reveals the significant contribution made by the cosmopolitan bourgeoisie to Warsaw's municipal and cultural infrastructure and their rationale for frequently, if not customarily, reinvesting their business profits in the locality. Chapter 7 appropriates Gerhart von Schultze-Gävernitz's general characterisation of nineteenth-century Russian industry as 'a piece of England on Russian soil'.[5] But although the empire's factories certainly relied on British machinery and skills, the chapter explains the reasons that new plants abroad were actually equipped to a far higher technological standard than their contemporary British counterparts. Chapter 9, entitled 'English foremen, English machinery and English business methods',[6] reflects a British-press description of the Marki venture and relies heavily on the letters and memoirs

[2] Starynkiewicz (the Polish translation of the Russian name) was Warsaw's 19th president from 1875–92.

[3] *Illustrated Weekly Telegraph*, Bradford, 19 March 1886, p. 1, Coningsby Dawson, *It Might Have Happened to You* (London: John Lane The Bodley Head Ltd, 1921), p. 111.

[4] J. Jedlicki, *A Suburb of Europe: Nineteenth-Century Polish Approaches to Western Civilization* (Budapest, New York: Central European University Press, 1999), p. 279.

[5] Gerhart von Schultze-Gävernitz, *Volkswirtschaftliche Studien aus Russland* [*Economic Studies from Russia*] (Leipzig: Verlag von Duncker and Humblot, 1899), p. 97.

[6] 'Edward Briggs' Obituary', *Yorkshire Weekly Post*, 12 March 1898.

of the Yorkshiremen – the skilled foremen and managers – who were recruited by the Briggs-Posselt partnership in the late nineteenth and early twentieth centuries.[7]

In researching this subject, two nineteenth-century Polish literary works have proved extremely informative. The title of Chapter 6, 'Your word is gold and your friendship a good security', is borrowed from the novel *Ziemia obiecana* [*The Promised Land*] by the Polish Nobel laureate Władysław Reymont.[8] In a fortuitous parallel with this case study, Reymont charts the fortunes of three international partners who established a factory in the industrial city of Łódź in the mid-1880s. The novel highlights the commonly held negative view of particularly German and Jewish industrialists and their apparently mercenary business behaviour. The influential Positivist author Bolesław Prus, known as the Polish Dickens,[9] provides particularly useful perspective on Warsaw's divided society in his seminal work *Lalka* [*The Doll*]. His subject matter is the clash of cultures between old and new money, class, cosmopolitanism and religion in the last quarter of the nineteenth century.[10]

Despite the appalling devastation of Warsaw and Marki during the Second World War some of the abundance of nineteenth-century Tsarist bureaucracy has survived to provide valuable insight for this case study. An 1883 petition by the Bradford partners' to Russian finance minister Bunge shows the industrialists' ambitions for Marki to achieve the scale and importance of Scheibler, the leviathan cotton manufacturer of Łódź and of the empire's foremost linen concern, Hielle and Dietrich of Żyrardów.[11] The records of the *Warszawskiego Komitetu Przemysłowego* [Warsaw Committee for Industry] reveal the venture capitalists' intention to create a monopoly for British worsted in the Russian empire.[12] The contemporary Polish press and state industrial surveys show Marki's growing workforce and productive capacity, whereas factory inspectors' and police reports detail the workplace and housing conditions in the industrial settlement. The British Foreign Office archive has been a significant source for this case study. The letters of the consul, Colonel Francis Cornwallis Maude, provide a rare firsthand account of the Bradford men's *modus operandi* in Warsaw: smoking cigarettes and reading the newspapers at the British consulate, fact-finding in Łódź and Białystok,

7 Most notably the letters and memoir of Marki's electrical engineer John Hinchcliffe.

8 Władysław Reymont, *The Promised Land* [*Ziemia obiecana*, 1898], trans. M.H. Dziewicki (New York: Alfred A. Knopf, 1927).

9 William John Rose, *Poland Old and New* (London: G. Bell and Sons, 1948), p. 221.

10 Bolesław Prus, *The Doll* [*Lalka*, 1887], trans. David Welsh (Budapest: Central European Classics, 1996).

11 AGAD, *Akta Warszawskiego Komitetu Przemysłowego z 1883 r* [Evidence of the Warsaw committee for industry for the year 1883] includes an undated letter written in French from the Bradford partners to finance minister Bunge in St Petersburg, signature 11/1883.

12 Ibid.

brokering deals with the local business elite and even sending a donation of rubles to Queen Victoria to mark her Golden Jubilee in 1887.[13]

This book is entitled *British Entrepreneurship in Poland*, but it must be acknowledged that this description is technically incorrect on two scores: this is a case study of Anglo-German entrepreneurship and Poland did not exist as an independent nation until the last two decades of the enterprise. Before 1918, Warsaw and the east of Poland constituted a region of the Russian empire known as either Congress Poland or the Kingdom of Poland, which is generally described as Russian Poland in English-language scholarship. However, there were both commercial and political reasons for the British branding of the business in the nineteenth century. The primary aim of the firm was to emulate the products of Bradford's industry as closely as possible and there was a palpable local prejudice against the products of national industry which were described in the Polish press as a fashionable 'mania for foreignness'.[14] At the same time, Poland's nineteenth-century business arena was dominated by ethnically German Protestant businessmen, but the ruling Tsarist regime, despite longstanding policies to attract foreign capital to the region, encouraged anti-German feeling among the Poles. Thus it was politic for the technically Anglo-German Briggs, Posselt and Co., of Marki to convey a strong British identity until the early twentieth century. Indeed the Posselt family, despite continuing close association with their homeland, maintained British citizenship until long after the Second World War. However, in an increasingly nationally charged political climate after 1905 and particularly in the interwar period '"Polishness" became the touchstone of respectability'.[15] Thus Chapter 11 shows the efforts of the region's industrialists to Polonise their image and reveals how second and particularly third generations of the Briggs family asserted their Polish credentials in order to maintain an integral place in the Second Polish Republic's business elite. Chapter 12, under the inscription 'the immensity of the calamity and the want of financial and material means',[16] considers the political legacy of long-term Tsarist rule, the Russian Revolution and the devastation of the First World War on the implementation of Polish independence after 1918. The asset stripping of the Marki plant and the owners' difficulties securing replacement equipment as the value of their reinvestment capital was progressively diminished by hyperinflation is described. Nevertheless, the resilience and resourcefulness of the surviving Briggs brother, Alfred, and his nephew, Charles Whitehead, to rebuild their Polish business in an entirely transformed economic environment is revealed.

---

13 FO640/12, log of correspondence, 12 May 1887, p. 80.

14 'Wystawa tkacka' ['Weaving exhibition'], *Gazeta Warszawska*, 4 February, 1888, p. 2.

15 Norman Davies, *God's Playground: A History of Poland Volume II 1795 to the Present* (New York: Columbia University Press, 1982), p. 404.

16 M. Bornstein Łychowska, *Ten Years Social Policy in Poland, 1918–1928* (Warsaw: Ministry of Labour and Social Welfare, 1928), p. 72.

Soviet accounts of Polish industrialisation generally betray a typically Marxist bias towards the growing politicisation of the working classes and stereotypical characterisations of the industrialists as 'blood-sucking' capitalists.[17] This attitude has arguably endured in the consciousness of Polish historians who favour cultural or military histories with a more positive national connotation than subjects of commerce and industry. The recent work of Janusz Miliszkiewicz and journalist Jerzy S. Majewski to record the integral part played in the history of Poland by the nineteenth-century cosmopolitan bourgeoisie has gone some way to redress the balance.[18] But despite local pride and a proliferation of local histories about Marki,[19] Ewa Wartalska's 1987 article in *Kwartalnik historii kultury materialnej* [*History and Material Culture Quarterly*] is the only published-previously scholarly work to explore the extraordinary achievements of the Briggs-Posselt partnership and their enterprise remains largely unknown outside Poland.[20] This book provides a comprehensive transnational account of the Marki venture, using British, German, Polish and Russian resources to inform its findings, to provide a fresh perspective on Polish industrialisation and the impact of British entrepreneurship abroad in the nineteenth and early twentieth centuries.

[17] Janusz Miliszkiewicz, *Polskie gniazda rodzinne* [*Polish Family Nest*] (Warsaw: ISKRY, 2003), note, Miliszkiewicz's chapter about the Briggs' great-nephew, Karol Whitehead, is entitled 'Uroczy krwiopijca' ['The charming bloodsucker'] to highlight the Soviet view not to perpetuate it.

[18] Ibid. and Jerzy S. Majewski, 'Dyskretny urok burżuazji przy Królewskiej' ['Discreet charm of the bourgeoisie on Królewska street'], *Gazeta.pl*, 11 June 2010, accessed at http://warszawa.gazeta.pl.

[19] Zbigniew Paciorek and Grzegorza P. Dudzika, *Mareckie zeszyty historyczne* [*Historical Record of Marki*] (Marki: Urząd Miasta Marki, 2007) and Czesław Brodzicki, *Marki koło Warszawy* [*Marki in the Area of Warsaw*] (Marki: Urząd Miasta Marki, 2002) among many more.

[20] E. Wartalska, 'Fabryka i osada fabryczna w Markach w latach 1883–1945' ['The factory and the workers' community at Marki 1883–1945'], *Kwartalnik historii kultury materialnej*, Warsaw (1987).

Chapter 1

'We may join together faithfully to raise our fortunes':[1] Britain's economic climate and the formation of the partnership in 1883

Bradford Mills at Marki, the factory and town built near Warsaw in 1883, was arguably established in response to three complex factors: the contemporary British socio-economic environment, personal motivations and the perception of growing prospects abroad. This chapter will consider Bradford's economic development and explain why industrialisation attracted foreign entrepreneurs to England during the nineteenth century. The commercial cooperation and financial interdependence that developed between these migrant traders and British industrialists will be described as a precedent for the Briggs-Posselt partnership. It will show the impact of growing competition on Bradford's industry and how the resultant drive to export and development of foreign raw-materials resources exposed manufacturers to the volatilities of world trade. The growing international acuity of British businessmen which led to significant capital export by the end of the nineteenth century will be highlighted.

Capital and Technology

Depictions of the practical men of England's northern cities, harnessing steam power and developing technology in dedicated factories, is a well-recognised portrayal of the Industrial Revolution. The accompanying transformation from a rural to urban existence for the majority of the population has been generally considered a matter of 'production rather than trade or finance'.[2] However, such stereotypes underestimate the central importance of capital – both cash and credit provision – to facilitate the explosive industrial and economic growth. Technology and capital were inextricably linked in the development of manufacturing and securing Britain's place as the hub of international commerce during the nineteenth century.

---

1 Menna Prestwich, *Cranfield: Politics and Profits Under the Early Stuarts* (Oxford: Clarendon Press, 1966), p. 72.

2 Stanley Chapman review of *Merchants to Multinationals: British Trading Companies in the Nineteenth and Twentieth Centuries* by Geoffrey Jones (New York: Oxford University Press, 2000), *Journal of Economic History*, 61: 4 (2001), pp. 1111–13.

In the pre-industrial era London was the institutional heart of the nation's economy where aristocratic landowners, educated in ancient public schools, subscribed to Conservative politics and controlled the national wealth.[3] During the nineteenth century a powerful middle class, a largely Liberal bourgeoisie, emerged particularly in the manufacturing strongholds of northern England. A social gulf developed between the so-called 'consumers' England' and 'producers' England'[4] that is often characterised as the north-south divide. This ideological difference between the 'gentlemanly capitalists'[5] who dominated banking and the provincial industrialists came to define British economic development in this period; in the seats of old money there was an 'institutionalized distrust of non-gentlemen'.[6] Thus in Manchester, Leeds and Bradford and in ports such as Liverpool and Hull, trade and industry flourished without the support of the traditional banking elite or the government, whose reluctance towards industrial investment and low opinion of commerce generally formed a strong literary theme in this period.[7] The manufacturers, despite their often extraordinary wealth and undoubted social aspirations, were not considered to 'speak the same language as the aristo-financial elite'.[8] This entrenched social hierarchy played a significant role in determining both the character of Britain's industrialising cities and creating opportunity for foreign-merchant financiers. New business remained outside the control of the old order, free to determine its own methods and culture; characterised by a political and religious non-conformity which 'symbolised a rejection of traditional values and an assertion of independence'.[9]

Bradford's Germans

Bradford's 'sudden leap from humble obscurity to the dignity of a trade metropolis'[10] was generated by industrialisation. In 1801 the town had just 6,000 inhabitants, but

---

3 C.H. Lee, 'The Service Sector, regional specialisation and economic growth in the Victorian economy', *Journal of Historical Geography*, x (1984), p. 154.

4 J.A. Hobson, 'The General Election', *Sociological Review* (1910), p. 113.

5 P.J. Cain and A.G. Hopkins, 'Gentlemanly Capitalism and British Expansion Overseas II: New Imperialism, 1850–1945', *Economic History Review*, New Series, 40: 1 (Feb, 1987) p. 1.

6 M. Lisle-Williams, 'Beyond the market: the survival of family capitalism in English merchant banks', *British Journal of Sociology*, xx (1984), pp. 246 and 254.

7 Elizabeth Gaskell, *North and South* (London: Chapman and Hall, 1855), Charles Dickens, *Hard Times* (London: Estes and Lauriat, 1890), Anthony Trollope, *The Way We Live Now* (London: Chapman and Hall, 1875).

8 Cain and Hopkins, 'Gentlemanly Capitalism', p. 6.

9 Rosemary E. Chadwick, *Church and People in Bradford and District 1880–1914: The Protestant Churches in an Urban Industrial Environment* (DPhil St Hilda's College, Oxford, 1986), p. 6.

10 J. Burnley, *West Riding Sketches* (Bradford: Hodder and Stoughton, 1875), p. 35.

abundant coal, iron and stone reserves and a local tradition of domestic spinning and weaving which supplemented agricultural incomes were the ingredients of its future prosperity. Burgeoning technology transformed this rural craft into city-based factory production and by 1881, with the inclusion of the districts of Bowling and Manningham, the census recorded a population of over 180,000. Early industrialisation was necessarily financed with steadily accumulated profits, but as technological development gathered pace, the swift adoption of new machinery, stock-piling of raw materials and general expansion became imperative to keep abreast of the competition. While the capital requirements of this rapidly growing industry were unmet by the existing banking system, the demand for larger and more diverse sales outlets to absorb the increasing output also escalated. Thus, the prospects for industrial investors and suppliers of credit developed in tandem with the need for national and international sales expertise.

Stanley Chapman observes that 'capital is mobile and moves to the international centre where it will earn most, and its owners commonly follow it there'.[11] Britain's entrenched social hierarchy and rapid industrial development combined to create a climate of extraordinary opportunity for foreign entrepreneurs and led to what J.B. Priestley described as a 'friendly invasion'[12] of notably German merchants. These economic migrants perceived a lack of mercantile experience to be exploited,[13] where the indifference of the English moneyed classes would allow them to take advantage of diverse commercial opportunities. From England's provincial cities, these foreign traders became instrumental in the formation of the modern international banking system and 'significant agents of economic growth'[14] for the host nation until the First World War.

The success of these nineteenth-century foreign businessmen is generally considered to lie in their international connections consolidated through extended-family ties, their wealth and banking expertise. Their superior technical education is often alluded to and their linguistic proficiency naturally set them apart from their British counterparts.[15] Although many of these attributes undoubtedly had a strong basis in fact, it must be considered that self-promotion was a substantial part of their strategy. Rather than fixed assets and manufacturing output, the merchants'

[11] Stanley Chapman, *Merchant Enterprise in Britain: From the Industrial Revolution to World War I* (New York and Cambridge: Cambridge University Press, 1992), p. 29, and P.L. Cottrell, *British Overseas Investment in the Nineteenth Century* (London: Macmillan, 1975), p. 28, 'capital flowed internationally to where it received the highest rate of return'.

[12] J.B. Priestley, *English Journey* (London: William Heinemann, 1934), p. 158.

[13] Geoffrey Jones, *Merchants to Multinationals; British Trading Companies in the Nineteenth and Twentieth Centuries* (Oxford: Oxford University Press, 2000), p. 288.

[14] Chapman, *Merchant Enterprise in Britain*, p. 4.

[15] F. Otto Metzenthin, 'Technical Education in Germany', *Yorkshire College Textile Students Magazine*, Leeds, J.W. Bean and Son, II: 1 (8 Nov 1895), p. 14 and in Michael Le Guillou, 'Technical Education 1850–1914', in *Where Did we Go Wrong? Industry, Education and Economy of Victorian Britain*, eds Gordon Roderick and Michael Stephens (Lewes: Falmer Press, 1981), pp. 173–84.

business was largely based on commercial intelligence, marketing and some less tangible quality which, in a modern context, might be described as interpersonal skills: the ability to instil confidence and forge friendships. A carefully honed reputation enabled them to build cooperative partnerships and political alliances, to improve the trading environment generally, develop new international markets and ultimately further their own profit potential. The customary trust-based dealing of this foreign contingent was similar to the manufacturers' habitual business behaviour. But their cosmopolitanism and superficially non-industrial activities that were 'associated with high status and gave access to political influence'[16] allowed them to form a useful intermediary group between Britain's industrialists and the moneyed elite.

Bradford's Germans are often presented as a homogenous group, their national origins, social activities and congregated operations in a district of the city known as Little Germany suggest united motivations and occupations.[17] In fact they were a diverse selection of predominantly Prussians and Germans of many religious denominations and political persuasions, from all social classes and with very broad-ranging business interests. While a few claimed sanctuary from religious or political persecution, the majority were either independent economic migrants or missives sent by foreign firms.[18] Despite the diversity of the group it is clear that the ambitious immigrants shared a single strategy to foster trust, develop prestige and successfully embed themselves in British commercial circles in the nineteenth century. All cast off their foreignness, played down less-acceptable religious affiliations and enthusiastically embraced British culture. A typical description was made of Nicolas Heydemann who arrived in Bradford in 1852 and reputedly 'associated himself with everything that was British. So much so that he became a naturalised Briton as soon as he could'.[19]

British citizenship, although regularly advanced as a veritable badge of national loyalty, did not preclude continuing German nationality. It was a standard requirement for a range of business activities such as operating a bank account or paying tax and also afforded the protection of the British state and law to international traders. However, beyond the practical efficacy of assuming British credentials, Humbert Wolfe, the son of a Bradford merchant, describes a more-concerted cultural adaptation by Bradford's German community who 'eagerly

16 Cain and Hopkins, 'Gentlemanly Capitalism', p. 18.

17 Norman Ellis, *Towards Little Germany* (Bradford: Low Moor Local History Group, 1997), A.A. Rollin, 'Builders of Bradford', *Jewish Historical Society of England*, Vol. XVII (1950/51), pp. 45–51.

18 Rosemary Ashton, *Little Germany: Exile and Asylum in Victorian England* (Oxford: Oxford University Press, 1986), J.B. Priestley, *Margin Released* (London: William Heinemann, 1962), p. 65 describes some as 'liberal refugees from Frankfurt and Leipzig'.

19 *N. Heydemann and Co., Bradford 1852–1952* (Bradford: privately published, 1952).

accepted all the habits of the English'.[20] His memoir recalls that, far from retaining their native tongue and continental customs, his father's contemporaries 'used Yorkshire phrases, and clipped their vowels ... The men at the weekends smoked unusually large pipes, drank whiskey-and-sodas, and wore Norfolk jackets, alarmingly checked, and the thickest of heather mixture stockings underneath their breeches'.[21]

It is impossible to generalise about individual motives, whether this studied assimilation was a matter of philosophical conviction or purely to achieve social acceptance, and Chapman does highlight that, despite a relative social tolerance, 'there was much hostility to Jews, who were widely regarded as dishonest'.[22] But Wolfe's account suggests that the determined integration was more than a business tactic and a genuine aspiration towards British culture which led immigrant businessmen of all religious persuasions to educate their children in the English virtues while the young men 'were experts on cricket averages'.[23] These businessmen liberally sponsored civic facilities such as art galleries, libraries, theatres and clubs, were enthusiastic participants in local sports and prolific donors to charities. Perhaps paradoxically considering their resolve to appear thoroughly English, the foreign merchants' cooperation in social and infrastructural investment is considered to have created a cosmopolitan character in cities such as Bradford, which became the focus of much retrospective pride for writers such as Wolfe and Priestley. The latter peppered his work with nostalgic descriptions of his home city where a 'dash of the Rhine and the Oder found its way into our grim runnel' and its suburbs 'reached as far as Frankfurt and Leipzig'.[24]

There are many common misconceptions about the nineteenth-century German merchants in Britain: that they were all Jewish, traded exclusively with Germany or confined their activities to one city. Similarly it has been generally accepted that their operations contrasted strongly with those of the industrialists: that their 'core ethos was to make profits from the use of other people's capital',[25] to charge interest on loans, speculate on commodities and deal in manufactured products rather than make fixed-capital investments. In fact these astute entrepreneurs constantly sought new revenue streams and local profit opportunities dictated their stock in trade. In Bradford, they specialised in various forms of wool dealing, in Manchester many of the same firms traded in cotton, whereas in Liverpool and Hull they were as instrumental in the development of the insurance and shipping industries, as they were to the international trade of raw and manufactured materials.[26]

20 Humbert Wolfe, *Now a Stranger* (London: Cassell and Company, 1933), p. 126.
21 Ibid.
22 Chapman, *Merchant Enterprise in Britain*, p. 45.
23 Wolfe, *Now a Stranger*, pp. 126–7.
24 Priestley, *English Journey*, p. 160.
25 Jones, *Merchants to Multinationals*, p. 288.
26 Chapman, *Merchant Enterprise in Britain*, p. 210.

In fact during the nineteenth century few successful businessmen – merchants or industrialists – confined their interests to a single line of business. Some diversification was born out of necessity as the development of services did not keep pace with the requirements of industry and manufacturers were often forced to supply their own needs. Thus, it was not uncommon for a worsted manufacturer to run a coal mine, while most derived supplementary income from rented property and land holdings provided vital collateral for securing credit. But whereas specialisation or monopoly would become a prominent feature of twentieth-century business, Victorian commerce generally employed a scattergun approach directed at any profit opportunity. Therefore merchants did not distinguish between their roles as bankers, dealers or salesmen and contrary to popular belief many made 'substantial manufacturing investments'.[27]

The Provision of Liquidity to Industry

In Bradford the merchants supplied raw wool to the worsted industry and sold yarn and cloth to a national and international customer base. However, it was their provision of financial liquidity to the manufacturers who had been shunned by British banks that proved key to their success and fundamental to the city's spectacular economic development. From the beginning of the factory system a hierarchy emerged, cash-rich manufacturers could fully process raw materials into finished goods and reap maximum profit, whereas the least-wealthy operations were forced to run the shortest lead times between outlay and remuneration. Undertaking only one or two manufacturing processes, a multitude of medium- and small-scale associated processors such as wool combers, top makers,[28] spinners, dyers and finishers, by adding only limited value to the final product, gleaned similarly restricted income. This state of affairs afforded a substantial opportunity to the merchants. They could carry stocks of components such as combed wool and yarn for ready sale or assume the role of converters and buy unfinished cloth from cash-strapped manufacturers at a relatively low price. They would then add value by dyeing and finishing the cloth before marketing it at an increased rate to the customer.

Only a handful of industrialists could afford the requisite investment to achieve the optimum business model known as vertical or full integration. This was the ability to fully process raw materials into a finished product and might be more simply explained as self-sufficiency. For the great majority, quickly off-loading yarn or semi-processed cloth to local merchants provided much-needed liquidity to their operations and simultaneously divested them of many commercial risks. By selling unfinished cloth they shed the responsibility of deciding the final colour or finish of the product and thus circumvented the vagaries of fashion. In some cases merchants collaborated so closely with manufacturers that they designed the

[27] Jones, *Merchants to Multinationals*, p. 288.

[28] 'Top' is scoured and combed wool fibre that has not been spun.

cloth which they would eventually market and sell, package, insure and ship.[29] But perhaps most importantly, by trading their products with local intermediaries, the industrialists avoided the risk of non-payment by inaccessible foreign customers. Thus, it is evident that financing manufacturing extended far beyond the provision of investment capital or credit. The merchants played a pivotal role in all stages of production from raw-materials supply to the sale of finished goods. By 1870 the sophistication of their dealings had increased and many offered currency-exchange services to their trading partners.[30] Operating internationally through so-called webs of enterprise, they made subcontracting arrangements, used direct investment to control the flow of raw materials and even placed 'liens on future output'.[31]

The Career of Ernst Posselt

Ernst Posselt arrived in England in 1858. Hailing from an affluent Heidelberg family, the ambitious twenty year old had disappointed his father's hopes of a career in academia when his 'inclinations were more towards commerce than scholastic pursuits'.[32] He was apprenticed to an export house in Brussels and spent some time in Antwerp before he perceived the opportunity unfolding in England's industrial north. Posselt was a self-made man of business and his obituary suggests how his character and commercial success were inextricably linked: the 'energetic young man found favour with suppliers and buyers alike, and everywhere he was known for his open, fresh approach to winning friends. Operating the business with zeal and energy it grew fast and soon became one of the leading firms of its kind'.[33]

The scarcity of records relating to nineteenth-century foreign-merchant operations has resulted in only a few men achieving lasting reputation and then usually for their contribution to British cultural or political life, rather than for commerce.[34] Therefore, the surviving records of E. Posselt and Co., Bradford not

---

29 John S. Roberts, *Little Germany* (Scarborough: Bradford Art Galleries and Museums, 1977), p. 15.

30 Jones, *Merchants to Multinationals*, p. 42.

31 Gordon M. Winder, 'Webs of Enterprise 1850–1914: Applying a Broad Definition of FDI', *Annals of the Association of American Geographers*, 96: 4 (December, 2006), p. 795.

32 *The History of E. Posselt and Co 1858–1958* (Bradford: privately published, 1958), p. 5, and Heidelberg Stadtarchiv, Ref Aus B 750d, *Stiftung des Geschwister Posselt im Andenken an Ihren Vater* (Bequest of the Posselt siblings in memory of their father).

33 Heidelberg Stadtarchiv, *Stiftung des Geschwister Posselt.*

34 The composer Frederick Delius (1862–1934), the poet and writer Humbert Wolfe (1885–1940) and the artist Sir William Rothstein (1872–1945) were all sons of Bradford merchants. Friedrich Eurich (1867–1945) became famous for his work to combat anthrax in the wool trade, while merchants Charles Semon (1814–1877), is remembered as Bradford's first German mayor and Jacob Behrens (1806–1889) is best known for his role in negotiating the Cobden Treaty.

only provide a remarkable insight into the activities of this firm, but also serve as a rare illustration for a whole generation of foreign venturers who were based in the city. Between his arrival in England in 1858 and his relocation to Warsaw in 1883, Posselt's dealings were characterised by a range of partnerships with his extended family and other associates. He had a short-lived alliance with a Prussian merchant Sigismund Zeno in Manchester,[35] longstanding affiliations with his brothers-in-law Hermann Quitmann, Julius Korff and most notably with his wife's family, the Peters of Elberfeld. His satellite interests both in England and abroad were invariably managed by Germans, including Theodor Bartsch, Emil Pahlke and Hugo Kolligs. But despite the number of partnerships and companies that he established, all generally traded under the Posselt name, to demonstrate his personal control over the extended network.[36]

Posselt displayed all the determined business networking and prolific charitable patronage typical of his contemporaries.[37] In 1864 he was elected to the Chamber of Commerce with fellow countryman and future Bradford mayor, Charles Semon, and members of the city's elite industrial families such as Holden, Foster and Oddy.[38] He was a member of Bradford's chess club,[39] showed his cattle at the Airedale Show at Bingley[40] and entered his company's team in local cricket matches.[41] Ernst Posselt was a founder trustee of Bradford's German-Evangelical Church, with, among others, Rudolph Delius, uncle of the great composer.[42] His Bradford business began with a trade in cloth and yarn,[43] but a range of national and international interests soon developed including several manufacturing businesses that long pre-date his enterprise with the Briggs brothers. He was

---

35 *Leeds Mercury*, 11 June 1861.

36 The various names of companies included: E. Posselt and Co., Derby, E. Posselt and Co., Manchester, E. Posselt, Paris, although later variations included Posselt, Peters and Co., and Briggs, Posselt and Co.

37 *Bradford Observer*, 14 June 1866, p. 1, notes Posselt's donation to the Jackson testimonial fund, *Freeman's Journal and Daily Commercial Advertiser*, Dublin, 7 April 1899, donation to the Royal National Lifeboats, *Bradford Observer*, 2 August 1866, p. 1, donation to Bradford Tradesman's Benevolent Institution, *Bradford Observer*, 15 November 1866, p. 1, to Derbyshire General Infirmary, *Derby Mercury*, 6 May 1874, to the Bradford Ladies Educational Society to establish a girls' school in Bradford, *Bradford Observer*, 1 January 1874, p. 1, to the Chicago Relief Fund, *Derby Mercury*, 29 November 1871, to Royal Lancaster Idiot Asylum, among many more.

38 *Bradford Observer*, 21 January 1864, p. 6.

39 Ibid., 30 November 1875, p. 4.

40 Ibid., 27 August, 1874, p. 8.

41 Ibid., 20 May 1873, p. 4 and 17 July 1873, p. 7 and 14 July 1875, p. 4, these cricket matches were regularly against teams from other German merchant companies such as Ahrons and Simonsen.

42 WYAS, Wakefield, Book 9, 14 March 1894, p. 155.

43 *History of E. Posselt and Co.*, pp. 5–6, 'stuff' refers to cloth.

co-owner of a prize-winning elastic factory based at City Road Mills in Derby,[44] he was partner in a Belgian tannery and in a 'steaming brick works in the Rhine Valley'.[45] From his office in Bradford, Posselt managed offices in Paris, Roubaix, New York, Heidelberg and Elberfeld.[46] In 1883 a trade journal described him as 'one of the most energetic and successful merchants in the British shipping trade'.[47]

The foreign merchant contingent were at the forefront of new technology improving their warehouse operations with the introduction of hydraulic hoists, steam-powered folding machines and sophisticated counter-balance lifting devices. They were also among the first businesses to use electric power in the 1890s and it is clear that they were no strangers to firsthand technical innovation as many registered patents for machinery, techniques and products as a commercial activity.[48] Without any formal technical education Posselt also applied for numerous patents for dyeing techniques, weaving methods and even for umbrella construction.[49]

Eric Sigsworth shows that in 1861, 40 per cent of Bradford's merchants were German and drew the conclusion that this reflected 'the importance of the German market for the worsted industry'.[50] However, Posselt's commercial-intelligence ledger reveals an extensive worldwide trade. His firm made numerous special arrangements with banks across Europe and as far afield as Australia, Egypt, India and the USA. Typical is the informal note that 'payable bills say drawn by us on Riga, Canada, Canaries made special discount when paying in, but as a rule they charge ½–1%'.[51] But Ernst Posselt was not extraordinary in the breadth of his international dealings; in 1842 and 1848 Lord Palmerston ordered censuses of commercial representation in foreign territories, which showed that a large proportion of recorded *British* trade was actually conducted by Germans resident in Manchester, Bradford and Liverpool.[52]

---

44 'Paris Exhibition', *Standard*, London, 3 July 1867, p. 6, 'Netherland Exhibition', *Morning Post*, London, 15 October 1869, p. 7. and 'Vienna Exhibition', *Morning Post*, 27 August 1873, p. 3.

45 WYAS, Posselt documents.

46 *History of E. Posselt and Co.*, p. 9.

47 'Notes of the Month', *Textile World*, Bradford, March 1883, p. 540.

48 Roberts, *Little Germany*, p. 18.

49 Posselt's patents included Patent Office references: No. 4656, 1 December 1876, a technique to form selvedges on fabrics, No. 4968, 23 December 1876, woven fabrics, No. 57, 7 January 1880, dyeing mixed textile fabrics and yarns, No. 445, 31 January 1880, dyeing cotton warps and cotton aniline black, No. 2503, 21 June 1880, dyeing cotton fabrics, No. 3475, 11 August 1881, umbrellas, parasols or sunshades. It is possible that his patents were the work of his employees.

50 E.M. Sigsworth, *Black Dyke Mills A History* (Liverpool: Liverpool University Press, 1958), p. 65.

51 WYAS Posselt documents, Commercial Intelligence Ledger.

52 Chapman, *Merchant Enterprise in Britain*, p. 98.

The Briggs of Briggella Mills

In the late 1850s, as the young Ernst Posselt arrived in Bradford, John Briggs, 'a type of true Yorkshire stock',[53] established his worsted-manufacturing business. Briggs began his career in the spinning mill of his uncle, Moses Bottomley, and married Eliza Ambler; the Bottomleys and Amblers were both prominent Bradford manufacturing dynasties. His brother, brother-in-law and later his five sons were all closely involved in his business, although Briggs remained the company's figurehead; 'enabled by his great industry, perseverance and bold enterprise to rise beyond his early surroundings and win both fame and fortune as a manufacturer'.[54] J. Briggs and Co. was financed in the classic manner without bank loans or credit, riding the wave of early industrialisation, and the founder rented Holme Top Mill until he had accumulated enough capital to build his own premises, Briggella Mills on Little Horton Lane. But an article in Bradford's *Illustrated Weekly Telegraph* perhaps better illustrates the firm's humble beginnings as it stated that Mrs Briggs 'by working at a hand loom ... succeeded in saving £200, a sum which formed the nucleus of her husband's business'.[55] The firm's operations expanded through the 1870s and with the acquisition of Newlay Dye Works at Horsforth in 1877, the optimum business model, full integration, was achieved.[56]

Figure 1.1 Briggella Mills, Little Horton Lane, Bradford, 1886
Source: Illustrated Weekly Telegraph, Bradford, 19 March 1886, p. 1.

[53] 'Messrs John Briggs and Co', *Men of the Period: The Records of a Great Country* (London: The Biographical Publishing Company, 1897), p. 143.

[54] Ibid.

[55] *Illustrated Weekly Telegraph*, Bradford, 7 September 1895.

[56] *Leeds Mercury*, 25 January 1877, shows that Newlay was acquired in 1877 by Jeremiah Whitaker, a cousin of the Briggs', and *London Gazette*, 23 June 1893, p. 3590 shows a pre-existing partnership between Whitaker and the Briggs brothers.

Like a generation of Bradford manufacturers, John Briggs prized practical education and believed there was 'no better school than the workshop'.[57] This enduring trait led Priestley to observe in the 1930s that 'there must be proportionately fewer university graduates in Bradford than in any other large town in England'.[58] At Briggella Mills the founder was proud to announce to the press in 1886 that,

> A marked characteristic of the firm from its inauguration to the present day should be noted. Each individual is a practical, hard working man, thoroughly trained in all the working details of manufacturing, and both willing and proud to 'put the brat on' and take his share of the hard work at the establishment.[59]

Cudworth's seminal *Worstedopolis* did much to promote the impression of worsted's dominance in Bradford.[60] But British wool supplies failed to keep pace with demand as mechanisation increased and the industrialists soon supplemented cheaper, readily available fibres. The introduction of cotton warps in the 1830s was considered a turning point for the Bradford trade, easing the limiting effect of poor wool supply on industrial expansion, 'it brought the mass market within reach of Bradford manufacturers'.[61] Thereafter the city experienced explosive economic growth as its reputation grew for mixed or lustre cloths which combined cotton with wool, alpaca, mohair or silk and could be produced cheaply in volume.

In the 1860s John Briggs confined his activities to spinning basic worsted yarn, but soon extended his repertoire to include a typical range of Bradford cloths: 'worsted coatings, dress goods and alpaca serges for the American market'.[62] By the 1880s the firm stood shoulder to shoulder with better-known manufacturers such as Titus Salt and John Foster. Although it has been argued that product diversification was a response to downturns in trade,[63] the activities of this firm suggest it was part and parcel of the natural expansion of successful businesses. By continually broadening their product base and manufacturing capabilities,

---

57 W.H.B. Court, *British Economic History 1870–1914* (Cambridge: Cambridge University Press, 1965), pp. 171–2.

58 Priestley, *English Journey*, p. 158.

59 *Illustrated Weekly Telegraph*, 19 March 1886, p. 1, a brat was a worker's apron or overall.

60 W. Cudworth, *Worstedopolis: a Sketch History of the Town and Trade of Bradford* (Bradford: W. Byles and Sons, 1888). Worsted is a smooth and fine quality of wool yarn and cloth used to make suits or dresses, as opposed to the heavy woollens which more usually create the characteristic tweed coatings and blankets of Scotland or South Yorkshire.

61 J. James, *History of the Worsted Manufacture in England* (London: Longman, Brown, Green, Longmans, and Roberts, 1857), p. 470.

62 *Men of the Period*, p. 143.

63 Roberts, *Little Germany*, p. 3, and Mary H. Blewett, *The Yankee Yorkshireman: Migration Lived and Imagined* (Urbana and Chicago: University of Illinois Press, 2009), p. 37.

industrialists could increase revenues, spread risk and ideally find a niche market to monopolise. Thus the Briggs became 'looked upon as amongst the leaders of the fancy yarn trade'[64] as well as 'world-famous for their umbrella cloths'.[65]

It is evident that in its basic organisational structure as a private family firm, its independent self-finance, development towards vertical integration, diversified product base and the timing of its trajectory to become one of Bradford's most successful firms, J. Briggs and Co. conformed to a local pattern. The founder epitomised the practical men of the Industrial Revolution by taking a characteristically hands-on or proprietorial approach to managing every aspect of his business. But contrary to the popular stereotype that Yorkshire industrialists were preoccupied with production and profit rather than aesthetics and 'for inspiration we are still beholden to the French',[66] Briggs' greater commercial acumen is suggested in census returns which show that two of his sons, Charles and later Alfred, were trained as pattern designers.[67]

Increasing Economic Pressure on Manufacturing Industry

As the nineteenth century progressed, the factors influencing Britain's commercial climate became increasingly complex. At the outset, resources and mechanisation were central to determining the pace and scale of industrialisation. It was sufficient for manufacturers to produce volumes of low-cost, generic products to make excellent profits and the British population represented their largest, wealthiest and most contiguous consumer. But the continuing expansion of industry depended on a commensurate growth in sales outlets. The fierce competition for domestic trade was well-illustrated by Joseph Benn's much-quoted comment to the 1905 Tariff Commission: 'we are all as thick as flies in summer in London trying to sell to the home market'.[68] In the latter nineteenth century a concerted cultivation of both colonial and other worldwide customer and supply bases began which exposed British industry to unprecedented political, economic and geographical uncertainties.

Free Trade policies and political stability were vital to maintain Britain's primacy and prosperity, but the world market was volatile and 'Britain's growing dependence on international trade increased her vulnerability'.[69] Formerly insignificant factors such as a new foreign import tax, a distant war or the opening of a far-flung transport link might suddenly have significant implications for England's provincial manufacturers. The consequences were by no means

64 *Illustrated Weekly Telegraph*, 7 September 1895.
65 *Men of the Period*, p. 143.
66 Sigsworth, *Black Dyke Mills*, p. 92 quotes *Bradford Observer*, 30 December 1889.
67 1871 and 1881 English Census.
68 Sigsworth, *Black Dyke Mills*, p. 103.
69 Cain and Hopkins, 'Gentlemanly Capitalism', p. 8.

predictable and whereas Bradford enjoyed a 50 per cent increase in worsted exports as a result of disruptions to French industry during the Franco-Prussian war,[70] Lancashire cotton weavers suffered a catastrophic collapse due to American Civil War embargoes on cotton export. Similarly, the exhaustion of a local coal supply or sudden shortage of raw wool, perhaps caused by a competitor's speculation in stock, or a 'drought in East Australia between 1893 and 1902 [which] culminated in heavy stock losses',[71] could drive the product price up and force closure on even well-established firms.

In addition, the aesthetic demands of both an ever more sophisticated domestic market and a culturally less-familiar international customer began to acquire greater significance, even dominance, for British manufacturers. By the last quarter of the nineteenth century, fashion – the question of cloth design, colour and quality – was the often-unacknowledged determinant of industrial success.[72] The staples of the Bradford trade, the so-called mixed or lustre cloths made with cotton warps and worsted wool, alpaca or mohair wefts became outmoded with the crinolines they were designed to cover. The press announced that 'events have fully shown that the lustre trade which was so profitable a dozen years ago, is now quite a thing of the past',[73] as a more streamlined-garment silhouette was introduced that demanded softer, draping fabrics. It is arguable that manufacturers, economists and journalists alike failed to address fashion as a serious issue in favour of debate in more familiar territory, such as factory and trade legislation or raw-materials supply. In the last quarter of the nineteenth century the challenges for British commerce were most commonly identified as the 'development of manufacturing abroad, aided by parental factory legislation at home'.[74]

Foreign Competition and Protectionism

In the second half of the nineteenth century foreign competition was increasingly blamed for undermining British economic success. Former customer nations did not simply supply their own national requirements for manufactured goods, or attack Britain's sales markets, but consumed their own formerly exported raw materials. Before the mid-nineteenth century England imported a large proportion of her wool requirements from Germany and only 23 per cent from the southern hemisphere. But by 1870 Germany had ceased to export wool which caused an acute

[70] Chadwick, *Church and People in Bradford*, p. 22.

[71] Stephen Brearley, *The International Wool Market 1840–1913* (PhD thesis, University of Leicester, 2004), p. 47.

[72] Quality, in this context, refers both to the composition of the cloth in terms of fibre and also to its weight and handle.

[73] 'Overgrowth of concerns', *Textile World*, Bradford, April 1885, pp. 221–2.

[74] 'Factory Legislation', *Journal of Fabrics and Textile Industries*, Bradford, 12 July 1883, p. 75.

shortage in the British market.[75] The impact of reduced resources was compounded by the growing politicisation of international commerce. The period from 1850 to 1875 'can reasonably be called the era of free trade',[76] but thereafter global policy-makers began to recognise the international movement of goods and commodities as an effective guide to legislation. The once-free market was increasingly rigged in favour of infant foreign industries as their governments placed levies on imported manufactures. These taxes, or tariffs, were typically applied to the highest-value products, for example fully processed cloth, which allowed developing industries to supply their requirements for imported components. Eventually, in the drive towards national self-sufficiency, the protective tariffs would be rolled out to include yarn and finally raw materials, until the only surviving imports would be nationally unobtainable commodities.

As protectionism became more prevalent, formerly dominant British industry was forced to shift emphasis to less-lucrative elements of the trade. But the industrialists' habitual commercial diversification and eagerness to trade in a variety of products and markets led the overall destructive impact to remain largely unacknowledged. Yarn sales boomed and new export markets for combed-worsted top emerged, at the expense of higher-revenue products. For British business communities under a 'great strain of competition to find new channels of trade',[77] export markets for raw materials and yarn, rather than for more profitable cloth, could not be ignored. Thus in 1874 the *Bradford Observer* qualified complaints about poor profits and high-wage costs with accounts of 'mills ... generally running full time; a great increase of machinery; an apparently sound trade; people well-employed; a very large consumption going on and stocks in this country very light; and it really is very difficult to reconcile these anomalies'.[78] Similarly, although British engineering companies and machine manufacturers were frequently accused of bolstering foreign competition by the international dissemination of technology, they could no more disregard a growing foreign market than the exporters of raw materials and components, especially in a climate of falling profits in which domestic industrialists had become less inclined to make further investment in new machinery.

It is evident that during the second half of the nineteenth century British industry came under very broad-ranging pressures which were of advantage to some sectors but generally had a negative impact. Even apparently positive developments could destabilise the precarious balance of the local trade. For

---

75 Brearley, *International Wool Market*, p. 30.

76 James Foreman-Peck, *A History of the World Economy, International Economic Relations since 1850* (London: Harvester Wheatsheaf, 1983), p. 55 and Cottrell, *British Overseas Investment*, p. 28.

77 'Review of the Bradford Trade for 1875', *Bradford Observer*, 30 December 1875, p. 7.

78 'The Wool Trade', *Bradford Observer*, 16 February 1874, p. 2 and in S.B. Saul, *The Myth of the Great Depression 1873–1896* (London: Macmillan, 1969), p. 46.

example, in 1859 Bradford's Chamber of Commerce led by Jacob Behrens determined to address the wool shortage which had dogged the worsted industry since before the mid-century. They successfully lobbied colonial wool growers to increase the southern-hemisphere supply of the long wools specifically required to make Bradford's characteristic worsteds. Within the next decade the wool press was introduced to compact cargoes, steam shipping developed and with the opening of the Suez Canal in 1869, transport costs dramatically decreased.[79] However, in 1882 the Bradford industrialist Thomas Illingworth forcefully attacked what he considered to be the true reason for persisting depression in the worsted industry. He disregarded all the standard arguments about foreign tariffs, changing fashion and the failure to modernise plant and stated emphatically that 'the gigantic increase in supply of wool is the primary cause'.[80] Over-supply of the vital commodity had destabilised prices and in an industry 'relying for profit on turnover, rather than high profit margins',[81] falling prices were as devastating as the increases caused by wool shortage.

Manufacturers' Tactics to Counteract Economic Depression

It is impossible to precisely define when the positive expansion of trade and industry, the dynamic diversifications of product and market, tipped over into a period of diminished profits and then to full-scale economic depression. Nevertheless, following a period of extraordinary growth between 1830 and 1860, there followed a tangible down-turn in which industrial communities were forced to dramatically rethink their strategies in order to survive. Debate on the merits of retaliatory tariffs intensified, while greater modernisation, improved technical education and even 'buy British' campaigns[82] were popularly advocated. By the last quarter of the nineteenth century structural changes to British industry began to emerge as the survival of the fittest saw smaller manufacturers either amalgamated to form cooperative monopolies in specialist trades, or knocked out of the market altogether.[83]

A culture of secretiveness became prevalent as industrialists boasted about the size of their mills but declined to discuss their products or share commercial intelligence. Conservative politician Henry Mitchell reported from the 1878 Paris Exhibition that there was 'a reluctance to join in anything like a display of

---

79 Brearley, *International Wool Market*, p. 146.

80 T. Illingworth, *A Sixty Years Retrospective of the Bradford Trade Indicative of the some of the Causes of the Present Depression* (Bradford: privately published, 1882).

81 Chadwick, *Church and People in Bradford*, p. 22.

82 Gary Firth, 'Bradford Trade in the Nineteenth Century', in *Victorian Bradford*, eds D.G. Wright and J.A. Jowitt (Bradford: City of Bradford Metropolitan Council, 1982), p. 25 mentions the Bective movement; a 'buy British' campaign established in 1881.

83 The most notable of these was the Bradford Dyers Association.

Bradford goods, the impression having got abroad that former displays of this description had tended rather to the advancement of our foreign competitors than to the advancement of the Bradford trade'.[84]

Reduced profits caused British businessmen to adopt a multi-faceted strategy to claw back income: they streamlined their operations, reduced social-overhead costs and spread risk with diversified investments.[85] Some bought into service industries such as transport, electricity generation and gas supply, but in view of the burgeoning success of foreign industry, many sought higher returns abroad. A vast amount of British industrial capital was ploughed into foreign infrastructure projects, particularly in the USA, Canada and Australia.[86] Philip Cottrell describes the acuity of British investors who by the late 1870s 'understood the relationship between the price of American railroad securities and the volume of cereal shipments on the American railway network'.[87] Between 1870 and 1913 foreign assets represented about a third of all British wealth and by the First World War 'foreign securities accounted for 48 per cent of the nominal value of all the issues traded on the London Stock Exchange'.[88]

The merchants, with their international connections and more liquid assets, were arguably better placed to capitalise on these global economic shifts than their industrialist partners. They were renowned for their 'ability to diversify into so many agency, transport, financial, mining, plantation, and industrial activities' and were said to thrive on 'the uncertainties of long-distance trade and erratic commodity markets'.[89] However, in the last quarter of the nineteenth century, the fluctuating supply and demand, price swings, rising international taxation and mounting competition threatened the livelihood of manufacturers and merchants in equal measure. But the merchants' problems were compounded by the failure of numerous cash-poor firms with which they had built a co-dependence in commercial centres such as Bradford. Simultaneously, the revised strategies of the dominant industrialists to reduce transaction costs by removing middlemen naturally impacted heavily.[90] The advent of the telegraph began to facilitate direct communication between suppliers and customers, thus raw wool, which had formerly been shipped to market in London or Bradford, could be traded at source without costly merchant or agent services.[91] As their customers became better informed, the bargaining position of merchant traders became weaker, and in order

84 Sigsworth, *Black Dyke Mills*, p. 85.

85 Cain and Hopkins, 'Gentlemanly Capitalism', p. 3.

86 A. Cairncross, *Home and Foreign Investment, 1870–1913* (Cambridge: Cambridge University Press, 1953), p. 2.

87 Cottrell, *British Overseas Investment*, p. 63.

88 M. Dintenfass, *The Decline of Industrial Britain 1870–1980* (London: Routledge, 1992), p. 40.

89 Chapman review of *Merchants to Multinationals* by Jones, pp. 1111–13.

90 Jones, *Merchants to Multinationals*, p. 50.

91 Ibid., p. 4.

to pre-empt entire exclusion, many took 'equity stakes in suppliers and customers or invest[ed] in entirely new activities to create new value-added chains'.[92]

The Briggs-Posselt Partnership

In 1883 this unpredictable economic environment formed the backdrop for two of John Briggs' sons, Edward and John junior, to enter into partnership with Ernst Posselt and venture a bold enterprise in the Russian empire. While the majority of their contemporaries took steps to reduce costs, spread risk and increasingly rejected the merchant role, these men formed a strategic alliance which would direct their combined professional experience and considerable accumulated capital at a very specific foreign opportunity. It might be assumed that Ernst Posselt, as an internationally experienced serial entrepreneur, instigated the scheme but all evidence suggests that Edward Briggs was the originator. The *Yorkshire Weekly Post* described that 'Mr Edward Briggs conceived the bold idea ... here he was joined by Mr E. Posselt'.[93]

There is no precise explanation for the acquaintance between Edward Briggs and Ernst Posselt. They did not share a religious affiliation or concurrent membership of the Chamber of Commerce and no longstanding commercial association between their two firms has been identified. Like Posselt, Edward Briggs was a prolific innovator and registered numerous patents for umbrella cloths, shower-proofing techniques, loom parts and even leg guards for cricketers.[94] Both men were in their mid-forties at the time of their partnership, both were sports enthusiasts and keen art collectors, thus it can only be assumed that these common pursuits forged their friendship. Indeed, in 1888 Briggs built an art gallery annex at his impressive moor-side villa, Westwood Lodge, in Ilkley, and in 1892 the *Pall Mall Gazette* alluded to his status as an art collector by describing him 'the Mr Tate of the Midlands'.[95] Posselt's lasting legacy is the priceless art collection that he bequeathed to the *Kurpfälzische Museum* in Heidelberg.

The alliance between these two men dispels many of the stereotypical characterisations of stolid northern industrialists and cosmopolitan foreign merchants, popularised in Victorian literature. It is evident that despite their apparently dissimilar social, religious and national origins, they shared both cultural interests and commercial aspirations. In 1883 Edward Briggs was well-

---

92 Ibid., p. 7.

93 'Mr Edward Briggs of Bradford', *Yorkshire Weekly Post*, 12 March 1898.

94 Edward Briggs' patents include Patent Office refs: No. 794, 27 February 1877, umbrella cloths or coverings, No. 2498, 21 June 1879, healds for weaving, No. 2292, 16 May 1882, for warps made of thrown silk, and with silk in the gum, and weft of spun silk and single thread, No. 3067, 17 February 1892, shower-proof fabric, No. 3096, 17 February 1892, umbrellas, No. 16492, 15 September 1892, leg-guards for cricketers.

95 'Art Notes', *Pall Mall Gazette*, London, 21 December 1892, p. 1.

established running the Bradford firm on behalf of his father and did not intend to move to Poland. In Posselt he sought a collaborator of sufficient wisdom, maturity and reputation, to guide the foreign enterprise locally with the youngest of the three partners, the 27-year-old John Briggs junior. Thus the company history of E. Posselt and Co. describes that Edward Briggs 'was very friendly with Ernst Posselt, and finally persuaded him to join in establishing a textile concern in Poland'.[96]

D.C. Coleman suggests that a fair analysis of business behaviour should 'avoid the presumption of a profit motive'.[97] Despite the characteristic political independence and religious non-conformity of Britain's northern industrialists, it is evident that 'social advancement was one of the most prized possessions to be bought by an English business fortune'.[98] Many Victorian industrialists sought acceptance among the aristocracy by acquiring large estates, they provided their sons with expensive educations, adopted the Anglican faith and joined the Conservative party. Building a foreign factory would not generate this sort of social capital, but such audacious entrepreneurship would certainly have brought a great deal of local prestige to the partners. Indeed the style of the Marki venture with its sizeable land holdings, workers' housing and impressive owners' residence suggests strongly the founders' aspiration towards the gargantuan ventures of Yorkshire's most-celebrated paternalists such as Salt, Akroyd and Crossley. In family firms the provision of meaningful employment for male heirs was an often-mentioned incentive to embark on new projects. Titus Salt reputedly told Lord Harewood at the opening of Saltaire that 'he had built the place to do good and to give his sons employment'.[99] Although the influence of family politics will be explored in more detail in the next chapter, it is worth noting here that an almost identical motivation was attributed to John Briggs by the *Illustrated Weekly Telegraph* in 1886.[100]

There was naturally a great deal of British press interest in the Briggs-Posselt partnership's foreign investment plan. The reportage falls into two clear categories: a sympathetic, arguably pro-protectionist, approach invariably suggests that they were forced to build a factory abroad to counteract losses to their Russian trade caused by the 'heavy protective tariff'.[101] The *Textile World* journal published quite specific details that 'Messrs Briggs of Horton, who, finding they cannot face a duty of £23,12s, 11d, per hundred-weight, are determined to embark their energies in

96 *History of E. Posselt and Co.*, p. 11.

97 D.C. Coleman, 'Gentlemen and Players', *Economic History Review*, 2:26 (1973), p. 96.

98 Ibid., p. 95.

99 Abraham Holroyd, *Saltaire and its Founder* (Bradford: Piroisms Press and Falcon, 1873), p. xii.

100 *Illustrated Weekly Telegraph*, Bradford, 19 March, 1886.

101 Ibid., 7 September 1895.

a part of the world more favourable, through its protection, to their industry'.[102] Nevertheless, there is little evidence to suggest that either of the partners' Bradford businesses had suffered any serious detriment through Russian protectionism. Their existing broad-spread interests, continuing investments throughout the period of depression and the significant capital they were able to export all tend to disprove the hardship supposition. The high-cost social-overhead model that they adopted for their foreign enterprise is perhaps the most conclusive evidence that it was not an act of desperation.

On the other hand, there were many critical reports about the reputedly growing phenomenon of British foreign direct investment which was said to employ 'English capital, and English thought and brains, combined with foreign machinery, and what is still more hurtful, foreign rates of wages'.[103] Considering rates of pay abroad and increasing factory legislation at home, Yorkshire's industrialists might well have concluded that 'an unquestionable advantage would thus appear to lie with manufacturers on the continent'.[104] But even appreciably lower wages abroad was an insufficient motivation for such high-cost and risky outlay.[105] In the 1890s James Baker was commissioned by the *Yorkshire Post* to investigate British enterprise in Europe. His conclusions reflect the commonly held view that building foreign factories was invariably for cheap offshore processing and that the foreign direct investors' sole purpose was to sell into existing markets at an unfair advantage. However, the Briggs-Posselt partnership, like fellow Bradford industrialists Titus Salt junior and Harrison Benn who established American factories in the following two decades,[106] never sought to undermine or close their existing concerns in favour of the foreign enterprise. Indeed, suggestions that these industrialists planned to transport their businesses 'bodily to the continent'[107] are preposterous when the majority of their family wealth had been laboriously built into the fixed assets of their Bradford firms over generations.

The strategy of their foreign enterprises was to identify new markets, to avoid the preserves of their domestic concerns and create additional, entirely independent, businesses. Therefore despite the readily bandied rumours that 'not less than ten firms – some of them very large ones, have left the neighbourhood, and dispersed their energy and capital over the continent of Europe',[108] the press rarely named

[102] 'Notes of the Month', p. 540.

[103] James Baker, *Our Foreign Competitors, Their Life and Labour* (London: Sampson Low, Marston and Company, 1892), p. 7.

[104] 'Factory Legislation', p. 75.

[105] WYAS, 10/D76/2/33/14/3, in the records of Bradford solicitors Vint, Hill and Killick, the venture capital of the Briggs-Posselt partnership was £68,000, equal to approximately £3.25 million in 2014.

[106] Salt bought a factory at Bridgeport, Connecticut, in the 1890s and Benn built a mill at Greystone, Rhode Island, in 1904.

[107] *Yorkshire Weekly Post*, 'Mr Edward Briggs of Bradford',12 March, 1898.

[108] 'Notes of the Month', p. 540.

those industrialists. In 1906 a Tariff Commission report criticised Benn's recently opened Rhode Island worsted mill and provoked an impassioned retort by the Bradford and District League Against Protectionism. The League accused the Commission of 'a travesty of the actual facts'[109] and strongly asserted that firms such as Holden's, Benn's and Briggs' that had undertaken foreign ventures were 'conspicuous for the rapid and continuous increase of their prosperity in Bradford'.[110]

In conclusion, this chapter has explored how an ideological conflict arising from the pre-industrial social hierarchy created opportunity for economic migrants such as Ernst Posselt during the nineteenth century. It has outlined how the expansion of international trade exposed British commerce to increasingly complex pressures which had both a destabilising and positive transformative effect on the industrial environment and business behaviour in the last quarter of the nineteenth century. The most successful entrepreneurs – both merchants and industrialists – adjusted to changing circumstances and prospered, despite the much-discussed economic depression.[111] Although Britain's prevailing economic climate undoubtedly influenced entrepreneurial decisions to make foreign investments and continued to exert a strong influence on the Briggs-Posselt partnership's strategy and mode of operation in Russian Poland, the next chapters will show that it was developing opportunities abroad rather than financial hardship at home which created the ultimate impetus. Mounting commercial opportunity had encouraged Ernst Posselt to base his international business empire in Bradford in 1858 and a similar temptation undoubtedly induced the naturalised Briton to relocate his young family to Warsaw in 1883.

---

109 'Bradford Woollen Industry Protectionism', *The Times*, 2 January 1906.

110 Ibid.

111 The Great Depression which began after 1873 and is generally considered to have continued into the 1890s but has been much disputed by contemporary businessmen, politicians and modern scholars.

Chapter 2

'An English company, of English registration':[1] The organisational form and financing of the foreign enterprise

In the last quarter of the nineteenth century British foreign investment was a growing trend, but the majority of capital outflow was concentrated in bonds, stocks and shares. These 'arm's length'[2] speculations were generally purchased by individuals or firms as a sideline to their core interests. Foreign direct investment – the commitment to build and run a business abroad – was by contrast fairly rare and the establishment of large-scale industrial plants with high-cost social-overhead infrastructure was very unusual. This chapter will consider how aspects of British business organisation and management translated within foreign direct investment. It will reveal that, despite shared ownership between unrelated partners, Briggs, Posselt and Co., Marki was an example of family capitalism, rather than the increasingly prevalent joint-stock model. Although the interlocking directorates of the domestic and foreign firms might suggest their interdependence, this chapter will show that the Marki venture should not be considered the branch of an international company but an independent concern which tailored its strategy and products to the host market.

The Legal Framework of Nineteenth-century Firms

In the nineteenth century partnership was the 'basic organising principle' of the British manufacturing industry.[3] This legal framework did not simply define ownership structure but arguably reflected a characteristic approach to the capitalisation and management of companies. The entrenched social attitudes

---

[1] Ellis T. Powell, *The Mechanism of the City* (London: King and Son, 1910), pp. 144–5.

[2] Mira Wilkins, 'The Free-Standing Company, 1870–1914: An Important Type of British Foreign Direct Investment', *Economic History Review*, New Series, 41: 2 (1988), p. 259 and Gordon M. Winder, 'Webs of Enterprise 1850–1914: Applying a Broad Definition of FDI', *Annals of the Association of American Geographers*, 96: 4 (December, 2006), p. 789.

[3] John F. Wilson, *British business history, 1720–1994* (Manchester and New York: Manchester University Press, 1995), p. 43.

towards trade and finance – that were described in Chapter 1 – galvanised self-reliance in the rising industrial classes, who centralised their business interests among family and close associates. These family capitalists tended towards a 'proprietorial' or 'personal' style of management in which the owners had direct control of the broadest range of functions within the firm including finance, purchasing, workforce management and sales.[4] Trusted employees might undertake certain responsibilities but real delegation of decision-making or operational management was negligible and although credit or working capital was usually generated through high-trust dealing in the locality, outside capital investors were rarely admitted into private partnerships.

After 1870 the dominance of private or family firms amongst new company registrations gave way to a prevalence of joint-stock, limited-liability concerns. The new business model was essentially a shared investment which insulated personal assets from professional losses. Cottrell suggests that this structural change was driven by the increasing capital requirements in the 'age of steel and electricity'.[5] But it is also evident that the introduction of more generous legislation to facilitate joint-stock status after 1865 coincided with a period of economic depression.[6] Thus depleted funds and risk aversion might have been equal incentives for British businessmen to pool resources and diversify their interests. By 1878 three to four new limited firms were registered each week in England including large numbers of social clubs, hotels and notably coffee houses.[7] The longstanding business culture was transformed as a new idea or invention, an aristocratic title[8] or simply available capital became the tickets to admit unknown partners into shared investment. The participants in these enterprises were not committed to the fixed assets or day-to-day running of their operations and could trade their stake without reference to the going concern. Although limited liability was undoubtedly attractive to British manufacturers, the palpable separation between ownership and control which characterised the joint-stock model, and particularly the insubstantial ties between investors, were anathema to their principles.

The sheer number of joint-stock companies created and the extensive modern scholarship devoted to them might suggest that, by the end of the nineteenth century, private enterprise was becoming outmoded. However, the age of unlimited liability further entrenched the family capitalists' commitment to personal control. They

[4] Ibid., pp. 12–13 discusses among others A.D. Chandler, *Scale and Scope: the Dynamics and Industrial Capitalism* (Cambridge, MA: Belknap Press, 1990).

[5] Cottrell, *British Overseas Investment*, p. 55.

[6] S.D. Chapman, 'British-Based Investment Groups before 1914', *Economic History Review*, New Series, 38: 2 (May, 1985), p. 244.

[7] H.A. Shannon, 'The Limited Companies of 1866–1883', *Economic History Review*, 4: 3 (1933), p. 291.

[8] Wilkins, 'The Free Standing Company', p. 266, describes them as 'ornamental directors'.

did not regard their 'individualistic and atomistic'[9] approach as restrictive but a proven formula for sustainability and success, most appropriate to an increasingly volatile commercial environment. Thus private partnership remained the preferred organisational form for British industrialists until well into the twentieth century. In 1913 the category 'manufacturing and commerce' only accounted for 7.1 per cent of the total value of securities quoted on the British stock exchange.[10]

Contemporary critics and modern historians alike have indicted the industrialists' apparently inflexible approach towards business innovations as central to Britain's declining primacy in world trade after the mid-nineteenth century.[11] Contemporary American and German economies were dominated by modern share companies whose ownership employed specialist managers or marketing experts to expand their enterprises into huge corporations. Whereas British industry was apparently limited by an old-fashioned proprietorial approach which disdained organisational or managerial innovations as well as new sources of capital. The negative stereotype was compounded with accusations that the industrialists were unwilling to update plant, reticent towards technical education and oblivious to the importance of marketing and design. But it must be considered that both strategic and structural changes to established businesses had to meet real challenges and reducing control of their core interests, even to increase capitalisation or introduce expertise, held no appeal for the leaders of the industrial revolution in an unpredictable commercial arena. In this context it was naturally considered imprudent to buy the modern machinery used by their foreign competitors when skilled British workers ran their existing plants efficiently. Nevertheless, in 1907 when a modified joint-stock model was introduced, in which private firms could attain limited liability and still retain all equity within a family or partnership, huge numbers of old-style companies subscribed, including J. Briggs and Co., Bradford.

Diversification of Assets

Although 'introverted family groupings still dominated most British firms'[12] well into the twentieth century, an apparently contradictory aspect of the industrialists' business behaviour is often overlooked. Membership of a private firm did not preclude tandem share-holding in numerous joint-stock enterprises. Despite their steadfast adherence to a traditional organisational structure for their core interests,

---

9 Wilson, *British business history*, p.131.

10 E.V. Morgan and W.A. Thomas, *The Stock Exchange: Its History and Functions* (London: Elek Books, 1962).

11 Dintenfass, *Decline of Industrial Britain*, Martin J. Wiener, *English Culture and the Decline of the Industrial Spirit 1850–1980* (Cambridge: Cambridge University Press, 1981).

12 Wilson, *British business history*, p. 120.

the family capitalists enthusiastically deployed both personal and company funds to make a range of auxiliary joint-stock investments.

In the latter nineteenth century manufacturers countered growing competition and lower profit yields with a multi-faceted strategy. Chapter 1 described how they reduced overheads, internalised manufacturing processes and dispensed as far as possible with agents and middlemen. Some increased the sale of components to service developing industries abroad, while others favoured difficult-to-manufacture products which their competitors would struggle to emulate. Although individual tactics varied according to the emphasis and preference of each business, when speculation in national or international transport or utility companies could achieve a greater return than reinvestment in their existing plants, it became a natural step for Britain's wealthy industrial elite. Spreading both personal and professional assets among a range of products and services which were affected by different market forces was both prudent and forward thinking in an uncertain economic climate.

Greater portfolio or direct investment in unrelated commercial activities was notably embraced by second and third generations of Yorkshire's textile dynasties, but it was rarely applauded as innovation and more readily characterised as a dilution of industrial capital and entrepreneurship. The north-south divide continued to impact on industrial society as the pioneers used their wealth to buy social preferment, if not for themselves then for their sons. In 1870 the *Bradford Observer* mocked the proclivity of 'manufacturers of the old school, many who speak in the dialect and have disdain for gloves and who, curiously enough, send their sons to be educated at the universities, whence they emerge gloriously incapacitated for business'.[13] But unlike their self-made fathers and grandfathers, the inheritors of the British manufacturing industry with established operations, attractive suburban homes and comfortable lifestyles had little opportunity to exercise any extraordinary individual skill within the family firms. This state of affairs was undoubtedly a significant motivational factor for Edward Briggs to undertake a foreign enterprise in the 1880s. But it is worth noting here that, at the beginning of the twentieth century, his son, Arthur 'Harry' Briggs, as managing director and majority share holder of J. Briggs and Co., Bradford, also sat on the board of directors of the newly formed Rolls Royce Motor Car Company and Bradford Football Club.[14]

By the twentieth century the successors to family capitalism were increasingly mere figureheads of the long-established manufacturing firms which financed their political, academic or military careers and their gentlemanly lifestyles. But for those who remained involved in company management, success was less based on

[13] *Bradford Observer*, 9 June 1870.

[14] C.W. Morton, *A History of Rolls-Royce Motor Cars: Volume 1* (London: G.T. Foulis, 1964), p. 226 and in A.J. Arnold, *A Game That Would Pay: A Business History of Professional Football in Bradford* (London, Duckworth, 1988), pp. 57–62.

the practical skills so prided by the founders and relied more on less tangible ideas about financial strategy, management and marketing.

The Scope of British Foreign Investment

Of the barrage of tactics British businessmen employed to counteract the economic pressures of the second half of the nineteenth century, capital export proved extremely popular. The accumulated profits of British industry were increasingly invested in foreign stocks, shares and government bonds while a few bold venture capitalists made the greater commitment into direct industrial investment abroad. The organisational principle of these undertakings naturally reflected domestic preferences and private partnership dominated, although the associated proprietorial approach to management naturally created practical difficulties in remote firms. The earliest British-owned foreign enterprises were generally an extension of an existing commodity trade and colonial plantations might be considered their precedent. These companies employed minimal fixed assets and undertook nominal manufacturing processes to extract mineral deposits, gold, silver, diamonds or coal, usually under the directorship of an expatriate member of the firm.[15] Manufacturing arguably constituted a second wave of more sophisticated foreign direct investment. Established in response to any combination of motivations, such as unexploited market opportunities or foreign government incentives, the early pioneers of this more capital-intensive undertaking also favoured family capitalism. These concerns became a much-imitated model for a wave of joint-stock and international partnerships to build foreign factories in the last decade of the nineteenth century, most notably in the USA. In the early twentieth century they arguably formed the prototype for a third phase of multinational corporations.

In the context of this evolution it is clear that Briggs, Posselt and Co., Marki was not the earliest foreign direct investment, but it was undoubtedly one of the largest and most ambitious of the period. However, in both its organisational structure as a private partnership and in its strategic aims, the Marki enterprise should not be classified as the division of an international firm. The later multinationals tended to develop foreign branches to supersede existing international trading relationships for a variety of transaction cost savings.[16] They integrated backwards into raw-material development and forwards to replace sales agents in foreign markets,[17] thus their foreign satellites were rarely fully vertical manufacturing plants. Just

15 Shannon, 'The Limited Companies', p. 305.

16 Stephen Nicholas, 'Agency Contracts, Institutional Modes, and the Transition to Foreign Direct Investment by British Manufacturing Multinationals before 1939', *Journal of Economic History*, 43: 3 (September 1983), p. 677.

17 John H. Dunning, *The Globalisation of Business: the Challenge of the 1990s* (London: Routledge, 1993), p. 57.

as the Briggs' Bradford company encompassed Briggella Mills, the Newlay Dye Works and nearby offices at Gordon Street to complete one fully integrated business, the multinational, with an overseas plantation, a foreign assembly plant and a sales or distribution unit abroad, operated as one fully vertical concern, albeit straddling many nations.[18]

It might be assumed that improving the efficiency and profitability of an existing trade was the standard rationale for all foreign ventures. But whereas some examples undoubtedly did move into existing export markets, it is evident that the Briggs-Posselt partnership led with a fundamentally different aim. Neither J. Briggs and Co., nor E. Posselt and Co., of Bradford had a significant Russian-export business but they perceived an unexploited market for worsted inside the Russian empire; a potential new *home trade* in which they might secure a monopoly. Despite the establishment of their Polish factory as 'an English company, of English registration',[19] its activities took on a far from international character. The directors intended to minimise the cross-border movement of products or money and operate as an autonomous, albeit foreign-owned, Russian-Polish business.

Notwithstanding their independent status, foreign direct investment did usually emanate from a parent company which was the source of both capital and entrepreneurial skill, and the founders typically had an ownership stake in both the domestic and foreign firms, but that is not evidence of co-dependence between the two businesses. As the majority of industrial wealth was fixed in leviathan factories, new outlets for goods, rather than cheap off-shore processing was the coveted solution to declining profits. The products and organisational structure of the foreign operations were likely to reflect the parent, but success for both the British and foreign interests lay in the directorship's ability to tailor a new strategy for their undertaking abroad that was appropriate to the host environment.

Targeting a separate market to the parent firm avoided erosion of domestic profits but several other practical factors led venture capitalists to reinvest the proceeds of their foreign ventures outside Britain. Chapman notes that the 'rate of interest continued at a higher, often much higher, level abroad'[20] in this period. However, the key reason was the protagonists' wholehearted belief in the greater profit potential overseas. Excess cash from their domestic concerns had been earmarked for diversification into foreign enterprise and profitability consolidated the perception of the preferential prospects abroad. As the entrepreneurs networked in new commercial circles, local opportunities presented themselves which they naturally pursued.[21] An early precedent for this business behaviour was John Foster's instruction to his New York agent Butterfield to reinvest the

[18] Geoffrey Jones, 'The Growth and Performance of British Multinational Firms before 1939: The Case of Dunlop', *Economic History Review*, New Series, 37: 1 (1984), pp. 35–53.

[19] Powell, *Mechanism of the City*, pp. 144–5.

[20] Chapman, *Merchant Enterprise in Britain*, p. 233.

[21] Chapman, 'British-Based Investment Groups', p. 232.

revenue from his export sales in American stocks and shares, rather than returning it to England.[22] Later the Scottish sewing-thread manufacturers J. and P. Coats, who opened numerous foreign branches at the turn of the twentieth century, were reputed to have 'continually invested in the shares of other companies and in 1917 this investment stood at £4.02 million'.[23]

If a foreign venture was well-placed to address unexploited opportunities while the domestic counterpart continued to negotiate the challenges of saturated markets in a competitive national industry, it was likely to outstrip the achievements of the parent fairly quickly. Perhaps, by their very decision to make an expensive and risky foreign direct investment, the owners considered their chances for expansion in their home trade to be limited. But despite the undoubted aspiration for foreign projects to prosper in tandem with the owners' British assets, the fact that many exceeded them and in some cases, despite the languishing and failure of the original firm, provides further evidence that early foreign direct investment, by contrast to later multinational-corporate ventures, was not designed to support the parent company. In 1886 the Yorkshire press implied the enormous success of the Briggs-Posselt partnership's Russian-Polish undertaking, stating that 'the premises at Marki are even more extensive than those of Briggella Mills and provision has been left for still further extensions which the success of the enterprise will render necessary in the immediate future'.[24] Similarly the foreign factories of, for example, Bradford venture capitalists Stephen Greenwood at Łódź or the Thornton family at St Petersburg were both eminently more successful in Russia than in Britain.

Categorising Foreign Direct Investment

The history of British foreign direct investment has been broadly researched but assessments of its characteristics and extent vary dramatically according to the parameters used to categorise it. Mira Wilkins highlights that a vast number of British-managed overseas companies have been erroneously described as foreign direct investment.[25] Some scholars question the inclusion of colonial enterprises, or those instigated by expatriates domiciled abroad and most discount merchant companies, reasoning that their core operations were international or because the ownership of many, despite British naturalisation, was basically foreign.[26] By contrast Chapman justifies his inclusion of merchant groups due to their

22 Sigsworth, *Black Dyke Mills*, p. 224.

23 Kirsten Kininmonth, 'The Growth, Development and Management of J&P Coats Ltd, circa 1890–1960: An Analysis of Strategy and Structure', *Business History*, 48: 4 (2006), p. 563.

24 *Illustrated Weekly Telegraph*, Bradford, 19 March 1886, p. 1.

25 Wilkins, 'The Free-Standing Company', p. 260.

26 Winder, 'Webs of Enterprise', p. 791.

central importance in the development of British overseas trade and finance in the nineteenth century.[27] However, it is evident that late nineteenth- and early twentieth-century international-investment groups and multinational corporations have been the subject of very much more extensive historical research than private businesses for a very practical reason. The unprecedented scale of these later operations, their remote activities and characteristic separation between ownership and control naturally required a well-documented legal basis.[28] By contrast, the independent foreign undertakings of private partnerships or family firms, based on informal agreements and developed in a culture of high trust, have proved more problematic to research. For R. and T. Elworthy of Elizabethgrad, makers and importers of agricultural machinery from 1874,[29] John Hughes' New Russia Company, an iron and steel works established in 1869 at Hughesovka [Iuzovka],[30] the 1860 Thornton Woollen Mill at St Petersburg,[31] for the machine makers and engineers Stephen Greenwood of Łódź,[32] John Holroyd in Austria[33] or indeed the Briggs-Posselt partnership at Marki, there were no effusive brochures to attract investors, no dividends were issued and no annual accounts were published. Much potentially useful information such as family or business correspondence, order books, accounts and so forth has been long since discarded or destroyed with the factories during the World Wars.

The Briggs-Posselt Partnership Agreement

In March 1883 the Briggs-Posselt partnership signed a four-point agreement drawn up by the Bradford solicitors Vint, Hill and Killick, which provides some rare insight for this case study. The liberalisation of England company law between 1855 and 1862 allowed the firm to be created in Bradford and subject to British regulations while its assets, management and two of the three owners would

[27] Chapman, 'British-Based Investment Groups', p. 232.

[28] Ibid., pp. 230–51, J.P. McKay, 'The house of Rothschild (Paris) as a multinational industrial enterprise, 1875–1914', in *Multinational Enterprise in Historical Perspective*, ed. A. Teichova (Cambridge: Cambridge University Press, 1986), pp. 74–86 and Jones, 'The Case of Dunlop', pp. 35–53.

[29] 'From Russia with Interest', *The Times*, 26 January 1987, p. 10.

[30] Colin Thomas, *Dreaming a City – From Wales to the Ukraine* (Ceredigion: Welsh Books Council, 2009). Hughesovka [Iuzovka] later became known as Stalino and is now Donetsk. See also Theodore H. Friedgut, *Iuzovka and Revolution: Vol. 1, Life and Work in Russia's Donbass, 1869–1924* (Princeton: Princeton University Press, 1994).

[31] Martin Varley, 'The Thornton Woollen Mill, St. Petersburg', *History Today*, 44 (December 1994) and some family correspondence preserved in the Russian Collection of at the University of Leeds.

[32] J. Kusiński, R. Bonisławski and M. Janik, *Księga fabryk Łodzi* [*Book of Łódź Factories*] (Łódź: Wydawn Jacek Kusiński, 2010), p. 206.

[33] 'Notes of the Month', p. 540.

permanently reside abroad; 'a legally distinct corporation for overseas activities'.[34] The brevity of the agreement, considering the scale of the shared investment and that construction of their foreign plant had begun already, suggests the very high level of trust between the partners. It recorded that:

> 1. E. Briggs J. Briggs the junior and E. Posselt establish themselves as spinners manufacturers and merchants at or near Warsaw or at such other place as they hereafter agree upon under the firm of 'Briggs Posselt and Co'.
>
> 2. The capital of the firm is £68,000 sterling.
>
> 3. All three partners have the right to sign the firm.
>
> 4. The contract is for six years from the 1st January 1883 ending 1st January 1889 then during the joint lives of the partners subject to determination by six months notice given by any of the three partners.[35]

Edward Briggs was not John Briggs' eldest son but apparently the most capable and when he assumed management of his family's Bradford assets in the last quarter of the nineteenth century, he certainly maintained the proprietorial style of the founder. He had been educated at Joseph Wright's school at Wibsey, a Weselyan institution famed for its practical and disciplinarian instruction. The boys were equipped to 'go out, chain in hand, measure a field, or a haystack, bring back the measurements to school and put down the correct results in their ponderous exercise books; write them out in neat hand-writing ... with crayon figure or illustration drawn to scale'.[36] The established nature of the family firm allowed Edward Briggs little freedom to exercise these technical skills except in the registration of product patents and minor modifications to machinery or process, however the foreign project let him implement all his planning and surveying expertise.

Although each partner was undoubtedly indispensible to the long-term success of the Marki business, Edward Briggs was the strategist who 'conceived the bold idea'[37] and directed its construction in a typically hands-on fashion. His practical grounding enabled him to realise the possibilities of the land at Marki, to regulate the water supply, establish power plants and, rather than emulating, dramatically improve upon his father's mid-century endeavours. But his willingness to introduce non-family capital – in the form of both money and expertise – and delegate local

34 Wilkins, 'The Free-Standing Company', p. 262.

35 WYAS records of solicitors Vint Hill and Killick, Ref. 10D76/2/33/14/3, transcribed here in full.

36 James Parker, *Illustrated History of Wibsey* (Bradford: Matthews and Brooks, 1902), p. 76.

37 'Mr Edward Briggs of Bradford', *Yorkshire Weekly Post*, 12 March, 1898.

management of the foreign firm to Ernst Posselt and John Briggs junior would seem to indicate a movement away from the personal management style of the founder to a more modern 'entrepreneurial' approach.

In the 1880s it was still largely accepted that prosperity lay in the industrialists' shop-floor management of their operations. Chapter 1 showed that the Briggs prided themselves on their intimate knowledge of 'all the working details of manufacturing',[38] and prior to the Russian-Polish venture, all members of the family firm had a direct role in running it, under the supervision of the founder. But Wilkins attributes the failure of many foreign direct investments to the decision-making authority being 'far removed from the area of economic activity'.[39] British-based directorships' lack of personal involvement in the remote commercial community, their failure to delegate responsibilities to local experts and basic delays in making crucial decisions led to unprofitability. Therefore, although Edward Briggs' status as founder and equal partner in the Marki concern might suggest his heavy involvement in running the foreign company, despite rapidly improving long-distance communications, it would have been considered unfeasible for him to manage the distant enterprise effectively from Bradford. Nor, as managing director of Briggella Mills, could he afford to loosen his grip on his existing interests. Thus, practical necessity, and arguably his firm commitment to the proprietorial approach of his father, forced Edward Briggs to entrust the foreign enterprise to his Warsaw-based partners and allow them to determine the longer-term strategic and practical adaptations necessary to capitalise on local opportunities in Poland.

Each of the Bradford partners enjoyed an equal right to 'sign the firm',[40] but one facet of their partnership agreement perhaps reveals a subtle difference in their individual long-term ambitions. It was usual for such contracts to stipulate terms regarding each participant's share in the profits or losses of a new concern and contract a minimum time period for the agreement. When a partner left a business, 'the most frequent outcome was that his capital and name were withdrawn from it'.[41] At Marki the Briggs brothers undoubtedly intended to engage in an enduring fixed-asset investment along the same lines as their Bradford family firm, whereas Posselt's career history would suggest that the Polish project was part of a habitual pattern of venture, profit and withdrawal in readiness for the next opportunity. Thus it seems likely that the minimum six-year contractual obligation was stipulated to tie Posselt to the new business. Although the former merchant certainly contributed a third of the capital, it was his skills rather than his cash that were of primary importance to the Briggs brothers. His eventual withdrawal from the foreign enterprise was almost certainly expected, even agreed, but his premature disengagement was a latent threat which the Briggs needed to legislate

[38] *Illustrated Weekly Telegraph*, Bradford, 19 March 1886, p. 1.

[39] Wilkins, 'The Free-Standing Company', p. 275.

[40] WYAS, Ref.10D76/2/33/14/3.

[41] Jones, *Merchants to Multinationals*, p. 21.

against. Six years must have been judged a sufficient period to make full use of his contacts and expertise, for John Briggs junior to establish his reputation in Russia and for sufficient profits to accumulate so that the German entrepreneur's stake could be released without detriment to the going concern. The fact that the partnership endured until 1897 strongly suggests that the returns were sufficient to encourage Posselt's continued participation and to finance his numerous other entrepreneurial activities.[42]

This distinction between the Bradford industrialists' and the German merchant's attitude to their shared investment clearly reflected some broader differences in the partners' cultural business behaviour. Although Posselt's Bradford firm retained his name until 1969, he actually dissolved his partnership with his brother-in-law Rudolph Peters when he relocated to Warsaw in 1883.[43] It is possible that this was a response to the growing pressures on the merchant role that were described in Chapter 1, or to fund his share in Edward Briggs' project, but it seems evident that Posselt had accumulated extraordinary wealth in England which he intended to devote wholeheartedly to Russian-empire opportunities. The course of Posselt's Russian career will be examined in more detail in Chapter 6, but it is worth noting here that within three years of his relocation to Warsaw, in tandem with his commitment to the Marki enterprise, he had established the first of several new manufacturing concerns: the *Zgierska Manufaktura Bawelniana* [Zgierz Cotton Factory].[44] Posselt went on to build the *Towarzystwo Akcyjne Tekstil* [Joint Stock Company Tekstil] manufacturing company at Riga,[45] a Warsaw-based silk factory the *Rosyjsko-Włoskiego Towarzystwa Akcyjnego Wyrobów Włoknistych* [Russian-Italian Joint Stock Company Fibre Products][46] and the *Warszawska Akcyjna Fabryka Dywanów* [Joint Stock Company of Warsaw Carpet Factories].[47] Thus, although he abandoned his traditional merchanting activities in favour of industrial fixed assets, Posselt's dynamic and broadly diversified approach to investment in different products, partners, markets and even nations remained. His core assets, the Marki and Zgierz firms and the Belgian tannery, were private partnerships, but later he embraced the joint-stock system. Indeed, in Russian Poland the poor capitalisation of industry made this a more typical organisational form for manufacturing businesses than in Britain.

42 *Yorkshire Daily Observer*, Bradford, 12 March 1897.

43 *Morning Post*, London, 3 January 1883, p. 6 and *York Herald*, 3 January 1883, p. 6.

44 *Rocznik polskiego przemyslu i handlu* [*Polish Annual of Industry and Business*] (Warsaw: Nakładem Polsk. Spółki Wydawnictw Informacyjnych, 1934), p. 559.

45 *Gazeta Losowań Papierów Publicznych*, Warsaw, No. 50, 16 December 1905, p. 3.

46 Wartalska, 'Fabryka i osada fabryczna w Markach', p. 655, W. Puś, *Przemysł włokienniczy w Królestwie Polskim w latach 1870–1900* [*Textile Industry in the Kingdom of Poland 1870–1900*] (Łódź: Zeszyty Naukowe Uniwersytetu Łódzkiego, 1976), p. 23.

47 *Kurjer Kolejowy*, Warsaw, No. 30, 1898, p. 2.

Family Politics and Business

The Briggs interests were, by contrast to their German partner, largely consolidated in one family enterprise. In the style of aristocratic primogeniture it was typical for elder sons to own a higher stake in nineteenth-century family firms.[48] This was considered to avoid dilution of the assets and incentivise entrepreneurship in younger generations who were encouraged to create auxiliary business activities to support the parent company. However, at J. Briggs and Co. a scrupulous fairness was initiated by the founder. All five of John Briggs' sons and his only son-in-law, Francis Whitehead, had an equal share of the Bradford firm which continued despite the permanent residence of his youngest sons John junior and Alfred Briggs in Russian Poland after 1883.

Family politics could be a powerfully destructive force in companies if proper leadership provision was not made before the death of the founder.[49] Edward Briggs' business acumen and ambition is certainly suggested by his instigation of the Marki venture in 1883 and his accession to leadership of the Bradford company over his four brothers. By the time his elder brother Moses had died in 1885, shortly followed by their father in 1886, Edward held managerial control of all the family's interests in Bradford and Marki. Thereafter, there is some evidence to suggest that he began to manoeuvre the ownership away from the egalitarian approach favoured by his father. The *London Gazette* shows that in 1893 Charles, the middle Briggs brother, bowed out of the family firm.[50] None of Moses' or Charles' sons inherited a stake in the ownership of J. Briggs and Co., and although the Warsaw-based brothers retained their share, their entrepreneurial interest had been effectively diverted into the foreign enterprise, whence their sister's only son Charles Whitehead was also dispatched in the 1890s.

The ultimate objective of Edward Briggs' strategy became more apparent on his death in 1898. A palpable divergence of family assets along national lines seems apparent, as his British business interests were left to his son Arthur 'Harry' Briggs and his brother-in-law Francis Whitehead,[51] whereas Polish records show that he bequeathed his share of Marki to his Warsaw-based brothers John and Alfred.[52] But some private understandings rather than contractual agreements amongst the family are evident as the 1907 obituary of Francis Whitehead emphatically states that 'he was also a member of the firm Messrs E. Briggs and Co., of Warsaw and

48 W.M. Mathew, *Keiller's of Dundee: The Rise of the Marmalade Dynasty 1800–1879* (Dundee: Abertay Historical Society Publication, 1999) and in Sigsworth, *Black Dyke Mills*.

49 Gillian Cookson, 'Family Firms and Business Networks: Textile Engineering in Yorkshire, 1780–1830', *Business History*, 39: 1 (1997), p. 15.

50 *London Gazette*, 23 June 1893, p. 3590.

51 Probate Register, 1907, p. 150, it should be noted that Edward Briggs bequeathed his British assets to his wife, son and brother-in-law.

52 PBN, *Księga wieczysta 'osada wójtostwa Marki'* [*Land and mortgage register of the settlement of the village of Marki*], No. 4980.

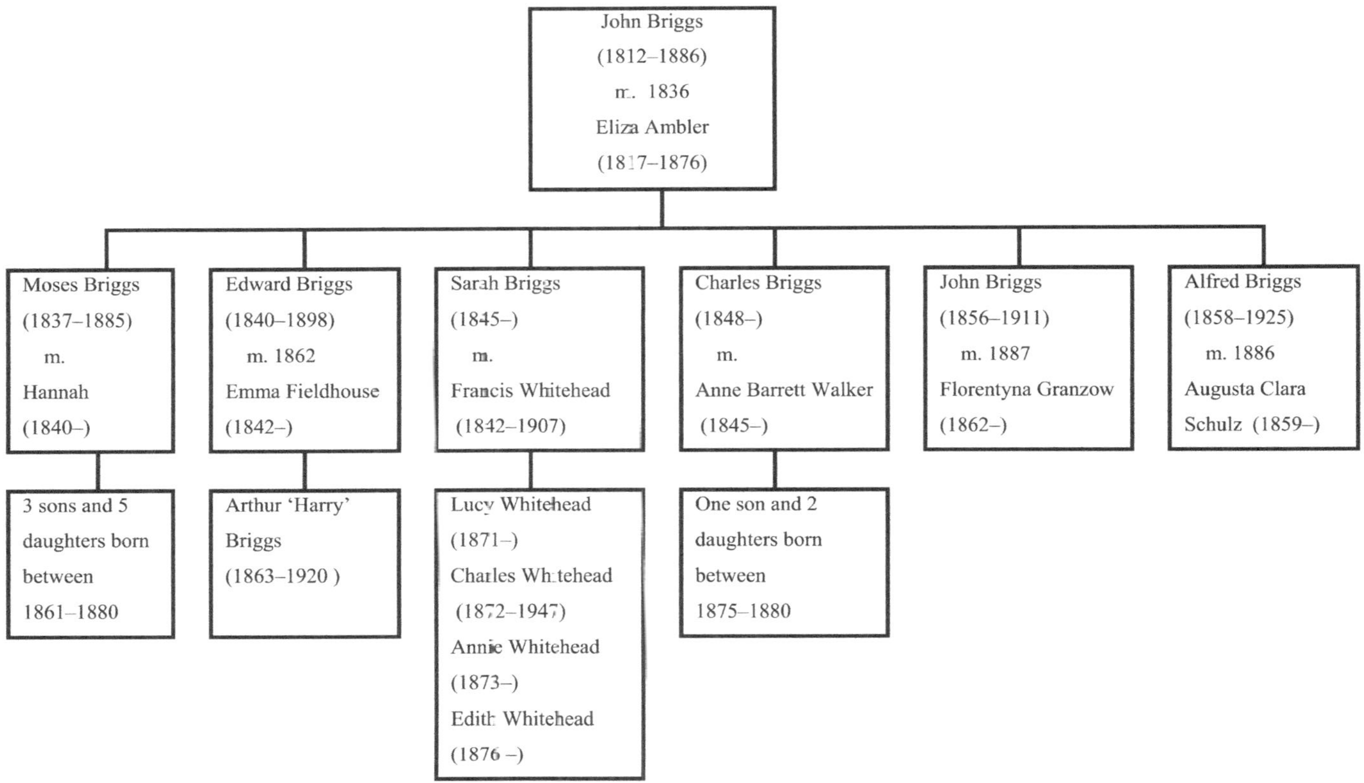

Figure 2.1 The Briggs' Family Tree
Source: Author's diagram

of Messrs Alfred Briggs and Co., of Gordon Street Mills, Bradford'.[53] Neither of the surviving partners in the Marki enterprise had any sons, therefore it seems probable, perhaps following Posselt's withdrawal from the partnership in 1897, that an agreement was reached with their brother-in-law Francis Whitehead that his only son Charles would inherit Bradford Mills at Marki, leaving the Bradford family firm to Edward's only son Arthur 'Harry' Briggs. Thus Charles Whitehead became sole proprietor of Polish enterprise after the deaths of his uncles, John in 1911 and Alfred in 1925.

Financing the Foreign Investment

After 1870, with the development of a secure international-banking network and rapidly improving communications 'flows of people, trade and capital created a "global economy" for the first time in history'.[54] But although the business of banking undoubtedly thrived on exchange-rate manipulations, commissions and interest charges, cash-rich entrepreneurs who established factories abroad sought to save not only agents' commission, import taxes, shipping and insurance costs, but also the charges associated with international banking. Other potential sources of investment capital such as merchant banks, company promoters and stockbrokers were 'wary of unproved foreign and colonial ventures, especially those in mining and manufacturing',[55] whereas the often state-controlled banks of developing nations, whether as institutionally unwilling as their British counterparts, rarely had the funds to support industry. Thus, the historically weak relationship between banks and industrialists persisted in British-foreign investment, and self-finance remained the norm.

By employing personal assets or ploughed-back profits from existing firms, entrepreneurs avoided the limiting effects of long-term interest charges or the jeopardy of securing loans against vital assets. But, as this chapter has highlighted, the key factor which made internal funding preferable was the industrialists' resistance towards any dilution of control over the direction of their business.[56] An outside investor might insist on a preferred supplier with whom they had a vested interest, or demand production of low-cost, high-yield goods to swiftly recover his outlay, despite the long-term detriment to the reputation of the new company. Reymont accurately describes this dilemma in his nineteenth-century novel *The Promised Land.* His cash-strapped protagonist Borowiecki resists taking on a wealthy partner who wants to manufacture shoddy; a cheap quality which used recycled wool and rags, in order to realise quick profits as he believes this would

53 'Mr Francis Whitehead of Bradford', *Yorkshire Daily Observer*, Bradford, 14 March 1907.

54 Jones, *Merchants to Multinationals*, p. 45.

55 Chapman, 'British-Based Investment Groups', p. 232.

56 Cottrell, *British Overseas Investment*, p. 55.

create a negative brand for his new firm. He complains: 'A factory I want to have; I want cash too; but I don't want to manufacture worthless stuffs'.[57]

Excellent capitalisation was essential to the Marki venture and the Briggs-Posselt partnership agreement suggests that in 1883, £68,000 was deemed a sufficient sum to establish a large industrial plant in Russian Poland. Few details exist to corroborate this assessment but it seems noteworthy that when a fire devastated the Thornton Woollen Mill at St Petersburg in 1892 the insurance settlement was a remarkably similar amount. Daniel Bateman Thornton wrote to his family in Bradford: 'we have had a settling up with the insurance company, no small matter considering the amount of damage ... £62,300'.[58] As Thornton already owned his land and the extent of the rebuild, machinery and stock replacement are unknown, this letter can only be considered a coincidental anecdote; nevertheless it does highlight a relevant point for this case study. An obvious assumption would be that venture capital would be roughly apportioned between land purchase, building materials, machinery, labour, raw materials and a reserve of cash to provide liquidity for the firm's dealings; an effective bridging loan between the project's outset, until production got underway and sufficient revenue could be generated to cover expenses. However, the value a company placed on its assets was largely theoretical and there was a considerable difference between the book cost and the hard cash required to secure them. It is more likely that the £68,000 cited in the Briggs-Posselt partnership agreement reflected a budgetary guideline, an indication of each partner's share and liability, or indeed an assessment for insurance purposes. In a commercial environment where reputations and trust could constitute a currency more potent than cash, nineteenth-century entrepreneurs developed an armoury of tactics to enhance the value of their capital and finance their plans. Extended credit terms might be negotiated with British suppliers, secured against the assets of the parent firm, and by fostering a culture of shared opportunity in Warsaw, local collaborators might similarly extend credit or exchange services to bolster the venture capitalists' initial fund or, indeed, minimise the outlay of real money.

Mutual Advantage Rather Than Cash

The terms under which the Briggs-Posselt partnership acquired the estate at Marki strongly suggest a mutual-advantage component. In January 1883, 70 per cent of the land was purchased from a joint-stock company owned by a consortium of Warsaw businessmen called *Folwark i cegielnia wójtostwa Marki* [Farm and brickworks of the village of Marki] while the final 30 per cent was retained by the vendors until

57 Reymont, *The Promised Land*, pp. 487–8.

58 Leeds Russian Archive, MS.1072/20, Daniel Bateman Thornton in St Petersburg to Mary Thornton in Bradford, 8 November 1892.

1886.[59] Although the records of the Polish land registry provide no explanation, this arrangement undoubtedly allowed the former owners to secure both the sale of land in a rural backwater and fulfil a large providential brick-supply contract into the bargain: thus a very competitive rate and extended credit terms, for both the bricks and the property were undoubtedly negotiated. In this way the Bradford partners secured the rights to the whole site with minimal capital outlay and post-dating completion until 1886 allowed the new business to accumulate sufficient funds before payment was finalised. The arcane nature of such agreements led few to be documented but this one instance suggests a probable pattern of finance for many aspects of the complex plant and accompanying town. Although it will be considered in more detail in Chapters 5 and 6, it is pertinent to note here that the Briggs-Posselt partnership also employed one of the shareholders of the land vendors' joint-stock company, the Warsaw architect Edward Lilpop, to manage their plant's construction.

In subjugated Russian Poland, exploiting political allegiances could provide an additional lever in transactions between like-minded traders who might invoice below market rates or exchange goods and services, to circumvent high taxation. Reymont cynically suggests that Łódź's cotton kings unscrupulously used their fiancées' dowries to fund their businesses and mocked what he saw as the mercenary intermarriage between manufacturing dynasties. However, he also highlights that speculation in raw materials was a common scheme to stretch venture capital. Reducing the circulation of vital components could drive up their price and thus the higher-value stock formed a useful currency to trade for goods, services or to provide collateral for credit or loans.[60] In the Yorkshire worsted industry, fixed-asset investments rarely accounted for more than 'forty-five per cent of a business's total capital, and often as low as twenty-five per cent',[61] while the remainder was held in raw-material stocks. Chapter 10 will describe how the Briggs-Posselt partnership devoted a great deal of 1883 to accumulating wool in the Russian empire.

By the turn of the twentieth century, Bradford Mills at Marki was a large and fully integrated yarn and textile manufacturing concern. Despite the ambitious style of the enterprise which included sizable land holdings, a model workers' community, private gas and electricity generation plants and a rail link to Warsaw, it is clear that the company was established on the same organisational basis as both J. Briggs and Co. and E. Posselt and Co. of Bradford. It was a private partnership based on the traditional family capitalism model which remained the most common configuration for British manufacturing firms until the First World War. The Briggs, like most British manufacturers, adopted a proprietorial approach to their interests and viewed the growing divorce between capital and control

59 PBN, No. 475 *do księgi wieczystej 'osada wójtostwo Marki'*, No. 4980.

60 Reymont, *The Promised Land*, p. 57.

61 P. Hudson, *The Genesis of Industrial Capital. A Study of the West Riding Wool Textile Industry, c. 1750–1850* (Cambridge: Cambridge University Press, 1986).

which characterised the up-and-coming joint-stock firms as both a threat to their familiar high-trust commercial culture and inappropriate to their requirements.

This chapter has shown that the foreign venture constituted a personal investment for Edward and John Briggs junior, in partnership with Ernst Posselt, rather than a company investment by J. Briggs and Co., Bradford. While useful cooperation between Bradford and Warsaw in the recruitment of staff and sharing of technical experience will be explored in later chapters, despite their interlocking directorates neither operation – domestic nor foreign – was intended to emulate or depend on the other. The Russian-Polish business was neither the source of cheap off-shore processing for the established operations nor a truly international venture, but an essentially British company which confined its operations to an adopted home country, tailoring its products and strategy to local demands and resources. Although Edward Briggs appears to display some key characteristics of a more modern entrepreneurial approach in his strategic management of the foreign venture – in the introduction of non-family capital and expertise, and a growing willingness to delegate responsibility – this has been shown to result from his firm commitment to the standard proprietorial form of management.

The British social and commercial climate which had galvanised self-reliance in Yorkshire's industrialists perfectly prepared the Bradford partners to capitalise successfully in the unfamiliar commercial arena of Poland. They favoured independent self-finance and were proficient builders of trust-based relationships which enabled them to achieve their goals without reference to the state, formal financial institutions or outside investors. In this context Ernst Posselt's role has been defined not primarily as the source of cash, but of vital human capital. His skills in commercial networking, his linguistic proficiency and ability to identify local opportunity would prove pivotal for the new enterprise. He would guide the younger Briggs brothers at Marki and advise Edward Briggs on local opportunities and necessary adjustments to the venturing firm's strategy.

Chapter 3

'To embark their energies in a part of the world more favourable':[1] Assessing the opportunity created by foreign protectionism

In the late nineteenth century it was frequently claimed that challenging economic conditions and increasingly restrictive factory legislation drove British industrial capital abroad.[2] This might present a compelling rationale for a rising incidence of overseas portfolio investment, but foreign direct investment was undertaken exclusively by industrialists who, in spite of the alleged hardships, had achieved extraordinary wealth and success. Therefore it is necessary to look beyond the supposed negative *push* factors in the home trade to understand their true motivation. Global developments in communications that established commercial infrastructure on an international footing in the last quarter of the nineteenth century certainly broadened the horizons of many businesses in terms of export markets and resourcing. However, it was a diverse range of nation- and industry-specific advantages, the *pull* factors, which enticed venture capitalists to build factories abroad and ultimately determined the style and location for clusters of British foreign enterprise. This chapter will consider the broad-ranging factors which made foreign direct investment in the Russian empire a particularly tempting proposition for the Bradford partners.

From a range of incentives which include the cheapness or greater availability of land and labour abroad, the attraction of untapped natural resources or markets, foreign direct investment has been most often attributed to protectionism. This book will not add to the very broad spectrum of academic debate on Free Trade, the proportionality or morality of legislative responses to growing international commerce which were intended to bolster foreign economies. Nevertheless, the evolution and implementation of tariff control must be considered to assess the opportunity that it created for venture capitalists. The supposition of Ewa Wartalska that the Bradford partners 'jumped over the tariff barrier'[3] will be tested along with Andrew Hutchinson Dawson's wider claims that the five largest factories established in Russian Poland in the 1880s, which included the Marki

---

[1] 'Notes of the Month', p. 540, and M. Edelstein, *Overseas Investment in the Age of High Imperialism: the United Kingdom, 1850–1914* (New York: Columbia University Press, 1982), p. 196.

[2] 'Factory Legislation', p. 75.

[3] Wartalska, 'Fabryka i osada fabryczna', p. 647.

venture, centrally 'sought profits through production within the tariff boundary of the Russian empire'.[4]

Tariff Control

Tariff control essentially fell into two categories: one comprised the import taxes levied on mainly luxury products such as 'wine, spirits, tea, sugar, and tobacco',[5] which were not part of the domestic product and generated revenue for the importer's national economy. On the other hand, protectionist tariffs were designed to weight the price of incoming goods which could be made locally. Creating artificially high prices for foreign products cushioned developing industry from world competition and in theory stimulated the market for local manufactures. Although both taxes – revenue or protectionist – were a duty imposed at the port of entry, there was a fundamental difference between them. Revenue taxes were not supposed to impact too heavily on a trade which was desirable for all parties concerned: producers or manufacturers, merchants, customers and the government. The British economy, for example, thrived on import duties and retail taxes of luxuries for an increasingly affluent population and the wealth of many high-ranking dignitaries rested on the colonial plantations producing them. However, national tastes could easily be influenced by prohibitively expensive goods; 'raise the tariff on wine and people will drink beer; the tariffs on coffee affect the patterns of tea consumption',[6] therefore it was critical to maintain the levy at the optimum level to sustain trade but generate maximum cash.

The same economic balancing act applied to protectionism, but despite a short-term increase in revenue, its goal was to progressively limit and ultimately stop the import of certain goods in order to stimulate domestic production. Nevertheless, protectionism was not an exact science and while the objective might have been to level global prices or appreciably advantage domestic industry, the significance of international trade to each nation, the size and wealth of populations, natural resources and industrial potentials were of course unequal. Within each economy quite different trades are interdependent, leading success or failure to have far-reaching implications. Thus the basically simple economic strategy became a field of complex calculations, as even subtle legislative changes could dramatically transform the fortunes of national economies, key industries, specific products and even individual businesses. As ex-Governor Seymour of New York suggested in 1881: 'if England should tax American grain imports to the extent of even so little

---

4 A. Hutchinson Dawson, *The Industrial Geography of Woollen Textile Manufacturing in Poland after 1870* (PhD thesis, University College London, 1966), p. 182.

5 John Vincent Nye, 'The Myth of Free-Trade Britain and Fortress France: Tariffs and Trade in the Nineteenth Century', *Journal of Economic History*, 51: 1 (1991), p. 36.

6 Ibid., p. 35.

as ten or twenty cents per bushel ... while allowing the grain of her own colonies to enter her ports free, she can bankrupt the farmers of the American North-West'.[7]

The Impact of Foreign Protectionism on British Industry

The basic principle of protectionism is a sliding scale based on the evolving needs of each country's industry. Large-scale import of particular merchandise highlighted the economic potential of the market, and to encourage the establishment or expansion of local manufacture those imports would be taxed. As national production capabilities advanced, the duty would be increased and then extended to components, until eventually only necessary raw materials and machinery would enter the borders at a workable rate. The regular amendments to product-specific tariffs provide a good illustration of both how the economic plan was implemented and its positive impact on the industries it protected, as they directly correlate to changing industrial requirements. For example, a revision to the Russian wool tariff published in the *Leeds Mercury* in July 1882 reveals a continuing requirement for raw materials, as dyed and undyed wool were taxed at a very low rate but the levy rose steeply for spun products, reflecting the growing proficiency of the Russian spinning industry: 'raw wool – undyed, 1rb per poud. Raw wool – dyed, 2rb per poud. Half spun wool – undyed, 3rb per poud. Half spun wool – dyed 4.5rb per poud. Spun wool – undyed, 7rb 50kp per poud. Spun wool – dyed, 9rb'.[8] The fact that no rates for cloth appear in this amendment suggests that by the early 1880s the tax had become so prohibitively high as to be entirely inconsequential to Yorkshire manufacturers, who had for the most part ceased to attempt the trade. In 1905 the Bradford businessman W.H. Mitchell bemoaned the progressive impact of protectionism on local trade, stating 'just as they replaced the import of fully manufactured goods in the first instance by the import of yarn to make goods themselves, so they are now proceeding to replace yarn by tops to spin into yarn for themselves'.[9] His complaints that protected foreign industries only bought raw materials or basic components in England and not finished products illustrate the way protectionism gradually deprived stronger economies of the highest margins for the most processed goods.

This was, however, by no means a new phenomenon, or one solely attributable to rising tariff control, as Sigsworth identifies in the pattern of trade between the Bradford industrialist John Foster and the German cloth manufacturer Louis Reichenheim. Before 1850 Foster enjoyed a significant direct trade, supplying the German weaver with worsted yarn, and even established a merchant partnership

[7] *National Fair Trade League Annual Report 1881–1882* (London, 1882), p. 23.

[8] *Leeds Mercury*, 8 July 1882. Note: a 'poud' or 'pud' was equal to 36 lb, 'rb' denotes Russian ruble, 'kp' denotes Russian kopek.

[9] Sigsworth, *Black Dyke Mills*, p. 102.

with him in Bradford in 1852.[10] When in July 1861 Reichenheim built his own spinning mill in Germany, he assured his British collaborator that it would only produce weft yarn, leaving the supply of more technically challenging and therefore expensive warp yarn to the Bradford firm.[11] But by 1865, Foster's letters reveal the closing stages of the once-lucrative trade when he wrote: 'we have no orders from [Reichenheims] for some time back and they hold out not much promise that they will be wanting much this season. The fact is we expect they will spin nearly the whole of what they want'.[12] Rapidly developing foreign industry represented a much-needed outlet for British industrialists, but serving its needs gradually came to dictate the focus of production for the formerly dominant manufacturing nation.

State Incentives to Attract Foreign Direct Investment

Until the late nineteenth century, policies to attract foreign capital, entrepreneurship and technology to underdeveloped fields of industry had largely consisted of the piecemeal apportionment of preferential government contracts to individuals, rather than legislation to create a conducive economic environment for natural commercial and industrial development. Foreign specialists were typically invited to fulfil individual contracts, for example the Tsar invited John Hughes to establish a modern iron works in Russia to furnish government-led expansion of the rail network in 1870.[13] In this unrefined approach the host nation recognised industrial and technological shortcomings, but sought to maintain control of enterprise and limit the activities of venturing entrepreneurs, with the result that only pockets of industrial advancement met the needs of individual projects. Protectionism provided the first broad-reaching system which was perceived to attract foreign investors generally. Its potential not just to increase business tax revenues, acquire foreign technology, but also to develop local infrastructure, led many governments to revise their trade policies and consolidate them with other incentives aimed specifically at prosperous foreign venture capitalists, rather than native businessmen. For example, in 1883 the Hungarian government advertised in the British press that they would exempt foreign entrepreneurs from: 'house tax and income tax till the end of 1895, and also from the taxes payable on the purchase of factory ground, and from stamp duty, and such dues as are leviable on the creation of new Joint-Stock Companies, and in the issue of shares'.[14]

---

[10] *N. Heydemann and Co.*

[11] Weft yarn does not have to be as strong or regular as warp yarn which is under constant tension during weaving, therefore it can be produced with less twist from cheaper raw materials at a lower cost.

[12] Sigsworth, *Black Dyke Mills*, p. 310.

[13] Thomas, *Dreaming a City*.

[14] 'A New Centre for English Enterprise', *Textile Recorder*, Manchester, 15 June 1883, p. 27.

In the last quarter of the nineteenth century the German Chancellor, Otto von Bismarck, became an enthusiastic proponent of protectionism. In the late 1880s his lead was notably followed by the Russian finance minister, Sergei Witte, who faced heavy criticism from more conservative voices in the Tsarist regime for his scheme to attract foreign capital to Russia. In the 1890s tariffs instigated by McKinley and later Dingley to bolster US industry led a wave of so-called tariff factories to populate the American industrial landscape.[15] For governments intent on enticing foreign investment and entrepreneurship, John P. McKay suggests that the desired economic results could be achieved by a 'quite subtle' combination of rail network improvement, high import tariffs and occasionally a marketing campaign to suggest the solidity of the regime and the trading climate.[16]

It is worth mentioning here that, by the twentieth century, many governments had devised a more sophisticated legislative tool to target specific and desirable foreign firms: foreign patents were disallowed unless the product was manufactured locally. In some cases British firms found foreign partners to assemble imported parts which enabled them to secure patent rights abroad, but Geoffrey Jones concludes that very often 'the desire to establish a strong patent position in a large market was the most important motive behind the firm's decision to make a direct investment'.[17] Threats of exclusion from large foreign markets were also used against powerful manufacturers to encourage them to build factories. For example, in the 1930s the Irish government ostensibly blackmailed both Cadbury and Dunlop to found local factories, by threatening to bar their products from the Irish market and offer monopolies to their competitors.[18]

The Russian-Polish Economic Environment

Although protectionism might have recommended itself as a panacea to stimulate economic growth, its implementation could produce a significant negative impact. In countries where poverty was rife and natural resources were minimal or unexplored, state treasuries relied heavily on import levies rather than personal or company taxation. The initial short-term financial gain provided by increased tariffs naturally led to a medium-term deficit as imports fell away. Creating a proportional increase in business tax quickly enough to fill the void was more difficult in practice than the theory suggested. In many countries which resorted to such legislative behaviour, the lack of industrialisation and impoverishment were both symptom and cause of an economic backwardness in which native capital

15 John P. McKay, *Pioneers for Profit Foreign Entrepreneurship and Russian Industrialisation 1880–1914* (London and Chicago: University of Chicago Press, 1970), p. 72.

16 Ibid., p. 7.

17 Jones, 'Growth and Performance of British Multinational Firms', p. 38.

18 McKay, *Pioneers for Profit*, p. 50.

and entrepreneurship were scarce. Thus, there was rarely an indigenous class of sufficiently capitalised or skilled businessmen to take advantage of the favourable commercial conditions which protectionism supposedly created and despite the introduction of this radical trade legislation to improve the situation, an entrenched culture of governmental control usually remained in place.

In 1883 the Polish Lands were under Russian military occupation and as such the administration faced an additional political dimension to the problem of stimulating economic development. Although 'the British example of using an income tax to supply the revenue requirements was not politically expedient',[19] it is clear that the endemic poverty of the region meant that the majority of the population had no money to pay taxes in any case. Heavy taxation of the aristocracy was, however, an integral part of the Russian programme of subjugation, to render any potential opposition leadership financially impotent or simply because they were the only source of cash. These policies created an economic environment that was the antithesis of the capitalist philosophy which had brought industrial progress and prosperity to Britain. Crushing taxation perpetuated a culture of conservatism in the moneyed classes which naturally tended to the ownership of land rather than industrial investment. In such circumstances foreign direct investment presented host governments with a significant short cut, to both capital and entrepreneurship.

It is arguable that the key to Bradford's success lay in the industrialists' freedom to manage local resources, establish infrastructure, run local government and lobby for national legislative improvements to the commercial environment. In Russian Poland, facilitating foreign ownership of industry was arguably a tactic to maintain a precarious political *status quo* in which native wealth was contained in agriculture and affluent foreigners, without any political axe to grind, were encouraged to finance industrial and infrastructural development, providing immediate access to technologies that had taken decades to progress abroad. For many foreign governments the vision of foreign direct investment was to instantly provide a broad-ranging and modern industry, create employment and thus greater wealth and contentment in the population, with minimal state expense. Demand for improvements in communications, water and power supply were created and often sponsored by the venture capitalists. Existing local trades enjoyed increased demand for their products and services, whilst auxiliary industries sprang up to support the primary employers and all benefited from the increased *per capita* wealth. Therefore, as a progressively more volatile international trading climate challenged the economic stability of longer-established industrial states, the governments of developing nations vied to attract the 'vast external pool of entrepreneurship, knowledge and capital waiting to be tapped'.[20]

---

[19] Foreman-Peck, *History of the World Economy*, p. 57.

[20] McKay, *Pioneers for Profit*, p. 12.

The British Free-trade Debate

Britain's stance as the staunchest Free Trade advocate in the nineteenth century and her attempts to influence, even police, the tariff strategies of her trading partners until after the First World War are frequently portrayed as a veritable moral crusade, rather than an economic issue.[21] However, it is evident that economic liberalism served the purposes of a nation with a strong industry, rich natural resources, heavily dependent on international commerce and that had developed British-owned assets abroad to produce commodities such as wool, cotton, rubber, sugar, even coal and iron to feed both expanding domestic industry and to trade abroad.

By the mid-nineteenth century, Chambers of Commerce had been founded in most English industrial cities on a mandate of enhancing the commercial climate and maximising exports. Bradford's Chamber typically served as a stepping stone towards social integration for venturing foreign merchants, who dominated its committee until the twentieth century, and a rite of passage for the sons of prominent industrialists.[22] But this forum which represented such a concentration of rich business leaders constituted a pressure group of significant political power. From its inauguration the association used its influence to lobby for, and even took an active role in, the negotiation of treaties with the city's primary trading-partner nations, France and the German *Zollverein*.[23] In the last quarter of the nineteenth century the minutes of the Chamber's meetings reflect its growing preoccupation with the local impact of American worsted tariffs and the global progression of protectionism as it infected Austria Hungary, Brazil, Spain, Italy, the Romanian Lands, Switzerland, Turkey, Portugal and Canada.[24] However, in 1880 when the prominent local industrialist Samuel Cunliffe Lister proposed a ballot urging the Bradford Chamber to press for 'reciprocity in the new Treaty [with France] and, failing that, countervailing duties upon all French manufactures imported into this country',[25] the overwhelmingly anti-retaliatory stance of the members was evident, as Lister's was the only vote in favour of the resolution.

'The ruinous impact of foreign tariff barriers upon the export achievements of Bradford manufacturers and merchants'[26] remains a convincing explanation for

[21] Foreman-Peck, *History of the World Economy*, p. 55.

[22] Michael Pratt, *The Influence of the Germans on Bradford* (MA thesis, Margaret MacMillan College, 1971), p. 23.

[23] Jacob Behrens, the chairman of the Bradford Chamber of Commerce, was famously active in negotiations which led to the Cobden Treaty in 1860. The German *Zollverein* was a coalition of German states formed to manage customs and economic policies within their territories.

[24] WYAS, WYB111/1/1/6, Bradford Chamber of Commerce Minute Book 1877–1883.

[25] E.M. Sigsworth and J.M Blackman, 'The Woollen and Worsted Industries', in *The Development of British Industry and Foreign Competition 1875–1914*, ed. Derek Aldcroft (London: George Allen and Unwin, 1968), p. 148, quotes Bradford Chamber of Commerce minute book, 20 January 1880.

[26] Firth, 'Bradford Trade in the Nineteenth Century', p. 29.

the changing fortunes of the worsted capital and British industry generally, after the boom years of the mid-nineteenth century. The National Fair Trade League agitated fiercely 'to neutralise the action of tariffs hostile to the products of British industry'.[27] But there were also influential voices that doubted the problems caused by foreign protectionism. In 1883 Bradford businessman and former mayor Henry Mitchell raised the alarm about the 'great falling off in the exports which had taken place during the last nine or ten years of goods from the Bradford district'[28] and blamed rapidly rising American and Russian import duties. On the other hand, the recently knighted Sir Jacob Behrens, chairman of Bradford's Chamber and one of the negotiators of the Cobden Treaty, suggested that any decline in the worsted trade was more than compensated for by increased woollen exports. The *Bradford Observer* joined the fray and famously dismissed the industrialists' despondency as the 'habit of comparing the present time with exceptional times'.[29]

Although foreign protectionism was the focus of a general dissatisfaction, it is evident that retaliation received little serious consideration from the majority of industrialists and national policy-makers who understood that the cause of Britain's economic difficulties was more complex. In the last quarter of the nineteenth century, rising domestic and foreign competition, progressive factory legislation, changing fashion as well as protectionism were all factors that had a transformative effect on British industry. In many cases they encouraged the entrepreneur to 'change and adjust, often for his own good':[30] to streamline production, reduce overheads, find specialisations, diversify market and product bases. The most successful relied on their own ingenuity rather than official agreements and capitalised on the new opportunities created. In 1905 a new ballot of Bradford Chamber members revealed increasingly divided views on Britain's international trade policy, but perhaps more interestingly, it highlighted the altered profile of local industry which had been effected by foreign tariff control. The votes were almost equally divided between those on whom 'the brunt of export decline had fallen, [who] were on-balance pro-retaliation, while those whose export trade had risen, spinners, yarn merchants and combers, were against'.[31]

---

[27] National Fair Trade League, *Annual Report 1881–1882*, p. 22. Established in 1881, this organisation claimed a national cross-industry membership and coordinated rallies intended to keep the protectionism at the forefront of political debate to influence British foreign policy.

[28] 'The Effect of Foreign Tariffs on the Bradford Trade', *Textile Recorder*, Manchester, 15 May 1883, p. 7.

[29] *Bradford Observer*, 30 December 1880.

[30] W. Kirchner, 'Russian Tariffs and Foreign Industries before 1914: The German Entrepreneur's Perspective', *Journal of Economic History*, 41: 2 (1981), p. 377.

[31] Sigsworth and Blackman, 'Woollen and Worsted Industries', p. 148.

European Tariff Wars

When protectionism is put forward as the central explanation for British industrial investment abroad, the argument tends to the presumption that the 'grass is always greener on the other side'. The unquestionable advantage enjoyed by foreign manufacturers was common rhetoric in the British press at the end of the nineteenth century.[32] In reality tariff control created an even less stable commercial environment for businessmen abroad, many of whom were less empowered than their British counterparts to lobby against the often haphazard and reactive legislation of their commercially inexperienced and autocratic governments. It is also evident that commerce was not always at the forefront of the policy-makers' minds and the efficacy of protectionism to motivate local industry vied with its usefulness as an instrument of foreign policy.[33] Indeed few successful trade treaties were negotiated based on purely economic arguments, whereas levies were frequently imposed to castigate or mollify neighbour states for objectionable foreign policy or military posturing. In the last quarter of the nineteenth century a virtual tariff war was in progress across continental Europe which stagnated international trade.[34] The anticipated positive impact of protectionism on industry was tempered by *quid pro quo* import-tax retaliations and the establishment of cartels, which restricted the output of certain products to maintain prices. However, such trade wars could often precipitate advantage for another national trading partner as an 1893 British consular report highlighted: 'in consequence of the maximum tariff now applied to Germany [by Russia], the importation of chemical products from that country has stopped, and that such articles as analine salts and required by the great manufacturing town of Łódź are now being imported from England'.[35]

In July 1881 the *Leeds Mercury* reported that 'the German Government seem to be not a little excited by the raising of the Russian tariff'[36] and anticipated reprisals of heavy duties on Russian corn and raw material. Walther Kirchner describes the resigned attitude of German industrialists who were 'by no means unprepared for, nor surprised by, the fact that any product which an industrialising country such as Russia greatly needed would sooner or later be imitated and manufactured there, and then protected by tariffs'.[37] Whereas trade treaties might have been useful to establish a legal framework for international patent rights, cross-border money transfers and consular representation, foreign entrepreneurs, like their British counterparts, relied on their own resourcefulness rather than any prospect of intergovernmental agreement to secure their individual interests.

---

32 'Factory Legislation', p. 75 and in 'Exhibition in Russia', *Textile World*, March 1883, p. 537.

33 Foreman-Peck, *History of the World Economy*, p. 55.

34 Ibid., p. 118.

35 FO65/1452, Henry Grant to the Secretary of State, 28 August 1893, p. 195.

36 'The Russian Tariff', *Leeds Mercury*, 1 January 1881, p. 7.

37 Kirchner, 'Russian Tariffs and Foreign Industries', p. 366.

Entrepreneurial Responses to Rising Protectionism

British worsted manufacturers did have a battery of practical responses to counteract the impact of protectionism, without going to the extreme of foreign direct investment. As has been shown, there were advantages to simply expanding production of the less-processed components that were increasingly required abroad; focusing on yarn sales instead of cloth and being ready to upscale production of tops as the progressive tariff took its toll. However, this strategy involved a change of emphasis in plant and skill requirements, investment in spindles, redundancy of looms, increased raw-material supply and labour to maintain returns. Most manufacturers favoured product diversification, balancing production between profit-rich wovens for Britain and the colonies, while yarn or components were exported to protected markets. Instead of producing large quantities of basic staples, in an increasingly price-competitive market, many moved to specialise in more difficult-to-manufacture items which were less subject to import tariffs and held their price: for example the Briggs brothers' development of their fancy yarn and umbrella-cloth trade. Fabric compositions could also be tailored to strategically circumvent the duties. Even in the twenty-first century British worsted manufacturers make some 52 per cent silk, 48 per cent worsted cloth qualities for export to the USA, to take advantage of a preferential American tariff for silk-rich cloth that was intended to benefit Far Eastern textile manufacturers.

One of the key problems which provoked the greatest indignation in British manufacturers was that the tariffs, devised by economists or politicians, were rarely implemented with sensitivity to the fine distinctions between products, which Behrens described as the 'really careless declaration and classification which took place in the Customs'.[38] In 1884 the Bradford Chamber of Commerce called on the Under Secretary of State, Lord Fitzmaurice, to mediate a dispute when the Russian customs authority demanded a Bradford exporter pay 'dyed duty' for a consignment of undyed yarn. The onus was on the manufacturer 'to prove the yarn was undyed and then after successful petition of the Russian government still had to get their shipper to apply back to Alexandrovna for reimbursement'.[39] Nevertheless, the inadequacy of the system also created a range of loopholes for the short-term exploitation of astute exporters. For example, a manufacturer might pass off a simple figured design as a complex Jacquard which was subject to lower duty.[40]

For greater ease of enforcement and given the technical limitations of customs officials, protectionist regimes experimented with various methods of applying

---

[38] 'The Effect of Foreign Tariffs on the Bradford Trade', p. 7.

[39] 'The Russian Customs Authorities and Undyed Yarns', *Journal of Fabrics and the Textile Industry*, Bradford, April 1884, p. 45.

[40] Quite complex patterns can be made on a simple shaft loom which could appear to an untrained eye to be woven on a specialist Jacquard loom.

the duty. Tax calculated on consignment value quickly led to double invoicing by cooperative export and import partners, who declared a reduced price at the border while the actual shipment value was reflected in a separate customer invoice. When Germany began to apply the tariff on the basis of consignment weight they compounded the problems for Bradford exporters in particular, as their relatively cheap but heavy worsted entered Germany at the same rate as the weighty-expensive worsted cloths of their arch rivals, the French. However, Sigsworth shows that this weight-based tariff simultaneously created a revival in the South Yorkshire woollen industry where exports were unexpectedly able to compete with the worsted sector.[41]

Loop-Holes of International Trade Legislature

The growing complexity of the tariff system naturally created numerous inconsistencies which could, quite legitimately, be appropriated by businessmen willing to endure some inconvenience. In 1883 the British consul at Budapest highlighted the misuse of an 1853 commercial treaty which allowed unfinished textiles to be exported from Hungary to Germany for finishing and then returned duty free. In the intervening years Hungarian merchants devised a profitable scheme of importing unfinished English cloth at a significantly reduced rate, finishing it in Germany, to re-enter Hungary without any tax liability. Legislation to check this and other abuses led the government to apply the general tariff to all imported and re-imported textiles.[42] Similarly, an incongruity led the Russian tariff on machine parts, intended to bolster its national component industry, not to encompass the import of complete machines. Therefore it was more cost effective and entirely legal for industrialists to import entire machines and dismantle them for parts. In the early twentieth century the US allowed cheap entry to used machinery, so wily industrialists set up their new equipment in Britain, France or Germany for a short period before sending it to their satellite ventures in America as second-hand equipment.[43] Few of these tactics provided a long-term solution to the problems created by escalating protectionism. Inevitably, as more exporters perceived the loopholes, they quickly became overexploited, identified by customs authorities and legislated against. As Chapter 1 described, in this period British industries experienced increased output, full employment and booming exports. But in an increasingly precarious economic environment the slightest amendment to a foreign tariff, or the closing of a legislative loophole, could spell ruin, especially for the largest manufacturers with the least flexible systems.

---

[41] Sigsworth and Blackman, 'Woollen and Worsted Industries', p. 156.

[42] 'A New Centre for English Enterprise', p. 27.

[43] Blewett, *Yankee Yorkshireman*, p. 52 also reported in *Wanganui Chronicle*, New Zealand, 25 March 1905, p. 2, 'The works of Messrs Benn in the States are completed. The machinery for which has been sent out "second-hand"'.

Naturally the contemporary press and political commentators directly linked protectionism with the increasing incidence of British foreign investment. The onerous taxes levied on British exports, the perceived benefits afforded to protected industry, the cheapness of foreign labour and also the increasingly restrictive domestic factory legislation were all understood to secure the advantage for less-regulated overseas industry.[44] These were abiding themes bandied to explain, even justify, the foreign investment decisions of reputedly desperate British industrialists. However, businessmen who were disenchanted with the British economic climate, or simply wanted to benefit from growing opportunities abroad, could have diversified their revenue bases much more easily with arms' length investments rather than building foreign factories. In fact, much evidence suggests that evading well-developed domestic, rather than growing foreign, competition was a substantial motivation for foreign direct investment. Establishing a factory within a tariff-controlled zone all but eliminated existing rivalries and 'in the face of numerous uncertainties, the fundamental assurance of no outside competition within Russia was very important to foreign businessmen'.[45] Typically emotive statements that 'the import duties levied by foreign governments which press so heavily upon English manufacturers, are giving a great impetus for the establishment by English firms of mills and factories in many European countries',[46] belied the true and broad-ranging rationale. Hence one of the rare British press reports of the Marki venture predictably points to protectionism as key to its instigation:

> The announcement that Messrs Briggs of Horton, near Bradford, have entered into contracts for the erection of a large manufactory in Poland is only another endorsement of the prevailing impression that the worsted trade is gradually leaving Bradford under the strong competition instituted mainly by foreign protective duties on British goods.[47]

Nevertheless, many industrialists who exploited this formulaic complaint about the stranglehold of tariffs, once successfully established abroad became notable exponents of protectionism in order to keep their British competitors out of the market. For example, Harrison Benn, who opened his New England mill in 1905, attempted to use his economic influence to prevent a reduction in the US worsted tariff that was proposed in the 1911 Underwood Bill. He was joined by 'other textile capitalists in Providence to lobby Congress for the preservation of high protective tariffs'.[48]

Contemporary journalists and modern analysts often conclude that the target nations for foreign direct investment were entirely dictated by the introduction

---

[44] 'Factory Legislation', p. 75.

[45] McKay, *Pioneers for Profit*, p. 78.

[46] 'A New Centre for English Enterprise', p. 27.

[47] 'Notes of the Month', p. 540.

[48] Blewett, *Yankee Yorkshireman*, p. 70.

of protectionism to an existing foreign market. That is, that an industrialist must necessarily have lost ground and thus been prompted to relocate inside the tariff-controlled zone to preserve an existing source of revenue.[49] For industrialists such as Benn, perhaps following historic losses in the French and German markets, the prospect of being shut out of the burgeoning US market was doubtless central. However, the Bradford industrialist's later actions show that protectionism alone was an intrinsically insecure basis for any large-scale foreign investment. Within six years of establishing his Rhode Island concern Benn began to vociferously agitate the US government for greater legislative support for his enterprise. Thus, although it must be acknowledged that protectionism was a central motivation for some British foreign investment, if the protectionism of existing export markets was the decisive factor for determining the location of all foreign enterprise then most British investment would have been made in France, Germany and later the US. Whereas the pattern is by no means consistent and notwithstanding some notable examples in those countries, the Bradford entrepreneurs chose Russia. At the time of the Marki venture, Russia still represented a potentially huge untapped market and although existing trade relations might have been beneficial, an entirely unexploited customer base was deemed to have the greatest profit potential.

The Questionable Advantage of the Protected Industrial Environment

This chapter has already outlined why protectionism, despite its useful elimination of existing competition, should not be assumed standard or sufficient as the primary incentive for foreign direct investment. It was an undoubted indicator of a set of socio-economic circumstances which constituted a significant opportunity, as well as signalling demand for specific products and likely host-government support for venture capitalists. But despite the prevailing impression in the British press that tariff control afforded foreign industry huge advantages, protectionism was largely the resort of states that were trying to improve the fortunes of an intrinsically inferior industry. As has been shown, protectionism was frequently the symptom of an economic backwardness which created a complex and challenging environment for venture capitalists. They routinely contended with a shortage of the most basic requirements, including water and power supply and the real probability that they would have to provide housing and education just to ensure the attendance of a largely unskilled workforce, however cheap they might be. The local undercapitalised and unsophisticated banking system could not provide liquidity for their commercial dealings and judicial support in the pursuit of debts could prove unreliable.

There were, nevertheless, many logistical benefits to moving into a target market rather than exporting to it: freight rates became negligible, import duties and local agents' percentages were no longer a factor in product price structures.

[49] Nicholas, 'Agency Contracts, Institutional Modes', pp. 675–86.

If the requisite raw materials were available locally the venturing manufacturer could develop the supply, but if sourcing crucial components in the host nation was unfeasible, the worldwide development of the commodity trade and communications facilitated imports which, under the rules of protectionism, would naturally be subject to the lowest duty. At the same time the testing local conditions presented a business arena which promised little local or international competition and thus cash-rich foreign entrepreneurs, who could afford to enter the field of industry in a dominant manner, could potentially enjoy the fruits of a monopoly.

Although relevant tariff control could provide a short-term boost to an establishing business, the industrialists' familiarity with the sudden gains and catastrophic losses even minute amendments to import duties could create meant that they could not depend on the constancy of the system or their power to influence future legislation in their favour. Despite the range of contributory incentives described here, which frequently accompanied protective legislation, the long-term sustainability of any enterprise centrally rested on the size and potential of the market and ideally on its achieving a monopoly, or at least oligopoly, in a specialist product. Therefore, although McKay might cite the tariff war between Germany and Russia, specifically the 1882 Russian tariff, as the central factor in the Bayer Chemical Company's decision to build premises in Moscow, or suggest that John Cockerill, the British-born Belgian entrepreneur, set up his cotton mill in Southern Russia through loss of Russian sales, it seems apparent that it was the potential monopoly, or at least the swift dominance of a growing market that could be achieved, that actually decided their actions.[50] It was the favourable socio-economic environment for entrepreneurial activity which often accompanied protectionism rather than the tariff barrier itself that was the primary catalyst. In the case of Russia, Fred V. Carstensen confirms that the impetus for foreign direct investment was not 'government initiative but was more prosaic and understandable: the opportunities intrinsic to a large, increasingly integrated market with steadily rising aggregate demand'.[51]

Market Demand and the Potential for Monopoly

To counteract the impact of foreign protectionism, as has been discussed, most British companies focused on domestic and colonial markets; however competition was fierce whereas the attraction of a new unexploited *home* trade was significant. Therefore, when considering the possibilities of a location for new enterprise, it

---

50 McKay, *Pioneers for Profit*, p. 81.

51 Fred V. Carstensen, 'Foreign Participation in Russian Economic Life: Notes on British Enterprise, 1865 to 1914', in *Entrepreneurship in Imperial Russia and the Soviet Union*, eds Gregory Guroff and Fred V. Carstensen (Princeton: Princeton University Press, 1983), p. 140.

is clear that the golden opportunity was a combination of market potential and monopoly, ideally accompanied by tariff control. The Bradford businesses of both the Briggs brothers and Posselt are likely to have suffered the impact of increased protectionism in significant customer nations such as France, Germany and the USA, but the well-developed worsted industries of those countries, which serviced both national and export markets, rendered them less attractive sites for foreign direct investment. By contrast, Hutchinson Dawson notes that in Russian Poland, 'the import of yarns countered a large deficit in domestic production and, in the absence of any domestic worsted spinning, provided the entire supply of this new yarn'.[52] Before the establishment of the Marki factory, Russian-Polish industry, the most rapidly growing industrial sector in the Russian empire at the beginning of the 1880s, was said to supply two-thirds of its worsted requirements from Germany and a third from France.[53]

It is worth mentioning here that existing histories of foreign direct investment tend to favour clusters of enterprises to provide comparison and give weight to analysis,[54] whereas lone cases, such as the Marki venture, are considered anomalies. However, as monopoly was their highest ambition, the unique cases that can be attributed to an individual perception of opportunity and rapid market domination which precluded all competitors arguably reflect the most successful examples. Whereas imitators or concentrations of so-called tariff factories, while more studied, reflect a less-secure investment strategy.

Even at its launch, it is evident that the Marki enterprise was the only fully vertical worsted spinning mill in Russian Poland and one of the leading textile-manufacturing plants in the Russian empire. For venturing entrepreneurs, even if they were the first to realise the commercial potential of a region, the scale and speed of their actions were critical to ensure instant command of the market and more particularly of local raw-material sources, to resist the growth of native, or other immigrant-investor, competition and ensure a failsafe position for their considerable investment. Although tariff control might minimise outside competition in the short term, the legislation was a blanket strategy intended to develop an autonomous national industry, rather than a prop for individual interests. In practice, as long as the goals of national self-sufficiency in the target products and economic development were met, protectionism did not preclude monopoly in favour of a broad-ranging competitive industry. It is arguable,

---

52 Hutchinson Dawson, *Industrial Geography of Woollen Textile Manufacturing*, p. 103 and this point is confirmed by W. Puś, *Przemysł włókienniczy w Królestwie Polskim w latach 1870–1900* [*Textile Industry in the Kingdom of Poland 1870–1900*] (Łódź: Zeszyty Naukowe Uniwersytetu Łódzkiego, 1976), p. 46.

53 Hutchinson Dawson, *Industrial Geography of Woollen Textile Manufacturing*, p. 103.

54 McKay, *Pioneers for Profit*, Kirchner, 'Russian Tariffs and Foreign Industries', Cairncross, *Home and Foreign Investment*, Cottrell, *British Overseas Investment*, Winder, 'Webs of Enterprise' and Wilkins, 'The Free-Standing Company', among many more.

therefore, that the success of the Marki enterprise, to meet Russian industrial demands for British worsted products, brought about the progressive increases to Russian worsted tariffs which were so resented in Bradford. By their own success and without lobbying the host government, the venturing worsted manufacturers were able to influence international trade legislation in their favour and remove all vestiges of foreign competition from their adopted home market while successfully dominating worsted production.

The Fine Distinction between Textile Products

In many assessments of industrial development, textile manufacture is deemed a single branch of industry. Some highlight the differences between wool and cotton production, but few address the critical difference in process, market and industrial development even between woollen and worsted manufacture, let alone between various branches of worsted production or products.[55] It is evident that the complex national differences in government, resources, contemporary industrial development and market had a strong bearing on the suitability of a location for foreign direct investment and the relative opportunity of these combined factors directly correlated to the proposed product of the venturing firm. A hypothetical Manchester cotton manufacturer would not have had a sufficiently unique product to establish a business in Russian Poland, despite the advantages of protectionism, adequate raw materials, cheap land and labour and access to the growing Russian market. However, in 1906 the Glasgow company J. and P. Coats did successfully establish a branch concern in Łódź, to manufacture spun cotton *thread* to supply tailors and mass garment manufacturers, rather than yarn to supply local cotton weavers.[56] The two superficially similar products used comparable raw materials and were subject to the same legislative protection, but the critical difference in quality, cost and customer base determined the difference between shortfall and oversupply and thus the feasibility of the enterprise which allowed Coats to secure a 'virtual monopoly on the Russian production of sewing cotton'.[57]

---

[55] Piotr Franaszek, 'Poland' in *The Ashgate Companion to the History of Textile Workers, 1650–2000*, eds L. Heerma Van Voss, E. Hiemstra-Kuperus, E. Van Nederveen Meerkerk (Farnham: Ashgate, 2010), pp. 397–420, Rosa Luxemburg, *The Industrial Development of Poland* [*Die Industrielle Entwicklung Polens*, 1898] (New York: Campaigner Publications Inc., 1977), Jacek Kochanowicz, *Backwardness and Modernisation: Poland and Eastern Europe in the 16th–20th Centuries* (Aldershot: Ashgate Publishing Limited, 2006).

[56] Kusiński, Bonisławski, Janik, *Księga fabryk Łodzi*, p. 196.

[57] Kininmonth, 'The Growth, Development and Management of J. & P. Coats Ltd', p. 558.

Individual Entrepreneurial Strategy

It has been argued here that the instigation of protectionism signalled both a national shortfall of specific products and accompanying favourable environmental factors for foreign direct investment, and the press or consular service might also publicise opportunity. However, as journalists generally provided retrospective commentary rather than recommendation and the worldwide economic policies designed to entice foreign investors came to prominence in the 1890s, neither can be argued to have directly informed the investment decision of the Briggs-Posselt partnership. Kirchner suggests that 'there has always been a difference between trade policy, as governments conceive it and ideologists describe it, and trade as the businessman conducts it'.[58] While there has been much research into global patterns of protectionism, the broad generalisations and statistical analyses of the impact of national legislation arguably fail to illustrate the significant entrepreneurial role in worldwide industry and trade. This case study provides a rare example of individual strategy, showing the relative importance of market potential as opposed to tariff control, highlighting the real rather than assumed advantages and difficulties for British foreign enterprise in the last quarter of the nineteenth century.

The Marki enterprise typifies many of the points already made in this chapter. Ernst Posselt had used membership of the Bradford Chamber of Commerce to build a local contact network but played no part in lobbying either the British or later Russian governments for changes to foreign policy. When establishing their Polish factory in 1883 the Briggs used the formulaic argument that foreign protectionism had driven them to invest abroad, stating 'at one time the firm did a large Russian trade but the severity of protective tariffs threatened to crush out this branch'.[59] But despite this casual allusion to diminishing exports, there is no evidence to suggest that Russia had any significance for either the Briggs or Ernst Posselt before the 1880s. The surviving customer accounts of E. Posselt and Co., Bradford show an insignificant Warsaw and Łódź customer base for spun yarns while the type of products manufactured at Briggella would suggest a typical spread of domestic, European and US trade.[60] Indeed their decision to embark on a costly foreign enterprise, the scale and the capital-intensive social-overhead model they employed all suggest that neither party had suffered any significant losses through global economic depression or foreign tariffs, in actual fact they had amassed significant, expendable capital. Rather than representing the final straw for the Bradford partners, increasing Russian import taxes and perhaps the tariff war between Russia and Germany signalled a climate of extraordinary opportunity to these affluent and visionary entrepreneurs.

58 Kirchner, 'Russian Tariffs and Foreign Industries', p. 378.

59 'Sudden Death of Mr Edward Briggs', *Ilkley Gazette*, 12 March 1898, p. 5, and 'Notes of the Month', p. 540.

60 *Illustrated Weekly Telegraph*, 7 September 1895.

The partners identified the growing demand for worsted in the Russian empire and a deficiency in technical capability to produce the Bradford specialty. They intended to create a dominant business that would cooperate rather than compete with the growing industry of the region and manufacture the 'sorts of yarns required to satisfy the needs of the Russian weaving industry'.[61] The more-advanced state of development of the Russian and Polish cotton industry, as opposed to worsted manufacturing, was surprisingly central to their plans. When the Russian tariff rose for the mixed-woven cloth qualities that were staple Bradford exports, it was the cotton weavers who, without any additional investment in plant or skills, could introduce worsted wefts to their cotton warps and emulate the typical Bradford exports. In a period when diversification was an increasing tactic to counteract rising competition, worsted yarn was the universal product to expand existing industry, allowing both cotton and woollen manufacturers to branch out into semi-worsted qualities which had been previously prohibitively expensive.

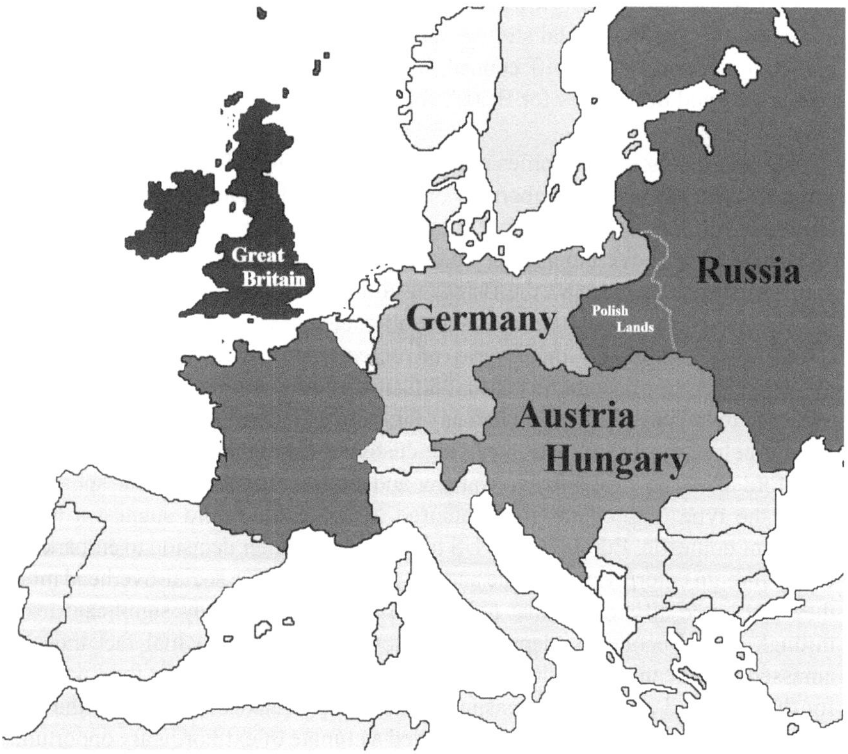

Figure 3.1 Map showing Europe circa 1883
Source: Author's diagram

[61] E. Litten, *Promyslennost Rossii w słowach i kartinach* [*Russian Industry in Words and Pictures*] (Łódź, 1897), p. 24.

In conclusion, it is clear that the Briggs-Posselt partnership's foreign investment decision was influenced by very complex factors. By the early 1880s in France, Germany and even the USA, despite a dynamic market for worsted products, competition was already too well developed for protectionism alone to entice these venture capitalists. In Russian Poland the significant advantages of cheap land, labour and local raw materials were to some extent offset by the expense of establishing the necessary infrastructure and social-overhead investment to exploit them. However, the combination of protectionism, undercapitalisation of Polish industry and unmet demand for their product in a potentially vast market constituted a real opportunity. For the Bradford partners, it is evident that potential product monopoly in a new market far outweighed the popularly cited domestic push factors or unpredictable protectionist advantage to provide a secure basis for their foreign enterprise.

Chapter 4
'Goods to the east and profits to the west':[1] Industrial development in Poland and the advantages of Marki

All evidence suggests that neither Edward Briggs nor Ernst Posselt had visited Poland before January 1883 and it remains a matter of speculation whether they had considered and discounted other protectionist states such as the USA, Germany or France. But during 1882 the combined advantages of Russian-empire market demand, the lack of established worsted manufacturing, progressive protectionism and various other socio-political benefits, which will be outlined in this chapter, encouraged the venture capitalists that Russian Poland would be an ideal location for their foreign direct investment. The optimal site within the target nation would undoubtedly be dictated by land, labour and resource availability, but existing distributions of industry, transport infrastructure and particularly water supply were also vital to determine the feasibility of industrial locations. During the dramatic industrial expansion of the Kingdom of Poland it is clear that differing priorities led some new businesses to favour clusters of enterprise while others chose isolated sites. General scholarship of industrialisation in Poland and Russia tends to focus on cotton manufacture as, by the end of the nineteenth century, this sector had the largest plants and was Russia's principal industrial employer. Although this chapter will focus on the practical and logistical requirements of a worsted-manufacturing enterprise, it will explore the opportunity that cotton's dominance in the region constituted for the Briggs-Posselt partnership.

Early Industrial Development in Poland

The historiography of the Polish lands is dominated by political instability and shifting borders. In the eighteenth century, Russia, Prussia and Austria competed for sovereignty over the region and between 1772 and 1795 increasing swathes of formerly independent Poland were claimed by these neighbouring states in three Partitions. In 1815 at the Congress of Vienna an amended demarcation of the territory was agreed in which central Poland, sometimes called Congress Poland or the Kingdom of Poland, was reunited around Warsaw but as an annex of Russia. Although the borders then held firm until after the First World War, the interstate

---

1 Jedlicki, *Suburb of Europe*, p. 279.

wrangling continued with the Polish lands forming the front line for military posturing and trade wars. Nevertheless, despite its common portrayal as 'the prey of three rival masters',[2] this chapter will explore how Poland's pivotal position between East and West, flanked by military and economic adversaries, positively stimulated its industrial development.

All nations have regional variations in economic activity and wealth which are largely dictated by basic geography. In the simplest terms arable agriculture dominates flat lands, pastoral farming prevails in rugged landscapes, concentrations of population and commerce build up near water courses and conglomerations of industry develop near natural resources. In Poland, however, additional political factors influenced the complex regional inequalities in industrial progress as well as the population's prosperity, ethnic composition and regional concentrations during the nineteenth century. Indeed Jacek Kochanowicz suggests that Polish industrialisation can be divided into two phases which were attributable either to state sponsorship or protectionism. The first industrial growth came in a period of relative administrative autonomy before 1830, when Congress Poland still had its own army and a progressive finance minister, Prince Ksawery Lubecki-Drucki. He 'established state iron works and supported a private wool industry, financing them by heavy taxation of the peasant population'.[3]

In this period the Kingdom of Poland was permitted free trade with both Russia and all the former-Polish territories, thus, as a conduit for West-East commerce, it became a focal point for industrial growth. A traffic in semi-processed goods paved the way to mass production as, for example, unfinished German manufactures could be sent through Prussian Greater Poland (also known as the Grand Duchy of Poznań) into the Russian Kingdom of Poland for final processing and then traded on into Eastern markets tax-free, as *Russian* products. The second phase of industrialisation in the last quarter of the nineteenth century is generally accepted to be the result of Tsarist protectionism.[4] As the previous chapter has shown, the relative advantage created by tariff control was more complex than the theory might suggest. However, it is evident that the development of Polish industry certainly owed more to political manoeuvres than to the practical factors of supply and demand which had stimulated Britain's Industrial Revolution.

State Incentives to Encourage Polish Economic Development

The first decisive move by Russia to capitalise on increased dominion in Poland through economic sanctions came in 1822. The introduction of a customs border between the Kingdom of Poland and Prussian Greater Poland prompted a wave of

---

[2] S. Stepniak, *The Russian Storm Cloud* (London: Swan Sonnenschein and Co, 1886), p. 165.

[3] Kochanowicz, *Backwardness and Modernisation*, p. 120.

[4] Ibid., p. 121, Luxemburg, *Industrial Development of Poland*, p. 92.

Figure 4.1 Map of the Polish Lands circa 1883
Source: Author's diagram

textile artisans from the West to settle in the Russian sector around Łódź, Pabianice and Zgierz. While this migration might be considered a simple consequence of a Russian scheme to bolster treasury revenues, the state's concurrent actions prove that the primary objective was to entice weavers and spinners particularly from Prussia, Bohemia and Austria. By allocating plots of land and building materials, offering the duty-free import of property, freedom from taxation and public charges for six years, in combination with protectionism, they intended to poach the industrial skills of neighbour states to establish artisan communities in a largely unindustrialised zone.[5] While the Polish aristocracy was forced to

[5] Kochanowicz, *Backwardness and Modernisation*, p. 128, see also I. Popławska and S. Muthesius, 'Poland's Manchester: 19th-Century Industrial and Domestic Architecture in Łódź', *Journal of the Society of Architectural Historians*, 45: 2 (1986), p. 150.

billet the occupying Russian militia, industrial enterprises were freed from this obligation for 3 to 6 years and the sons of immigrant craftsmen were exempted from military service.[6] Polish municipalities were required to provide the foreign artisans with rent-free land and, in this way, the first concentrations of industry in Russian Poland took on a distinctly German character.

It might be assumed that such partial policies would have been strongly resented by the native populace, but there is little evidence that the arrival of these first foreign cloth manufacturers had any disruptive effect on the existing *status quo* in the short term. The immigrants cooperated rather than competed with the largely agricultural commercial activity of the Kingdom of Poland. They provided luxury goods to the nobility, a market for locally grown wool or flax and some employment opportunities. On the other hand, the industrialists of central Russia lobbied vociferously for inter-regional tariffs to check what they saw as the rise of state-sponsored international competition. But as long as the dynamic growth of Polish industry served the economic purposes of Russia, the Tsarist administration was unmoved and the Kingdom of Poland enjoyed a growing status as the workshop of the empire. Nevertheless, despite the obvious economic advantages of union with the dominant state, a palpable philosophical divergence between economic and nationalist ideals began to emerge. Industrial expansion and improving regional prosperity provided no consolation for a lack of Polish independence and in 1830 the failed November Uprising against annexation eventually led Russia to apply punitive economic sanctions in the Polish territories. By moving the tariff border east of Warsaw, the Kingdom of Poland was economically ostracised from the empire with the consequence that industrial growth stagnated.

Eastward Economic Migration

This retaliatory state action naturally impacted heavily on the recently established industries of the Łódź area. Exports sank by two-thirds between 1834 and 1850.[7] Norman Davies highlights that the Polish weavers also lost their vital contracts to supply broadcloth to the Polish army, which was disbanded after 1830.[8] However, the statistics belie the true state of affairs; industry resides in the skills of people, not in fixed locations. A significant number of Poland's textile artisans were first-generation immigrants who simply repositioned their businesses inside the newly defined tariff zone to maintain access to the Russian market. Thus a policy which effectively ruined the economy of Łódź in the second quarter of the nineteenth century simultaneously created a new and essentially *Polish* textile industry further east at Białystok.

6 Luxemburg, *Industrial Development of Poland*, p. 85.

7 Ibid., p. 90.

8 Norman Davies, *God's Playground: A History of Poland Volume II 1795 to the Present* (New York: Columbia University Press, 1982), p. 172.

This economic migration might be considered a precedent for the Briggs-Posselt enterprise, but prior to the factory system the cross-border transfer of a national industry simply involved dismantling and reassembling numerous small-scale workshops in the nearest suitable location. Given the legacy of political instability in the region, the manufacturers had developed a product and lifestyle which virtually embraced an itinerant existence. Native textile production was largely a domestic handicraft, in which smallholders grew flax to seasonally spin or weave, as a supplement to their core agricultural income: by contrast, the incoming German artisans were professional manufacturers with a specialisation in woollen cloth. Their product as their primary source of income was more expensive and sophisticated, but most importantly did not tie them to land holdings to supply raw materials. Wool could be purchased from markets, merchants and growers in any region, enabling these cloth workers to freely pursue market demand and political advantage.

Although protectionism undoubtedly indicated favourable conditions to venture capitalists later in the century, scholarship of the industrialisation of Poland invariably gives great emphasis to additional state incentives such as the tax breaks, immunity from military service, land allocations which have already been described. While undoubtedly revealing the intent of the Russian government to poach foreign skills, these inducements did little to encourage mass immigration or spur industrialisation. Indeed intrinsic to the acceptance of such sponsorship was an unwelcome measure of confining state control and regulation. Davies describes the 1820 scheme of Rajmund Rembieliński, the prefect of Mazovia, who advertised the standard benefits: 'land, free materials for building a house, and six years exemption from rent, taxation, and military service',[9] to attract unemployed Saxon and Silesian weavers to Łódź after the Napoleonic wars. Nonetheless, only ten weavers arrived in three years before he rolled out his offer to flax weavers in 1824 and cotton manufacturers in 1828.

The real basis of individual decisions to move east, into the Russian-ruled territories, was undoubtedly a positive assessment of long-term economic advantage, rather than the possibly fickle enticements of a foreign government. Russia's lack of industrialisation and the potential of its unexploited markets, which contrasted with the relatively mature and highly competitive mercantile economy of the German states, were central determinants for relocation. These same factors, market and monopoly, continued to determine the viability of large-scale foreign direct investment at the end of the nineteenth century. This argument is further substantiated by what might be described as the second wave of economic migration; the transfer of Polish industry from Łódź to Białystok after 1830, when no land was allocated or tax relief provided, yet large numbers of manufacturers pursued the market opportunity into Russia.

---

[9] Ibid.

Regional Variations in the Technical Advancement of Polish Industry

National generalisations regarding industrial development in the Polish lands are problematic given 'the vagaries of the borders of a long non-existent state';[10] therefore research is generally confined to specific towns, regions or industries.[11] However, when Gryzelda Missalowa used Poland's modern borders as the basis for historical analysis, dramatic regional variations in the technical advancement of industry became apparent.[12] The 1822 separation of Prussian Greater Poland from the Russian-held lands established a pattern in which the most technologically advanced manufacturing regions of western Poland, ostracised from a key market, experienced a mass exodus of skilled artisans. Remaining workshops struggled to compete with the tax-free prices of their newly established rivals inside Russia, whose modernisation of plant improved their quality and speed of output.[13] This model of progressive industrial decline in the West and eastward skills-drain was similarly replicated in the Łódź area after 1830. But in 1851 Russia's abolition of its customs border with the Kingdom of Poland, combined with British reforms to permit machinery export, brought unprecedented industrial modernisation to the Kingdom of Poland. The focus of investment returned to Łódź, where manufacturing was upscaled from workshop to factory production, and with the general implementation of steam power came a pressing demand for the exploitation of local natural resources such as coal. Imported cotton fibre superseded wool and flax to meet the increased raw-material demands of mass production.

Although it has been argued here that Polish industry was developed by individual manufacturers in pursuit of market opportunities, it is evident that the regional shifts in urban and industrial development, the progress from artisan to mass production and even the evolution of product from domestic flax weaving, to woollen workshops, cotton factories and finally worsted plants, can all be loosely

---

10 Lawrence Schofer review of *Uprzemysłowienie ziem polskich w XIX i XX wieku* [*The Industrialisation of the Polish Lands in the Nineteenth and Twentieth Centuries*], ed. Irena Pietrzak-Pawlowska (Wrocław: Studia i materialy, 1970), *Journal of Economic History*, 31: 4 (December 1971), pp. 986–8.

11 Janusz Kubiak and Teresa Szyburska, 'Urbanystka i architektura Żyrardowa – Jej wartosci i problemy konserwatorskie' ['Urban planning and architecture of Żyrardów – its value and the problems of conservation'], *Kwartalnik Architektury i Urbanistyki*, Panstwowe Wydawnictwo Naukowe, Warsaw (1984), pp. 95–111, Ewa Markiewicz-Kozańska, 'Rozwój przestrzenny wielkich i dużych zespołów fabryczno-mieszkalnych na terenie Łodzi w drugiej połowie XIX wieku' ['Spatial development of great and large groups of industrial flats in Łódź in the second half of the nineteenth century'], *Kwartalnik Architektury i Urbanistyki*, Panstwowe Wydawnictwo Naukowe, Warsaw (1984), pp. 137–44. Popławska and Muthesius, 'Poland's Manchester', pp. 148–60.

12 G.Missalowa, 'Przemysł włókienniczy do 1918 roku' ['The textile industry until 1918'], in *Uprzemysłowienie ziem polskich w XIX i XX wieku* [*The Industrialisation of the Polish Lands in the Nineteenth and Twentieth Centuries*] pp. 219–76.

13 Kochanowicz, *Backwardness and Modernisation*, p. 119.

charted against Russian-tariff amendments. Regardless of the state's intent to bolster or penalise, protectionism significantly boosted the progress of technology across the Polish lands and by the second half of the nineteenth century 'the main textile manufactories of Russian Poland had outstripped the production of the Prussian and Austrian partitions combined'.[14]

The re-establishment of Łódź after 1851 with unprecedented investment in technology and greater cooperation between industrialists, merchants and suppliers for shared investment in commercial infrastructure facilitated exceptional productivity. But a significant transformation in manufacturing culture should also be noted, as the scale-over-skill philosophy of mass production led Poland's industrialists to abandon their itinerant status in favour of permanent settlement. Given the legacy of political instability in the region, the risks of the strategy were palpable but the potential rewards proved irresistible and the former-immigrant industrialists invested heavily in fixed assets and embraced Russian nationality.

This somewhat pared down analysis of Poland's industrial development illustrates the complex pattern which had been established before the 1880s. The Russian regime had encouraged the wholesale import of industry from abroad and consequently the Russian-Polish industrial environment was defined by an ethnic, linguistic and religious identity largely at odds with both the native populace and the ruling regime. By contrast to the German communities in nineteenth-century England, in Russian Poland there is little evidence of any cultural assimilation by the incomers, arguably because there was no commensurate Polish commercial class for the venturing entrepreneurs to join and because the political status and thus economic prospects for Germans in Russian Poland were more favourable than for native Poles. Industry thrives in cooperation and investors naturally prefer the most accessible commercial environment, in terms of location, culture and language. Thus, the long-term legacy of Tsarist economic policies in the Kingdom of Poland was a growing trend for particularly German foreign direct investment. Rosa Luxemburg describes 'the great upswing in value of production'[15] in the last quarter of the nineteenth century which she attributes to the arrival of industrialists from Saxony and Silesia who chose to invest in the fundamentally German commercial communities of Poland, rather than in central Russia.

Extraordinary Economic Growth in the Kingdom of Poland

Thus, despite systemic protectionist policies designed to enhance the entire industry of the Russian empire, the value of production in the Kingdom of Poland rose by 12 per cent between 1870 and 1876 in comparison to an only 2 per cent

[14] Davies, *God's Playground*, p. 174.

[15] Luxemburg, *Industrial Development of Poland*, p. 99.

increase in the Russian heartlands.[16] An 1885 British Consular report described that 'shielded against foreign competition by high rates of duty, the manufacturers of Central Russia still find themselves unable to struggle successfully against the internal competition they encounter, on the part of cotton mills established by Germans at Łódź'.[17] The following year the Russian economist Ianzhul published a bitter diatribe claiming that with few natural resources, a scant indigenous skills base amongst a largely peasant populace, Polish industry should be described as nothing more than the 'fruit of government protection'.[18] However, as the whole empire was subject to the same trade policies, roughly similar social conditions, natural resources, products and especially markets, it is important to consider the reasons for the marked variation in economic development and industrial progress in Poland as compared to central Russia.

Notwithstanding the evident intricacies which determined the establishment of Polish industry, two basic academic arguments persist in accounting for its success: Russian protectionism and foreign entrepreneurship. These standard explanations which imply national passivity and exploitation formed a rallying cry for both nationalist and socialist activists in the nineteenth century. They were perpetuated later by Soviet historians who routinely describe industrialists as 'blood suckers' and promote the determinist power of the proletariat as central to industrial success.[19] Therefore in the 1970s Wiesław Puś emphasised the contemporarily acceptable reason for Poland's rapid industrialisation as the 1864 emancipation of the Polish peasants which he claimed was the basis for a growing home trade which stimulated local growth.[20] But as these liberated serfs provided both labour force and a potential market across the Russian empire, his argument provides no clear explanation for the particularly meteoric rise of Polish industry. Kochanowicz's post-Soviet analysis further refutes this argument by suggesting that Poland entered the industrial revolution with 'an impoverished peasantry that could not form a strong domestic market'.[21]

The proximity of the Polish lands to the Russian empire's western border was undoubtedly a significant advantage for economic development, given both the industrial advancement of neighbouring states in contrast to its rural tradition and the relative lack of exploitation of the Russian market. However, Russia's heavy military presence in the region is frequently credited with providing a market for wool cloth and associated products such as leather, as well as endowing

---

16 Kochanowicz, *Backwardness and Modernisation*, p. 120 and Hutchinson Dawson, *Industrial Geography of Woollen Textile Manufacturing*, p. 96.

17 Diplomatic and Consular Report, Annual Series, Russia, No. 73, 1885, p. 6.

18 Ivan Ivanovic Ianzhul, *Przemysł fabryczny w Królestwie Polskiem: studyum ekonomiczne* [*Manufacturing Industry in the Kingdom of Poland: An Economic Study*] (Petersburg: Trenke and Fusnot, 1887), p. 84.

19 Miliszkiewicz, *Polskie gniazda rodzinne*, pp. 44–7.

20 Puś, 'Przemysł włokienniczy', p. 4.

21 Kochanowicz, *Backwardness and Modernisation*, p. 120.

the region with a superior transport infrastructure which facilitated the easy movement of goods and exploitation of natural resources.[22] The militia, whether Polish or Russian, was the main customer for a range of wool products including uniform cloth, blankets and upholstery in the nineteenth century.[23] Luxemburg also highlights the significant role that the Crimean War had in restoring Poland's status as a conduit for trade, when Russian ports were embargoed and foreign goods were redirected through the Polish Kingdom.[24]

Many other factors have been proposed to account for the disproportionate progress of Polish industry in comparison to the rest of Russia. Luxemburg offers the somewhat sweeping generalisation that 'the Polish worker is first of all more intelligent and better educated'[25] than their Russian counterpart. Although her assertion might seem superficial, it is evident that under Russian subjugation, a class of Polish intelligentsia, that in different political circumstances would have led government, native entrepreneurship or engaged in a host of professions subsequently closed to Polish nationals, were forced into industry as engineers, middle management and even skilled workers. Indeed Davies suggests that by the end of the nineteenth century landownership had ceased to be a profitable enterprise and 'one quarter of the *zaścianki* [petty nobility] enjoyed a lower standard of living than the average serf'.[26]

It must also be considered that the periodic relocations of industry caused by shifting customs borders entrenched competitiveness, resourcefulness and flexibility in Russian-Polish manufacturers which contrasted strongly with the heavily subsidised, state-controlled and hierarchical nature of Russian industry and industrialists. Therefore, rather than any partiality towards the Kingdom of Poland, a range of social privations caused by Tsarist policies might account for the greater dynamism of the Polish economy in the nineteenth century. In the same context, the heavy taxation of the wealthiest sections of Polish society might be construed as a form of ethnic protectionism, which was as significant an attraction to immigrant entrepreneurs as the removal of international competitors from their target market. German management combined with Polish labour characterised industry throughout the Polish lands. However, in Prussian Greater Poland and Austro-Hungarian Galicia Polish noble landowners were not persecuted; 'only in Russia did the authorities take active measures to repress an estate which they regarded as incurably hostile to Tsarist order'.[27] Thus a minority, notably German, industrial bourgeoisie was able to become the most powerful and affluent section of the Russian-Polish populace, while the estate lands of the beleaguered Polish

22 Ibid., p. 121 and Luxemburg, *Industrial Development of Poland*, p. 90.
23 Davies, *God's Playground*, p. 172.
24 Luxemburg, *Industrial Development of Poland*, p. 93.
25 Ibid., p. 136.
26 Davies, *God's Playground*, p. 182.
27 Ibid., p. 182.

aristocracy struggled to meet Russian tax dues and a recently displaced and impoverished peasant majority provided an ideal industrial workforce.

Patterns of Industrial Development in Poland

Apart from the political factors which influenced the location of urban concentrations in Russian Poland, there were also some more pragmatic, industry-specific factors which determined the site and character of Poland's industrial towns. As has been shown, native textile manufacture in common with Bradford's early industry had developed out of agriculture and as the secondary occupation of rural workers it was located on scattered smallholdings. By contrast, the migrant artisans centralised their activities to share dyers', finishers' and merchants' services and the advent of the factory system increased the urbanisation of existing settlements. However, the large plants which became an increasing feature of the Polish industrial landscape at the end of the nineteenth century and employed a vertically integrated system had less need of strategic cooperation. Collaboration offered no cost-saving advantage to companies managing all manufacturing processes in-house, thus fresh parameters determined their location.

In a competitive trade, proximity to raw materials, customer base, energy supply or transport networks could constitute the essential commercial advantage. Some large plants were still established in or around existing industrial clusters to make continued use of the established commercial infrastructure and concentrated customer base. For example Scheibler's factory town of Księży Młyn was built as a suburb of Łódź, while others such as Dietel favoured new sites at Sosnowiec and Częstochowa close to the expanding coalfields of Dąbrowa. However, the establishment of modern industrial plants did not entirely supersede the earlier forms of manufacturing unit. In the late 1870s the declining artisan and workshop trade still accounted for two-thirds of manufacturing firms in Russian Poland although they produced less than one-third of the national output.[28] Piotr Franaszek shows that domestic, dual-economy manufacture persisted, even alongside the factory system and some of the largest Polish manufacturers, including Scheibler and Poznański, still employed an estimated 8 per cent of outworkers using domestic looms into the 1890s.[29]

[28] Hutchinson Dawson, *Industrial Geography of Woollen Textile Manufacturing*, p. 79.

[29] Franaszek, 'Poland', p. 403. See also in Hutchinson Dawson, *Industrial Geography of Woollen Textile Manufacturing*, p. 51.

The Polish Wool Industry

Although the majority of studies of industrial expansion in the Russian empire focus on cotton manufacture, this case study must consider the specific factors which would have influenced the location of a worsted plant in the last quarter of the nineteenth century. The differentiation is important as worsted had quite different raw materials, manufacturing technique, market and product price, although there were undoubtedly some overlapping requirements such as transport, energy, water and labour supply. Hutchinson Dawson's research on the geographical distribution, employee numbers, output and ethnic origins of the mill owners, despite a lack of differentiation between the woollen and worsted branches of the industry, provides an invaluable snapshot of the Russian-Polish wool industry at the time of the foundation of the Marki enterprise. He shows that in the early 1880s there were only a handful of factory-scale wool manufacturers including Heinzel established in 1879, Kunitzer and Meyer both in Łódź and Kindler at Pabianice (later acquired by Silberstein of Łódź);[30] all were steam-powered and employed several hundred workers but none had the capability to comb and spin worsted.[31] However, it is worth noting here that in 1895 Heinzel's firm was amalgamated into the joint-stock company of Kunitzer and Meyer and thereafter advertised as exclusively cotton spinners and weavers.[32]

In January 1883 the Bradford partners undertook a fact-finding mission to Russian Poland. A swift and accurate assessment of the existing industrial environment was required to ensure the long-term success of their endeavour. Although their central aim was to purchase a suitable site for their plant, the venture capitalists also needed to familiarise themselves with the potential customer base, to advertise their intentions and forge cooperative relationships locally. Whereas existing industrial concentrations could signal the feasibility of an area, the potential market and the availability of necessary services, they might similarly highlight disincentives such as market saturation, competition for resources, land and labour. Weighing potential advantages and disadvantages was essential as, for example, clusters of firms might compete for water but their collective purchasing power would mean they paid less for coal than a lone company.

30 Kusiński, Bonisławski, Janik, *Księga fabryk Łodzi*, p. 240.

31 Hutchinson Dawson, *Industrial Geography of Woollen Textile Manufacturing*, p. 70.

32 Kusiński, Bonisławski, Janik, *Księga fabryk Łodzi*, p. 212.

The Rise and Fall of Białystok

On 20 January 1883 the Bradford men visited Białystok; the traditional centre of the Russian-Polish wool industry.[33] This town's particular product specialisation can be attributed to the pursuit of military-supply contracts by wool weavers, after the disbandment of the Polish army and withdrawal of the Russian customs border in 1830. Despite few natural advantages, Białystok then enjoyed 20 years of rapid industrial development. However, in 1851 the abolition of the punitive inter-regional tariff marked the onset of the town's decline. At that time the resurgence of Łódź promoted self-perpetuating improvements such as rail communications, which by-passed Russian Poland's old wool capital. Thus new investors with the latest technology disregarded Białystok in favour of either flourishing centres or undeveloped sites elsewhere. In the last quarter of the nineteenth century most of the town's workshops and factories only undertook one process of manufacture; fewer than five engaged in two, such as spinning and weaving, and there were no fully integrated factories.[34]As has been shown in relation to Bradford, cash-poor businesses engaged in the fewest processes of manufacture and achieved low profits. Thus Białystok's once up-to-date industry became increasingly antiquated and its capital resources sank.

The story of Białystok's decline is not so clear-cut and, as has been shown in British industry, when market advantage was lost either through competition or protectionism, the first response of business was to seek solutions. With a lack of capital to invest in updating plant, manufacturers typically resorted to a strategy of specialisation or cost reduction. By introducing coarse or recycled wool and rags to their cloth, the manufacturers of Białystok reduced their prices and created a niche for basic woollen cloth and blankets which allowed the town's industry to survive.[35] Thus, Poland's most profitable textile manufacturers grew by supplying the vast Russian market with long runs of finer and more expensive cloth, whereas more parochial local demand for coarse, cheap cloth became the preserve of the workshops and small factories of Białystok.[36]

---

[33] FO393/16, Francis Maude to Izydor Blum, merchant in Łódź, 20 January 1883, p. 105, confirms that on 20 January Briggs and Posselt were in Białystok and on 21 January they went to Łódź.

[34] Hutchinson Dawson, *Industrial Geography of Woollen Textile Manufacturing*, p. 55.

[35] Białystok's fate resonated strongly with Yorkshire towns such as Dewsbury or Barnsley that were left behind by the meteoric rise of Bradford's worsted or Manchester's cotton trade.

[36] Hutchinson Dawson, *Industrial Geography of Woollen Textile Manufacturing*, p. 91.

Łódź: the Manchester of Poland

In 1883, Łódź, the thriving centre of Poland's cotton industry, might have seemed an obvious site for new investment. Frequently described as the Manchester of Poland, the epithet is as misleading as Bradford's popular label *Worstedopolis*,[37] as both industrial centres produced a very broad range of manufactures. Indeed the *Księga Fabryk Łodzi* [*Book of Łódź Factories*] catalogues the history of over 1,000 businesses, from vast textile manufacturing empires, to co-existing medium- and smaller-scale firms, machine manufacturers, finishers, bleachers, dyers and merchants as well as numerous clothing, hat and haberdashery companies.[38] In the last quarter of the nineteenth century a growing fashion for worsted and semi-worsted cloth qualities emerged in conjunction with increasing Russian tariffs to control their import which resulted in a rising demand for locally combed wool yarn. Thus Łódź cotton weavers such as Silberstein started to advertise their diversification into the '*wollener und halbwollener waaren*'[39] [woollen and half-woollen goods].

Between 1870 and 1883 the value of production for the Łódź textile industry increased by 500 per cent and by the mid-1880s it employed almost 63 per cent of Polish textile workers.[40] While an influx of foreign investors might account for some of the extraordinary growth, many long-established, small and medium-sized companies also experienced their most dramatic expansion at this time.[41] In a pattern which resonated strongly with contemporary Bradford average business sizes increased markedly as the largest mills thrived and drove out smaller concerns.[42] The period was characterised by high numbers of start-up ventures alongside countless business failures; a volatile dynamism where three-quarters of the mills operating in 1876 had shut by 1893. British trade journals bandied the statistics for any aspiring venture capitalist to read that 'the woollen industry of Russia has lately increased immensely … [Previously] Russian Poland alone had 564 weaving mills with 3204 hands and yearly production worth 5,520,000francs. In 1880 the number of these had sunk to 287 and the value of annual production had risen to 75 million francs'.[43]

In January 1883 the ground conditions created by such rapid industrialisation would have presented a less-encouraging prospect to the British entrepreneurs who visited the city than the statistics suggested. During Poland's pre-industrial

37 Cudworth, *Worstedopolis*.

38 Kusiński, Bonisławski, Janik, *Księga fabryk Łodzi*.

39 Ibid., p. 240.

40 Franaszek, 'Poland', p. 410.

41 Markiewicz-Kozańska, 'Rozwój przestrzenny', pp. 137–44.

42 Hutchinson Dawson, *Industrial Geography of Woollen Textile Manufacturing*, p. 139.

43 *Textile World*, September 1884, p. 62, quotes the figures of the *Moniteur Officiel du Commerce* in France.

period Łódź had been divided into parcels of land, each measuring approximately 21 m by 300 m, which was deemed sufficient to accommodate a workshop and to cultivate flax. The vision was to provide a well-organised artisan community and led the population to increase from 800 to 15,000 between 1820 and 1850. However, by the end of the 1870s Łódź had 100,000 inhabitants and had become an 'agglomeration of dense blocks of speculative housing, stores, and small and medium-sized trades and factories'.[44] The once strongly administered city plan was abandoned after 1851 and few regulations were imposed to control building or address any urban and industrial infrastructure requirements. The only limitations were those practically dictated by the city's historic grid layout and a stipulation that the width of streets must remain sufficient to allow a fire engine to turn. Many of the largest factory complexes were bisected by public streets.[45] Expanding businesses competed to acquire adjoining plots of land in order to develop their manufacturing capabilities, but more often the expansion of one area of production had to be made at the cost of another.[46] The shortage of land led to a proliferation of multi-storey buildings and the lack of regulation meant that incidences of building collapse during construction, or under the weight of heavy machinery, were commonplace. Indeed a British electrical engineer who visited Łódź in March 1910 described a 'regrettable feature was the sight of a multi-storey building, which had collapsed upon the builders, during its erection'.[47]

By the early 1880s the city of Łódź reflected a developmental crisis which had characterised Bradford or Manchester 30 years earlier and forced greater municipal legislation to regulate urban planning. Water supply vied with land availability as a primary consideration for textile manufacturers; indeed these were the two main determinants which encouraged British industrialists such as Titus Salt to relocate to rural sites.[48] Despite its name, for Łódź literally means boat, the early nineteenth-century administration had allocated the area for industrial development largely because it was agriculturally unproductive and a key reason for this was a lack of water. Under the historic urban plan, based on the vertically disintegrated workshop system, the state built municipal bleaching works and dye-houses in the south of the city where the main water supply was located,[49] leaving all other industry to compete for the scant resource. In contemporary Britain,

[44] Davies, *God's Playground*, p. 171, Popławska and Muthesius, 'Poland's Manchester', p. 151.

[45] Markiewicz-Kozańska, 'Rozwój przestrzenny', p. 138.

[46] Dr Piotr Jaworski, senior curator of the *Centralne Muzeum Włókiennictwa* [Central Museum of Textiles] in Łódź, made this point in conversation April 2010.

[47] Hinchcliffe's memoir.

[48] L. Caffyn, *Workers' Housing in West Yorkshire 1750–1920*, West Yorkshire Metropolitan County Council, Royal Commission on the Historical Monuments of England (London: Her Majesty's Stationery Office, 1986), p. 18 and J.A. Jowitt, *Model Industrial Communities in Mid-Nineteenth-Century Yorkshire* (Bradford: University of Bradford, 1988), p. 44.

[49] Davies, *God's Playground*, p. 172.

textile manufacturers bemoaned the consequences of the 1876 Rivers Pollution Prevention Act which had kept 'almost stationary the number of concerns which carry on bleaching, dyeing and other finishing processes',[50] while the number of spinners and weavers constantly grew and increased demand for these services. This resulted in a clear monopoly for the wet processors as 'effective as if it had been brought about by a high protective tariff'.[51] The central importance of water supply to the Bradford partners is well illustrated by a 1904 conveyance deed for a parcel of land adjacent to Briggella Mills. This document outlines the purchase of some mill buildings and warehouses in the briefest detail but emphasises the acquisition of 'the reservoir ... and sole and exclusive right to the uninterrupted flow of water from and through the land of the vendors'.[52]

The Bradford partners' plans were for a large and fully integrated production facility. Capital rich, they intended to undertake all manufacturing processes in-house in order to reap the maximum return from their new business, therefore any limitation to water supply or land for future expansion would have been unthinkable. Despite its popular epithet, the Promised Land, the disadvantages of Łódź far outweighed any perceived benefits in its concentrated customer base, available skilled workers or well-developed transport services. Indeed the construction of the Łódź *Fabryczna* [Factory] rail link with Warsaw in the 1860s afforded remote suppliers ease of access to the city's industry. Therefore, having gathered enough commercial intelligence about their competition and potential customer base in Łódź, the Bradford men set their sights on Poland's former capital.

Warsaw in the 1880s

In 1883 Warsaw was a burgeoning commercial and banking centre with a population almost three times that of Łódź. The headquarters of the Russian administration of the region and the focal point of transport links with Western Europe, central Russia, the Baltic lands and Austria Hungary,[53] Warsaw was considered one the Russian empire's five main trading centres alongside Riga, Moscow, Odessa and St Petersburg.[54] Although it had a thriving garment-making and merchant trade, the city was essentially dominated by light industries such as sugar refining,

[50] 'The Rivers Pollution Act: How it is affecting manufacturers of fabric' [sic: The Rivers Pollution Prevention Act 1876], *Journal of Fabrics and Textile Industries*, 12 December 1883, p. 133.

[51] Ibid.

[52] WYAS, Conveyance and assignment, 10 August 1904, Vol. 36, No. 227, p. 36.

[53] Direct rail connections between Warsaw and St Petersburg were established in 1862, with Moscow in 1870, Kiev in 1871 and southern Russia in 1877.

[54] W. Blackwell, 'The Russian entrepreneur and the Tsarist period', in *Entrepreneurship in Imperial Russia and the Soviet Union*, eds G. Guroff and F.V. Carstensen (Princeton: Princeton University Press, 1983), p. 24.

tanning and engineering and it owed much of its economic dynamism to its status as a military stronghold.[55]

Russian legislation technically applied to the entire Polish territory but some regional variations were evident and following the abortive January Uprising of 1863 Warsaw, considered the heart of Polish cultural, intellectual and political life, found itself more heavily under the Tsarist cosh than, for example, provincial German Łódź. Russian was imposed as the language of administration, the judiciary and education; thousands of Poles were removed from the civil service to be replaced by Russians.[56] Polish economic power and especially political authority were curbed in a concerted campaign of Russification designed to eliminate the 'last vestiges of Polish autonomy'[57] and prevent further insurrection. The city's local management was 'strictly subordinated to the Ministry of Internal Affairs in Petersburg'.[58] Infrastructural development focused on military rather than social requirements, but even this was hampered by disagreements between, for example, the Ministry of Communications which was prevented by the Ministry of War from building bridges in the city.[59] From 1870, health and education services, building control, population movement, the judiciary and even the management of charities came under the control of the city's Russian chief of police. The beleaguered local municipality was left to manage markets, pavements, cemeteries and public parks on a very limited budget, while local taxes were largely expended on maintaining the Russian police force.[60] Thus the urban infrastructure of Warsaw was little better than that of Łódź and certainly lagged far behind contemporary London, Bradford and other Western European cities.

The impact of capital shortage on economic development is widely discussed in Polish historiography. State sponsorship and private finance by the nobility had played a significant role in industrial investment before 1830. However, autocratic control and the heavy taxation of Poland's landowners and rural overpopulation coupled with low land productivity all contributed to a deficiency of native capital and a disincentive to entrepreneurship. Long-term lending to industry was controlled and periodically banned by the Tsarist regime, so whereas British banking had evolved to a sophisticated international footing by the last quarter of the nineteenth century, the Bank of Poland, heavily regulated by the state, had barely a decade's experience. Some private banks were established in the 1870s by Russian-Polish business leaders, such as Kronenburg's *Bank Handlowy* [Business

---

55 Kochanowicz, *Backwardness and Modernisation*, p. 114.

56 Robert E. Blobaum, *Rewolucja: Russian Poland 1904–1907* (Ithaca and London: Cornell University Press, 1995), p. 4.

57 Theodore R. Weeks, 'Defending Our Own: Government and the Russian Minority in the Kingdom of Poland, 1905–1914', *Russian Review*, 54 (1995), p. 540.

58 Anna Słoniowa, *Sokrates Starynkiewicz* (Warsaw: Państwowe Wydawnictwo Naukowe, 1981), p. 16.

59 Ibid., p. 21.

60 Ibid., p. 16.

Bank] which was a conduit for French capital and the *Bank Diskontowy* [Discount Bank] which was owned by a consortium of Warsaw merchants connected to the Deutsche Bank.[61] There is no suggestion that these were cooperatives intended to provide private finance to business, but rather a diversification for the wealthy elite. In the same way, many owned a brewery or sugar refinery, invested in land, coal mines or railway interests.

Unsurprisingly, Warsaw commerce, like that of Łódź, was dominated by non-Polish businessmen. However, there was a clear distinction between Warsaw's cosmopolitan blend of second- and third-generation gentlemen traders originating in Prussia, Germany, Austria, Switzerland and Italy who derived their incomes from diversified interests and professions, as bankers, lawyers, architects, landlords and press magnates and the so-called *Łódźermenschen*,[62] those formerly itinerant self-made men whose fortunes developed from the artisan trade. These characteristic differences between the two commercial communities bore many similarities to England's north-south divide; the 'money-ocracy' versus the 'mill-ocracy'.[63]

The longstanding Russian policy to poach industrial skills and capital from abroad has already been described, but in the last quarter of the nineteenth century it is clear that the possibilities of large-scale foreign direct investment became the focus of increased debate in St Petersburg. In September 1880 the future finance minister Bunge petitioned the Tsar to make legislative reforms which would assist the manufacturing industry. Instead of the standard interventions which favoured selected industrialists with state contracts or tax exemptions, Bunge advocated the 'issuance of laws adapted to the modern development of the economy'.[64] Nevertheless, the ideological conflict between capitalist ideals and autocratic control provoked heated debate amongst the progressive and traditionalist elements of the Tsarist government. While foreign ownership of Polish businesses could not be allowed to curtail Russian sovereignty or facilitate the export of profits, fostering the preconditions for greater industrial, and so economic, expansion might prove invaluable to improve social conditions, bolster military investment and thus secure political power in the potentially rebellious western region of the empire.

---

61 Davies, *God's Playground*, p. 175.

62 *Łódźermenschen* literally means 'Łódź people' but in its linguistic mixture of Polish and German, it aptly describes the melting pot of the city's industrial society. However, the connotations of the label are now somewhat derogatory and often used to describe the predominance of Jews amongst Łódź industrialists.

63 Cain and Hopkins, 'Gentlemanly Capitalism', p. 13.

64 Boris V. Anan'ich, 'The economic policy of the tsarist government and enterprise in Russia from the end of the 19th through the beginning of 20th century', in *Entrepreneurship in Imperial Russia and the Soviet Union*, eds Gregory Guroff and Fred V. Carstensen (Princeton: Princeton University Press, 1983), p. 128.

The Advantages of Marki

It has been argued in this chapter that late nineteenth-century Russian Poland had become a hothouse of economic development in spite of largely adverse political conditions and *not* as a result of positive discrimination by the Russian state. Nevertheless, the high profile of Bunge's recommendations, which closely coincided with the Briggs-Posselt partnership project, certainly suggests a tolerance, if not predilection, towards foreign direct investment within the Russian administration. But it must be considered that local business culture also had a bearing on the Bradford partners' choice of a site near Warsaw. In 1875 the appointment of the politically moderate and progressive Warsaw president, General Sokrates Starynkiewicz, transformed the prospects of the local economy. Starynkiewicz's unprecedented attempts to circumvent Russian bureaucracy and enfranchise local business leaders to manage and finance infrastructural developments will be explored in greater detail in Chapter 6. However, it should be noted here that the projects he instigated – a modern sewage system and water supply, the first telephone exchange, metalled roads and tramways – were not insignificant factors in creating a climate of opportunity which led to a 'wave of dynamic industrial development' in Warsaw during the 1880s.[65]

Although documentation of the Bradford partners' business plans is scarce, their ultimate choice of Marki stands as evidence of their priorities. They chose an isolated location rather than an industrial conglomeration such as Łódź to ensure plentiful building land and future unconfined expansion. For businessmen prepared to consider remoter property, the high taxation of agricultural land and resulting impoverishment of Polish landowners made rural estates cheap, and cash the king. Although Marki's transport communications were meagre compared with those of Russian-Polish cities, they could be developed and sole use of the small river would have been viewed as a distinct advantage. Indeed, as Marki was only a few miles from Warsaw's eastern suburb Praga, with its busy port and rail links which made it the 'focal point for communication between Warsaw's factories and the huge market which the empire represented for them',[66] the village arguably had better direct access to both Warsaw and Russia than either Łódź or Białystok.

Polish Opposition to Foreign Industrial Investment

Despite the tolerant attitude of the Tsarist state and Warsaw's local administration towards foreign direct investment, the Polish stance towards venture capitalists was overwhelmingly negative. At the time of the Marki venture the subjugation of

---

65 Wartalska, 'Fabryka i osada fabryczna', p. 648.

66 Stephen D. Corrsin, *Warsaw Before the First World War: Poles and Jews in the Third City of the Russian Empire 1880–1914* (New York: Columbia University Press, 1989), p. 47.

Russian Poland was in no doubt: the local administration, army and police force were Russian and Cossack regiments were regularly deployed to quash dissent. Workers' associations were illegal and private enterprise was heavily regulated. The dissenters of England's industrial north, without political franchise, had turned their talents to business, but in Russian Poland the cash-strapped, politically impotent and deeply divided factions of Polish society could only debate and philosophise. Whereas open discussion of Russian oppression was dangerous, the social transformations caused by industrialisation and particularly a perceived influx of foreign industrialists, apparently under the sponsorship of the Tsarist authorities, provided an ideal platform for commentators of almost every political persuasion to expound their views. Although the rhetoric formed only a thinly veiled protest against Russian rule, it was clearly tolerated. In a divide-and-rule approach to managing local politics, the Tsarist regime actively encouraged Polish hostility towards incoming foreign elements or indeed any non-Polish minority. As the British consul observed in 1886: 'one must come to the conclusion that the Russian government looks with complacency on the unfriendly feelings, which it allows to be ventilated in the newspapers'.[67]

In 1883 the *Tygodnik Ilustrowany* voiced the local perception that the traditional 'exploiters closest to our hearts were our nearest neighbours the Germans',[68] but highlighted that more recently French, Belgian and, in an undoubted reference to the Briggs-Posselt partnership, even English industrialists were increasingly settling in the Kingdom of Poland. The *Kurjer Warszawski*, in an article entitled 'The English in Poland', used a similar metaphor of devouring exploitation, suggesting that the region had become 'a gourmet colony for British industrialists'.[69] Jerzy Jedlicki identifies the very broad spectrum of late nineteenth-century Polish political viewpoints, including Populists, Positivists, Organicists, Liberals, Socialists, Right Wing Radicals and Nationalists amongst many more. Each was represented by a dedicated press ready to expound their views on the industrialisation of the Kingdom of Poland: the Socialists advocated rebellion against the dehumanising effects of industry which reduced the workforce to a commodity, whereas the Marxists argued in favour of greater investment before they seized the capitalist wealth for the people.[70] The Catholic Church, arguably the only unifying voice of the Polish nation, roundly rejected modernity as morally corrupting. The *Przegląd Katolicki* pointed an accusatory finger at the superficiality of American society and described England, the seat of the Industrial Revolution, as 'tormented and perplexed by materialism, atheism, moral degradation, heresy and godlessness'.[71] But even the non-sectarian press such as the Krakow daily *Czas* [*Time*] subscribed

67 FO65/1277, Grant to the Secretary of State, 13 August 1886, p. 8.

68 Wartalska, 'Fabryka i osada fabryczna', p. 647.

69 'Anglicy w Polsce' ['The English in Poland'], *Kurjer Warszawski*, 26 March/ 7 April 1883, p. 2.

70 Jedlicki, *Suburb of Europe*, p. 248.

71 Ibid., p. 215.

to the view that 'scientific, industrial and social revolution was the antithesis of civilisation; it was the beginning of catastrophe'.[72]

The Polish Positivists represented the most progressive attitude to industry, 'with firm belief in reason, science, material progress and education as keys to the nation's future'.[73] They disregarded calls for violent revolution in favour of *praca organiczna* [organic work] and advocated social reform and reasonable cooperation with the state, to alleviate poverty. Superficially, their outlook had much in common with the Liberalism of British industrial employers, but they too spoke out against increasing foreign investment. In 1873 prominent Positivist Eliza Orzeszkowa renounced the foreign ownership of industry which she argued perpetuated the peasant status of the population. In quasi-religious idiom she claimed that Polish workers would 'tend and pasture the flocks of our lord, on rivers which flowed with honey and gold, but not for us'.[74] The same view was more belligerently expounded by Aleksander Świętochowski, the outspoken editor of numerous Warsaw newspapers, who in 1880 proclaimed that the region's industry 'exported goods to the east and profits to the west, and thus only made foreigners rich'.[75] He refused to publish advertisements for large industrial companies whom he labelled as sharks.

The extreme fragmentation of Polish political thought in this period provided a rich source for the writer Bolesław Prus who caricatures Warsaw's entrenched philosophical, ethnic, religious and social divisions in his classic novel *The Doll*. He presents a bourgeois-merchant protagonist, Wokulski, alongside a caricature cast of old-fashioned Polish romantics, militant nationalists, poverty-stricken aristocracy, persecuted Jewish money lenders, at odds with their assimilated sons. However, generalisations regarding nineteenth-century socio-political groupings in Poland are almost impossible given the illegality of political parties and heavy subjugation of social and religious affiliations. Some of the most strident views were expounded in anonymous publications by one group, masquerading as another; most commonly radical intelligentsia posing as united workers. This tactic was even embraced by the authorities in attempts to influence local opinion. For example, in 1889 the British consul described a pamphlet entitled 'A Voice from the People on the Polish Question, by a Peasant'[76] as blatant Tsarist propaganda. It set out the advantages of Russian rule, reproached the self-interested motives of the nobility, emphasised the shared cultural legacy of the Slavic nations and warned of the threat posed by Austria and Germany to Polish nationality.

---

72 Ibid., p. 216.

73 Blobaum, *Rewolucja*, p. 33 and Lucjan Blit, *The Origins of Polish Socialism: The History and Ideas of the First Polish Socialist Party* (Cambridge: Cambridge University Press, 1971), p. 12.

74 Jedlicki, *Suburb of Europe*, p. 228.

75 Ibid., p. 279 quotes A. Świętochowski, editor of *Przegląd Tygodniowy* [*Weekly Review*], *Prawda* [*Truth*] and *Niwa* [*The Field*].

76 FO65/1370, Grant to the Secretary of State, 19 July 1889, p. 19.

When ethnic origin, religion and wealth had such a strong bearing on social standing, relative political enfranchisement and economic potential, it was inevitable that foreign ownership of industry would become a contentious issue. Through the medium of Wokulski, Prus voiced the contemporary obsession regarding German domination of Poland's business arena:

> I am quite ready to enumerate for you factories in which the entire administration and all better paid workers are German, in which the capital is German, and managing directors all reside in Germany; in which our workers have no opportunities of bettering themselves, but are badly paid labourers, badly treated and totally germanised.[77]

The complexity of the issue is perhaps better illustrated by an 1887 government survey of woollen and worsted manufacturers published in the *Dziennik Łódźki* which highlights that only 1 per cent of these companies were in Polish ownership, 23 per cent were designated Jewish and 39 per cent under the ownership of ethnically German industrialists who had resided in the Kingdom for more than 25 years. It is likely that, while the government highlighted the alien status of these industrialists, many considered themselves entirely Polish and had long-held Russian nationality. The survey determined that 37 per cent of woollen and worsted mills were owned by 'foreigners'.[78] Despite administrative control and military dominance, the Russian section of the Polish populace was its smallest and most transient component. These Russian expatriate administrators and militia were least likely to capitalise on the economic opportunities unfolding in Russian Poland and thus less committed to the region than the foreign industrial investors.

Although this chapter has devoted some attention to a largely hostile local attitude towards foreign venture capitalists, it is evident that the venomous reportage of the contemporary Polish press had only a subtle influence on business behaviour. Adept at overcoming any obstacle to their economic ambitions, the Bradford men would not view the relatively impotent local censure of their plans as an insurmountable inconvenience, but the stimulus for a carefully staged public relations campaign. Marki was undoubtedly selected primarily for the suitability of land; nevertheless, the Bradford partners' choice might also have reflected a desire to disassociate themselves from the unpopular and parochial German industry of Łódź. It suggests that they aspired to the cosmopolitan 'money-ocracy' of Warsaw not the 'mill-ocracy'[79] of established industry.

This review of industrial development in Poland has inevitably revisited the issue of protectionism, as the region's unique political status, vacillating between economic ostracism and integration with the Russian empire, was so instrumental

---

77 Prus, *The Doll*, p. 154.

78 Hutchinson Dawson, *Industrial Geography of Woollen Textile Manufacturing*, p. 127.

79 Cain and Hopkins, 'Gentlemanly Capitalism', p. 13.

to its economic progress. By the time of the Marki enterprise it might be argued that existing patterns of industrial settlement and internal politics had little bearing on new investments, as the full integration of plants and wealth of the industrialists largely removed them from state control and the need for strategic cooperation. But in reality it is almost impossible to separate the practical-logistical issues which dictated the site of new ventures from a historic legacy which continued to exert significant influence. It is evident that the most basic requirements for land and water primarily attracted the Bradford partners to Marki, but these were perhaps plentiful and cheap as a result of longstanding Russian oppression of the Polish nobility. Similarly, comparing the greater dynamism of Poland's industrial development with that of Russia has suggested some historic-cultural reasons for the Bradford men to target the Polish part of the empire in particular. In 1883 when these entrepreneurs intended to both buy and sell in Russian markets, proximity to Western Europe cannot have been as important as it had been for venturing German artisans in 1820, who needed to maintain access to suppliers across the border. However, that early state-sponsored immigration had led business in Russian Poland to be largely conducted in German, rather than Polish or Russian, and thus enabled the swift integration of this Anglo-German partnership, which would have been entirely unfeasible in Moscow or St Petersburg.

Chapter 5

'British interests will be in no way served':[1] The role of the British consul to assist foreign direct investment

By the end of 1882 the Bradford partners had their sights firmly set on Russian Poland as the ideal location for their foreign enterprise. The last chapters have described their rationale for seeking an unexploited market and have shown that they did not follow an investment trend or solely respond to any state incentive. But despite their obvious independence and combined entrepreneurial skill, they could not realistically establish a business abroad without the assistance of local intermediaries to provide commercial intelligence and create vital trust for them in the host nation. This chapter will identify the first of several Warsaw-based mediators and reveal how each contributed to the launch of this foreign enterprise.

On 11 December 1882 Edward Briggs wrote to the British consul at Warsaw expressing his intention to build a factory in Russian Poland. Foreign Office correspondence has been an invaluable source for this case study, revealing the Bradford entrepreneurs' evolving plans, their intelligence-gathering tactics and even their physical movements in the lead up to purchasing land outside Warsaw in January 1883. Despite growing parliamentary condemnation of British capital export and the bitter complaints of British industrialists regarding the unfair advantages that lower wages, less factory legislation and most notably protectionism afforded their foreign counterparts; this chapter will reveal the pivotal role played by British consular officials to assist foreign direct investment in the late nineteenth century.

The Consular Mandate

Supposedly impartial to the profit of individuals, the consul's basic function was to represent British interests abroad. His responsibilities were loosely grouped as: 'consular', providing local assistance to expatriates, including the issuance of birth, marriage and death certificates; 'political', detailing matters with possible international implications such as military manoeuvres; and 'commercial', the scope of which was less well-defined but historically involved ensuring the

[1] FO393/16, Maude to Messrs John Briggs and Co., Bradford, 14 December 1882, p. 99.

rights of Britain's merchant traders in foreign ports and latterly came to entail fact-finding for the British state. However, this chapter will explore the complex reasons that consular officials habitually exceeded, even contravened, their brief. Using the authority and local knowledge accumulated through their official duties, they assisted both British and foreign-owned companies abroad, which made no contribution to the British economy.

The consul's standing is markedly different from that of the ambassador who represents the British monarch abroad. Disraeli's 1842 description of consulates as 'a refuge for the destitute', for those 'broken in fortune and reputation',[2] was a caricature which endured in the minds of politicians and businessmen to impact negatively on the status of the service. In 1858 *The Times* made no attempt to disguise its contempt, stating that consuls were 'the pariahs of the diplomatic body'.[3] Overtones of the nineteenth-century obsession with social hierarchy seem evident in such indictments. They reflect the longstanding prejudice that only gentlemen or military officers were truly trustworthy, whereas administrators and tradesmen were afforded little respect. It remains debateable whether the government discriminated against business professionals who applied for consular office, or was slow to acknowledge the growing usefulness of the consuls' commercial function to the domestic economy. But, by the late nineteenth century, the routine recruitment of ex-military officers was certainly resented by critics in Parliament who contrasted the growing importance of the consuls' business-related mission with an apparent lack of qualifications in the majority of appointees. Nevertheless, contrary to popular belief, this chapter will show that an officer's title in no way precluded an enthusiasm for commerce.

Salaried and Unsalaried Consuls

One of the main issues which provoked domestic censure was the difficulty of controlling the consular officials abroad. Remote from state regulation, there was a common perception that the posting was 'the most efficient means of making what is a fortune in the provinces'.[4] Historically, consuls had undertaken their responsibilities unpaid, charging fees for their official duties and simultaneously developing their own interests. It was not until the 1820s that a reform led by Lord Canning recommended that some consuls general were put on the Civil List to receive a salary which might focus their energies primarily on state matters. However, those excluded from the Civil List were 'allowed to engage in trade in their spare time'.[5] The inadequate enforcement of the directive led continuing

2 *HC Debate*, Consular Establishment, 8 March 1842, Vol. 61, cc. 229.

3 *The Times*, 22 May 1858, p. 10.

4 Ibid.

5 John Dickie, *The British Consul: Heir to the Great Tradition* (London: Hurst and Company, 2007), p. 14.

substantial objections to be raised in Parliament that trading by both paid and voluntary British government officials abroad would lead to a 'diminution in consular influence with local authorities, and the temptation to advance private interests at the expense ... of public duty'.[6] In 1872, a Select Committee restated the ruling more firmly; salaried consuls were restricted from trading and any fees that they charged should be paid to the Exchequer while the volunteers were permitted to retain office expenses.[7] The persistent mistrust and disagreements about the emphasis of their role resulted in pay freezes and a gradual reduction of consular wages during the nineteenth century. But in 1901 when Alex Murray protested that his £900 stipend was 'altogether inadequate' considering the rising cost of living in Warsaw, he received short shrift from the Secretary of State.[8] In a mocking reply Sir Villiers Lister stated that 'it strikes me that with rent at £125 a year, with meat at 4d per lb and man-servants wages at £24 a year, Warsaw must be one of the cheapest places in the world!'.[9]

Despite Murray's complaints, there was no shortage of candidates eager to assume consular duties unpaid.[10] For example in 1886, Julius Winzer, a 30-year-old native of Staffordshire who claimed to speak Russian, Polish, French and German, applied for the position of consul general at Warsaw. Winzer declared himself 'well acquainted in English and Russian mercantile matters'[11] and on good terms with the civil and military authorities in the city, as well as 'the representatives of all foreign powers'.[12] Yet he stated 'as head of the largest wholesale establishment in Poland, salary is not so much an object to me'. [13] Despite an inexorable characterisation of consuls as the poor relations of the diplomatic service, that businessmen such as Winzer so actively sought the role strongly suggests its lucrative personal possibilities. Indeed Platt argues that 'unpaid consular posts were much sought after for their social or indirect financial advantages'.[14] For former military men or local expatriates, beyond the basic pecuniary advantages – the state salary, housing, central office and fees – was a perception that the title afforded authority. The administrative tasks of office provided legitimate insight into the private dealings of a broad range of social and commercial contacts. Thus, an astute official was in a unique position to identify opportunities: to match local

[6] D.C.M. Platt, 'The Role of the British Consular Service in Overseas Trade, 1825–1914', *Economic History Review*, 15: 3 (1963), p. 498.

[7] *HC Select Committee Report*, Diplomatic and Consular Services, No. 314, 16 July 1872, Vol. 212, cc. 1241–2.

[8] FO65/1633, Alex Murray at Warsaw to Secretary of State, 30 September 1901, p. 38.

[9] FO65/1633, Sir Villiers Lister to Murray at Warsaw, 16 October 1901, p. 41.

[10] The year-end report for the Warsaw consulate shows that only the Consul General received a salary, all vice-consuls were unpaid.

[11] FO65/1277, Julius Winzer to the Secretary of State, 4 February 1886, p. 84.

[12] Ibid.

[13] Ibid.

[14] Platt, 'Role of the British Consular Service', p. 498.

businessmen with British partners, to recommend suppliers and agents or find employment for a relative or the son of a friend.[15] He could circulate information to curry favour, profit from unofficial consultancy and take a speculative share in numerous private enterprises.

Commercial Reports for British Business

The focus of the consuls' responsibilities naturally varied from post to post according to local needs, just as the character and interests of individual incumbents could shape the role. In Latin America frequent revolutions led mediation and the granting of asylum to be normal consular activities.[16] But as foreign competition was increasingly held culpable for the rising pressure on the British economy, the government's demands of its Foreign Office officials grew and commerce was endorsed as their 'principal object'.[17] Despite an enduring archaic directive to 'give his best advice and assistance … to his Majesty's Trading Subjects, quieting their differences, promoting peace, harmony and goodwill amongst them',[18] by the end of the nineteenth century consuls were expected to analyse new trade legislation and scout out quite specialised opportunities for British businessmen. For example, in 1883 Edmund Phipps, the consul general at Budapest, detailed changes to the Austro-Hungarian tariff in Manchester's *Textile Recorder* which he viewed as a significant opportunity for British venture capitalists. He highlighted the poor capitalisation of Hungarian industrialists, the 'exceptional favours offered by the Government'[19] to encourage foreign direct investment and even projected a 10 to12 per cent return on capital. Late nineteenth-century consular briefings were thus peppered with foreign governments' calls for expert contractors; for example that 'the municipality of Warsaw are prepared to receive tenders for the electrical exploitation of the town, such as lighting and tramways'.[20]

After 1886 all British consulates were required to prepare an annual report detailing economic and industrial statistics, local commerce and trade legislation

---

[15] FO393/16, Vol. I, Miscellaneous Correspondence 1881–85, Maude to Mr Beauclerk, 20 October 1882, p. 84: 'since I wrote last I have had a long talk with Mr Winzer about Winnie … he would probably at first be employed in pricing goods and then when he picked up the language, he would be put into the office as a clerk. He would be treated with courtesy from the first by the other employees. Mr Winzer said emphatically to me that he will have nothing at all menial, or unbecoming to a gentleman to perform and if he is an intelligent boy he is sure he will get on well'.

[16] Platt, 'Role of the British Consular Service', p. 495.

[17] Ibid., p. 494.

[18] Dickie, *The British Consul*, p. 30.

[19] 'A New Centre for English Enterprise', p. 27.

[20] FO65/1565, Murray to Secretary of State, 16 February 1898, p. 277 and on 30 September 1898, p. 315, Warsaw's municipality invited tenders to build the city's market hall.

from their districts. Although some of the data was issued by the host government or garnered from the press, the consul was expected to glean the most valuable intelligence from his own observations and, above all, from British expatriates in his jurisdiction. But unsurprisingly, as their operations became the focus of greater interest for the British government and, more particularly, their home-trade competitors, these businessmen became reluctant to supply the necessary facts. Late nineteenth-century Foreign Office correspondence reveals a plethora of complaints from consuls worldwide that, for example, the 'merchants and shipping firms that are in a position to supply information for Consular Annual Reports are obliged to decline to help us owing to keenness of competition'.[21] When tasked with providing local insight for the Associated Chambers of Commerce in England in 1896, Henry Grant made the excuse that he would be 'confronted by manufacturers interested in misleading me as they would see me as a British agent collecting information for the benefit of their English rivals'.[22] In 1902 Murray justified his request to pass advice from the British consul in Persia to the Briggs brothers by suggesting that: 'it helps me very considerably to be able to render a small service of this sort to a big local … firm who are often able to give most useful hints for reports'.[23]

At the end of the nineteenth century it is evident that a confused, even contradictory, directive was seriously impacting on the effectiveness of Britain's consuls. An official who only complied with his basic mandate to protect the rights of British nationals abroad, to provide passport renewals and issue certificates, was entirely ill-equipped to fulfil the growing requirement for pertinent commercial insight. Indeed in 1918, George Michel, the consul at Para, questioned how such clerks could 'be expected to be in touch with British sentiment, business methods or needs?'[24] The authority afforded them as representatives of the Foreign Office proved insufficient to demand commercially sensitive intelligence, but any consular involvement in trade which might have informed their reports was considered essentially corrupt by the vociferous critics in the British Parliament. The dilemma was succinctly highlighted by Lord Rosebery in 1886 when he asked: 'how much further we can go in the direction of developing and assisting commerce by means of diplomatic and consular agency, without running the risk of possible connection with private firms or enterprise, and the consequent lowering of the standard and repute of those services'.[25]

---

[21] Platt, 'Role of the British Consular Service', p. 500.

[22] FO65/1522, Grant at Warsaw to Secretary of State, 9 November 1896, p. 48.

[23] FO65/1652, Murray to Mr Law in the Foreign Office, 3 December 1902, p. 126.

[24] Dickie, *The British Consul*, p. 29 quotes George Michel, Consul at Para, to Sir Arthur Peel, Minister for Brazil, forwarded to the Secretary of State, Arthur Balfour, 10 August 1918.

[25] Platt, 'Role of the British Consular Service', p. 507.

Credit Checking and Debt Collecting

In order to counter domestic criticism and justify their role, consuls increasingly needed a strategy to acquire industrial, economic and trade data. Although the service has been described as under-paid, under-staffed and sternly criticised, microanalysis of Foreign Office correspondence reveals that the officials routinely undertook tasks which exceeded their official mandate.[26] For example in 1890 the British attaché to Russia suggested it was acceptable for the consul to advise a businessman on matters of law and 'recommend him to a trust-worthy lawyer',[27] but that they should resist requests to advise on the financial standing of potential business partners. Nevertheless, collecting debts and supplying credit references did occupy a considerable amount of their time. British firms expected their consulates to check the credentials of foreign agents and potential business partners, while the enquiries of foreign nationals who hoped to cultivate British associations are equally ubiquitous in consular correspondence.[28] By making himself indispensible to expatriate and foreign businessmen alike, a shrewd consul could furnish himself with an unrivalled commercial insight and a network of advantageously beholden local contacts. Although this might have been necessary simply to inform his official reports, it also created an invaluable resource for new investors in the area.

Consular Mediation of Foreign Direct Investment

Consuls often played a significant role in the facilitation of British enterprise abroad, but their intermediary status has been largely overlooked in studies of British foreign investment. They were neither party to the venturing firm nor agent of the local government, yet their contribution could prove crucial, both to the success of an individual company and to economic development of the host nation. Consular participation provided a professional diplomacy to negotiations, and the cachet of his connection with the British government lent weight to his recommendations, engendering trust for venture capitalists with foreign traders and local governments. The Briggs-Posselt partnership proposed a vast, capital-rich undertaking in Russian Poland, but Foreign Office records reveal numerous smaller-scale British foreign enterprises were mediated by the Warsaw consul in the same period. For example in 1882 Mr Johnstone of London sought a Warsaw partner for his sack-making company[29] and in 1902 two Glasgow pork butchers

[26] Ibid., p. 494.

[27] Ibid., pp. 503–5.

[28] FO393/16, Maude to John Fowler and Co., Leeds, 21 November 1882, p. 91.

[29] FO393/16, Maude to Robert J. Johnstone Esq., 30, Leadenhall Street, London, 20 September 1882, p. 74.

'visited Warsaw with a view to establishing a bacon factory'.[30] These were among many private undertakings which provided no conceivable benefit to the British state, but were significantly assisted by a Foreign Office official.

Between 1876 and 1887 the consul general at Warsaw was Colonel Francis Cornwallis Maude, a retired army officer who in many ways conformed to the critic's view of applicants to the post. Awarded the Victoria Cross for his heroics during the Indian Mutiny,[31] he left the army in 1866 to establish the Malta Ice Works which was the first in a series of failed commercial enterprises.[32] He returned to England bankrupt in 1867 where he founded the Free Labour Registration Society, an anti-trade union movement which he claimed had 'fought twenty-six pitched battles with trade unions over a period of eighteen months'.[33] In 1870 he purchased 600 acres of land in Canada where he cleared forest for three years, but returned to England where he farmed in Hampshire and was chairman of the Southsea Co-operative stores. He then spent a year in France before taking up the post of consul general in Russian Poland.[34]

In December 1882 Edward Briggs wrote to Maude for information. As a significant British taxpayer it is likely that the industrialist considered himself entitled to the expert advice of a Foreign Office official. However, the consul's reply was emphatic:

> The matter appears to me to be of a purely personal nature, and in no way forming part of my consular duties. By which I mean that British interests, in general, will be in no way served by the establishment of such a factory as you contemplate, but rather the contrary will be the case.[35]

Maude's understanding was quite clear; the proposed venture would not benefit the British exchequer and would further the development of competing foreign industry. But far from rejecting the industrialist's overture, the consul promptly laid out the terms of his participation: 'to do full justice to the business it will be desirable that I proceed to Łódź myself ... This will naturally involve some expense and inconvenience'.[36] Thus the official defined his involvement as a private arrangement and demanded confirmation by telegram of a 40-pound fee. Later correspondence suggests that this was an exorbitant price as in 1885,

30 FO65/1652, Murray to Secretary of State, 15 April, 1902, p. 92.

31 Francis Cornwallis Maude and John Walter Sherer, *Memories of the Mutiny* (London: Remington, 1894).

32 *London Gazette*, 24 December, 1867, p. 7051.

33 Roger T. Stearn, 'Maude, Francis Cornwallis (1828–1900)', *Oxford Dictionary of National Biography* (Oxford: Oxford University Press, October 2005).

34 Ibid.

35 FO393/16, Maude to Messrs John Briggs and Co., Bradford, 14 December 1882, p. 99.

36 Ibid.

when commissioned by the Secretary of State to make a six-week political fact-finding tour, Maude estimated that 'as a great part of my time will be spent in travelling and hotels, the extra expenses of pocket, which such a journey will entail, will hardly be covered by 10 rubles (£1 per day). But that sum will be sufficient for my requirements'.[37] Further perspective for the charge is provided by the consulate's year-end account for 1883–84 in which 'the gross amount of all fees and remuneration received at the British consul-general of Warsaw' totalled only £11, 12s, for the whole year.[38]

Colonel Maude intended to leave the Bradford entrepreneurs in no doubt of his value to their project as he confidently asserted 'whatever information I send you will be verified by the opinion of manufacturers and foremen, both here and at Łódź'.[39] Of particular significance for this case study is the revelation that the partners originally intended to locate their new business in the large industrial city of Łódź. It was a plan that the consul had no hesitation in authoritatively opposing: 'I am of the opinion that another locality would be more suitable for the erection of such a mill as you describe'.[40] Finally, Maude requested clarification of the projected acreage and estimated number of employees that would be required.

Colonel Maude's Fact-finding for the Bradford Partners

The correspondence of the following weeks forms as much a case study of the consular role in the facilitation of British overseas ventures as it does about the foundation of this enterprise in particular. Colonel Maude used a variety of tactics, calling in favours and exploiting his authority, to persuade the businessmen of his locale to provide information for the Bradford men. He made a three-day visit to Łódź from 21 to 23 December, but subsequently addressed all Edward Briggs' questions to a textile agent, Izydor Blum:

> Dear Sir,
>
> I shall fall much obliged to you if you will send me a brief answer to the following queries at your earliest possible convenience, in order to enable me to complete any report for Messrs B.
>
> 1. How do spinners and manufacturers pay for their goods, that is, what credit do they get from the parties they buy from?

[37] FO65/1227, Maude to the Secretary of State, 28 September 1885, p. 18.

[38] FO65/1193, Count Morsztyn, secretary to the British consul at Warsaw to the Secretary of State, 31 March 1884, p. 48.

[39] FO393/16, Maude to Messrs John Briggs and Co., 14 December 1882, p. 99.

[40] Ibid.

2. How do they (the spinners and manufacturers) get paid by the parties to whom they sell, and what credit do they give?
3. Do bankers allow overdrafts, and what commission do they charge?
4. What kind of money do customers pay in?
5. If customers neglect to pay, what sort of law is there to compel payment?
6. Are there any bankruptcy laws, and if so, how do they work?

Again thanking you for your kind attentions … Francis C. Maude.[41]

While usefully highlighting the venture capitalists' key concerns to be their legal and financial standing in Russian Poland, this letter shows that, despite all his authoritative posturing, the consul was not sufficiently conversant with the fine detail of trade to respond without canvassing opinion. The reasons that Blum diligently supplied information, against the broader backdrop of resentment to consular enquiries already described, is perhaps explained by his personal circumstances. The Russian-Jewish textile agent had become a naturalised Briton in 1873, but was declared bankrupt in Manchester and returned to Łódź in 1878.[42] As a Jew his British credentials afforded him a measure of security against the periodic punitive actions of the Tsarist state. Indeed in 1887 Blum made a desperate appeal to Maude's successor to intercede with the authorities when, contrary to an international agreement to protect British traders in Russia, Blum found himself subject to a new law that Jewish merchants of the Piotrków district must either pay a crippling first-class merchant's tax or quit the country.[43]

Whereas Maude could use his authority to gain Blum's cooperation, proffering the prospective enterprise as an investment opportunity proved a potent tactic to offset the reluctance of other informants and furnish himself with the advice of powerful industrialists and financiers. At the end of December he relayed that 'a large manufacturer of Italian cloth'[44] based in Warsaw had confirmed the growing market for fine worsted yarn and extended a £10,000 investment to the Briggs-Posselt enterprise. This offer illustrates the considerable trust that the consul's participation engendered and while it might seem astonishing that a Warsaw businessman would attempt to buy such a substantial stake in a new concern, without even meeting his potential partners, there were sound reasons for this course of action. Naturally the chance to diversify business interests would have been fundamental but, in this case, the unnamed manufacturer also hoped to influence the product base of the new firm, to stipulate his own requirements and secure supply, undoubtedly at a preferential rate. The prestige of association

41 FO393/16, Maude to Blum, 24 December 1882, p. 102.
42 *London Gazette*, 27 August, 1878, p. 4908.
43 FO65/1308, Grant to Secretary of State, 7 March 1887, p. 84.
44 FO393/16, Maude to Messrs John Briggs and Co., 27 December 1882, p. 102. Maude does not mention the name of this contact but it is possible it was one of the Bonacossa brothers that Posselt collaborated with later.

with cash-rich foreign investors should not be underestimated as a motivational factor; it would have bolstered the participant's reputation and possibly provided the opportunity to piggy-back the venture capitalists' credit arrangements with local suppliers and banks. On the other hand, if the new venture rivalled his firm, it would be prudent to be as intimately involved as possible, to rein in any elements that might challenge his existing interests.[45] The arrival of the wealthy British investors would undoubtedly have attracted the interest of other local parties, thus securing an association ahead of the pack would have been advisable. Given their much-prized independence, it is highly unlikely that the northern industrialists asked Maude to seek shareholders and despite the sizable offer equivalent to almost 15 per cent of the company's capital, no additional partners are mentioned in the agreement signed by the Briggs brothers and Ernst Posselt later in 1883.

Shortly after receiving the consul's report the British entrepreneurs made the visit to Warsaw, Białystok and Łódź, as described in Chapter 4, to make their own assessment of the potential of each area. Maude's unguarded letters to Blum, while providing an amusing insight into his way of life, reveal some resentment that he was apparently excluded from Bradford men's plans:

> They came at about noon when I was in bed, having been at Madame Wernicka's ball until half past five in the morning: and Count Morsztyn (who received them) asked them to wait while I dressed, which occupied some twenty five minutes, meantime he supplied them with newspapers, and cigarettes and small talk. I offered them luncheon but they refused stating they were going to Lublin, I suppose they did not want me to know they were going to Łódź.[46]

Blum fuelled the contretemps by suggesting that Posselt had complained about Maude's fee. He wrote: 'that fellow even insulted you, telling Mr Gaud that you got £40 for your journey, and that you claim £100, but they will not give you another penny'.[47] The consul's fury was palpable as he vowed to 'give it to them *hot*'[48] when he next met the Bradford men. However, two days later he forwarded a conciliatory note to Ernst Posselt requesting an appointment to 'clear up' the affair at his earliest convenience.[49] It is certain that Maude saw the importance of smoothing over any bad feeling, to protect his good name and salvage any future benefit of association with the prosperous and influential businessmen. Similarly, whether the venture capitalists valued his advice or not, it was important for them to remain on good terms with the consul. Maude could be a powerful advocate for the new firm and in the first month of 1883 is shown to have provided at least one

45 Wilkins, 'The Free-Standing Company', p. 267.

46 FO393/16, Maude to Blum, 20 January 1883, p. 105.

47 Ibid.

48 Ibid.

49 FO393/16, Maude to Posselt at the Hotel Mühl in Warsaw, 22 January 1883, p. 107.

vital credit reference for them to Winzer, in his capacity as import agent. He stated 'I am morally convinced that they are good for any engagements they enter into'.[50]

As news of the Bradford partners' plans spread in Warsaw, consular correspondence shows that Maude was approached by several contractors and potential employees who sought introduction to the new firm. Of particular note and perhaps revealing the local importance of the enterprise was a letter 'from Mr Robert Lindley, the renowned engineer, who is at present conducting the canalization and water works of Warsaw'.[51] The consul similarly conveyed the applications of ordinary workers, for example in 1884 he wrote to Posselt: 'the bearer of this letter is ... a very sad case indeed. I have given him some temporary assistance, but it would be a great kindness, and charity, if you could find him employment at your factory. He is a weaver by trade'.[52]

It remains a matter of speculation whether, in his first letter to Bradford, Maude advocated 'another locality'[53] already having the estate of Marki in mind, but there is a compelling indication. In November 1882, only a few weeks before Edward Briggs' letter, the British consul wrote to John Tomlin about a proposed sack-making enterprise in Russian Poland:

> I am happy to announce to you that Mr Wm E. Rau of this city, one of the richest men in Russia, and a very large iron and steel manufacturer (Lilpop, Rau and Loewenstein) has agreed to join you in the sack business ... as Mr Rau speaks English perfectly well, and is besides a most agreeable, gentlemanly fellow, any person who really means business, would find him a most charming partner.[54]

In January 1883 the Briggs-Posselt partnership acquired the land at Marki from a joint-stock company *Folwark i cegielnia wójtostwa Marki* [Farm and brickworks of the village of Marki],[55] owned by a consortium of Warsaw businessmen including the architect Edward Lilpop, nephew of Rau's business partner Stanisław Lilpop. Maude's earlier recommendation of Rau to Tomlin shows that the engineering firm of Lilpop, Rau and Loewenstein were well known to him and he would undoubtedly have discussed the Bradford partners' plans with this influential industrialist financier. Although this chapter has exposed the consul's somewhat haphazard fact-finding methods and his financial motivation has been implied strongly, with this one introduction Colonel Maude positively influenced the entire course of the Briggs-Posselt partnership's Russian-Polish enterprise and undoubtedly proved his worth.

---

50 FO393/16, Maude to Julius Winzer, 25 January 1883, p. 107.

51 FO393/16, Maude to Messrs Briggs and Co., 17 February 1883, p. 113.

52 FO393/16, Maude to Posselt, 13 November 1884, p. 228.

53 FO393/16, Maude to Messrs John Briggs and Co., 14 December 1882, p. 99.

54 FO393/16, Maude to John Tomlin Esq., 15 November 1882, p. 90.

55 PBN, No. 475 *do księgi wieczystej 'osada wójtostwo Marki'*, No. 4980.

Rau, Lilpop and Marki

Maude's description of the German-born Warsaw industrialist, Wilhelm Ellis Rau, as 'the richest man in Russia'[56] was no exaggeration. Thomas C. Owen presents statistics of wealth among leading corporate founders in Russia and in the period 1879 to 1886, Rau is ranked in first position with interests in sugar beet, iron and machinery manufacture.[57] Rau and Lilpop's importance to the foundation of Bradford Mills at Marki cannot be underestimated. Edward Lilpop was immediately engaged by the British venture capitalists to manage the construction of their factory. Chapter 6 will describe how the association with these influential businessmen secured not only suitable land, but also all the necessary suppliers and building contractors for the project.

The usefulness of these secondary intermediaries, however, far exceeded the provision of land, supplies and local human capital. Every study of entrepreneurship within the Russian empire stresses the importance of cooperation with regional and national government. Jedlicki makes the point at length that joint-stock enterprises could not be established without a state permit, railway companies needed a treasury guarantee, coal mines required licences and large factories could not survive without government orders and customs privileges for importing machinery and raw materials.[58] Relations with the local authorities were as important as those with the St Petersburg and 'one of the highest compliments that could be given a foreign manager was that he knew how to treat officials correctly'.[59] In 1897 the British consul similarly highlighted the business culture of Russian Poland where 'greasing the wheels',[60] in other words, bribery, was standard business practice.

When the Bradford men proposed their investment at Marki, the Russian authorities convened the *Warszawskiego Komitetu Przemysłowego* [Warsaw Committee for Industry].[61] This panel of influential local businessmen would advise the Ministries of Internal Affairs and Finance in St Petersburg on the prudence of authorising the planned company and, among other things, the propriety of offering tax exemptions for the importation of machinery. The reliance of the Tsarist state on the counsel of Russian-Polish, invariably ethnically German, business leaders provided an easy strategy for the Bradford entrepreneurs and their local collaborators to gain approval of their plans. Indeed, the *Polski*

56 FO393/16, Maude to John Tomlin, 15 November 1882, p. 90.

57 Thomas C. Owen, *Russian Corporate Capitalism from Peter the Great to Perestroika* (New York: Oxford University Press, 1995), p. 184. It is worth noting that, according to the *Oxford Dictionary of National Biography*, Maude also had sugar-beet growing interests in Russia.

58 Jedlicki, *Suburb of Europe*, p. 275.

59 McKay, *Pioneers for Profit*, p. 280.

60 FO65/1542, Murray to Secretary of State, 22 July 1897, p. 120.

61 Wartalska, 'Fabryka i osada fabryczna', p. 649.

Słownik Biograficzny shows that Wilhelm Rau was himself a member of the panel at this time.[62] By engaging the vested interests of the tightly knit Warsaw business community, the new enterprise ensured that the evidence gathered by the influential committee was overwhelmingly positive. Perhaps predictably, it was a representative of the machine-making firm Lilpop, Rau and Loewenstein who underlined the importance and uniqueness of the venture and insisted that 'none of the required machinery to start production at Marki could be acquired in either the Kingdom of Poland or Russia'.[63]

In the committee's testimony, local industrialists spoke with one voice, highlighting the revenue potential, the technological advancement and emphasising the ways the worsted factory would consolidate existing industry. The scale of the new plant was compared to the largest textile manufacturers of the region. Marki, in the future of the wool industry, was predicted to 'play the same role as the Żyrardów business of Hielle and Dietrich and the Łódź company of Scheibler'.[64] Salzman, the owner of a local dye-house and laundry, justified the employment of foreign technical staff as the introduction of valuable new skills to Russia. He asserted that 'a combing facility for the preparation of raw wool, which only processes spun worsted ... does not currently exist in this country'.[65] In 1884 the *Gazeta Rzemieślnicza* defended the unpopular employment of foreign staff by a German entrepreneur in broadly similar terms: 'this new factory, specialising in nickel products is the first in our country, therefore the founder has already brought a contingent of foreign artisans'.[66] Having substantiated the importance of the Marki project in commercial terms, its advocates exploited the fears of the Russian administration. In a veiled reference to the importance of wool products for military purposes, they suggested that the establishment of the worsted-spinning mill would protect Russian weavers if war led to a blockade of their current foreign yarn and raw-materials supplies.[67]

The Fast-track Establishment of Foreign Direct Investment

The accumulated evidence of this case study suggests that, in spite of the heavily bureaucratic control of the Tsarist administration, the Marki enterprise was

62 *Polski Słownik Biograficzny*, 'Wilhelm Ellis Rau (1825–1899)', Vol. 30, p. 646.

63 AGAD, *Akta Warszawskiego Komitetu Przemysłowego z 1883 r.*, signature 11/1883.

64 Wartalska, 'Fabryka i osada fabryczna', p. 649, Hielle and Dietrich were the country's foremost linen manufacturer and Scheibler was the wealthiest cotton king in this period.

65 Wartalska, 'Fabryka i osada fabryczna', p. 650, *Nottinghamshire Guardian*, London, 19 May 1894, p. 3, shows that Salzman employed a British director for his works William George Kirkland.

66 'Nowe fabryk' ['New factory'], *Gazeta Rzemieślnicza*, No. 2, 1884, p. 10.

67 AGAD, *Akta Warszawskiego Komitetu Przemysłowego z 1883*, signature 11/1883.

proposed, researched and initiated within six weeks. In Briggs' letter to Maude in December 1882 it is clear that a suitable location had not been identified, yet according to Wartalska 'the legal formalities had been dealt with and the agreement of the local authorities had been obtained', allowing construction of the new plant to commence at the end of January 1883.[68] Kirchner argues that the fast-track establishment of foreign direct investments related to the scarcity of Russian industrial capital which 'gave the advantage to financially strong foreigners, even in dealing with the Russian government'.[69] In the Kingdom of Poland, heavy bureaucratic control of native entrepreneurship has already been shown as a subjugation tactic. An 1882 consular briefing effectively described the usual state of affairs in which, for example, a railway-construction project that 'has been for several years the subject of assiduous application, on the part of the would-be-concessionaires, who comprise some of the principal Polish landowners, and the permission was finally granted last year by his Imperial Majesty'.[70] In this context the rapid launch of the Bradford worsted manufacturers' venture seems astounding. However, although the British press later applauded Edward Briggs' skilful negotiation of 'the iron bound officialism and prejudice of the Russian Government',[71] it is evident that it was the partnership's considerable capital in combination with the united efforts of Warsaw's influential business elite that won swift authorisation for their plans.

In the last quarter of the nineteenth century parliamentary disapproval for the growing trend of capital export was palpable and British economic depression was generally blamed on the rise of foreign industries. Yet, through the medium of Foreign Office correspondence, this chapter has shown the vital role played by British consuls to facilitate foreign direct investment. Although a profit motive has been implied strongly, it is evident that complex circumstances explain the consuls' actions, not least the increasing hunger of the state for commercial intelligence. Whereas Colonel Maude might have hoped that his initial large fee would establish the level of future remuneration in a continuing close association with the Briggs-Posselt partnership, the infrequency of future correspondence would suggest that the northern industrialists dispensed with the consul's services once they were successfully established in Warsaw. Indeed, like their wise-expatriate contemporaries, they consciously avoided giving him information that might prove useful to their competitors. The next chapter will describe how, through Rau and Lilpop, the Bradford partners embedded themselves in Warsaw's elite commercial community and paved the way for the long-term success of their Russian-Polish enterprise.

[68] Wartalska, 'Fabryka i osada fabryczna', p. 648.

[69] Kirchner, 'Russian Tariffs and Foreign Industries', p. 373.

[70] FO65/1146, Maude to Secretary of State, 31 December 1882, p. 103.

[71] 'Sudden death of Mr Edward Briggs', *Ilkley Gazette*, 12 March 1898, p. 5.

Chapter 6

'Your word is gold and your friendship a good security':[1] Social and commercial networking in Warsaw

The foundation stone of the Bradford partners' strategy in Russian Poland, even before land acquisition and plant construction, was to forge trust-based relationships among Warsaw's commercial elite. The cooperation of local suppliers and contractors, as well as the long-term success of the enterprise, rested on their effective integration into the local business network. However, as the cultural and administrative hub of the Kingdom of Poland, Warsaw's economy was dominated by banking and light industries, not by textile manufacture. This chapter will consider how, with little common ground in the field of commerce, the Briggs-Posselt partnership adapted the age-old tactics of international merchant venturers to embed themselves in Warsaw's business community and realise their plans for Marki. Far removed from their familiar milieu of woolmen, it will reveal the rich and diverse opportunities that the host nation presented to the venture capitalists.

International Trust-based Dealing

Over centuries of developing international commerce, kinship ties, shared ethnicity and religious affiliation played essential roles in creating trust between associates. These links swiftly integrated immigrants among their compatriots abroad: regardless of the origin of the entrepreneur, creating 'a common business culture based on shared aspirations and interpersonal contacts was a key ingredient in determining the operational framework of individual firms'.[2] Local cooperation did not undermine the fundamentally competitive nature of trade but, 'founded upon tenets of common interest and collaboration',[3] smoothed business interactions generally. Sharing commercial intelligence broadened the scope of opportunity and joint investment significantly improved the trade environment for the larger

---

1 Reymont, *The Promised Land*, p. 81.

2 Robert Lee, 'Commerce and Culture: A Critical Assessment of the Role of Cultural Factors in Commerce and Trade from c. 1750 to the Early Twentieth Century', in *Commerce and Culture: Nineteenth-century Business Elites*, ed. Robert Lee (Farnham: Ashgate, 2011), p. 3.

3 Cookson, 'Family Firms and Business Networks', p. 1.

group. Indeed the success or failure of an entrepreneur could often be determined by his standing in the local community and its influence on national government.

Many well-known merchant and banking dynasties were created by a relation or trustworthy employee being sent abroad to prove himself. It was not uncommon for the emissary to succeed beyond expectation so that 'before long London or Manchester exchanged places with the home town as centre and satellite of the family's trading activities'.[4] In the period before easy long-distance communications, it is clear that such international undertakings could be managed most reliably by extended family, or in the absence of suitable relatives, by members of the same ethnic or religious group. By the late nineteenth century infrastructural improvements, secure international banking networks and greater trade legislation across the world might feasibly have superseded the importance of trust-based dealing in such enterprises, but the ingrained 'view that family connections held a monopoly on trust'[5] endured. Thus, trust-based relationships continued to mediate most business transactions into the twentieth century.

The main reason for this continuing state of affairs was that the pioneer international concerns, whether in banking or commodity dealing, were essentially a single firm comprised of numerous tightly interconnected branches, thus the fortunes or failings of each element would impact on the whole. Despite improvements to global financial and trade-related legislature in the late nineteenth century, formal institutions could not be relied upon to arbitrate legal disputes with remote partners; indeed the length of time court proceedings might take in any country could be ruinous.[6] Contractual obligations offered little security if the actions of an unscrupulous associate or employee in a foreign branch brought down the whole firm. Posselt's international interests were dominated by familial relationships with his many brothers-in-law, but his son William described the catastrophe caused, when in 1875 'the manager of his branch office in Paris was found guilty of such large embezzlements that it almost ruined the firm'.[7] The Marki venture, on the other hand, was an independent company, not the branch of an international enterprise. Its product or profits were not fed back to bolster a British or German parent company, thus any failure would only have had consequences for the investor partners. Nevertheless, relationships built on trust were vital to bind the partners, local suppliers, customers and to some extent management in informal contracts of mutual obligation.

4 Chapman, *Merchant Enterprise in Britain*, p. 12.

5 Cookson, 'Family Firms and Business Networks', p. 1.

6 Christof Dejung, 'Bridges to the East: European Merchants and Business Practices in India and China', in *Commerce and Culture: Nineteenth-century Business Elites*, ed. Robert Lee (Farnham: Ashgate, 2011), p. 109.

7 William Posselt, *Gottfried Posselt 1693–1768, sein Leben, seine Vorfahren und seine Nachkommen* [*Gottfried Posselt 1693–1768, his Life, his Ancestors and his Descendants*] (Munich, 1926), p. 202.

The Rationale for Assimilation

By the early nineteenth century a strong tradition already existed for enclaves of, for example, Greek or Italian merchants to trade their national commodities in commercial centres across the world. These expatriates tended to maintain their national identity as an effective brand for their products and to create a commercial mystique which might deter local merchants from dealing with their homeland. However, by the mid-nineteenth century international traders increasingly chose to cast off their foreign identity and assimilate. It might be assumed that the political attitude of the host nation influenced this behaviour; that a more liberal regime encouraged adherence to foreign traditions of faith, dress and behaviour whereas assimilation was more general in intolerant societies. But it is evident that the growing sophistication of the tradesmen's ambitions accounted for the transformation in behaviour and even in politically moderate regions economic migrants sought to assimilate.

Despite a relatively liberal political climate in mid-nineteenth-century Bradford the 'friendly invasion' of Germans described by Priestley invariably strove for integration.[8] Although their commercial connections in Germany and linguistic fluency undoubtedly provided inroads to the city's rapidly growing industry, these international entrepreneurs had broader ambitions. They relocated to profit from a burgeoning global trade which encompassed commodity speculation, manufacturing and banking; in this context a strongly defined foreign identity tended to work against their interests. When the young Ernst Posselt came to Bradford in 1858, he did not intend to trade from the confines of a German ghetto or limit himself to transactions with his homeland, anymore than he intended to restrict his dealings to worsted. Posselt was typical of a 'world-wide cosmopolitan bourgeoisie'[9] which developed its trade in England but operated 'webs of enterprise overseas'.[10] Bradford's German émigrés arrived at the grass roots of industrial development and were instrumental in creating the city's economic success, but their commercial aspirations could only be realised with the highest level of social acceptance in the host nation.[11] Assimilation allowed them to win the trust of Yorkshire business partners and wield sufficient political power to lobby both local and national government for improvements to the trading environment.

The specific political climate of each nation undoubtedly had a bearing on entrepreneurial behaviour, but even the most inhospitable regime would not discourage a determined entrepreneur if an opportunity was identified; they simply needed to adjust their strategy to meet local needs. In Warsaw under

---

8 Priestley, *English Journey*, p. 158.

9 Foreman-Peck, *History of the World Economy*, p. 50.

10 Winder, 'Webs of Enterprise', p. 795.

11 M. Casson, 'Entrepreneurship and Business Culture', in *Entrepreneurship, Networks and Modern Business*, eds J. Brown and M.B. Rose (Manchester: Manchester University Press, 1993), p. 42.

Russian rule, the activities of both Jews and Catholics were tightly controlled whereas the minority of Protestant businessmen, of predominantly German origin, constituted an ostensibly neutral political group. The combination of their natural entrepreneurial bent and relative freedom from Russian oppression allowed them to dominate commerce. The group's success perpetuated a measure of state support as they provided a rich source of revenue for Russia. Indeed Warsaw's bourgeois bankers and industrialists accounted for only 4 per cent of the population in the late nineteenth century but provided 65 per cent of the city's income tax.[12] The outspoken newspaper editor Świętochowski derided the privileges afforded to the Kingdom's German contingent and attributed Polish economic impotence to an 'inability to communicate and work together, because of the lack of freedom of association'.[13] The extent of political leverage wielded by Warsaw's business leaders cannot in any way be compared with, for example, Bradford merchant Sir Jacob Behrens' central role in negotiating the Cobden Treaty.[14] Yet the political oppression of Jewish competitors and the heavy taxation of the Catholic aristocracy, who would have led property ownership, banking and enterprise in other political circumstances, constituted a significant opportunity akin to protectionism for members of Warsaw's Evangelical-Augsburg community.

Warsaw Commerce and the German-Evangelical Church

The most ambitious of Warsaw's businessmen and new arrivals to the city alike typically sought to join the German-Evangelical Church. Some romantic assertions have been made that, for example, the celebrated architect Henryk Marconi 'converted to the Evangelical-Reform faith out of love for his wife Małgorzata Heiton'.[15] But it is evident that the young Italian's religious conversion facilitated not only his marriage, but a prestigious career sponsored by Warsaw's wealthiest patrons. The Jewish publisher Salomon Lewenthal, later known as Franciszek Salezy Lewenthal, changed his religious adherence after purchasing the *Kurjer Warszawski*, reportedly 'so as not to hurt the paper among its Christian readership'.[16] Indeed Warsaw's economic arena was dominated by some 'great assimilationist entrepreneurial families, such as the Kronenberg, Natanson,

---

[12] Słoniowa, *Sokrates Starynkiewicz*, p. 33, Corrsin, *Warsaw Before the First World War*, p. 2.

[13] Jedlicki, *Suburb of Europe*, p. 236.

[14] J. and H. Behrens, *Memoir of Jacob Behrens 1806–1889* (Bradford: Percy, Lund, Humphreys and Co., 1925), p. 50. Behrens appeared before the commission at Paris as a witness from the English worsted trade and assisted Richard Cobden in negotiations for the 1861 treaty and corresponded with Disraeli on the subject of tariff control.

[15] Tadeusz Stegner, *Ewangelicy warszawscy 1815–1918* [*Warsaw Evangelicals 1815–1918*] (Warsaw: Semper, 1993), p. 158.

[16] Corrsin, *Warsaw Before the First World War*, p. 36.

Wawelberg, and Epstein families and Jan Bloch';[17] all formerly Jewish members of the Evangelical-Augsburg Church.

The success of one religious group and the tendency of incomers to join it depended on both its 'traditional religious dominance, and the effectiveness of religious discrimination'.[18] While it might be a leap of the imagination to suggest that the inclusive policies of the Evangelical-Augsburg Church had a commercial motive, it is evident that the strength of the institution and the wealth of its members were significantly bolstered by state persecution of other religious adherents. The congregation comprised a local network of trust through which business transactions were mediated safely. Cooperation produced numerous palpable advantages: participants were insulated from outside competition, an exchange of services might circumvent taxable transactions, credit could be secured, commercial intelligence was shared and the group's accumulated experience could negotiate the bureaucracy of local government and procure lucrative state contracts.

By the late nineteenth century the role of religious institutions globally as a focal point for business interactions and directing civic affairs had become arguably as important as their spiritual function. It is unsurprising that Ernst Posselt joined Warsaw's Evangelical-Augsburg confession as he came from a long line of Lutheran scholars and was a trustee of Bradford's Evangelical Church.[19] But the Briggs brothers' attachment to this German institution, rather than the British-Anglican ministry at Warsaw, strongly suggests that their religious allegiance related less to faith and more to a social or commercial motive. When trade interactions in a foreign country required verification of reputation and reliability, shared religious affiliation with potential business partners provided a valuable reference. In Britain's industrial cities chapels were considered 'social centres for the well-to-do',[20] but in Warsaw, where every aspect of public life was heavily regulated by the Russian state and the formation of secular chambers of commerce was prohibited, the role of the Church took on even greater importance. The Evangelical-Augsburg Church was an effective club for the business elite which would play a critical role in the establishment and success of the Marki venture.

Beyond friendship or capital, the practical necessity for swift assimilation into Warsaw society might further explain the Briggs brothers' uncharacteristic admission of a non-family investor into partnership. Ernst Posselt had a successful track record in establishing foreign enterprises; he naturally spoke German, Warsaw's language of business, but additionally had a strong association with the religious hub of Warsaw commerce. There is also a suggestion, although not proven, that Posselt may have had a pre-existing contact in Warsaw. His Derby

17 Ibid., p. 56.

18 Lee, 'Commerce and Culture', p. 16.

19 Heidelberg Stadtarchiv, 100 Years Posseltslust (1881–1981) and WYAS Wakefield, 14 March 1894, Book 9, No. 75, p. 155.

20 Lee, 'Commerce and Culture', p. 12.

partnership with Theodor Bartsch, a Prussian merchant and industrialist with connections in St Petersburg, was mentioned in Chapter 1.[21] It may be purely coincidental but the contemporary pastor of Warsaw's Evangelical-Augsburg Church, editor of the *Dziennik Warszawski* and author of many articles on his travels in the Middle East, was one Henryk Bartsch.[22]

Warsaw's Evangelical-Augsburg Congregation

In contrast to Bradford's Germans, Warsaw's Evangelical-Augsburg congregation were not recent immigrants. The majority had been born in the city and many came from families that had been resident since the eighteenth century. The church's administrative body was elected from lawyers, doctors, architects, publishers, industrialists and bankers. Most are shown to have had a broad range of professional, commercial and intellectual interests such as the Gebethner brothers, merchants and well-known collectors of Polish art, who ran a pianoforte-manufacturing company and published the influential *Kurjer Warszawski* and *Kurjer Codzienna* between 1868 and 1887.[23] Leon Loewenstein, Wilhelm Rau's partner in the engineering company Lilpop, Rau and Loewenstein, had worked for his uncle the banker Leopold Kronenberg before becoming a significant property owner with extensive interests in sugar refineries and railways. Wiktor Hausbrandt, a lawyer and playwright, was editor of Warsaw's legal journal the *Gazeta Sądowa*. Indeed the group was characterised by the range of their business interests and interlocking directorates. The same family names appeared year after year elected to the church's governing body, they were predominantly native Poles of German descent and tradition, long established as Warsaw's trading elite.

This case study provides a fascinating insight into the practical advantage of mediating business through this religious institution. The role of the prominent Protestants Lilpop, Rau and Loewenstein in recommending the Briggs-Posselt partnership's plans to the Warsaw Industrial Committee was highlighted in the last chapter.[24] Their engagement of Edward Lilpop as project manager has already been described, but Evangelical-Augsburg connections can be traced for almost all the contractors who worked on the Marki plant: carpenters the Bevensee brothers and Konstanty Rudzki who provided the ironwork were contemporary

---

[21] *Bradford Observer*, 21 December 1865, p. 5, *Bradford Observer*, 29 April 1869, p. 8, *Derby Mercury*, 24 May 1876, p. 2 and *Derby Mercury*, 9 May 1877, p. 8.

[22] Mieczysław Albert Krąpiec, *Studia polonijne* [*Polish Studies*] (Lublin: Towarzystwo Naukowe Katolickiego Uniwesytetu Lubelskiego, 2000), p. 67. Theodor and Henryk Bartsch, although of a similar generation, were definitely not brothers but it is highly probable that there was a kinship tie between them.

[23] Feliks Gebethner was on the congregational committee of the Evangelical-Augsburg Church in 1883 and his brother Gustaw followed in 1885.

[24] Wartalska, 'Fabryka i osada fabryczna', p. 650.

members of the congregational committee. Aleksander Sikorski whose quarries at Szydłowc provided the stone was associated closely with the Lilpops; indeed all these men had all been involved in building the grand *Świetej Trójcy* [Holy Trinity] Evangelical Church itself.[25] With such a large proportion of their cooperative circle profiting from the Marki venture, it is safe to assume that the favourable press coverage of the enterprise can be attributed to those publishers among the ranks of the church membership. For example Ludwik Jeneke, contemporary president of the congregational committee and longstanding editor of the *Tygodnik Illustrowany*, published an overwhelmingly positive report on the Marki venture in 1883 which will be detailed in Chapter 7.[26]

Dynastic Intermarriage

Religious affiliation opened the doors of opportunity but intermarriage cemented local business ties. Reymont ridiculed the mercenary nature of marital alliances between families of the Łódź cotton kings with numerous cynical references to the cold-blooded form of these arrangements. He portrayed an ambitious man's persuasive argument to a prospective father-in-law: 'you will be investing your daughter at 100 per cent', and the father's miserly reply: 'in principle, I agree, only we must deduct my expenses: the wedding, the trousseau and the cost of her education'.[27] However, such calculated intermarriage was not confined to nouveau-riche industrialists, for centuries it had been an accepted strategy to secure the interests of dispersed international traders and to protect the assets of the aristocracy. Marriage strengthened existing community bonds and provided a fund of human capital to extend familial interests when 'competent sons and cousins were sometimes in short supply'.[28] It is worth noting here that Julius Winzer, whose impressive application for the role of British consul was outlined in the last chapter, owed his local standing to his marriage into the Warsaw firm of Lesser Gebruder.

By the 1880s the pattern of conjugal association between earlier generations of Warsaw's business community was apparent. Under the umbrella of the Evangelical-Augsburg Church it is possible to identify several clear dynastic sub-groups: the elite bankers such as Bloch, Kronenberg, Natanson and Epstein were closely related. A second clan of notable architects and wealthy intelligentsia such as the families of Lilpop, Heurich, Anders, Werner, Hausbrandt, Marconi and Lanci is also evident. While a third faction comprised a significant number of iron and steel producers, engineers, tanners and builders included Granzow, Temler,

25 Stegner, *Ewangelicy warszawscy*, p. 173.

26 J.I. Starożyk, 'Nowa fabryka sukna i kortów pod Warszawa' ['New Cloth and Yarn Factory outside Warsaw'], *Tygodnik Ilustrowany*, No. 37, 1883, p. 165.

27 Reymont, *The Promised Land*, p. 519.

28 Lee, 'Commerce and Culture', p. 29.

Pfeiffer, Hoesick and later manufacturers such as Briggs, Posselt, Whitehead and Wedel.[29]

Warsaw's tannery-owning empires are an excellent example of one monopolistic dynasty. It was said that 'if Pfeiffer, Temler and Schwede were the princes of Warsaw's tanneries, Karol J. Szlenkier was the king'[30] and marriages, as well as cooperative partnerships, between all these families can easily be traced. Such professional-familial alliances were not exclusive, however, as there is evidence of both intermarriage and overlapping commercial interests between all of the groups. The bankers built factories, manufacturers invested in banks and cases of quite diverse business partnerships often emerged, for example in 1912 the joint-stock company Granzow, Temler and Wedel united a brick manufacturer, tanner and chocolatier, all of whom were connected to the Briggs brothers by marriage.[31] Whether the more tightly interknit Evangelical families constituted hierarchies of wealth or profession, or whether the marriage contracts maintained a line between Protestants and assimilated Jews is hard to determine, but it is evident that intermarriage consolidated the entire clan under the auspices of the Lutheran Church.

In Bradford, most strategic alliances were formed inevitably between families engaged in the textile trade. Hierarchies of wealth and influence developed through mutually advantageous unions such as the marriage of the Briggs brothers' niece Annie Whitehead to Isaac Smith, the industrialist son of the Bradford Mayor. The upwardly mobile social aspirations of young men eager to secure their future with a mill owner's daughter were also in evidence. But whereas the well-established Edward Briggs could perhaps afford the luxury of a love-match with Emma Fieldhouse, a Briggella Mills weaver, his Warsaw-based brothers needed to secure their foreign prospects with prudent marital connections. However, influential cloth manufacturers were rare in Warsaw; thus, it seems likely that it was Posselt who had the task of identifying suitable brides for the young Briggs among Warsaw's closely interconnected banking, publishing, engineering, tanning and building dynasties.

Kazimierz Granzow and the Królewska Elite

Since the establishment of his Kawęczyn brickworks in the 1860s, Kazimierz Granzow's wealth and reputation had risen on the wave of Warsaw's nineteenth-century urban development. Between 1874 and 1884 he was *Starszego Cechu Majstrów Murarskich* [Senior Master of the Guild of Masons].[32] He supplied the

---

29 *Polski Słownik Biograficzny* and BMD records.

30 *Gazeta.pl*, 'Cm.Ewangelicko-Augsburski – Szlenkierowie' ['Evangelical-Augsburg Cemetery – Szlenkier'], 14 April 2008, accessed at http://fotoforum.gazeta.pl.

31 *Polski Słownik Biograficzny*, 'Kazimierz Granzow (1832–1912)', Vol. 8, p. 552.

32 Ibid. describes Granzow's brickworks as 'the largest in the Kingdom'.

bricks and managed the construction of the majority of Warsaw's most prestigious building projects, including the palaces of fellow Evangelical-Augsburg adherents Wilhelm Rau (designed by Leandro Marconi, son of the aforementioned Henryk) and the residence of the so-called king of the tanners, Karol Jan Szlenkier. Indeed, his products were so commonly used that generic bricks were dubbed 'Granzówki' in this period.[33]

By the late 1870s Granzow was firmly established amongst the highest echelons of Warsaw society when he acquired a plot of land on the city's most desirable street, Królewska. The location was close to the stock market, opposite the *Ogrod Saski* [Saxon Gardens], adjacent to the Evangelical-Augsburg Church and neighbouring the palaces of celebrated bankers Kronenberg and Bloch. Granzow commissioned the bankers' architect, Witold Lanci, to design a residence that would overshadow his neighbours' in luxury.[34] He employed the fashionable Polish sculptor Teodor Rygier to create '12 statues set on the railings of balconies which represented various branches of art and industry'.[35] The popular local artist Józef Buchbinder was engaged to create 'a magnificent ceiling over a monumental marble staircase'.[36] In 1884 when a group of Lwów architecture students made a tour of Warsaw's most important new buildings, they were described as the factories of 'Lilpop, Rau and Loewenstein ... the firm Orthwein, Markowski and Karasiński, the filter station at the sewage works [by Lindley], the houses of Messers Szlenkier on Zielona Square, Granzow on Królewska and the ones constructed by Mr Józef Huss'.[37]

In 1856 Granzow's sister Emilia married the tanning industrialist Aleksander Temler. Two years later, shortly after the death of his first wife Karolina Jaeger, Granzow married his sister Klementyna Temler and cemented his connection with numerous influential dynasties of the Lutheran confession. The family's portraits were captured by the society photographer Jan Mieczkowski whose sitters included President Starynkiewicz, the revered educationalist Dr Józef Mianowski and the newspaper editor Aleksander Świętochowski.[38] Their local standing is shown

---

33 Granzow most notably built the *Wielka Synagoga* [Great Synagogue] on Tłomackie Square designed by Leandro Marconi, the *Szpital Dzieciątka Jezus* [Hospital of the Infant Jesus] designed by Julian Ankiewicz, the *Teatr Mały* [Small Theatre] by Jan Bereżecki which was also known as the Granzow Theatre. The only surviving apartments to have been built by Granzow are 22 Ujazdowskie Avenue designed by Karol Kozłowski and 72 Marszałkowska Street designed by Edward Goldberg. Tadeusz S. Jaroszewski, *The Book of Warsaw Palaces* (Warsaw: Polish Interpress Agency, 1984), pp. 139 and 151. Stegner, *Ewangelicy warszawscy*, p. 173.

34 Majewski, 'Dyskretny urok burżuazji przy Królewskiej'.

35 Ibid.

36 Kawęczyń Brick Company 'K.Granzow' SA, 12–18 Chełmżyńska Street, accessed at http://madein.waw.pl.

37 *Gazeta Warszawska*, No. 184, 1884, p. 2.

38 Ryszard Wojtkowski, *Wykonywa się fotografie* [*Photgraphs Are Taken*] (Warsaw: Miasto Stołeczne Warszawa, 2008), pp. 52–60.

by an 1884 description of a charitable bazaar on behalf of the *Warszawskiego Towarzystwa Dobroczynności* [Warsaw Charitable Society]. The wives of the ruling Russian officials 'Mrs General Starynkiewicz, Mrs General Tołstoj, Mrs General Doepp and Mrs General Schweder'[39] ran a stall for mercerised cotton goods beside members of the Polish aristocracy 'from the family of Prince Woroniecki, Mrs Stanisław Lasocka with her daughter, Mrs Count Władysław Łubieńska with her daughter Helena, and from the family of Wielogowski baroness Krauzowa', then 'Emilia of the Temler family now Mrs Pfejfer, with her sister Anna Temler and Miss Florentyna Granzow' were mentioned.[40] The wealth, reputation and local influence of the Granzows undoubtedly made their only daughter Florentyna, known as Flora, an extremely desirable match for Warsaw's aspiring young businessmen.[41]

Chapter 5 described how the Bradford men began to forge relationships through the British consul with Wilhelm Rau and Edward Lilpop. In 1883 Rau, Granzow and Aleksander Temler all held leading positions on the board of Warsaw's Evangelical-Augsburg Church where they undoubtedly welcomed Posselt; the affluent trustee of Bradford's German-Evangelical Church.[42] While John Briggs and his younger brother Alfred lived in Marki, Posselt took up residence at Królewska 10, in the aforementioned building designed by Huss for Messers Lesser and Strasburger, which by that time was also owned by Kazimierz Granzow. Indeed the Marki firm's adverts for staff and suppliers invariably called for applications and enquiries to be sent to the prestigious addresses of either 6, 8, 10 or 12 Królewska, in one case clarifying that number 10 was 'the house of Mr Granzow'.[43]

It is worth noting here that the banker Edward Natanson also lived at Królewska 10. Natanson, in partnership with his neighbour Leopold Kronenberg, owned two important industrial concerns the *Towarzystwo Akcji Mirkowski Fabryk Papier* [Mirkowski Joint Stock Paper Company] and the *Warszawskie Towarzystwo Fabryk Cukru* [Warsaw Sugar Company] in addition to his directorship of Warsaw's *Bank Handlowy* [Business Bank].[44] Natanson, like Posselt, was a

---

39 *Gazeta Warszawska*, No. 286, 1884, p. 2.

40 Ibid.

41 Klementyna Temler was a well-known patron of the arts; she sponsored the artists Buchbinder, Redlich and Lenartowicz and made generous donations to the *Museo Astronomico Copernicano* [Copernicus Astronomical Museum] in Rome.

42 'Wybory' ['Elections'], *Gazeta Warszawska*, No. 142, 1883, p. 2.

43 WYAS, Poss/54, Commercial intelligence ledger, Posselt's address is sometimes noted as Królewska 10–12. *Kurjer Warszawski*, 29 September 1884, p. 8, advertises for staff to apply to Królewska 6, while the foreign office consular records FO640/12 show 'Briggs Posselt & Co., Ernest Haigh, passport for his wife to Królewska 8', 22 August 1892, p. 115. *Gazeta Warszawska*, No. 15, 1883, p. 5. On Flora Granzow's marriage certificate her address is stated as Królewska 16 which suggests that this property was also in her father's ownership in 1887.

44 Miliszkiewicz, *Polskie gniazda rodzinne*, pp. 36–41.

prodigious art collector who reputedly displayed work by Cranach, Gainsborough, Gauguin, Pissarro, Rubens and Van Gogh, amongst many others, in his luxurious Królewska apartment.[45] The enduring bond between the Natanson and Posselt families will be revealed in Chapter 12, as during the First World War Posselt's nephew Arnold Korff appealed to the German authorities on behalf of his bankers, the Natanson family.

Through the efforts of Ernst Posselt and his 'open, fresh approach to winning friends',[46] the Bradford partners were admitted into a mutually advantageous relationship with Kazimierz Granzow. He introduced the venture capitalists to building contractors and provided an impressive central-Warsaw address, and in return the brick manufacturer enjoyed the prestige of association with the British venture capitalists and a supply contract for the specialised terracotta pipes required for the Marki water filtration system.[47] In August 1887 the relationship was ultimately secured when John Briggs junior married Flora Granzow. The timing of the betrothal undoubtedly indicates the growing success of the Marki enterprise and Granzow's confidence in the young Yorkshireman's prospects and wealth. The continuing friendship between Granzow and Posselt is further suggested by the marriage in May 1896 of Posselt's eldest son William, who had been born at Bradford in 1871, to Granzow's niece Mania Jaeger. In 1906 the Briggs' nephew Charles Whitehead secured his place in Warsaw society, as well as a longstanding commercial cooperation for his uncles' firm, by his marriage to Eleonora Wedel, the daughter of Poland's foremost chocolate manufacturer Emil Wedel.

Interlocking Directorates

The value of the social network extended far beyond the provision of local contractors and spouses for the Briggs in Warsaw. Through their matrimonial associations it is clear that all the Bradford partners developed some significant longstanding commercial collaborations. However, a characteristic difference between the Briggs' approach and that of their cosmopolitan merchant partner seems evident. The Briggs exploited the opportunities created by their extended family to consolidate their Marki interests. They used their estate and plant to supply the enterprises of their Polish relations and cooperated with local businessmen to improve the immediate locality, for example the shared investment to create the Marki railway. By contrast, during his two-decade residence in Warsaw an obvious decentralisation distinguished Posselt's investment in numerous companies, international partnerships and products.

There is no question that Ernst Posselt worked with practiced efficiency and due diligence on behalf of the Marki venture. From his eminent address in

45 Ibid., p. 37.
46 Heidelberg Stadtarchiv, *Stiftung des Geschwister Posselt.*
47 Wartalska, 'Fabryka i osada fabryczna', p. 665.

Warsaw he continued to promote the state-of-the-art worsted manufactory among the newspaper magnates, bankers, building contractors and engineers. But his heavy financial commitment, administrative and public-relations work for this primary venture did not preclude him simultaneously developing a series of Russian interests in his own right. By 1886 Posselt had established the *Zgierska Manufaktura Bawelniana* [Zgierz Cotton Factory] where he was joined in another longstanding British partnership with Walter Buckley.[48] In the following decade he started both a silk company, the *Rosyjsko-Włoskiego Towarzystwa Akcyjnego Wyrobów Włoknistych* [Russian-Italian Joint Stock Company Fibre Products] with Italians Giuseppe and Primo Bonacossa, and the *Warszawska Akcyjna Fabryka Dywanów* [Joint Stock Company of Warsaw Carpet Factories] with Polish-German partners Gerson Markus and Maks Baender.[49] In the same period he established the *Towarzystwo Akcyjne Tekstil* [Joint Stock Company Tekstil] to manufacture textiles at Riga.[50]

The array of his endeavours suggests that the entrepreneur formulated a comprehensive investment plan which included both local staples such as cotton and unexploited specialities such as silk, carpet and worsted to create a balanced portfolio for himself. In almost every case Posselt built a factory (although he acquired existing premises for the silk firm) with worker housing. He favoured international partnerships with specialists in the field of manufacture to run the enterprise, thus Buckley became managing and technical director at Zgierz, the Bonacossas with several other Italian directors ran the silk mill and Maks Baender managed the carpet firm. Posselt's far-reaching business empire had been consolidated through family relationships from long before his collaboration with the Briggs. Thus in Russia he put each new venture on a firm footing with a majority of his own capital combined with at least one technically expert partner and, predictably, family members or trusted friends were introduced to each directorship. His sons Ernest and Gustaw were engaged at Zgierz, the Riga factory was run by William Posselt and Ernst's son-in-law Henrik Laerum, a native of the Baltic city.[51] His nephew Arnold Korff joined the board of the carpet company and his son's German father-in-law Otto Stuck joined the board of the Italian silk firm.

Apart from revealing his own extraordinary entrepreneurial talent and *modus operandi*, Posselt's Russian investments effectively illustrate the complex pattern of interlocking directorships which linked commerce across the Kingdom of Poland at the end of the nineteenth century. Through the original Bradford partnership Posselt took a leading role in the administration of the Warsaw Wool

---

48 *Rocznik polskiego przemyslu i handlu* [*The Polish Annual of Industry and Business*] (Warsaw: Nakładem Polsk. Spółki Wydawnictw Informacyjnych, 1934), p. 559.

49 Wartalska, 'Fabryka i osada fabryczna', p. 655, Puś, *Przemysł włokienniczy*, p. 23, *Kurjer Kolejowy*, Warsaw, No. 30, 1898, p. 2.

50 APW, Zespół 87, 'Firma Arnold Korff w Warszawie', Group 4, Arnold Korff to Lieutenant Herr Waldemar Bernhoff, 3 February 1916, p. 73.

51 L.P. Lochner, *Fritz Kreisler* (London: Rockcliffe, 1950), p. 60.

Fair during the 1880s where he was joined by the merchant Bronisław Werner.[52] Werner, another Evangelical-Augsburg devotee, was a director of both his family's engineering firm *Norblin, Bracia Buch i T. Werner* and the *Miejskiego Towarzystwa Kredytów Wzajemnych* [Municipal Mutual Credit Society].[53] The Werners, by virtue of their relation to the Temlers, were part of Granzow's extended clan but Bronisław was also Edward Lilpop's brother-in-law. Thus he was admitted to the directorship of Posselt's *Rosyjsko-Włoskiego Towarzystwa Akcyjnego Wyrobów Włoknistych* [Russian-Italian Joint Stock Company Fibre Products]. But it is worth noting that he and Edward Lilpop were simultaneously on the board of the Kalisz cotton-spinning firm *Towarzystwo Schlösserowskiej Przędzalni Bawełny i Tkalni* [Schlösser Cotton Spinning and Weaving Joint Stock Company] with Edward Herbst, co-owner of the gargantuan Łódź enterprise of Karol Scheibler and also the cotton king's son-in-law.

Interfaith Collaboration

This chapter has shown that the Protestant minority dominated Warsaw commerce and their interlocking directorships united manufacturing and banking interests across the Kingdom of Poland. But a significant role in the local economy was also played by rich Catholic aristocrats such as Polish Counts Krasiński, Zamojski and Przeździecki as well as many Jewish entrepreneurs. Despite the preponderance of purely Protestant enterprises, interfaith partnerships and shared investments were not uncommon. For example, the Briggs joined Polish nobleman Adam Dzierżanowski, Jewish entrepreneurs Manas Ryba and Julian Różycki as well as the Jewish financiers Halpern and the Goldfeder brothers in the *Spółka udziałowa kolejki wąskotorowej* [Joint stock company of the narrow-gauge railway].[54] However, in an environment of stultifying Tsarist bureaucracy, many entrepreneurs sought partnership with an influential Evangelical-Augsburg Church member to facilitate state authorisation for their plans.

Business and politics were intimately connected in commercial centres worldwide, but in nineteenth-century Warsaw entrepreneurs faced some particularly complex challenges. Chapter 4 outlined the extreme dissonance of Polish society in this period with its religious, ethnic and class divides which became a central theme for the positivist author Bolesław Prus. His novel *The Doll* has been shown to have voiced heavy criticism of the German character of Warsaw's trade

52 'Kronika ekonomiczna' ['Economic bulletin'], *Gazeta Warszawska*, 7 June 1890, p. 3.

53 Tomasz Markiewicz, Tadeusz Władysław Świątek, Krzysztof Wittels, *Polacy z wyboru, rodziny pochodzenia niemieckiego w Warszawie w XIX i XX wieku* [*Poles by Choice, Families of German Origin in Warsaw During the Nineteenth and Twentieth Centuries*] (Warsaw: Wydawnictwo Dom Spotkań z Historią 2012), p. 241.

54 Wartalska, 'Fabryka i osada fabryczna', p. 654.

arena.[55] Despite relative freedom from Tsarist oppression, the Protestant business leaders were constantly prey to an aggressive undercurrent of Polish nationalism. Thus, interfaith collaboration and shows of Polish nationalism proved a potent assimilation tactic particular to the Russian-Polish commercial arena. Bronisław Werner's local reputation was undoubtedly enhanced by his five-year exile in Orenburg following his valiant efforts in the 1863 Warsaw Uprising.[56] Indeed Prus invented an extraordinarily similar back-story for his fictional merchant Wokulski. Many Protestant employers increased local esteem by employing Polish scholars unable to work in academia due to the Russification policies. Thus the offices of the Warsaw-Vienna railway became known as the asylum for Polish learning, the *Bank Dyskontowy* [Discount Bank] was sometimes called the Polish Academy of Sciences and the *Bank Handlowy* [Commercial Bank] was known as the Polish Literary Club.[57]

In Russian-occupied Warsaw private trade-related initiatives and associations invariably found themselves under the chairmanship of one of Warsaw's Tsarist administrators. Hence the annual Warsaw Wool Fair was overseen by General Starynkiewicz and in 1885 the *Towarzystwo Wyścigów Konnych* [Horse Racing Association], under the presidency of Governor General Gurko, organised Warsaw's industrial and agricultural exhibition.[58] By contrast charitable associations remained largely unsupervised and provided a useful front for both political and commercial alliances. For example, the Mianowski Fund was established in 1881 by a collective of prominent Warsaw intelligentsia, financiers and industrialists including Bolesław Prus, Henryk Sienkiewicz, Stanisław Przystański, the Kronenbergs, Natansons, Jan Bloch, the Counts Krasiński, Zamoyski and Przezdziecki, Edward Lilpop, Karol Strasburger and Karol Dejke, among many more. It honoured Dr Józef Mianowski, the rector of the Warsaw *Szkoła Główna* [University of Warsaw], who shielded his students from Russian reprisals after the 1863 January Uprising and thus was considered to have created a 'refuge for patriotic youth'.[59] Outwardly the fund sponsored research and published scholarship in the humanities and sciences, but its underlying politics was evident.

Charity, Cultural Patronage and Reputation

Charity and sponsorship of civic facilities were key components of venture capitalists' standard strategy to raise their profile and build a positive reputation

55 Prus, *The Doll.*

56 Markiewicz, Świątek, Wittels, *Polacy z wyboru*, p. 241.

57 Corrsin, *Warsaw Before the First World War*, p. 61.

58 'Odezwa komitetu wystawy' ['Appeal by the committee of the exhibition'], *Gazeta Warszawska*, No. 38, 1885, p. 2.

59 Piotr Hübner, Jan Piskurewicz and Leszek Zasztowt, *History of the Józef Mianowski Fund*, Warsaw, 1992, accessed at http://www.mianowski.waw.pl/history.htm.

abroad. The nineteenth century saw a global development in non-sectarian associations, clubs and societies which served to develop networks of trust which 'transcended religious or ethnic boundaries and for integrating urban elites'.[60] Bradford's industrialists and merchants collaborated to fund the St George's Hall and in 1881 Posselt donated a painting of 'The Pyramids of Gizeh' by Albert Zimmermann to a collection which would eventually be displayed in the Cartwright Hall.[61] In Warsaw the *Towarzystwa Zachęty Sztuk Pięknych w Królestwie Polskiem* [Society for the Encouragement of Fine Arts in the Kingdom of Poland], or *Zachęta*, was established in 1860 by among others prominent Evangelical-Augsburg congregationalists Aleksander Lesser and Wojciech Gerson. By 1883 it had a membership of 4,300 and existed under the sponsorship of numerous bankers and industrialists, including Kazimierz Granzow who donated 100,000 bricks to build the gallery which would ultimately neighbour his Królewska home.[62] The *Zachęta* was a supposedly non-political, religiously and socially inclusive association, but in the climate of oppressive Russification and disaffection with German economic dominance, it provided a useful platform for the bourgeoisie to display strong support for Polish culture. Thus, Briggs, Posselt and Co., the Natansons, Hielle and Dietrich and K. Rudzki and Co. were among several donors of art for a charity tombola in 1892.[63] Indeed the Bradford partners became well known in Warsaw, not simply for their reputed philanthropy at Marki but also for donations to the *Łódzkie Żydowskie Towarzystwo Dobroczynności* [Łódź Jewish Charitable Society].[64] In 1890 they provided Praga's hospital with 'equipment for the operating room and surgical instruments to a value of 276 rubles'.[65] At the beginning of the twentieth century John Briggs presented the first motorised ambulance to Warsaw named after his wife, Flora.[66]

General Starynkiewicz and Warsaw's Business Leaders

In Bradford, prominent businessmen, even foreigners, ran local government and controlled the decision-making authority. Thus the city's incorporation in 1850 was arguably an extension of an existing culture of cooperation and shared investment by industrialists and landowners to develop local resources and facilities. By contrast in Warsaw, under Russian rule, meaningful political influence was hard

---

60 Lee, 'Commerce and Culture', p. 32.

61 *Leeds Mercury*, 14 December 1881, p. 5.

62 *Gazeta Warszawska*, No. 53, 24 February 1886, p. 2.

63 'Tombola artystyczna' ['Art Tombola'], *Gazeta Warszawska*, No. 55, 1892, p. 3.

64 'Z łódzkiego żyd. tow. dobroczynności' ['From the Łódź Jewish charitable society'], *Rozwój*, Łódź, No. 222, 30 September 1903, p. 3.

65 'Podziękowanie' ['Acknowledgements'], *Gazeta Warszawska*, No. 330, 1890, p. 3.

66 Jerzy S. Majewski, 'Do wypadku co koń wyskoczy!' ['To the accident at a horse's gallop'], *Warszawa Gazeta.pl*, 28 January 2011, accessed at http://warszawa.gazeta.pl.

to acquire. The extraordinarily wealthy naturally enjoyed a measure of power over their tenants or employees and they had considerable leverage in negotiating municipal service contracts, but real political enfranchisement was largely impossible. Nevertheless, following his appointment to the role of president in 1875, Starynkiewicz took the revolutionary step of involving local business leaders in Warsaw's municipal development for the first time.

The Tsarist General took up office in a city with appalling social problems, undergoing a population explosion that was unmatched by infrastructural investment. Starynkiewicz's vision was to have a modern sanitary system, water supply, street paving, lighting and proper transport facilities; in short for Warsaw to stand alongside the modern cities of Europe. While it might be assumed that the president would have had power to manage investment as he saw fit, in truth his role was largely ornamental and the Russian police chief ran the city under a mandate of oppression and Russification, not infrastructural improvement.[67] State contributions to Warsaw's budget were negligible and any expenditure over 1,000 rubles had to be authorised by the Ministry of Internal Affairs in St Petersburg, whereas the cost of a new sewer system and waterworks would run into millions.[68] Further to this, the local hegemony of affluent landowners and financiers, including bankers such as Jan Bloch, opposed his plans through prejudice or fear of the cost. Thus the president realised that an autocratic approach to urban development would not work in Warsaw and he would need both the cooperation and cash of the local bourgeoisie to realise his vision.

Starynkiewicz is still revered by Varsovians for the apparently democratic approach he took in his determination to improve their city. He published the British engineer Lindley's plans for the waterworks and sewer system in the press alongside cost estimates in both Russian and Polish.[69] He reasoned with critics and rejected cost-cutting measures that would undermine the integrity of the project. For example, he 'decided to use only the English cement coming from Szczecin, instead of Silesian cement, which is somewhat cheaper but could prove more expensive in the long run as it is less durable'.[70] Rather than awaiting protracted authorisation from the Russian state for each minute detail from budget approval, to the appointment of an engineer, contractors, raw-materials acquisition, compulsory land purchase and so forth, the President pressed St Petersburg for over two years to allow him to devolve control to a committee of local businessmen which would supervise these matters on behalf of the state.[71]

The *Społeczny komitet budowy wodociągów i kanalizcji miasta Warszawy* [Joint committee for building of the waterworks and sewer system for the city of

---

67 Słoniowa, *Sokrates Starynkiewicz*, p. 16.

68 Ibid., p. 63.

69 Ibid., p. 60.

70 'Kanalizacja i wodociągi' ['Sewer system and water works'], *Gazeta Warszawska*, No. 5, 1885, p. 2.

71 Słoniowa, *Sokrates Starynkiewicz*, p. 67.

Warsaw] included 20 citizens led by, perhaps the greatest coup for Starynkiewicz, the financier Jan Bloch who had initially 'committed his personal authority in the fight against the project for a domestic sewer system'.[72] The municipal engineer Grotowski and unsurprisingly many from the Evangelical-Augsburg congregation, including project manager for the Briggs-Posselt partnership Edward Lilpop, made up the board.[73] This committee had unprecedented powers to buy land, to approve suppliers, construction tenders and to settle disputes. In 1885 their negotiations with disgruntled landlords were reported in the press when 'invited citizens Ręczlewski, Fajan, Granzow and Bevensee'[74] were called to assist in the valuation of properties on Miodowa Street that would be compulsorily purchased for the canalisation work. The heavy pressure exerted by the committee on behalf of the municipality is suggested as the report threatened that an agreement was expected because legal action 'would be very pitiful, longwinded and achieve questionable results'.[75]

The acuity of Starynkiewicz's plan is evident; well-off landlords such as Kazimierz Granzow financed the canalisation through a loan-share scheme initiated by the president. They were motivated to resolve opposition and engender the cooperation of local landowners by the promise of lucrative supply contracts. Thus Granzow had a monopoly on brick supply for the first phase of the project, providing 5.1 million in 1883 and tendered for a further 3 million brick-supply contract in 1885.[76] Like the Marki venture, the realisation of Starynkiewicz's vision, which might have been thwarted by Russian bureaucracy, local opposition or lack of funds, was guaranteed by engaging the economic interests of Warsaw's business elite. Thus the ambitious and costly municipal improvement was brought to fruition and simultaneously improved the local economy.

In conclusion it is evident that the Bradford partners' strategy to develop and consolidate their interests in Warsaw rested on three basic principles that had been used by economic migrants for generations: religious affiliation, intermarriage and naturalisation. Through local intermediaries, Rau and Lilpop, they joined the influential German-Evangelical Church which provided all their immediate practical requirements and 'a mechanism for developing commercial and financial opportunities'.[77] The next chapter will explore the positive public-relations capital generated by employing contractors and suppliers from this cooperative network

---

72 Ibid., p. 62.

73 Ibid., p. 68.

74 *Gazeta Warszawska*, No. 173, 1885, p. 2, all these men were members of the Evangelical-Augsburg church committee during the 1880s apart from Fajan who is likely to have been a part of the congregation.

75 *Gazeta Warszawska*, No. 173, 1885, p. 2.

76 'Kanalizacja i wodociągi', p. 2.

77 Ikaros Madouvalos, 'The Entrepreneurial Activity of Dimitrios and Stephanos Manos in Central Europe in the Nineteenth Century', in *Commerce and Culture: Nineteenth-century Business Elites*, ed. Robert Lee (Farnham: Ashgate, 2011), p. 145.

to construct the Marki plant. Intermarriage soon bound the Bradford men to Kazimierz Ganzow, cementing their ties with each other and the most influential commercial dynasties of Warsaw. Less is known about Alfred Briggs' 1886 marriage to Augusta Clara, the daughter of William Schulz, a German landowner and factory proprietor. However, the fact that his brother-in-law, Rudolph Schulz, became cashier for the Marki firm illustrates the enduring view that positions of trust could be managed most securely by family.[78] The longstanding importance of this relationship is suggested by Rudolph's burial alongside Alfred in the Briggs' family grave at Warsaw in 1927. The Bradford men engaged in charitable, cultural and civic sponsorship, as was customary, to bolster their reputation in the host community. But their standing with the Russian state and with foreign banks was only guaranteed by naturalisation, which provided the rights and protection of citizenship. Thus John Briggs assumed Russian nationality and during the interwar period his brother Alfred and nephew Charles Whitehead became Polish. Despite Warsaw's complex political environment, this chapter has revealed a well-capitalised and sophisticated commercial scene, populated by a long-established business elite and some significant international entrepreneurs such as Wilhelm Rau. Examination of the Briggs' and particularly Posselt's developing commercial connections in the Russian-Polish business arena has exposed the heavily concentrated ownership of numerous diverse firms among this group.[79]

[78] WYAS, Conveyance and assignment, 12 October 1908, Vol. 46, No. 207, p. 513.

[79] Winder, 'Webs of Enterprise 1850–1914', p. 795.

Chapter 7
'A piece of England on Russian soil':[1] Building, equipping and marketing the foreign factory

'State of the art' was a label invariably applied to foreign direct investment projects. Indeed it was commonly attributed to a range of businesses and products in the Victorian period to excite interest and build consumer confidence as a promotional, rather than a necessarily accurate, description.[2] This chapter will examine the genuinely groundbreaking facets of the Marki plant in comparison with both contemporary British and Russian-Polish standards. It will show how an image of technological progressiveness, in place of real product innovation, could be used to great advantage to market new firms abroad. In a period when scientific developments were aimed at greater economy and reduced skill requirements in manufacturing, this chapter will explore their particular instrumentality in facilitating British foreign direct investment. As headline reports focused on the unprecedented plant sizes, giant engines, huge employee numbers, larger and faster machines of industrial enterprises abroad, this chapter will separate the fact from the fiction to reveal some fundamental pillars of the Briggs-Posselt partnership's strategy in Russian Poland.

Product Innovation Versus Modern Marketing Techniques

In the last quarter of the nineteenth century, growing disposable income and status consciousness in the middle and working classes created a culture of consumerism in the industrialised world which became the stimulus for greater industrial growth. The burgeoning market naturally led to increased competition as the number of manufacturing firms escalated. Nevertheless, despite a contemporary thirst for novelty and drive towards product development, innovation was not an exact science and designing new products often proved costly, with an uncertain outcome. But as the largest factories had been designed to mass produce generic

---

1 Schultze-Gävernitz, *Volkswirtschaftliche Studien aus Russland*, p. 97.

2 Blewett, *Yankee Yorkshireman*, p. 58, and Dave Pretty, 'The Cotton Textile Industry in Russia and the Soviet Union', in *The Ashgate Companion to the History of Textile Workers*, 1650–2000, eds L. Heerma Van Voss, E. Hiemstra-Kuperus and E. Van Nederveen Meerkerk (Farnham: Ashgate, 2010), p. 427, amongst others.

goods, they were often limited by their plant's fixed capabilities. Therefore the majority of firms manufacturing standard products in a price-competitive market increasingly used marketing techniques to distinguish their offer from those of their competitors. Descriptions such as *state of the art* or *patent* were liberally applied whether the claims were valid or not: that is to say, employing a new way to sell old or standard goods often proved an easier, cheaper and more effective method to influence customer behaviour than actual innovation.

The manufacturing possibilities of entirely new companies, such as the Marki factory, were not constrained by existing plant limitations. Nevertheless, foreign direct investment invariably introduced a tried-and-tested specialism to an unexploited foreign market rather than an unproven innovation. Their strategy was to achieve a monopoly by dominating both raw-material supply and sales markets in order to forestall competition. As their products had been previously imported, the prohibitively high cost had logically restricted the scope of market penetration. Thus the founders used the same promotional techniques as their compatriots to court publicity and raise the profile of less well-known manufactures abroad. Once disengaged from the domestic price war, the Bradford partners could largely determine the price of worsted in the Russian empire. For although their initial investment in the new plant would be factored into the costing, relocation radically reduced transaction and manufacturing costs. But customer perceptions played a vital role in determining the local product value. The challenge for the venturing entrepreneurs was to reduce the product price to exclude any residual competition from imports, but maintain the premium and high-end product image that the international trade had created.

Common patterns of entrepreneurial behaviour can be discerned in the promotion of foreign enterprises worldwide, such as the social and commercial networking that was explored in the last chapter. Venture capitalists needed to generate interest and engender trust as complete unknowns to develop the untapped-market potential of target nations in order to justify their vast investments. But it is clear that local political and product-specific factors had a significant role in determining the strategy and public image each presented. Harrison Benn could afford to be bullish about his British credentials in promoting his US venture in 1905, but the Briggs-Posselt partnership needed to steer a careful course to avoid attracting the damaging label applied to many German-owned companies in Russian Poland of foreign exploiters.[3] The right publicity could pre-empt political opposition, bolster their reputation and at the same time attract suppliers, contractors, customers and labour. Technical innovation provided a politically neutral platform on which to promote a new enterprise abroad; an irreproachable positive brand to attach to a business. By highlighting the modernity of their plant, their business credentials and prosperity the entrepreneurs could capitalise on local perceptions of foreign wealth, success and technical progress. They could

[3] 'Wyzyskiwacze przemysłu' ['Exploiters of industry'], *Gazeta Rzemieślnicza*, No. 2, 1884, p. 1.

spin an ideal company and product image to market basic worsted yarns which saturated the market in Bradford as the product of cutting-edge foreign technology in Russian Poland.

Two almost contradictory impressions of the Marki firm had to be circulated: the Polishnesss of the venture and the extraordinary opportunity it presented for local contractors and labour had to be highlighted. At the same time a potential industrial clientele had to be convinced that the new firm's cheaper, domestically made offer was equal to expensive foreign imports, and essentially British. The contemporary local prejudice against the products of national industry was vividly described in a report of Warsaw's 1888 weaving exhibition as a fashionable 'mania for foreignness'.[4] Indeed the British consul drew attention to the fraudulent labelling of Polish-made goods, which 'although bearing labels in English ... is clearly made in various factories in Warsaw'.[5]

In the spring of 1883 an overwhelmingly positive appraisal of the Bradford partners' Marki project appeared in Warsaw's *Tygodnik Ilustrowany*; the newspaper under the editorship of Ludwike Jeneke, contemporary president of the Evangelical-Augsburg congregational committee. The journalist J.I. Starożyk set the scene with details which were undoubtedly designed to impress: 'a finished building already stands, five floors high, with one hundred front windows, for the spinning mill ... In the future three such buildings of five floors will be built in a square, over an area measuring 18 morga. The finished chimney will be 155 feet high'.[6] Despite local hostility towards foreign investment, there was a keen interest in science and technology. Therefore, the article focused on the modern land drainage, water filtration and sewer systems that were being installed. The Polishness of the contractors was emphasised: 'the building works are directed by Mr Gołębiewski, master mason, carpentry by Mr Bevensse, the stone is from the firm of Sikorski. The iron parts of the factory are supplied by the firm of Mr Rudzki. The building works employ about 300 people'.[7]

Starożyk set out the stall on behalf of the Bradford entrepreneurs, presenting their investment as a unique opportunity. He described how 100 local children aged 12 to 15 had been sent to England by the firm 'with the aim of teaching them spinning work'.[8] When educational possibilities were scarce and an estimated 70 per cent of the Polish population were illiterate,[9] the promise of training and subsequent employment was noteworthy. Similarly, the assertion that the children would be taught both English and Polish was an extraordinary public-relations

4 'Wystawa tkacka' ['Weaving exhibition'], *Gazeta Warszawska*, 4 February, 1888, p. 2.

5 FO65/1691, Murray to Secretary of State, 27 February 1904, p. 238.

6 Starożyk, 'Nowa fabryka sukna i kortów', p. 165. *Morga* is a unit of measurement roughly equivalent to an acre.

7 Ibid.

8 Ibid.

9 Słoniowa, *Sokrates Starynkiewicz*, p. 28.

Figure 7.1 Bradford Mills at Marki circa 1910
Source: By kind permission of Ralph Haigh

coup, when their native language was banned from schools in their own country. Without providing any real information about the new firm's strategy or products, but aggrandising the size and modernity of the investment, Starożyk created a glowing image for the foreign firm. To drive his point home he insisted that 'this act of founding a plant in Marki deserves positive recognition. They are not importing foreign workers but rather sending the local youth abroad where along with professional training they receive moral care'.[10]

A drip-feed of positive propaganda about the company continued throughout 1883 which reiterated the unassailable reputation of the founders and the contribution of local firms to the building works. Despite the large-scale import of British-made machinery, the company's local purchases, such as 2,000 Polish-brand light bulbs, were emphasised.[11] At the end of the year the *Gazeta Warszawska* included an update on the Marki project in a seasonal farming and weather report. It described the prospects for root crops, winter corn and the impact of over-wintering costs on the price of livestock and then concluded:

> The largest building project of the current year is the great spinning mill at Marki which is almost complete. The workshops for the most part have been set up. The children that were sent to England earlier in the year have already returned and the little workers are in good health, satisfied with the trip. Work in the spinning mill is due to begin soon.[12]

State-of-the-Art Equipment and Foreign Direct Investment

The promotional value and prudent public-relations rationale for characterising foreign-owned factories as technically progressive has been presented. Cheap marketing tactics instead of expensive innovation were employed to promote unremarkable staple goods abroad as the product of the latest foreign technology. But as foreign direct investment generally introduced an established field of expertise to an unexploited market, real product novelty was rare. However, there are well-founded reasons for venture capitalists to unfailingly equip their new factories with the most modern machine technology available.

In the nineteenth century, as manufacturers habitually met challenges to efficiency and economy with continual fine-tuning and occasional revolutionary inventions, the factory became a testing ground for modern technology. The modifications and enhancements encompassed every area of business, not just motive power and machinery but raw-materials source development, process, labour-force organisation, marketing and distribution. The *Bradford Observer* succinctly described it as 'a constant perfection of mechanical appliances and

10 Starożyk, 'Nowa fabryka sukna i kortów', p. 165.
11 Wartalska, 'Fabryka i osada fabryczna', p. 651.
12 *Gazeta Warszawska*, 5 November 1883, p. 2.

an economy of labour and expenditure'.[13] But whereas some improvements were protected as secret recipes to create an advantage over competitors, the tempting commercial value of the most effective led them to become cross-industry standards. British-owned foreign plants were invariably a distillation of manufacturers' customary behaviour to constantly improve their operations. Thus in 1886 a Bradford trade journal pointed out that,

> It does not often fall to the lot of any manufacturer to build more than one weaving mill, it is evident that the experience gained by his first essay is to a considerable extent lost to the public. We have met with few who, if they had to build over again, would not have made most material alterations to the construction of the mill.[14]

For those who could afford foreign direct investment, it was not simply a chance to launch an old product in a new market, but provided the rare opportunity for the instigators to bring all their experience to bear, to create the optimum manufactory, in terms of labour, management, equipment and power. Therefore, although the Russian-Polish industrial arena lagged far behind Britain and the most basic equipment, or British cast-offs, might have sufficed to equip a secondary foreign factory, the Bradford entrepreneurs did not intend to emulate Briggella Mills at Marki, but to dramatically improve upon it. The high-cost and high-risk nature of the instant foreign factory contrasted sharply with the British industrial culture of cautious trial and prudent reinvestment. Nevertheless industrial venture capitalists had to work with speed and decisiveness, on an unprecedented scale, in order to monopolise foreign opportunities.

The Role of British Engineering Firms in Russian Industrialisation

Although the combined skill and ambition of the Bradford partners was undoubtedly central, a radical change of direction taken by British engineering firms in the last quarter of the nineteenth century had an important role in facilitating the successful establishment of the Marki plant. As foreign industry presented a growing threat to British primacy in world trade, the press and successive government enquiries consistently levelled criticism at British manufacturers' apparent refusal to update plant.[15] Comparisons revealed that new factories abroad had instant scale, greater average motive power and the

---

13 Sigsworth, *Black Dyke Mills*, p. 113 quotes *Bradford Observer*, 29 December 1887.

14 'The Construction and the Ventilation of Weaving Sheds', *Textile World*, June 1886, p. 171.

15 Royal Commission on the Depression of Trade and Industry carried out surveys in 1884 and 1886 and this suggestion of technical conservatism is central to the argument of Dintenfass in *Decline of Industrial Britain*.

newest machinery, whereas piecemeal development and antiquated practices characterised domestic industry. The evidence seemed irrefutable; the state-of-the-art approach was better and allowed foreign industrialists to claw away British profits. But the outspoken critics centrally misunderstood the workings of industry and based their conclusions on superficial evidence. Across the world the principle of the factory was the same, a single unit composed of machinery and labour. But the balance of requirements for each of these elements varied according to local conditions and, in the simplest terms, deficiencies in one had to be made up by the other. In newly industrialising countries, modern production methods could compensate for a potentially damaging lack of skills. By contrast, the large, price-competitive and highly skilled labour force of established industry rendered many machinery updates superfluous. Thus British manufacturing was based on skilled people, whereas the emphasis abroad fell to *skilled* machinery. Very broad-ranging economic factors increased the pressure on British industrialists in this period and cost-effective solutions had to be found; despite the critics' verdict, replacing tried-and-tested equipment was not the panacea.

The charges of technological conservatism against the industrialists were coupled with the supposed anomaly that the quality and innovation of British textile machinery went almost unchallenged in the international market. The machine-making sector had developed as a service to domestic industry, but once the local clientele had been equipped, the expense and durability of these products meant that repeat orders were few and far between. Like any other branch of industry at the end of the nineteenth century, British engineering firms sought a broader sales catchment, new revenue streams and innovative ways to sell. These astute engineers, with a wealth of experience in meeting challenges to industrial efficiency and economy, naturally set their sights on the huge potential of export markets. They adapted existing technologies to work efficiently with the different types of fuel or raw material and to emulate British quality without skilled operatives. Thus foreign markets came to dictate the strategy and products of British machine makers in this period and groundbreaking inventions such as the highly efficient ring spindle were developed in Lancashire but exported while the British cotton industry persisted with the longstanding mule.

The revised tactics of Britain's heavy-industry sector proved successful because their speciality products were hard to replicate abroad and thus they were always the last target of foreign protectionism. Indeed this was one of the few fields of British manufacturing that was significantly enhanced by international tariff control which stimulated industrialisation abroad and thus created huge demand for machinery. In the 1860s Poland's most valuable import was British machinery and this state of affairs remained unchanged until well into the twentieth century.[16] But British engineering firms, like foreign direct investors, could not capitalise on the foreign opportunity without commercial intelligence and local intermediaries. The German economist Gerhart von Schulze-Gävernitz highlights the role

[16] Puś, *Przemysł włókienniczy*, p. 16.

played by one ambitious nineteenth-century entrepreneur to encourage Britain's engineering firms into the Russian market. Ludwig Knoop trained in Manchester where he realised that great profits could be made if the different technical needs of Russian industry could be met. He forged close links with Lancashire engineering firms such as Mather and Platt, Hick Hargreaves, Dobson and Barlow, Howard and Bullough and Platt Brothers of Oldham and negotiated exclusive rights to sell their products in the Russian empire. As the industrial-equipment market was for occasional and very large investments by individual companies, rather than a broad spread of moderately priced repeat orders, it was vital to capitalise on a client's initial investment period. Knoop encouraged his British partner-suppliers to extend their ranges to service the instant-factory market. By offering not just engines, spinning equipment or looms, but fire precautions and electric lighting systems, they maximised sales and increased their profit yield from each customer. If the buyer had confidence in the supplier, putting all their eggs in one basket was both convenient and cost-effective. They could negotiate favourable prices based on the order size and ensure coordinated delivery times, while the agent might ease them through local bureaucracy, arrange transportation and installation by experienced professionals. Thus Knoop's agency became a one-stop shop to equip Russian-empire industry with both British machinery and skills.

Despite the contemporarily popular Russian proverb that there was 'no church without a priest, no factory without a Knoop',[17] the industrial magnate's name has never previously been connected with the Briggs-Posselt enterprise. However, a review of the branded technologies adopted at Marki – the Hick Hargreaves steam engines, Mather and Platt's Grinnell Sprinkler system, the Edison electric dynamo and the Green's Economiser – reveals that all were in Knoop's portfolio.[18] The Bradford entrepreneurs were evidently advised by Knoop on the primary building blocks for their foreign plant: the optimum British source for engines that could provide fuel efficiency using Polish coal and the processing equipment which would be most appropriate to the lack of local skills. Having established the relationship, the agent could then encourage his customers towards some possibly unplanned innovations such as turbines to provide electric lighting which would allow shift work, or the latest sprinkler system to protect their investment from fire and reduce insurance premiums. Thus, the inevitable shortfalls in the Bradford partners' local knowledge were compensated with the experience of Knoop's agency. Indeed the products sold by the German-born Russian entrepreneur were so ubiquitous in the Russian-Polish industrial arena that Reymont mentions them in his classic novel. He describes the fictional industrialist Borowiecki 'stopped

[17] Schultze-Gävernitz, *Volkswirtschaftliche Studien aus Russland*, p. 92.

[18] 'Maszyna olbrzym' ['Giant machine'], *Kurjer Warszawski*, No. 153, 1892, p. 4. James E. Brittain, 'The Early Diffusion of Electrical Power Technology, 1870–1920', *Journal of Economic History*, 34 (1974), p. 111.

for a time in front of the Mather-Platt oxydizing apparatus, through which the goods already printed and dyed had to pass'.[19]

Bradford Mills at Marki

Determining which modern innovations would best serve the enterprise and which standards of domestic industry would suffice, regardless of prestige or novelty, was central to the venturing entrepreneurs' business skill. Analysis of contemporary industrial practice and this case study in particular reveal that all facets of the plant, buildings and labour-force management were instigated to meet one or more of the following criteria as part of an overall strategy to maximise the firm's profits: 1. to facilitate optimum scale of output;[20] 2. to ensure reliability of production and consistent quality;[21] 3. to provide maximum economy in fuel and raw materials;[22] 4. to protect the fixed assets and reduce insurance premiums;[23] 5. to create the most favourable processing conditions simultaneously maintaining buildings and machinery.[24]

Power and Transmission

Motive power generation was central to the productive capability of any manufacturing firm. The engine was the heart of the mill and its type and size, in conjunction with the transmission system, dictated the scale, speed and cost of output for manufacturers. For this reason the steam engine was the focus of experimentation and modification throughout the nineteenth century. Like the height of the chimney or the breadth of the factory facade, the engine was a universally understood measure of the relative size, modernity and importance of nineteenth-century industrial firms. After 1870 the horizontal engine began to supplant the earlier beam engines due to its increased speed, 'smooth and economical running'[25] and it dominated until the end of the steam-power era. During the 1880s Salt's

[19] Reymont, *The Promised Land*, p. 25.

[20] For example, employing vast motive power, processing equipment suitable to unskilled workforce and the pioneering use of electric lighting to facilitate shift work.

[21] Particularly with reference to the isolation of the plant and lack of local support services, self-sufficiency in components was vital.

[22] For example, the Green's economiser, heat sharing, water filtration and purification.

[23] For example, the Grinnell system, fire brigade, electric lighting instead of gas and workforce insurance or sick funds.

[24] For example, ventilation or heating systems and hydro-extractors for drying large amounts of yarn or cloth also prevented damp in buildings and improved health of workers.

[25] Colum Giles and Ian Goodall, *Yorkshire Textile Mills 1770–1930* (London: H.M.S.O. Royal Commission on the Historical Monuments of England, 1992), p. 141.

Mill replaced two beam engines with one horizontal engine,[26] Briggella Mills at Bradford had a pair of horizontal engines and Bradford Mills at Marki had two horizontal and one vertical engine from the outset.[27]

The contemporary press predictably focused on the size and generative capacity of the Marki steam engines but their reports are inconsistent. For example, in 1884 the *Gazeta Handlowa* described that Briggs, Posselt and Co. had 'three steam engines and four generators', providing a total of 1,500 hp.[28] By contrast Bradford's *Illustrated Weekly Telegraph* only mentions two engines, 'one being 650 hp and the other 250 hp. In addition to these another engine of 400 hp is now in progress of conveyance to Poland for erection in the mills'.[29] In 1887 the *Przegląd Guberni Warszawski* [Review of the Warsaw Province] reported that the Marki plant had four steam engines but only with a motive power of 650 hp,[30] whereas the British Consul announced 1,000 hands and 1,000 hp at Marki.[31] In 1892 a new five-storey building was constructed by the firm with a dedicated engine generating 1,000 hp,[32] but in 1897 Edward Litten described the overall cumulative power of the plant as: 'six steam engines of 3000 hp, namely four large ones – 1000, 800, 700 and 250 hp and two small ones for the extra production and electricity. The spacious boiler house has eight massive Russian boilers'.[33] Factory inspectors' reports consistently mention three engines with combined power of 2,100 hp until 1900 when they reduced their estimation to 1,850 hp.[34] When Russian-government surveys often note the number and not the generative capacity of steam engines per firm, rendering regional inter-firm comparisons unviable, the press occasionally provides the missing local context. For example, in 1892 the *Kurjer Warszawski* remarked on the new Hick Hargreaves engine at

[26] Ibid., p. 135.

[27] APW, *Starszy Inspektor Fabryczny Guberni Warszawskiej* [Senior Inspector of Factories for the Warsaw District], signature 375, report for the year 1896–97 – Briggs, Posselt and Co., Marki, p. 004.

[28] Wartalska, 'Fabryka i osada fabryczna', p. 651 quotes *Gazeta Handlowa*, Warsaw, No. 64, 1884, and the same information was confirmed retrospectively in *Przegląd Techniczny*, Warsaw, No. 28, 8 July 1914, p. 379.

[29] *Illustrated Weekly Telegraph*, 19 March 1886, p. 1.

[30] J. Łukasiewicz, *Przewrót techniczny w przemyśle Królestwa Polskiego, 1852–1886* [*Technical Development in the Industry of the Kingdom of Poland*] (Warsaw: Państwowe Wydawn Naukowe, 1963), p. 399 quotes *Przegląd Guberni Warszawski* [Review of the Warsaw Province] 1887.

[31] NA, Diplomatic and Consular Reports, Annual Series, Issues 82–160, 1887, p. 37.

[32] 'Maszyna olbrzym', p. 4.

[33] Litten, *Promyslennost Rossii.*

[34] APW, *Starszy Inspektor Fabryczny Guberni Warszawskiej*, signature 375, Briggs Brothers and Co., Marki report for the year 1 May 1896–1 May 1897, p. 004, Briggs Brothers and Co., Marki report for the year 1 May 1900–1 May 1901, p. 043.

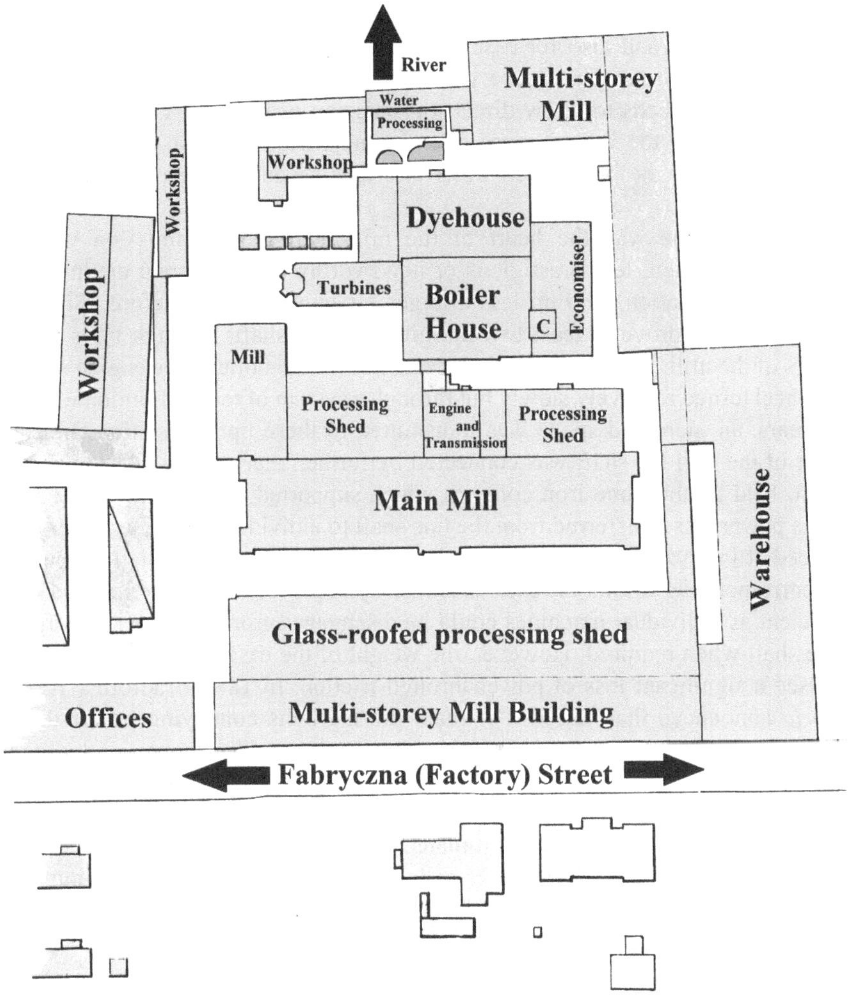

Figure 7.2 Layout of the Marki factory compound circa 1900
Source: Author's diagram

Marki that, 'if we are not mistaken larger machines are only possessed by the cotton companies of Heinzel and Kunitzer, Scheibler, and Poznański in Łódź'.[35]

In conjunction with the engines, the Green's Patent Economiser was gaining popularity amongst innovative mill owners in this period as an 'indispensable ajunct [sic: adjunct] to steam boilers'.[36] In the standard configuration of mill

35 'Maszyna olbrzym', p. 4.

36 *Textile World and Yorkshire Inventor*, March 1883 (no page number is assigned to advertising pages).

complexes boilers were housed in a separate building adjacent to the mill, as a fire precaution and also for ease of delivery of fuel from railway sidings in the mill yard. The engine house was located between the main building and the production sheds to allow direct transmission of power.[37] The economiser, located between the boiler house and chimney, used exhaust gases from the furnaces to heat the boiler-feed water and thus saved between 20 and 25 per cent fuel.[38]

If the engine was the heart of the mill then the transmission was its circulatory system, less prestigious or newsworthy than the great engines, but integral to operations and no less a target for improvement. Before 1880, the factory engine drove at least two upright cast-iron shafts through traps in the floors of the mill. Powered directly by steam from the boilers, the engine's large flywheel turned relatively slowly but through a system of toothed-pinion wheels, or gears, an increased speed was transmitted to these upright shafts. On each floor of the mill the shaft was connected by further gearing to a horizontal line shaft, held by the same iron columns which supported the ceiling. In the final stage power was transferred from the line shaft to individual machines by drums, spaced at intervals along the line shafts above the machinery which connected to corresponding drums on each machine by ropes or belts. The method was efficient as individual machines could be disengaged from, or knocked off, the line shaft when required. However, the weight of the cast-iron shafts and gears caused a significant loss of power through friction. In 1885 Bradford's *Textile World* announced that 'the use of main driving-belts conveying power direct from prime movers [engines], has largely supplanted the agency of toothed-wheel gear. The largest and most modern mills are now geared with belting which has proved, both as regard increased speed and economy, worthy of the reputation it has gained'.[39] The estimated savings of the new belt-drive system were the natural focus of British press interest. In 1884 a French spinning mill was described 'in which toothed gearing driving 18,000 spindles was replaced by belts, with a saving of 20 per cent in friction, or 3½ per cent on the effective driving power transmitted'.[40]

The superior fuel economy of the belt drive was indisputable, but its sheer practicality in terms of cost and ease of maintenance led to its domination at the end of the nineteenth century. For an isolated factory, reliance on belts manufactured on site, as opposed to precision iron shafts and gears which had to be supplied from abroad, proved vital. Thus the system was naturally adopted at Marki where:

37 Giles and Goodall, *Yorkshire Textile Mills*, p. 144.

38 Ibid., p. 150.

39 'Leather Belting', *Textile World*, February 1885, pp. 168–9.

40 J.A.J. Schultz, 'Belting', *Journal of Fabrics and the Textile Industry*, 12 June 1884, p. 64.

> The accelerating wheels [of the engines] are 7 English feet wide, the total discharge power is not moved by ropes, but with the help of two belts of 3-inch and a second of 4-inch widths which run to the ground and second floors, from where belts, in a separate belt chamber specially furnished for this purpose, also transfer power to all other floors.[41]

Cities such as Bradford or Manchester included many belt-manufacturing firms as part of a booming service sector to local industry. But the length of time, perhaps more than the expense of acquiring British components, led the Marki enterprise to include several quite specialist departments including a tannery, belt factory and a wire-brush workshop to provide vital card clothing.[42] Each of these activities constituted a separate specialised trade in more industrialised regions, but where a manufacturer could undertake the production on-site, there was an economy in component and transport costs, a reduction in expensive stoppages and a consequent improvement in product prices.

It is evident that modifications to the configuration, or lacing and width of the belts, to increase efficiency continued after the initial installation of the belt-drive system. In 1897 a United States consular report described experiments at Briggella Mills at Bradford in which '2-inch belts were at first substituted for the old 3-inch belts, but now, inch and a half' belts had reduced the motive-power requirements by as much as 50 per cent.[43] It is also evident that technical experimentation carried out at Marki was later introduced in the Bradford company. For example, an invention to 'entirely supersede leather covered rollers in drawing and spinning machinery' by Richard Temmel of Berlin was 'worked out to its practical success in the mills of Messrs. Briggs, Posselt & Co., Warsaw … has recently been introduced on a large-scale at Briggella Mills, Little Horton'.[44]

Economy, Recycling and the Environment

Fuel efficiency was a primary goal of the modern engines, economiser and transmission installed at Marki but in the late nineteenth century trade journals also expounded new ways to utilise industrial waste with an almost evangelical zeal. Bradford's *Journal of the Textile Society* went as far as to say it was 'the duty of the enterprising manufacturer to … make way for the utilisation of waste

---

41 'Maszyna olbrzym', p. 4.

42 Litten, *Promyslennost Rossii*.

43 United States Bureau of Foreign Commerce, Consular Reports: Commerce, Manufactures, Vol. 53, Issue 3574, 1897, p. 47.

44 United States Bureau of Manufactures and Bureau of Foreign Commerce (1854–1903), United States Department of Commerce and Labor, Bureau of Statistics, US G.P.O., Monthly consular and trade reports, Technology & Engineering, Vol. 54, Issues 200–203, 1897, p. 45.

substances',[45] as growing scientific knowledge dramatically increased the scope for salvaging previously discarded materials. Sizeable new industries emerged to process old clothing and waste wool, potash and wool fat, coal ash, clinker and perhaps most notably the coal tar created in furnaces. Improvements to spinning techniques combined with the constant search for cheap raw materials allowed manufacturers to supplement expensive fleeces with the shorter or broken fibre from used wool. In the early twentieth century, J.H. Clapham observed that 'wool made from rags is no longer an occasional ingredient of a few despised fabrics, but a standard raw material for a considerable section of the trade'.[46] In 1900–01 recycled qualities accounted for approximately 20 per cent of the weight of output from the Marki factory, although the value of this branch of production was not recorded.[47]

Recycling provided obvious economic benefits, but the environmental implications were also important. In Marki there were no municipal services to remove household, let alone industrial waste, therefore pollution had to be kept to a minimum or the mill owners had to meet the cost of removal. Even in Warsaw wealthy landlords were forced to pay for frozen sewage to be cut and removed from the open sewers on their property in winter.[48] However, when General Starynkiewicz first set out his plans for an urban sewage and water system, many property owners objected on account of the loss of income which salvaged sewage provided as fertiliser.[49] Thus natural waste would have been collected to fertilise company-owned estate lands at Marki and the copious amounts of ash and clinker produced by burning coal could be used to create black lime mortar, providing both a cost saving in building materials as well as a practical means of disposal.

Managing the Quality and Supply of Water

Water was essential to most factory operations: to generate steam-power, for wet-processing,[50] for basic sanitary requirements and in reserve for fire fighting. Industrial clusters generally formed around a water source, but rapid industrialisation during the nineteenth century quickly led demand to exceed supply. When natural variations in flow rates and rising competition for the scant resource began to impact on the profitability of the factories, the ingenuity

---

45 D. Dixon Marshall, 'The Utilisation of Waste Products', *Yorkshire College Textile Students Magazine and Journal of the Textile Society*, Bradford, Vol. 1, 8 November 1895, p. 39.

46 J.H. Clapham, *The Woollen and Worsted Industries* (London: Methuen and Co., 1907), p. 26.

47 APW, signature 375, p. 043.

48 Słoniowa, *Sokrates Starynkiewicz*, p. 35.

49 Ibid., p. 61.

50 The wet processes are essentially scouring, dyeing and finishing of yarn and cloth.

of the industrialists focused on developing methods to control, reservoir and recycle supply. The location of new industrial plants was generally determined by a proximate and plentiful water supply. Saltaire, for example, was strategically located between the River Aire and the Bradford branch of the Leeds-Liverpool canal both for ease of transport and water supply. The Briggs brothers' Newlay Dye Works at Horsforth was described as 'bounded on the north by the Midland Railway ... on the south east by the towing path of the Leeds Liverpool Canal and on the west by the River Aire'.[51] Nevertheless, management of the resource remained critical to the effectiveness of any new operation and underground storage tanks, as well as bore holes, became commonplace in British factories.[52]

Abraham Holroyd described 'an enormous tank or reservoir, and filter, with 500,000 gallons of water, into which through a number of conduits, the rain is carried' for manufacturing at Saltaire.[53] River water was siphoned in through a tunnel under the buildings to supply the company's boilers and out through another series of tunnels. The Marki plant had a comparable system: 'water for the requirements of the factory, will be directed by channel through double terracotta pipes 18 inches in diameter, fitted together at the appropriate angle and running into three pools the whole length [of the factory] for pre-filtering'.[54] Despite the allusion to this being a technically sophisticated arrangement, it actually reflected fairly rudimentary engineering principles and filtration involved nothing more than a simple settling tank to separate river sediment from usable water. It is evident that the system was primarily designed to guarantee water supply rather than regulate the river as during unseasonably wet weather in August 1913 a British employee wrote that 'the mill yard was like a lake, and several parts of the mill were flooded; one portion was waist deep and the water stopped one of the engines'.[55]

One of the key reasons that wool manufacture had thrived in the north of England was the geological conditions which provided ideally soft water for scouring, dyeing and cloth finishing as well as preventing lime-scale damage to boilers and pipe work.[56] Tailoring water quality through the addition of chemicals was an important, yet less high-profile, technology that the Bradford industrialists brought to Marki. But whereas a consistent standard of incoming water could be created, factory outflow was not generic. It roughly separated into three categories: relatively clean water passed out of the motive power system and could be returned to source or reused without treatment; water used in wet-processing (other than dyeing) would emerge

51 WYAS Wakefield, Conveyance and Assignment, Vol. 17, 31 January 1896, p. 256.

52 Giles and Goodall, *Yorkshire Textile Mills*, pp. 116 and 152.

53 Abraham Holroyd, *Saltaire and its Founder* (Bradford: Piroisms Press and Falcon, 1873), p. 22.

54 Starożyk, 'Nowa fabryka sukna i kortów', p. 165 and Wartalska, 'Fabryka i osada fabryczna', p. 665, notes that these terracotta pipes were made by Granzow.

55 Hinchcliffe, 24 August 1913.

56 'The Purification of Water for Manufacturing Purposes', *Journal of Fabrics and Textile Industries*, August 1883, p. 94.

contaminated with high levels of soap, wool fat and simple chemicals such as lime (added to create the optimum pH); whereas the effluent from the dye-house would be irretrievably polluted. Wartalska suggests that both a mechanical and chemical system was introduced at Marki to purify factory effluent and local historians have drawn the modern eco-conscious conclusion that this was to prevent river pollution.[57] However, press coverage of increasingly rigorous anti-pollution laws in Britain reveals that no methods existed at all at that time to produce 'satisfactory effluent at a reasonable cost'.[58] Legislation to prevent the contamination of rivers did not exist in Russia at this time and Benn's 1904 enterprise in Providence, Rhode Island, reportedly took advantage of the lack of US control and 'emptied its black waste into the river'.[59] For the Marki firm, the usually slow flow rate of their water source meant that effluent discharged downstream could easily surge back to sully the clean supply. Therefore it seems most likely that a sink hole was used to contain Marki's dye-house pollutants. Despite these precautions, drinking water still had to be imported to Marki daily from a mile away.[60]

Processing less-dangerously contaminated, used water from factories to recover wool fat, soap and chemicals became a lucrative sideline for many industrial firms, as well as the basis of numerous new plants in this period. In Bradford Whetley Mills and Cumberland Works were established in the early 1880s exclusively to make paints, ointments, lubricants and manure from the volume of dirty water created by local factories.[61] The Marki plant, with plentiful waste water and huge demand for both soap and grease, used a chemical treatment to recover all useful elements from scouring water to supply their soap factory.[62]

Electricity and Fire Prevention

The early use of electricity is the most-cited evidence for the technological progressiveness of the Marki plant and even in the context of worldwide industry it was a worthy headliner. Electrical technology was still in its infancy in 1883 and the first international electrical exhibition was held in Paris only two years before the Briggs-Posselt partnership established the Marki plant.[63] Several key

[57] Wartalska, 'Fabryka i osada fabryczna', p. 652. Local historian Zbigniew Paciorek made this suggestion in conversation in April 2010.

[58] M. Keighley, *Wool City* (Bradford: Wool Publishing, 2007), p. 12.

[59] Blewett, *Yankee Yorkshireman*, p. 154.

[60] N.B. Peel, 'Briggella in Poland', *The Bod-kin*, No. 22, March 1991, p. 13.

[61] Giles and Goodall, *Yorkshire Textile Mills*, p. 113.

[62] J. Edward Litten, *Die Englische Wollspinnerei der Firma Briggs, Posselt and Co. in Marki bei Warschau* [*The English Wool-Spinning Factory of the Firm Briggs, Posselt and Co., at Marki by Warsaw*] (Warsaw: Alexander Ging, 1896), p. 6.

[63] Brian Bowers, *A History of Electric Light and Power* (Stevenage: Peter Peregrinus, 1982), p. 120.

figures competed to develop industrial-scale electric lighting in the UK including Edison, Swan and Crompton, whereas continental engineers such as Siemens and Duprez concentrated on the potentially bigger prize of implementing electricity as a motive power. But although some American mills ran entirely on electricity by the 1890s, the earliest British example was not until 1907 and most Yorkshire mills remained steam powered until the 1930s.[64]

Early prototypes for electric lighting presented difficulties in running several lights from a single motor which was a key requisite for large-scale use. Crompton led the field and managed to equip Kings Cross Station in 1882 with a generator that supplied more than one arc lamp and 'all generators were driven by a single steam engine'.[65] In the following year the new factory at Marki installed a comprehensive electric-lighting system, which comprised 2,000 arc lights operated by an overhead network of 40 small generators producing 26 hp each. It was almost certainly the Edison system marketed by Mather and Platt. *Przegląd Techniczny* shows that only one electricity generation plant predated that of Bradford Mills at Marki in the Russian empire.[66] It was installed at the Sosnowiec factory of German wool manufacturer Henryk Dietel in 1882. The considerable investment in this virtually untried technology at Marki is testimony to its advantages. The quality of electric light was far superior to gas,[67] facilitating long working days and even shift work throughout the dark winter months and the reduced fire risk was a considerable benefit.

Fire was the single greatest threat to the increasingly capital rich and complex factory plants of the nineteenth century and preventative measures were naturally the subject of much experimentation. Stone or brick-vaulted ceilings, supported by cast-iron columns and beams, had long since replaced wood as building materials and substantial iron doors which opened onto stone staircases were intended to isolate each department. An optimum arrangement of buildings segregated high-risk areas such as the foundry, boilers and dye-house from the multi-storey mills. High-temperature processes such as combing, which could not be isolated from the power sources in the main building, were accommodated in adjoining single-storey sheds to minimise the fire risk. Improvements to this basic construction were regularly marketed by innovators worldwide. In *The Promised Land* Reymont's protagonist rejects the new costly Monier system, which combined modern concrete and steel with the traditional vaulted constructions, whereupon a devastating fire broke out in the drying room which destroyed the entire building.[68] The fiction reflected reality as in 1897 Poznański's Łódź cotton mill perished by

64 Giles and Goodall, *Yorkshire Textile Mills*, p. 163.
65 Bowers, *History of Electric Light and Power*, p. 110.
66 *Przegląd Techniczny*, Warsaw, 8 July 1914, p. 379.
67 Bowers, *History of Electric Light and Power*, p. 110.
68 Reymont, *The Promised Land*, p. 390.

fire and was subsequently rebuilt with 'transverse iron arches and brick vaulting'.[69] At Marki the vaulted construction was naturally favoured for its fire-proof qualities and the additional advantages of excellent load-bearing strength and impermeability. Thus heavy machinery could be installed on all floors and it would not be adversely affected by damp from the basement scouring departments.[70] The firm's internal rules reflect the emphasis on fire prevention as the highest fines were levied against workers who touched the electric lighting, allowed rubbish to accumulate near their machines or smoked anywhere on site. By contrast the sanctions for disobeying the foremen, sleeping or fighting at work were nominal.[71]

Despite managerial and structural precautions, the description provided by Daniel Thornton of a fire at his Thornton Woollen Mill at St Petersburg in 1892 reveals the potential speed of devastation. He wrote that the blaze was sparked from the transmission end of the fifth floor, but as hydrants were placed on the stone staircases, the fire-proof doors had to be opened to direct the water jets. Then 'the roof fell in with an awful crash, the machinery began to fall through the floor … so taking the fire lower and lower into the mill'.[72] Despite a considerable pay-out by their insurance company of £62,300, the firm was forced to lay off 1,500 workers, losing rental income from company housing in the short term, permanently losing some skilled staff and forfeiting vital orders until they could rebuild. As winter approached it was a race against time to get a roof back on the mill and salvage any usable machinery or components. Thornton described the scene with 'men working night and day, by night we had electric light but it is a slow and dangerous performance at best'.[73]

Fire-preventative structures, water reservoirs and well-drilled company fire brigades were usual in nineteenth-century textile firms including Marki, but Briggs, Posselt and Co. were the first firm in the Kingdom of Poland, and very likely in Europe, to install the Grinnell Sprinkler system. Invented in the USA, manufactured by Mather and Platt in Lancashire and marketed in Russia by Ludwig Knoop, this system was first demonstrated in England in 1881. The *Bolton Evening News* described how a shed was built in Bolton market square and packed with combustible materials:

---

[69] Popławska and Muthesius, 'Poland's Manchester', p. 153. There is the suggestion that Reymont's protagonist Borowiecki was modelled loosely on Poznański and certainly Andrzej Wajda's 1975 Academy Award-nominated film adaptation was partly filmed in Poznański's Łódź palace.

[70] Giles and Goodall, *Yorkshire Textile Mills*, p. 34.

[71] APW, signature 375, internal regulations for workers of the Briggs factory, 3 February 1910, pp. 017–022v.

[72] Leeds Russian Archive, MS1072/20 Daniel Bateman Thornton in St Petersburg to Mary, 8 November 1892.

[73] Ibid.

> Fire was set to this inflammable material in five places, and in 58 seconds one of the caps had burst off and the Sprinkler was at work. The flames had no sooner appeared to be getting hold, and from the open doorway could be seen leaping to the ceiling, then they were hidden to sight in a cloud of smoke, and in three minutes the fire was practically quelled.[74]

Whether this groundbreaking installation served to reduce insurance premiums for the Marki firm is unknown, but clearly the entrepreneurs were convinced that it was a worthwhile investment to secure their fixed assets and prevent loss of business through fire. Their far-sightedness is reflected in the fact that such sprinkler systems remain a primary safeguard against fire not just in factory buildings but offices, schools and hotels worldwide. However, in 1897 a little-reported incident at Marki was described in the British press which shows the consequence of the company's unwise use of a new building before the sprinkler system had been installed:

> Every block but one was provided with automatic sprinklers and another set was at Hull last week shipped in order to equip that block also. Unfortunately, however, the fire broke out in that mill and the building was gutted. The stock was of a floating character, and the precise amount of damage is not yet known, but it is expected to be about £100,000.[75]

Heating and Ventilation

Creating the optimum environment for production, buildings and machinery maintenance was another aspect of the factory design to which increasing attention was given at the end of the nineteenth century. The impact of damp particularly, but also excessive heat or chemical contamination could threaten the overall sustainability of the business. Wartalska suggests that the installation of heating, ventilation and air humidifiers at Marki was 'intended to create good working conditions for the workers'.[76] Although there was a growing consciousness amongst British industrialists about employee health and more particularly employer liabilities,[77] this investment was certainly made primarily to maximise efficiency, not for the comfort of the labour force. Industrialists building an optimum manufactory needed to weigh up the relative benefits of damp conditions

74 *Bolton Evening News*, 30 June 1881.

75 'Fire at Bradford Mills, Warsaw', *Leeds Times*, 17 April, 1897, p. 7.

76 Wartalska, 'Fabryka i osada fabryczna', p. 652.

77 'Employers' Liability on the Continent', *Textile World*, December 1886, p. 291 and in 'Employer's Liability Act (1880) Amendment', *Textile Recorder*, Manchester, 15 May 1883, p. 3.

for the fault-free production of yarn,[78] against its detrimental effect on machinery or labour. Department by department they needed to create, sometimes diverse, ideal conditions for each process. Dyeing and finishing departments could operate with a simple louvered vent system to release steam and fumes, whereas modern hydro-extractors and drying machines could increase throughput and save space, as they dispensed with the need for a dedicated drying house.[79]

The Flexible Capabilities of the Marki Plant

The general opportunity discerned by the Bradford partners has already been outlined: worsted yarn was both in great demand and short supply in the Russian empire in 1883. Worsted spinners were largely reliant on semi-processed fibre imports while woollen and cotton weavers could incorporate this yarn to extend their product offer without further investment in plant or skills. Therefore the unique selling point of the Marki venture, in the regional context, was that it could sort, scour and comb raw wool to make tops for local sale to spinners, spin the standard yarn qualities required by the national weaving industry or ultimately adopt the fully vertical approach and produce cloth.

The greatest breakthrough for factory-scale worsted production, arguably on a par with the introduction of steam power, had been the mechanisation of the combing process around the mid-century. Mechanical combs superseded the highly skilled hand process to meet growing demand from increasingly large spinning and weaving companies. Further modifications had increased combing speeds by up to 30 per cent by 1888.[80] Combs provided the semi-processed raw material that was the basis of all worsted yarn. Spinning equipment, on the other hand, took several forms: fly or later cap frames were generally used in the worsted trade and mules usually equipped British cotton mills (although the French produced a softer worsted yarn using the mule system). But an American innovation, the ring spindle, developed and brought to market in this period most notably by Lancashire manufacturers Howard and Bullough,[81] could be applied to either the cotton or worsted trade and was almost universally adopted abroad. The advantages of this modified method of introducing twist to yarn and winding it onto bobbins were clearly outlined in an 1884 comparative study entitled 'Ring Spinning versus Mule Spinning'. It described that the mule produced 29 hanks per spindle in a 56-hour week, whereas the ring produced 48 hanks: 50–70 per cent more spindles could fit on the same floor space with a 15 to 30 per cent reduction

[78] Damp conditions act as a lubricant which aids spinning and weaving processes, humidifiers or more sophisticated oiling or sizing processes are now commonly used in spinning, especially for finer counts or poor quality raw materials.

[79] Giles and Goodall, *Yorkshire Textile Mills*, p. 4.

[80] Firth, 'Bradford Trade in the Nineteenth Century', p. 30.

[81] Howard and Bullough traded as Tweedales and Smalley after 1891.

in running costs. Two to five per cent less waste was created and the resulting yarn was of an improved quality and consistency. However, the key advantages of the ring spindle were that,

> Skilled labour is dispensed with, as young girls can, with very little practice, become as expert as the best mule spinner, and at a cost of less than one third ... Each girl is able to mind 400 to 500 spindles, according to the counts and quality of yarn in progress ... Lastly, there is a further saving in insurance, the premium for which is much less than with the mule, the risk of fire being reduced to a minimum.[82]

By the early 1880s, the Bradford partners were experienced worsted manufacturers but their enterprise at Marki was subject to exactly the same conditions as any foreign firm: labour was plentiful, cheap and largely unskilled. Thus, rather than installing the familiar British cap or fly frame which was operated in Bradford by second- and even third-generation industrial workers, they introduced the ring system at Marki for their core business. The state-of-the-art innovation offered the fastest running speeds, optimum space and labour economy but primarily had the least skills requirement. Nevertheless, there is evidence that the firm also introduced two other spinning systems to maximise the productive capabilities of its foreign plant.

For the rationale behind the Bradford partners' investment in a second spinning system at Marki, it is necessary to look again at the contemporary impact of foreign competition on the British wool trade. Bradford's worsted industry was essentially based on spinning hard or long wools, to make fine lustrous yarns which were ideal for firm dress cloths to fit over crinolines, hard-wearing suits and coats. As was described in Chapter 1, this yarn was combined with cotton or other fibres, to mass produce relatively cheap, durable but lightweight mixed cloths. The French, on the other hand, favoured softer short wools such as merino which were mule spun and woven into more expensive all-wool fabrics. In the last quarter of the nineteenth century, changing dress fashions which abandoned the crinoline in favour of a more fluid silhouette rendered the Bradford staples outmoded and French worsteds gained popularity in the unprotected British market. Although a few manufacturers such as Ramsden of Great Horton adopted the French spinning system,[83] the home trade virtually relinquished the ladies' dress market because any 'attempt to compete with the French would have required a total reorganisation of the trade, as well as re-equipping and modifying the nature of the labour force'.[84] Instead most Bradford firms diversified into men's suiting

---

[82] 'Ring Spinning versus Mule spinning', *Journal of Fabrics and Textile Industries*, 12 March1883, p. 34.

[83] Wright and Jowitt, *Victorian Bradford*, p. 22.

[84] J.A. Jowitt, 'Textiles and Society in Bradford and Lawrence, USA, 1880–1920', *Bradford Antiquary*, 5 (1991), pp. 3–24.

qualities, overcoat cloths and furnishing fabrics simultaneously increasing exports of yarn and combed tops. But it is evident that the devastating economic impact of this particular branch of foreign competition, in combination with changing fashion, remained a preoccupation for British industrialists in 1883: 'a great deal has been said and written upon the subject of the French versus the Bradford method of worsted spinning, and yet, the topic is still uppermost in the minds of practical men'.[85]

This was another instance in which a foreign enterprise could aspire to the ideal and rectify an impediment to their domestic concern. The Briggs-Posselt partnership opted to equip the new firm to spin both relatively cheap Bradford staples in long wool, as well as the more expensive French-spun soft merinos using the mule.[86] It may be no coincidence that in 1883 Platt Brothers of Oldham, another firm represented by Knoop in Russia, launched their 'French System of Worsted Spinning' at the Huddersfield Fine Art and Industrial Exhibition.[87] Several trade journals described the arrangement which, contrary to the ring, was extraordinarily complex, involving 19 separate processes. Despite the intricacy and expense, the flexibility that the French spinning system offered the Marki firm undoubtedly increased its hold on the Russian-empire worsted market.

Thus the Bradford partners equipped their Marki plant to mass produce relatively cheap Bradford staples using the ring spindle and expensive French-style soft worsted utilising local merino wool with the mule. But, almost ten years after founding their worsted company, the entrepreneurs took the decision to move on the Russian-Polish woollen market. In 1892 the *Kurjer Warszawski* reported that the firm was building another five-storey mill to card and spin 'thick woollen yarn'.[88] Several contributory factors undoubtedly influenced this decision: firstly woollen-yarn manufacture largely existed on an artisan basis in Poland, therefore the potential for a bulk manufacturer of cheap and consistent woollen yarn or cloth, for industrial supply or particularly to fulfil military contracts for coats or blankets, was enormous. Secondly, by 1890, as intensifying competition from Moscow threatened to edge Polish cotton goods out of the Russian market, the Łódź manufacturers 'decided to embrace the demands of Russia's far eastern and Siberian markets for the cheapest of finished goods'.[89] For the first time large

85 'Messrs Platt Bros. and Co's French System of Worsted Spinning', *Textile World*, August 1883, p. 675.

86 Litten, *Englische Wollspinnerei*, p. 4.

87 'Messers Platt Brothers of Oldham show the French System of Worsted Spinning', 'The Huddersfield Fine Art and Industrial Exhibition', *Journal of Fabrics and Textile Industries*, 12 August 1883, p. 93. Wartalska, 'Fabryka i osada fabryczna', p. 652, made the assumption that the machinery for this department was imported from France, rather than 'French system spinning machinery' manufactured in England.

88 'Maszyna olbrzym', p. 4.

89 Laura A. Crago, 'The "Polishness" of Production: Factory Politics and the Reinvention of Working-Class National and Political Identities in Russian Poland's Textile Industry, 1880–1910', *Slavic Review*, 59: 1 (2000), p. 33.

factories began to mass produce rustic textiles for export to Russia which had been the former speciality of the Białystok home trade. They developed *sztuczna wełna* or *wełna odpadkowa* [shoddy] and a new, exclusively Polish cloth known as *wigón* [a vicuna-cotton mix] all of which combined wool and cotton rags with raw wool to make thick loosely woven, cheap textiles. This was an opportunity for the Marki firm to get a foothold in a new market and profitably utilise inferior parts of a fleece and recycled wools which were unsuitable for worsted spinning. However, it is clear that commercial pragmatism and providence played equal parts in the Briggs-Posselt partnership's diversification. When the Zgierz firm of C.A. Meyerhoff was liquidated Marki acquired not only woollen carding equipment and looms but the expertise of their former owner who 'will develop products for this company'.[90]

The Buildings and the Architect

Just as machine technology was subject to constant fine tuning throughout the nineteenth century, the planning of mill compounds was also undergoing greater rationalisation and being tailored to the requirements of production. But certain standards characterised industrial plants worldwide, for example at least one multi-storeyed building usually in an Italianate style was annexed by single-storey sheds, a gated fortress-like quadrangle was filled with outbuildings and more often than not the plant lay parallel to a water source. The single-storey processing sheds, usually for combing or weaving had been introduced in 1829, but endured well into the twentieth century.[91] This practical structure could fit any plot of land, was both economical and uncomplicated to extend or relocate. The saw-tooth profile roof had a glazed section which faced north in order to cast an even light on the interior workspace.[92] This style of building was as ubiquitous in Russian Poland as it was in England and Harrison Benn remarked on the its merits for accommodating heavy machinery without any detriment from vibration, when he built his American plant in 1905.[93] After 1875 the majority of Yorkshire's mills comprised a central four- or five-storey building of 'ten to seventeen bays long and had between 1,000 and 4,000 m² of working space'.[94] Bradford Mills at Marki did not compare in stature with Salt's or Manningham Mills in Bradford, but it certainly exceeded this British norm even before the extensions of 1892, with 30

---

90 *Prawda: Tygodnik Polityczny, Społeczny i Literacki*, Warsaw, No. 52, 24 December 1892, p. 10.

91 Giles and Goodall, *Yorkshire Textile Mills*, p. 39.

92 Ibid., p. 107.

93 Blewett, *Yankee Yorkshireman*, p. 58.

94 Giles and Goodall, *Yorkshire Textile Mills*, p. 37.

bays and a working area of more than 20,000 m^2 which reflected the plentiful land, vast capital and the ambition of the founders.[95]

In the construction of new mills 'a closer approach to an ideal layout was possible [than] in mills where integration was achieved by piecemeal addition'.[96] The challenge for the architect was to design a range of buildings which enabled a logical flow of manufacturing processes and the most efficient use of power. Thus the planning of mills was a highly specialised field and central to the economic success of any new venture. The architects and engineers needed a profound understanding of the workings of the industry and the particular requirements of their clients. Titus Salt employed Bradford's leading architectural firm, Lockwood and Mawson, and prominent engineer, William Fairbairn, to create the works at Saltaire. The 1886 factory-building boom at Oldham was the work of only three architectural firms who were considered to have the accumulated experience to 'perfect many points, and to avoid many of the defects which exist in the earlier mills'.[97]

Although some integrated factory complexes did pre-date the Marki enterprise in the Polish lands, they focused on cotton or linen manufacture. Scheibler's great cotton mill at Księży Młyn, described by Popławska and Muthesius as 'a leap into the most up to date English methods',[98] was designed in the 1870s by the prolific architect Hilary Majewski. On the other hand, Jan Kacper Heurich was a contemporary proponent of workers' housing and built the palace of the Lilpops on Ujazdowski Avenue in Warsaw. His local prestige and Evangelical-Augsburg-Church connections would suggest him to have been a contender to design the Marki mill, yet the less-experienced Edward Lilpop was engaged by the Bradford men. However, Starożyk describes Lilpop as the 'executor of the plans'[99] rather than the architect and several factors strongly suggest that the British entrepreneurs arrived with blueprints from Bradford, for which the Polish architect assumed management. The specialised nature of the plant, Lilpop's lack of industrial experience and the speed of the project's inauguration all cast doubt on his being the designer. Indeed, Chapter 5 highlighted that the Bradford partners did not buy land until January 1883 but their plans had been authorised and building work had already begun by the end of the month.[100]

The swift construction of factories was not unusual in this period for two key reasons: firstly, 'when a manufacturer determines to erect a mill it is generally when the trade is what the Yankees call "booming" and he is naturally in a hurry to have the mill built, so that he may have machinery at work and take advantage of

95 *Illustrated Weekly Telegraph*, Bradford, 19 March 1886, p. 1.
96 Giles and Goodall, *Yorkshire Textile Mills*, p. 101.
97 'The Construction and the Ventilation of Weaving Sheds', p. 171.
98 Popławska and Muthesius, 'Poland's Manchester', p. 153.
99 Starożyk, 'Nowa fabryka sukna i kortów', p. 165.
100 Wartalska, 'Fabryka i osada fabryczna', p. 648.

the good time'.[101] Foster's Black Dyke Mill took only 'ten months from the cutting of the first sods in Black Myres Field to the point at which the spindles first began to turn in the new mill'.[102] Secondly, it was imperative that the minimum of time should elapse between capital outlay on land, building materials and machinery and the realisation of profit. Reymont portrayed the desperation of an industrialist who had 'sunk 40,000 rubles in the factory yet cannot get it started'.[103] The construction period represented a financial dead-time for investors, thus speed from initiation to activation was one of the key advantages of well-capitalised foreign investors entering a market with potential. But whereas speed in mill construction was usual, hasty planning by an inexperienced foreign designer is entirely improbable in this case. Like their fellow industrialists in Bradford or Oldham, the Briggs-Posselt partnership would only have entrusted their huge investment to one of a handful of specialist architects. By the 1880s Mawson and Lockwood had passed their prime, whereas the firm of Milnes and France was prolific. These architects had designed several plants near Briggella including Illingworth's Whetley Mills, Princeville Combing Mill and Bank Top Mill in the Horton area as well as Oak Mills at Clayton and seem the most likely originators of the Marki plans. The firm was also credited with the Bradford Tradesmen's homes in 1885 and a large number of the warehouses in Little Germany including those of the prominent merchants Behrens and Semons.

In conclusion it is evident that British state-of-the-art technology provided both a convenient platform on which to promote the Marki enterprise, as well as a sound strategy to maximise profits. The numerous groundbreaking innovations installed by the Briggs-Posselt partnership to create an optimum manufactory in Russian Poland can easily counter any charges of technological conservatism made against British industrialists in this period. However, despite their objective to manufacture staple Bradford products, the new factory did not emulate British industry but far exceeded it in technical modernity and efficiency. This chapter has shown that Russian-empire industrialisation and the late nineteenth-century export achievements of British engineering firms rested heavily on the intermediary role of Ludwig Knoop. That is not to detract from the entrepreneurial skill of the Briggs-Posselt partnership for whom innovation and rationalisation of their operations remained integral to their approach at Marki. Thus the observations of Starożyk in 1883, Litten in 1897, Hinchcliffe after 1910 and Karol Whitehead's recollections of the interwar period reveal continual steady expansion, diversification and improvements to the plant.

This chapter has focused on the buildings, power generation, transmission and processing machinery installed at Marki, but it must be considered that technology encompassed a great deal more than the firm's fixed assets. Modern business analysts now recognise a more broadly defined concept of technology

---

[101] 'The construction and the ventilation of weaving sheds', p. 171.

[102] Sigsworth, *Black Dyke Mills*, p. 171.

[103] Reymont, *The Promised Land*, p. 487.

which includes skills and organisation. Robert Grosse identifies 'at least three types of technology: product, process and management'[104] and cites many modern firms for whom 'creativity, marketing skills and client relationships were a key technology'.[105] Chapter 8 will consider some of these less tangible aspects of venturing industrialists' business plan – their employment policy and managerial practices – as significant indicators of their groundbreaking approach.

104 Robert Grosse, 'International Technology Transfer in Services', *Journal of International Business Studies*, 27: 4 (1996), p. 782.

105 Ibid.

Chapter 8
'The Polish Bournville or Port Sunlight':[1] Paternalism, the model industrial community and employment policy at Marki

The town of Marki with its company housing, shops, school and church might be considered a typical British-style model industrial community, less developed and without the fine infrastructure of Bournville or Port Sunlight, but essentially the same. Indeed the nineteenth-century Yorkshire press described it as 'a second edition of Saltaire'.[2] However, just as the plant was intended to improve upon contemporary British industrial practice, the planned town was also a carefully considered response to Russian-Polish social conditions; part and parcel of the Bradford entrepreneurs' strategy to create the optimum manufactory. At Marki the entrepreneurs made every effort to correct the deficiencies which had limited the profitability of their domestic concerns and might reduce the sustainability of the new enterprise. With reference to evolving techniques of workforce management in Britain, this chapter will show the central importance of paternalism, social-overhead investment and employment policy to the Briggs-Posselt partnership's Polish enterprise.

Industrial Paternalism and Workforce Management

When manufacturing moved out of the domestic setting and into dedicated industrial sites, 'the point was not the machinery but the organisation, the factory included labour and equipment as one integral unit'.[3] Each department had to accomplish set tasks at a given speed in order to feed the next section with work, and this production line foundered if the workers were not as synchronized as the machinery. In general, the complexity of processes increased throughout the mill. Primary operations, such as scouring, required minimal labour and equipment to produce sufficient throughput to supply the spinning department, whereas later processes, such as weaving, required a variety of complex machinery and many skilled operatives to prevent a back-up of costly semi-processed stock. But this flow of production was not an exact science and some flexibility in the system was essential. Variations in the quality of raw material might have a knock-on effect, calling for greater attention

1 Dawson, *It Might Have Happened to You*, p. 111.

2 *Illustrated Weekly Telegraph*, 19 March 1886, p. 1.

3 Cookson, 'Family Firms and Business Networks', p. 12.

in spinning to produce useable yarn, slower weaving or extra hours in the mending department to make the resultant cloth saleable. Similarly an unreliable or absent worker, like a missing cog in any machine, could impact on the smooth running and overall profits of the business. Reymont mocked this factory ethos with the words of a desperate labourer: 'I am a man, not a machine', and his protagonist's sardonic reply: 'at home you are ... here you are but a machine like the rest of us'.[4] But by the late nineteenth century, with increasingly large capital outlay on plants and rising competition, maximising profits was imperative. The owner's income, the gargantuan running costs of the factory and the livelihoods of all employees relied on every worker playing their part efficiently. Thus the flow of production and workforce management, like engines and machinery, were subject to constant review and were arguably less costly to modify and improve.

The advent of the factory system fundamentally changed industrialists' approach to employment. In early dispersed manufacturing, entrepreneurs sought to minimise both fixed and working-capital commitments by subcontracting or outsourcing work. By assuming as little responsibility for their workers as possible they remained 'highly attuned and responsive to market needs'.[5] These first industrialists essentially merchanted generic products, but as demand, competition and the sophistication of requirements increased, dedicated factories better met their needs. But with no experience of regulating mass employment, these pioneers experimented with 'methods of organizing the social relations of production',[6] which would maximise efficiency but maintain owner control. A hierarchy which created 'submissiveness of subordinates, and reciprocity of personal loyalty and obligation'[7] proved most effective. From this principle, industrial paternalism and the ambitious concept of the model workers' community emerged. Early examples such as Robert Owen's New Lanark experiment revealed that, if an industrialist provided housing, education and healthcare, he could engender the loyalty of whole families and mould the community's behaviour to meet his needs. In a controversial lecture delivered at Bradford's town hall in 1864, John Ruskin perceptively observed that the industrial community allowed the wealthy bourgeoisie to inculcate a moral order in which workers would 'never drink, never strike, always go to church on Sundays and always express themselves in respectful language'.[8] Thus the factory owner became the 'single autonomous legislator, the judge and the executor of his own regulations'.[9]

---

[4] Reymont, *The Promised Land*, p. 26.

[5] Cookson, 'Family Firms and Business Networks', p. 4.

[6] Nicholas Abercrombie and Stephen Hill, 'Paternalism and Patronage', *British Journal of Sociology*, 27: 4 (December 1976), p. 419.

[7] Ibid., p. 420.

[8] J. Ruskin, *The Crown of Wild Olive: Four Lectures of Industry and War* (London: George Allen, 1900), pp. 105–6.

[9] Victoria E. Bonnell, *The Russian Worker: Life and Labour under the Tsarist Regime* (Berkeley, Los Angeles, London: University of California Press, 1983), p. 118.

Paternalism flourished in the early phase of industrialisation as a direct response to the employment of unskilled workers.[10] But by the end of the nineteenth century a changing socio-economic and political climate in Britain began to undermine its effectiveness. Greater industrial experience, improved living standards and a competitive labour market meant that workers became less amenable to the total control of their employers. At the same time, the industrialists' great wealth and local influence made them a natural target for emerging political groups who competed for the allegiance of the labouring classes. Paternalism which had so effectively smoothed the transition from agrarianism to urban industrialism had brought a significant sector of the population under the control of an affluent minority. Thus rising socialist parties attempted to undermine the employers' reputations by expressing suspicion of their motives. The well-known captains of industry were particularly accused of self aggrandisement; for getting 'brilliant names as philanthropists by giving a few pounds to some chapel or church or to the funds of some society not worth a pin from the economic point of view'.[11] Thus the fleetingly harmonious interdependence of labour and capital – the old order of Britain's northern industrial towns – was increasingly pilloried or labelled as exploitative.

In reality, the employees of Owen in the 1830s, Salt or Akroyd in the mid-century and later those of the Briggs-Posselt partnership at Marki enjoyed greater job security, superior living and working conditions to their contemporaries in the urban factories of Glasgow, Bradford or Łódź.[12] However, changing social attitudes perhaps explain a gradual evolution in the professed motives of the founders of so-called model towns as the nineteenth century progressed. Early examples were invariably promoted as philanthropy as their owners claimed a 'common belief in the need to alleviate the social, political, and moral problems thrown up by ... industrialization',[13] whereas later instigators increasingly relied on a religious justification for their regimes for social control and some openly declared their social-overhead investment was a tactic to pre-empt worker revolt. For example, the German steel magnate Alfred Krupp candidly stated during the construction of his industrial housing at Essen that 'when the whole country goes on a general revolt, with the working classes against the employers, we will be the only ones that they will save'.[14] Pullman, a workers' community built between 1880 and 1884 by the eponymous rail-car company on the outskirts of Chicago, was reputedly a direct response to growing conflict between capital and labour. The firm's owners

10 Abercrombie and Hill, 'Paternalism and Patronage', p. 417.

11 *Yorkshire Daily Observer*, Bradford, 28 March 1904.

12 Abercrombie and Hill, 'Paternalism and Patronage', p. 419.

13 Jowitt, *Model Industrial Communities*, p. 7.

14 Walter Bolz, *Krupps-Siemens: Nebenerwerbssiedlung fur Kurz- und Vollarbeiter* [*Krupps-Siemens: Part-time Settlement for Short- and Full-time Workers*] (Berlin: J. Springer, 1934), p. 61, in Kubiak and Szyburska, 'Urbanystka i architektura Żyrardowa', p. 96.

visited Saltaire and modelled their housing project on the Yorkshire community, but their highly skilled and sophisticated American workforce rebelled against the paternalistic scheme as a form of coercion.[15]

Despite the various professed motivations of the founders, assuming entire responsibility for the housing, health and education of a workforce and their families was primarily a business tactic to ensure reliable productivity and facilitate greater profit. But by the last quarter of the nineteenth century British manufacturers faced multi-faceted challenges which, in combination with changing social attitudes, made the huge investment in model industrial communities an unsound proposition for textile factory owners in Britain. Indeed Edward Akroyd and John Crossley, the initiators of the Yorkshire towns of Akroydon, West Hill Park and Copley, left Halifax in straightened circumstances during the 1870s and the Salts were bankrupt by 1892.[16] Thus, in 1883 when the Briggs-Posselt partnership began to construct housing at Marki, the trend amongst their Bradford contemporaries was to reduce social-overhead investment. Nevertheless, the ideal of the model industrial town remained aspirational for some businessmen and notable examples such as Bournville and Port Sunlight were certainly established long after Marki or Saltaire. However, the rising market for luxury products such as soap and chocolate arguably made viable the high-cost social-overhead investment of William Hesketh Lever at Port Sunlight and the Cadbury family at Bournville.

The Appropriateness of British Industrial Paternalism in Nineteenth-century Poland

At the end of the nineteenth century the Russian-Polish industrial environment was reminiscent 'of scenes in England a century before'.[17] Russia's punitive policies to neglect municipal investment following the 1863 January Uprising led Warsaw's infrastructure to lag far behind contemporary West European standards, at the same time, the emancipation of the Polish peasants led the city's population to increase by 263 per cent between 1866 and 1914.[18] Most migrants came to Warsaw 'straight from the plough';[19] few were literate or had any skills apart from farming. Overcrowding and homelessness were rife and the lack of clean water supply or basic sanitation led to regular outbreaks of cholera.[20] But despite the atrocious conditions peasant workers clung to a belief of improved prospects in

---

15 Robert M. Lillibridge, 'Pullman: Town Development in the Era of Eclecticism', *Journal of the Society of Architectural Historians*, 12: 3 (1953), p. 22.

16 Jowitt, *Model Industrial Communities*, p. 85.

17 Davies, *God's Playground*, p. 197.

18 Anna Żarnowska, *Workers, Women and Social Change in Poland, 1870–1939* (Aldershot: Ashgate Variorum, 2004), p. 289.

19 Ibid., p. 294.

20 'Cholera', *Gazeta Warszawska*, No. 286, 28 October 1893, p. 4.

the city. By the early 1880s the majority of Warsaw inhabitants were single people living a hand-to-mouth existence and the British consul noted 'great numbers of persons are out of work and in great distress'.[21]

In this environment, the concept of the model community applied extraordinarily well. Paternalism, largely derived from the traditional social code of the landed estate,[22] offered the security of the recently disbanded system of serfdom, with the industrialist assuming the role of manorial lord. His presence and personal involvement in industrial towns reinforced the paternalistic ethic and proved 'a tried and tested way of checking destabilising forces that threatened the firm from outside'.[23] In other words, isolation generally improved the employer's prospects for workforce control but the traditionally servile attitude of the Polish peasant and their enduring belief in the 'inviolability of social hierarchy'[24] also constituted a distinct advantage to the Bradford men at Marki.

Some nineteenth-century Russian-empire factory towns, particularly those instituted by foreign investors, have certainly been characterised as model industrial communities. But whereas housing and other facilities at Marki, Saltaire and Bournville were built simultaneously with the factory to create a complete town (although increased investment followed in stages to meet the needs of a growing workforce), the Russian examples invariably made social-overhead investment long after the associated business had been established. For example John Hughes' New Russia Company was instituted in the 1870s but frustrations at constantly having to recruit and train itinerant labour only led the firm to provide permanent dwellings in the early twentieth century. Similarly the French founder of the Gorlovka Coal Company, Edgar de Sinçay, has been described as 'a pioneer in the development of family housing',[25] but not until long after his mining activities in southern Russia had begun. A notable Russian-Polish industrial settlement which pre-dated Marki is Scheibler's Księży Młyn, which added to the urban conglomeration of Łódź over decades; 'a town within a city'[26] rather than an autonomous community. In fact a clear pattern emerged in the late nineteenth century for established businesses in Russia to extend their social provision and apply the promotional language of British paternalists to their existing concerns.

In the Kingdom of Poland, Żyrardów most closely resembled a British model industrial community. It was founded in 1833 by the Łubienski brothers who built a linen factory under the technical direction of the French engineer Philippe de

---

21 Jedlicki, *Suburb of Europe*, p. 241. FO65/1227 Maude to the Secretary of State, 3 March 1885, p. 50, Żarnowska, *Workers, Women and Social Change*, p. 303.

22 Jowitt, *Model Industrial Communities*, p. 89.

23 David J. Jeremy, 'The Enlightened Paternalist in Action: William Hesketh Lever at Port Sunlight before 1914', *Business History*, Vol. 1 (1991), p. 77 and in Jowitt, *Model Industrial Communities*, p. 109.

24 Żarnowska, *Workers, Women and Social Change*, p. 300.

25 McKay, *Pioneers for Profit*, p. 262.

26 Crago, 'The "Polishness" of Production', p. 20.

Girard, for whom the town was named. In 1847 the firm was sold on by the Bank of Poland to a joint-stock consortium led by the Austrian entrepreneurs Hielle and Dietrich.[27] Although the present-day town, resulting from almost a century's piecemeal development, appears comparable to Port Sunlight or Saltaire and has received a great deal of scholarly attention for its exemplary workforce provision and paternalistic management practices,[28] Żyrardów was not established as a model town, but was rebranded as one in the last quarter of the nineteenth century when most of its infrastructure was developed.

Hielle and Dietrich may have been influenced by progressive ideas in workforce management and determined to improve local conditions, but the evidence suggests that the firm's promotion as an exemplar of paternalistic care in the 1880s resulted from entirely different circumstances. In April 1883, as construction at Marki was underway, the owners of the great linen factory were forced to call in Cossacks to suppress a worker revolt. A Bradford journal suggested that 'the proposal of the firm to reduce wages'[29] had caused the dispute which ended 'in riots and loss of life'.[30] A swift improvement of local facilities followed which might reflect the owners' attempts to make amends and rehabilitate their reputation as caring employers. However, it is more probable that the consequence of their request for armed intervention, which revealed the extreme discontent in the town, was heavier state scrutiny and regulation. Thus Krzysztof Zwolinski asserts that 'it was not Dietrich's "paternal" care for his workers, but the necessity of complying with government orders and purely economic calculations, which led him to build factory housing, organise canteens, a hospital, ambulance, baths, laundry, schools, orphanage and install equipment for ventilation and humidification in the production halls'.[31]

The Local Influence of the Bradford Partners' Scheme

In Warsaw the wealthy elite frequently sponsored hospitals, orphanages and homeless shelters to alleviate the dire social conditions in the city. Nevertheless,

---

27 Kubiak and Szyburska, 'Urbanystka i architektura Żyrardowa', p. 95.

28 Paweł Hulka-Laskowski, *Mój Żyrardów: z dziejów polskiego miasta i z życia pisarza* [*My Żyrardów: the History of a Polish City and the Life of a Writer*] (Warsaw: Czytelnik, 1958), Jacek Grzonkowski, Wojciech Adalbert Maślarz and Barbara Rzeczycka, *Żyrardów miasto wielu narodów* [*Żyrardów City of Many Nations*] (Żyrardów: Muzeum Mazowsza Zachodniego, 2006), Irena Pietrzak-Pawłowska, *Żyrardów, 1829–1945: praca zbiorowa* [*Żyrardów, 1829–1945: a Collective Work*] (Warsaw: Państwowe Wydawn Nauk, 1980). A. Wójcicki, 'Instytucje fabryczne i społeczne w przemyśle Królestwa Polskiego' ['Factory institutions and industrial society in the Kingdom of Poland'], *Ekonomista*, XIV (1914).

29 *Textile World and Yorkshire Inventor*, June 1883, p. 617.

30 FO65/1167, Maude to Secretary of State, 27 April 1883, p. 16.

31 Krzysztof Zwolinski, *Zakłady Żyrardowskie w latach 1885–1915* [*The Mill at Żyrardów in the Years 1885–1915*] (Warsaw: Książka i Wiedza, 1979), p. 166.

the programme of social provision introduced by the Bradford partners in 1883 was perceived as an entirely new concept locally. In 1892 the *Gazeta Warszawska* acknowledged the efforts of firms such as Szlenkier, Rudzki, Lilpop and Rau, Temler and Szwede and of Łódź manufacturers Scheibler, Kunitzer, Heinzel, Poznański and Hielle and Dietrich of Żyrardow to improve the welfare of their workers. But Marki was singled out as the manifestation of British philanthropic practice in which 'a worker is taken care of by his employer'.[32] Indeed the article urged Polish manufacturers to heed this foreign example and introduce its beneficial approach to their own businesses. Whether the Bradford men actually introduced a new concept in workforce provision at Marki, or simply revealed the value of directing existing charity to facilitate workforce control, is debateable. But in the late nineteenth century, their local influence was evident among their close circle: Granzow built a settlement for his brick workers at Kawęczyn with shops, a laundry, a reading room, a nursery and school which housed 650 people by 1896. Similarly, Posselt's neighbour Edward Natanson established a workers' town by his Mirkowski Paper Factory at Jeziorno in 1887, which his son later described as an industrial community 'in the English style'.[33]

Although model industrial communities were virtually unheard of in the Russian empire, the provision of accommodation for factory workers was not unusual in 1883. The Russian workforce typically divided its time between the factory and farming on remote rural homesteads. Thus, dormitories or barracks within the plant compound, where beds were shared between day and nightshift workers, were the norm, and before the 1880s employers were under no obligation to provide separate-sex quarters.[34] In Russian Poland the majority of peasant migrants went into domestic service where they were required to remain single.[35] Thus when marriage and a family home were an 'unattainable luxury for the average worker',[36] even low-status factory work which provided these opportunities represented an ambitious step up the social hierarchy, particularly for women.

Worldwide industrialists seemingly described their investment in model communities with one voice. The virtual formula which included housing, schools, churches and parks conformed to a middle-class notion of a rural idyll. But despite a superficial similarity in the range of amenities, a uniform standard was not evident either nationally or internationally; model was a relative term. It has been suggested

32 'Gazetka' ['Newsletter'], *Gazeta Warszawska*, No. 147, 1892, p. 3.

33 Miliszkiewicz, *Polskie gniazda rodzinne*, p. 40 and in E. Pustoła-Kozłowska and E. Wartalska, 'Historia papierni w Jeziornie' ['The history of the paper mill in Jeziorno'], *Kwartalnik historii kultury materialnej*, XXXIV, No. 1 (1986), p. 75.

34 Bonnell, *Russian Worker*, p. 124.

35 Anna Żarnowska, 'Working Family in the Kingdom of Poland at the end of the C19th', in *Polish Population Review 10, Household and Family on the Polish Territories in Historical Perspective*, ed. C. Kuklo (Warsaw: Polish Demographic Society, 1997), p. 73.

36 McKay, *Pioneers for Profit*, p. 266.

Figure 8.1 Main street of Marki circa 1910
Source: By kind permission of Ralph Haigh

that the quality of accommodation in British examples reflected the industrialists' sense of moral obligation to their employees.[37] But realistically, local social conditions and the competitiveness of the labour market determined the level of provision necessary to secure a workforce. Twenty years before the Marki venture Edward Akroyd condemned the housing at Haley Hill in Halifax, 'with only a single living room and chamber, however numerous may be the inhabitants',[38] as inferior and announced his plans for a model village. Given the overcrowding and homelessness in Russian-Polish cities, the security of regular employment and a relatively improved standard of living were wholly adequate to attract and retain a workforce at Marki. Thus the Briggs-Posselt partnership's worker accommodation conformed exactly to Akroyd's rejected inferior standard. Successful applicants to the firm received a single room with a fireplace and a shared standpipe outside. Despite extensive land holdings the Bradford men built economical back-to-back blocks of flats typical of Yorkshire's inner-city developments. Nevertheless, these were solidly built brick residences, unnecessarily adorned with gables, pleasingly located outside the factory gates and, in a regional context, rightly deserved their reputation as modern and convenient.

It is worth noting here that Saltaire, Akroydon or Port Sunlight did not typify British housing in the Victorian era. Municipalities only introduced more stringent planning regulations for new buildings in the 1870s and Lord Salisbury sparked fierce debate when he attacked the government for condoning construction projects which displaced or more tightly concentrated the working class. He argued that 'thousands of families have only a single room to dwell in, where they sleep and eat, multiply, and die ... It is difficult to exaggerate the misery which such conditions of life must cause'.[39] A Royal Commission on the Housing of the Working Classes was initiated in 1884 but Salisbury's opponents rejected his ideas as state socialism which strangled 'the spirit of independence and the self-reliance of the people ... destroying the moral fibre of our race'.[40] Thus Marki's company housing, which far exceeded the provision made by Russian industrialists, conformed to a general British standard while the few high-quality British model towns were anomalies against a back drop of more basic housing stock.[41]

Company Housing and Payment in Kind

Housing was absolutely integral to the paternalists' strategy for social control as it ensured an attendant and compliant workforce. The Briggs-Posselt partnership,

---

37 Caffyn, *Workers' Housing in West Yorkshire*, p. 68, made this assertion with reference to Copley, Akroydon, West Hill Park and Saltaire.

38 Jowitt, *Model Industrial Communities*, p. 79.

39 Andrew Roberts, *Salisbury: Victorian Titan* (London: Phoenix, 2000), p. 283.

40 Ibid., p. 286.

41 Popławska and Muthesius, 'Poland's Manchester', p. 156.

like the Lever brothers at Port Sunlight, ultimately maintained discipline 'by the threat of dismissal and with that the loss (within one week) of a house rented in the village'.[42] In 1913 when a strike at Harrison Benn's New England factory led to a wage increase being agreed in his absence, the Bradford industrialist telegraphed orders 'to raise house rents in Greystone by 13 per cent',[43] which was the exact equivalent of the pay rise his workers had negotiated. But beyond basic social control there were also many pecuniary advantages for employers to provide housing. Barter, exchange and credit have been shown as fundamental for financing nineteenth-century businesses. Mutual advantage rather than cash was the preferred currency and this philosophy naturally extended to wages. Low rents constituted a form of payment in kind which favourably reduced the owners' working-capital requirements and increased worker dependency.[44] Giving 'subsidies in aid of wages'[45] was outlawed in Britain and by 1886 payment 'other than in money' was also forbidden in Russia.[46] But industrialist landlords continued to boast moderate rents as a fringe benefit and by the late nineteenth century, property rental was a popular form of diversification for many Russian-Polish industrialists. It provided a new land use and fresh revenue stream for employers who could recoup building costs through captive tenants and as such it was viewed as 'a perfect form of investment'.[47] Poznański was praised for the quality of his workers' tenements built in central Łódź in the 1890s and proudly announced an annual 2 per cent profit on them.[48]

It is worth noting that the Briggs-Posselt partnership took a surprisingly liberal attitude to the subletting of company accommodation. The sub-tenants had to be factory employees who, if they were made redundant, must vacate within seven days like the main tenant.[49] But in 1887, as Marki rents were between 50 kopeks and 1.5 rubles per week and the average woman earned just 50 kopeks a day before fines, it is evident that subletting was an economic necessity for the workers. It also served the purposes of the company who needed to accommodate a growing workforce, ideally without further investment in housing. Thus in April 1887 a total of 907 workers lived in the 150 company flats at Marki, making the average occupancy more than six people per room.[50]

---

42 Jeremy, 'The Enlightened Paternalist', p. 63.

43 Blewett, *Yankee Yorkshireman*, p. 76.

44 Sigsworth, *Black Dyke Mills*, p. 152.

45 Caffyn, *Workers' Housing in West Yorkshire*, p. 128.

46 Theodore H. von Laue, 'Factory Inspection under the "Witte System": 1892–1903', *American Slavic and East European Review*, 19: 3 (1960), p. 349.

47 Antoni Szram, 'The impact of the investor on the work of the architect taking as examples the activities of factory owners in Łódź – J.K. Poznański and K. Scheibler', *Kwartalnik Architektury i Urbanistyki*, 29 (1984), p. 281.

48 Popławska, and Muthesius, 'Poland's Manchester', p. 157.

49 APW, signature 375, pp. 017–022v.

50 APW, Ref.1, 159/1887, No. 125, Factory Inspector W. Swiatłowski to the governor of Warsaw N. Medem, 23 April/5 May, 1887, pp. 2–3.

Figure 8.2 Worker housing in Marki
Source: Author's photograph

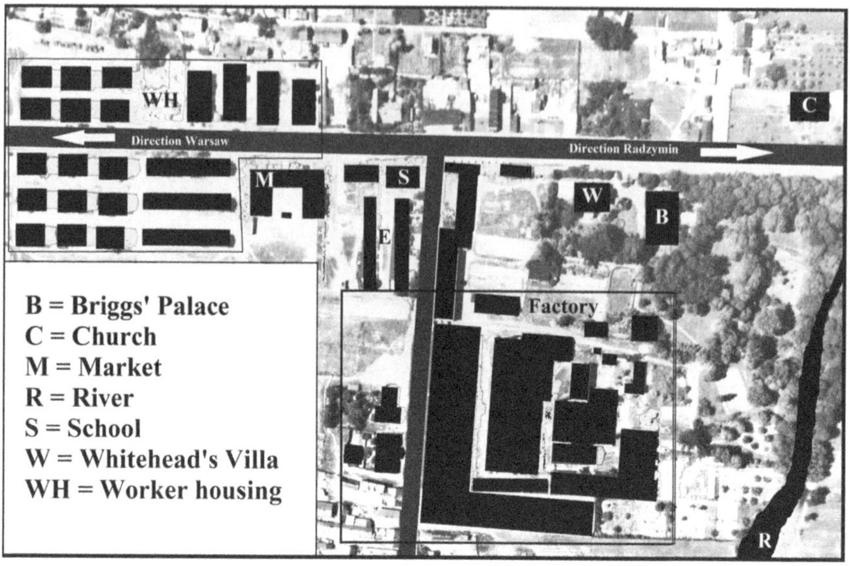

Figure 8.3 Town plan of Marki during the interwar period
Source: Diagram drawn from an aerial photo kindly provided by Urząd Miasta Marki

The isolation of many factory settlements, long working hours and poor transport facilities meant that local shops were essential and these were invariably run or sublet by the firm. The income from company stores was often of secondary importance to the owners, whose workers recycled their pay straight back into the company coffers at the end of the working week. As wages routinely fluctuated as a result of short hours or fines, workers sought credit in the shop which in turn increased their indebtedness to the firm.[51] The Briggs-Posselt partnership let both a bakery and grocery in Marki for annual rents of 1,500 rubles to serve 'clientele of the factory and surrounding area'.[52]

Each worker was provided with a small allotment so that they could supplement their earnings with home-grown food or even keep livestock. But any middle-class perception of gardening as a healthy form of recreation was entirely misplaced when factory workers had been uprooted so recently from an agrarian existence. In Russia, such land allocations were a common tactic to embed workers beside factories and pre-empt their seasonal retreats to the countryside.[53] The allotments also served as an insurance policy for employers, who in times of short work

[51] Bonnell, *Russian Worker*, p. 138.

[52] *Kurjer Warszawski*, 29 September 1884, p. 8 and *Kurjer Warszawski*, 9 December 1885, p. 9.

[53] Anna Żarnowska, 'Religion and Politics: Polish Workers c. 1900', *Social History*, 16: 3 (1991), p. 301.

might retain their skilled workforce without pay by providing this basic means of subsistence alongside low-cost housing.

Factory Legislation and the Russian Inspectorate

Rising factory legislation in England was a significant bone of contention for British manufacturers; restrictions dogged their every attempt to expand or manage their workforces autonomously. Even quite reputable employers such as the Briggs brothers found themselves at the sharp end of the law for 'not having young hands properly registered and certified'.[54] In 1863 the *Bradford Observer* reported the firm's misdemeanours and apparent disdain for the regulations: when 'Serjeant Cumberland served his summons on the defendants, someone in their employment refused insolently to give him any information ... and threatened to kick him out of the factory'.[55] By contrast the Russian 'owners or managers of mills and factories have been free to deal with their workpeople, without let or hindrance'.[56]

British manufacturers naturally bemoaned the advantage to their Russian counterparts who 'are not hampered with trade unions; nor is there any disposition on the part of the authorities to handicap the mill owners with unnecessary burdens or harassing interference'.[57] In Russia, factory regulation and workers' rights were not seriously considered until industrial unrest forced them onto the agenda in the 1880s. Thereafter the law vacillated between allowing powerful industrialists' autonomy and measures 'toward the political pacification of the workers'.[58] But although British trade journals heralded the first Russian factory laws as 'most gratifying',[59] it is evident that their implementation was flimsy and inconsistent. For example, the employment of children under the age of 12 was forbidden in 1882, but the law 'tolerated work for minors aged 10 to 12'.[60] The work day could extend to 18 hours and employers' liability for workers' illness, invalidity or death was not addressed until the twentieth century.[61]

---

54 *Leeds Mercury*, 12 May 1863, p. 3.

55 *Bradford Observer*, 14 May 1863, p. 5. The court fined the firm a total of £18, 2s, 6d.

56 'Social Legislation in Russia', *Journal of Fabrics and the Textile Industry*, 12 February 1884, p. 16.

57 *Textile World*, November 1882, p. 437.

58 Frederick C. Giffin, 'The Formative Years of the Russian Factory Inspectorate, 1882–1885', *Slavic Review*, 25: 4 (1966), p. 644.

59 'Social Legislation in Russia', p. 16.

60 Jürgen Rojahn, 'Poland', in *The Formation of Labour Movements, 1870–1914: An International Perspective*, eds Marcel Van Der Linden and Jürgen Rojahn (New York: E.J. Brill, 1990), p. 492. Kubiak and Szyburska, 'Urbanystka i architektura Żyrardowa', p. 107.

61 Rose L. Glickman, *Russian Factory Women: Workplace and Society 1880–1914* (Berkeley, Los Angeles, London: University of California Press, 1984), p. 5, Franaszek, 'Poland', p. 404.

In 1882 a Russian factory inspectorate of former doctors, teachers, engineers and lawyers was formed to monitor working conditions, but their inadequate number underlined the government's lack of real intent to enforce standards. Indeed in 1885 only 19 per cent of establishments placed under supervision were actually inspected.[62] Subsequent expansion of the office never kept pace with industrialisation and in 1899 each official was responsible for 5,000–8,000 factories.[63] Thus, inspections were cursory and usually relied on management questionnaires rather than the worker interviews that were recommended by the state. The primary task of the inspectorate was to monitor the observance of child labour laws but their mandate soon encompassed supervising the issue of labour contracts, regulating pay scales, checking fire precautions and reviewing housing, schools, baths and shops under company management. When Russian finance minister Witte came to office he made further demands for regular information on industrial development: 'on the type of fuel used, on the costs of production, on prices and market conditions'.[64] Industrialists naturally resented the interference of the inspectorate and were suspicious of its intelligence-gathering motives, but their workers equally mistrusted the agency whose role was perceived to restrict their earning potential but fell short of protecting their rights.

The late and insubstantial establishment of the Russian factory inspectorate meant that many firms had a customary mode of operation in place which they were reluctant to change in order to satisfy the state. Industrial employers rightly considered themselves invulnerable to prosecution, for although penalties for transgression of the factory laws existed in principle, they only applied if the contravention led to unrest and, for example, only 5 per cent of such offences led to prosecution in 1901.[65] Indeed Russian law invariably favoured the tax-paying factory owner who was always 'able to find a legal reason to fire a worker'.[66] Employees could be evicted from their homes and jobs if the firm was unable to procure raw materials or fuel, or for more subjective infringements such as 'bad behaviour, unexcused absence, or contagious disease'.[67] Most Russian factory laws provided exploitable loopholes: for example it was illegal for minors and women to perform night shifts, but this could be authorised under an ambiguous proviso that 'the process of manufacture cannot have a bad influence on the health'.[68] In 1897 when an engine broke down at Marki and 800 workers were threatened with

62 Giffin, 'Formative Years of the Russian Factory Inspectorate', p. 643.
63 Von Laue, 'Factory Inspection under the "Witte System"', p. 355.
64 Ibid., p. 352.
65 Ibid., p. 359.
66 Bonnell, *Russian Worker*, p. 142.
67 Von Laue, 'Factory Inspection under the "Witte System"', p. 350.
68 'Social Legislation in Russia', p. 16.

redundancy this law was suspended on the pretext that forbidding night work might lead to worker protest.[69]

It is evident that the Bradford men instituted many employment practices at Marki that were considered progressive by Russian standards and pre-empted many state laws. For example they never employed children under the age of 12 and by 1901 no one under the age of 15 worked in the factory.[70] The working day was restricted to 12½ hours except in the dye-house where 14 hours was standard and these hours significantly reduced in the twentieth century. The owners generally allowed a free day on Sunday, respected the numerous Catholic holidays and thus maintained a regular 295-day annual employment until the early twentieth century. They housed their workers, paid medical expenses and built a school long before it became a state requirement.

Employment Policy at Marki

The model workers' community and paternalistic management framework were central facets of the Briggs-Posselt partnership's strategy to create the most efficient factory and profitable business. The approach, which developed in early British industrialisation, has been shown to have adapted well to the Russian-Polish socio-economic climate, but it was hardly groundbreaking in a global context. However, the Bradford partners' social engineering went much further than the tried-and-tested model pioneered by Owen and Salt. It is evident that they intended to populate their model town, as far as possible, only with women and advertised that 'widows with children especially females from 12 years, can find beneficial and lasting occupation and housing at the spinning factory of Briggs and Posselt in Marki. Apply to Królewska 6'.[71] After 1870, 32 orphanages were founded in Russian Poland and 16 of them were in Warsaw.[72] Life expectancy was extraordinarily low, not exceeding an average 40 years at the end of the century,[73] nevertheless these institutions were populated with more abandoned children than orphans, as dire poverty rendered parents unable to support dependents. Thus it is likely that the word 'widow' in the Briggs-Posselt partnership's advert may have been a euphemism for single mothers generally.

---

[69] APW, Ref. 1A II/1897, *Starszy Inspektor Fabryczny Guberni Warszawskiej*, W. Miropolski, inspector of factories for the Warsaw area, to N. Ivanisov the senior factory inspector about new regulations at Briggs, Posselt and Co., Marki in relation to the breakdown of steam machinery, 5/17 March 1897, pp. 39–41.

[70] APW, *Starszy Inspektor Fabryczny Guberni Warszawskiej*, signature 375, report for the year 1901–02 E. Briggs Brothers and Co., Warsaw, p. 001.

[71] *Kurjer Warszawski*, 28 September 1884, p. 11.

[72] Kubiak and Szyburska, 'Urbanystka i architektura Żyrardowa', p. 108.

[73] Davies, *God's Playground*, p. 181.

The simplest explanation for the Bradford men to employ this most vulnerable social group was that women were the cheapest workers. There was already a huge income gap between Britain which had the highest pay *per capita* worldwide and Russia which had the lowest in the middle of the nineteenth century.[74] No Russian regulations existed to specify a minimum wage but in Poland women tended to earn 75 per cent, and juveniles only 20 to 30 per cent, of a man's pay.[75] This estimation is confirmed by an 1887 report for Marki which shows that minors were paid 1.5 rubles and men received 4.5 rubles per week,[76] and as has already been mentioned, female workers earned on average 50 kopeks per day before fines.[77] But the scheme did not simply reflect a desire to economise on wages; women were also considered less politically active and more controllable than male workers. Indeed the 1914 annual report of the General Union of Textile Workers in Britain blamed low levels of unionisation on the large number of female employees in the textile industry.[78] In Russia and Poland the patriarchal tradition certainly instilled a sense of subordination in women and their low social status rendered them much less likely to risk unemployment through organised protest or general misbehaviour. Nevertheless, to fully understand the rationale behind the Marki industrialists' radical employment policy, it is necessary to consider a longstanding management issue of British manufacturing industry.

The 'Skill Trap' of British Industry

From the beginning of the factory movement, the absolute control that industrialists sought to achieve maximum productivity was compromised by their reliance on skilled craftsmen from the independent artisan tradition. By virtue of their indispensability, these essential workers negotiated a measure of counter-control in which they could dictate employment terms and wages, subcontract work and direct operations generally. In other words, to secure necessary skills, 'British employers relinquished much of their authority over the production methods employed in their works'.[79] The most skilled protected their hierarchical supremacy by 'artificially restricting their numbers through apprenticeship',[80] their methods 'acquired the status of custom'[81] and attempts to challenge them

---

74 Foreman-Peck, *History of the World Economy*, p. 47.

75 Franaszek, 'Poland', p. 405.

76 APW, Ref.1, 159/1887, pp. 2–3.

77 APW, signature 375, pp. 017–022v.

78 Jowitt, 'Textiles and Society in Bradford and Lawrence', pp. 3–24.

79 Dintenfass, *Decline of Industrial Britain*, p. 28.

80 Deirdre Busfield, 'Job Definitions and Inequality: the "unskilled" women workers of the West Riding textile industry 1850 to 1914', *Textile History*, 19 (Spring 1988), p. 69.

81 Dintenfass, *Decline of Industrial Britain*, p. 29.

were strongly resisted. This state of affairs, which has latterly come to be known as the 'skill trap', was deeply entrenched by the second half of the nineteenth century.

Standard functions within the factory had a designated grade which determined not just the pay but also the status and sex of the operative. The convenient social ideal of the male breadwinner endured from preindustrial times and permeated the definition of factory roles to undermine the validity of certain skills. It was accepted wisdom that men took on more physically demanding occupations whereas women earned pin money with lighter work, with the consequence that traditional male roles had a higher status and pay. In reality women were employed in equally arduous work such as wool scouring, or highly skilled work such as burling and mending,[82] but the difficulty of these processes went unrecognised. At the same time, activities such as wool combing or hand weaving, which before mechanisation had been physically demanding, highly paid and male-dominated, continued as such after mechanisation, even though the strength or skill requirement had become negligible.

As the economic pressures on manufacturers increased in the latter nineteenth century, the character of industry changed; with larger investments in more complex plants, the optimal flow of production rather than individual skills became central to profitability. Flexibility became vital but whereas greater economy might be achieved if an employer could hire and fire at will, or move workers between departments depending on demand, the legacy of the skill trap was workers' inflexible adherence to 'exclusive practices'.[83] Thus temporarily idle staff had to be paid but refused to pick up the slack in an overworked section, while overtime rates were laid out to another department. Michael Dintenfass succinctly describes the industrialists' dilemma: 'to acquiesce to this state of affairs was to consign the firm to suboptimal efficiency. To resist it was to court industrial unrest'.[84] This institutionalised lack of compliance came to characterise British employer-employee relations and the only solution to circumvent its costly confines was to employ more women; not centrally because women were cheaper or because the allotted tasks now required less skill, but to thwart the existing male-dominated organisational restrictions and provide the necessary fluidity to factory operations. Thus in the late nineteenth century, Bradford's mill owners endeavoured to increase the ratio of women to men in their employ which by 1880 exceeded 2:1 in worsted manufacture.[85]

The Marki venture provided the Briggs-Posselt partnership with an opportunity to impose the most advantageous employment policy and management framework on a largely peasant, ideally female, workforce. Hand-in-hand with the most technologically advanced machinery, they engineered the cheapest and most

---

[82] Burling and mending is an operation which removes yarn defects or impurities and fixes weaving faults by hand sewing.

[83] Busfield, 'Job Definitions and Inequality', p. 65.

[84] Dintenfass, *Decline of Industrial Britain*, p. 29.

[85] Chadwick, *Church and People in Bradford and District*, p. 27.

flexible employee profile possible. The proportion of female workers at Marki consistently exceeded 70 per cent compared with a Kingdom-of-Poland average of 40 per cent of industrial workers at the end of the nineteenth century.[86] Apart from the aforementioned incident when the breakdown of one engine in 1897 threatened to make half the workforce redundant for 8 weeks, the firm appears to have maintained full employment until the twentieth century. The majority of departments worked for 12½ hours from 5.30 am to 7.30 pm with a 30-minute break for breakfast and 45 minutes for lunch. In the scouring and carding departments work continued until 9 pm.[87] In 1898 the hours reduced to 11½ and by 1908 the firm's standard regime comprised a 10-hour day from 6 am to 6.12 pm including a half-hour breakfast and a generous 1½ hours for lunch.[88] These adjustments may reflect state directives or prudence in a period of economic depression. However, the Marki entrepreneurs' success at thwarting the British skill trap seems evident in twentieth-century factory-inspectors' reports which show, in periods of short or fluctuating orders, the firm was able to curtail or extend the working day department by department to their best advantage. In August 1907 they reduced production generally to a four-day week 'due to lack of orders'.[89] In 1909 they were once again operating a 60-hour week but in August work in the spinning department was increased to a two-shift system which maintained full production from 4 am until 10 pm daily.[90] In October the dyers were put on short time and a similar pattern is reflected in all the available data leading up to the First World War. But despite the central importance of women workers to the success of the Bradford partners' foreign enterprise, the socially acceptable myth that Marki was 'a successful experiment in housing workmen in healthy surroundings' persisted.[91] In the interwar period, the author Coningsby Dawson visited the town and described a romanticised vision of the settlement laid waste by war, where 'three thousand willing workers are idle, and all the women and children who are dependent on them starve';[92] even though the majority of Marki's workforce were actually those women.

---

[86] Żarnowska, 'Working Family in the Kingdom of Poland', p. 64.

[87] APW, Ref.1, 159/1887, pp. 2–3.

[88] APW, *Starszy Inspektor Fabryczny Guberni Warszawskiej*, signature 375, p. 008v, although the finish time of 6.12 pm looks incongruous, it is likely to have ensured that a worker did not leave their workstation early in order to 'clock off' from the time office at the main gate at 6 pm.

[89] APW, signature 375, announcement by W. Zawiszewski of E. Briggs Brothers and Co., approved by Factory Inspector Goncharov, 27 August 1907, p. 005.

[90] Ibid., 17/30 August 1909, p. 014v.

[91] Dawson, *It Might Have Happened To You*, p. 111.

[92] Ibid., p. 115.

Instilling Factory Discipline

The chapter has considered the Bradford partners' general strategy to select the most favourable workforce and the instrumentality of housing to instil a sense of obligation in their employees, but inside the factory a carefully designed code of practice was instituted to maintain order and maximise productivity. Just as early British manufacturers had transformed rural labourers into tools of industry, the Briggs-Posselt partnership had to force a fundamental adjustment in lifestyle on their Polish workforce. Former peasants were required to conform to the dictates of the clock, not the season or the weather, and undertake unvarying repetitive tasks with efficiency for six days every week. It is arguable that the main reason that the Polish children were sent to England in 1883 was to familiarise a core of young workers with factory discipline, that they might set an example to the rest of the workforce. The fact that the Bradford men had to provide these young employees with decent clothes and shoes for the journey well-illustrates the extreme poverty of their target workforce.[93]

When new recruits joined the Marki factory, they received a rule book which laid out the terms of their employment, hours, pay and particularly their obligations to the firm. The start and finish of the working day was signalled by a steam whistle. Since the advent of the factory system manufacturers had progressively developed a method to ensure the devoted attention of their workforce. They paid their employees for piece work, that is, not by the hour but by output. Incomes were generally maintained at a level sufficient to cover basic necessities, thus a fine system discouraged misbehaviour or lack of productivity. Penalties were incurred for lateness, absence, untidiness, disobeying the foreman's orders, for being in a department where they did not work, or lingering in the toilet or yard. Levies were naturally applied for poor workmanship such as 'damage to the ring if the wrong amount of fibre is introduced' or 'hand spooling yarn'.[94] The system facilitated the abuse of particularly female employees who were at the mercy of foremen who apportioned work and time-office managers who logged attendance. If equipment faltered they were reliant on skilled mechanics to fix their machines quickly so that they could maintain their earnings.[95] The eagerness to avoid inactivity is reflected in the company rules which heavily emphasised that workers must not attempt to repair their own machines, or replace belts on the belt drive by hand, remove guards or clean machines when they were running.

Although conditions at Marki were undoubtedly well above contemporary standards –well-lit, adequately heated, fire-safe and not overcrowded – the brutal workplace culture, typical of most Russian and British factories, was prevalent. In 1892 the Polish press described a terrible incident at Marki in which a female

93 Wartalska, 'Fabryka i osada fabryczna', p. 651.
94 APW, signature 375, 3 February 1910, pp. 017–022v.
95 Glickman, *Russian Factory Women*, p. 205.

worker was found to have disposed of a baby in the mill's toilets.[96] This could just be a sad anomaly, but it might equally reflect a company culture in which women had no chance to retain employment and housing while caring for infants, under their employers' relentless determination to maintain a local demographic which best served the needs of the firm.

In 1887 factory inspector Swiatłowski reported that 'almost all workers interviewed by me indicated that the English foremen resort to fist violence'.[97] The unwillingness of the owners to remove the two worst offenders until their contracts had ended suggests that corporal punishment was considered necessary to maintain order. The effectiveness of the Briggs-Posselt partnership's methods is nevertheless suggested by an 1893 log of workers' grievances which showed, of 29 complaints made against foremen and time keepers for beatings, bribery, verbal abuse and the refusal of work or medical assistance, only 10 were made by women.[98] The figure seems disproportionately low considering the 70-per-cent-female workforce but the fact that only two women received compensation compared with the damages paid to 16 of the 19 male complainants suggests both the higher status of male workers and the perception that discontented men were more likely to cause trouble.

The realities of life in the model community of Marki were evidently far removed from the public image used to promote the enterprise. But the regime was arguably accepted by a workforce, mindful of the very great personal benefits they derived from towing the company line. Thus the glowing press reports which highlighted the generous philanthropy of the Bradford men at Marki stand at odds with the somewhat ambivalent conclusion of the factory inspector who reported in 1887:

> Altogether the attitude of the factory owners to the workers cannot be called criminal [but] does leave one with a negative impression and it can also be said that the relationship is not based on the feelings of humanity and justice on the one side and … trust and respect on the other side.[99]

Education and Positive Public-Relations Propaganda

The school was a central pillar of every model community and in Marki it was built in a typical Yorkshire style, with a clock tower that could be seen throughout the town. It was a prime example of window dressing for the British entrepreneurs which they often promoted to differentiate themselves from their competitors, even in a commercial context. For example the 1888 Warsaw Weaving Exhibition

[96] *Gazeta Warszawska*, No. 34, 1892, p. 3.
[97] APW, Ref.1, 159/1887, pp. 2–3.
[98] APW, Ref.IV, 4/1893, pp. 162–5.
[99] APW, Ref.1, 159/1887, pp. 2–3.

Figure 8.4 Marki school
Source: Author's photograph

catalogue announced that 'the large factory of Briggs, Posselt and Co., at Marki near Warsaw employing over 1000 workers is showing off wool and yarns. Next to this factory there are houses for workers and schools for girls and boys'.[100] At Port Sunlight the factory owner's regular visits to the school were intended to instil his benevolent image in the minds of the town's youngsters, who would eventually take their place in the ranks of company workers.[101] But at Marki there is a strong suggestion that the patrons' visits were primarily intended to create a favourable impression on local society. Each year the Warsaw press and other guests were invited to enjoy recitals by the Marki schoolchildren. The event provided the industrialists with an opportunity to advertise the significant improvements they intended to make to the school and show off its 'very desirable garden'.[102] But despite the symbolic importance of the institution and the public-relations capital

[100] 'Wystawa tkacka' ['Weaving exhibition'], *Gazeta Warszawska*, 4 February, 1888, p. 2.

[101] Jeremy, 'The Enlightened Paternalist', p. 74.

[102] 'Szkółka w Markach' ['Village school in Marki'], *Gazeta Warszawska*, No. 164, 1890, p. 2.

it generated, it is evident that few children actually received an education in Marki's school.

In the late nineteenth century only 20 per cent of children aged seven to 14 attended school in the Kingdom of Poland. By the First World War the figure was still only 25 per cent and a third of Warsaw's children were educated in illegal Polish schools.[103] The insufficiency of schools was symptom of both the unwillingness of the Tsarist state to make social investment and Warsaw's soaring urban population. Nevertheless, the fact that very few working-class children received an education rested more on the families' pressing need for their income and a perception that education did not improve employment prospects when Russian migrant workers occupied the best-paid clerical jobs in Poland. In 1885 the Russian finance minister Bunge sought to address the situation, arguably to preclude the illegal Polish-nationalist education many children received. But instead of allocating state funds, he urged private industrial enterprises to build schools.[104] The effective bartering of Polish children's education in return for commercial opportunities inevitably led to a flawed implementation, as schooling work-age children stood in direct opposition to the industrialists' financial interests.

The Marki school was established long before the Russian state's insistence, but the Briggs-Posselt partnership only agreed to educate children that worked in the mill, if their work schedule permitted; thus in 1887 only 30 of 82 eligible young workers actually attended school.[105] The industrialists were under no legal obligation to teach younger children but as the Bradford men had made every effort to populate the town only with those of working age, the issue was not under discussion. Despite the law's stipulation that minors should work no more than four hours without a break, the state's collusion with the cash-rich foreign investors is evident as the factory inspector reported: 'on the whole minors work in two shifts, one before lunch, the other after. Each shift lasts six hours in a row, which is allowed at Briggs' and Posselt's factory by a special decree of the finance minister'.[106]

Although school attendance at Marki was appalling, it was significantly higher than in the majority of Russian-empire factories which provided less than 10 per cent of children with an elementary education in 1885.[107] By the 1890s the government's interest in welfare provision was in greater evidence but proof of company expenditure, rather than effective execution of education and healthcare, satisfied the state's bureaucratic demands. Thus it was reported in 1897 that 96 boys and 85 girls were educated at Marki at a cost of 2,030 rubles and a 20-bed

---

[103] Żarnowska, *Workers, Women and Social Change*, p. 142 and Anna Żarnowska, 'Education of Working Class Women in the Polish Kingdom', *Acta Poloniae Historica*, 74 (1996), p. 143.

[104] Giffin, 'Formative Years of the Russian Factory Inspectorate', p. 646.

[105] APW, Ref.1, 159/1887, pp. 2–3.

[106] Ibid.

[107] Giffin, 'Formative Years of the Russian Factory Inspectorate', p. 649.

hospital with a doctor and medical attendant came to 5,600 rubles annually. By that time the firm's provision also included a day-care nursery for children up to the age of seven and a concert hall which were both described as philanthropy.[108]

Healthcare, Insurance and Employers' Liability

Free healthcare was integral to the paternalists' program for workforce control in the nineteenth century. So-called sick funds were generally financed through a percentage deduction from wages and supplemented by fines.[109] Although they were presented as a form of insurance, as Russian law legitimised fining workers for absence when sick and even dismissal for serious or infectious illnesses, the fund was often a thinly veiled tactic to reduce earnings. In cases of extreme injury, the fund could be redistributed without additional expense to the employer and most firms withheld compensation if an accident was deemed to result from carelessness. The Marki sick fund was instituted in 1883 and despite being a legal requirement in Russia after 1866 it was still described as a form of philanthropy on factory inspectors' reports at the end of the century.[110] In 1887 the firm deducted 3 per cent from wages to finance the fund but Swiatłowski highlighted 'the illegal character of these extortions'[111] as they were used to pay a doctor's salary.

By the 1890s the firm had reduced the worker contribution to a 'voluntary two per cent of wages'.[112] Sick workers received a quarter of their average pay and there was a small hospital with a company doctor at Marki. The firm would meet the cost of medicine and funerals for both workers and their families.[113] By 1910 there had been a dramatic improvement in welfare provision as, in addition to the doctor, the firm employed a medical assistant and midwife and would pay for any specialist care required by workers in one of Warsaw's hospitals. As claims for pre-existing injuries were commonplace, new employees underwent a medical examination and accidents had to be reported to the factory manager immediately. The doctor had a daily surgery at the factory but he would visit very ill workers at home, in which case employees were reminded that 'the patient and others in attendance should behave decently'.[114]

In addition to the worker-financed sick fund and the company medical team, the Briggs-Posselt partnership paid an annual premium to the St Petersburg

---

108 APW, signature 375, p. 004.

109 Franszek, 'Poland', p. 405.

110 APW, signature 375, annual report for E. Briggs Brothers and Co., 1898 to 1899, p. 003.

111 APW, Ref.1, 159/1887, pp. 2–3.

112 APW, signature 375, p. 004.

113 Ibid.

114 APW, signature 375, pp. 017–022v.

Insurance Society of 3,225 rubles to compensate employees for serious injuries.[115] By the 1880s, British employers' liability for worker injuries was increasingly under discussion. In cases of litigation the Manchester *Textile Recorder* reported:

> In determining in any case the amount of compensation payable ... the court shall take into consideration the value of any payment of contribution made by such employer to or for the injured person in respect of his injury, and also the value of any payment or contribution made by such employer to any insurance fund or compensation fund.[116]

In this era workplace accidents which did not result in death were all too common. For example, in 1890 the *Gazeta Warszawska* recorded that a 15-year-old worker at the Marki factory, 'Karolina Piszczalska, crushed her hand while feeding yarn under the rollers'.[117] A catalogue of bone fractures and hand mutilations sustained at Briggs, Posselt and Co. during 1893 reveals three fractures, usually to the operatives' collarbones, were caused by blows from machine belts and there were five cases of severed or crushed hands from combing or carding equipment in that one year.[118] The Briggs-Posselt partnership's insurance policy paid two-thirds of an employee's wages for short- or long-term incapacity and six times their salary for full invalidity caused by a workplace accident. Three times their salary would be paid to a worker's family in case of death. An 1888 press report provides some insight into the implementation of the firm's medical care and insurance:

> As a result of his own carelessness Stanisław Lasocki who worked in the spinning factory of Brucks and Poselt [sic: Briggs and Posselt] in Marki, fell under the driver wheel and his hand was broken, his spine and chest damaged. Lasocki was taken to the hospital at Praga but died there within a few hours. As the company insures the lives of their workers, the family of the deceased will receive more than 1,000 rubles.[119]

Loyalty Schemes and Sobriety Incentives

Another facet of the industrialists' 'managerial armoury'[120] was a range of loyalty or incentive programs which were based largely on the hierarchical importance of the employee. Industrialists claimed some complex motivations for instituting

---

115 Ibid., p. 004.

116 'Employer's Liability Act (1880) Amendment', *Textile Recorder*, Manchester, May 1883, p. 3.

117 *Gazeta Warszawska*, 1890, No. 1, p. 2.

118 APW, Ref. IV, 4/1893, pp. 162–5.

119 *Gazeta Warszawska*, No. 325, 1888, p. 2.

120 Jeremy, 'The Enlightened Paternalist', p. 58.

these schemes but their general purpose was to control behaviour or tie senior staff to the firm. Edward Akroyd, a key figure in the development of the Yorkshire Penny Bank Movement, argued that 'high wages often tempted a man to undue social indulgences'[121] and many British firms tried to encourage 'habits of thrift, prudence and sobriety'[122] in their workers in this period. Titus Salt was well known for the temperance policies he imposed at Saltaire, whereas at Marki, although alcohol was naturally forbidden at work, the rules were more relaxed. In Russian industry, drunkenness and Monday absenteeism were common problems among men but rare in women, thus savings funds were more usually introduced to withhold excessive cash from the foremen and skilled machinists on whose attendance the company relied, rather than to reward their compliant female employees.[123]

Hielle and Dietrich prided themselves on the accounts they offered to their 'best workers' with a deposit of 50 rubles on which the company paid 6 per cent interest annually.[124] Nevertheless, general mistrust of employers led very few eligible staff to join the scheme. The terms and conditions of a similar incentive program at Marki perhaps reveal the true character of the perk. Briggs and Posselt reserved the right to withhold employees' savings for two months if they did not give a proper term of resignation, or entirely if their removal from the company was the result of 'improper behaviour or a crime such as theft, fighting etc.'.[125] For top-level management and skilled technicians these loyalty schemes were the first step towards more sophisticated rewards such as profit sharing, share-holding and directorships which gradually transformed the ownership structure of many industrial firms in the twentieth century. At both Briggella Mills in Bradford and at Bradford Mills in Marki the firms remained essentially family-owned, but by the early twentieth century some non-family members were rewarded with a place on the board of directors.

Religious Instrumentality and the Russian State

Marki mirrored the model-community formula established in Britain in almost every respect except for the use of 'religious instrumentalities' for community control.[126] A church or chapel was considered the social cement that united British factory towns and their provision was considered a traditional role for

121 E. Akroyd, *The Yorkshire Penny Bank* (Leeds: Longmans, Green, 1872), p. 22.

122 Samuel Smiles, *Thrift* (New York: Harper & Bros, 1875), p. 179.

123 Bonnell, *Russian Worker*, p. 148.

124 APW, Ref. IV, 9/1893, K. Bekman on the board of the Joint Stock Company Manufacturers of Żyrardów Hielle and Dietrich to the inspector of factories P. Koszłakow, 6/18 March 1893, pp. 41–2.

125 APW, Ref. IV, 9/1893, Izdebski at Briggs and Posselt Co. to the inspector of factories P. Koszłakow, 5/17 March 1893, pp. 38–9.

126 Jeremy, 'The Enlightened Paternalist', p. 77.

the paternalist whether he was a local land owner or an industrial entrepreneur. Model industrial communities were meant to emulate 'the old English notion of the village'[127] where the 'squire and parson between them shared oversight of the parish'.[128] In many cases the professed religious conviction of industrialists was little more than a socially acceptable tactic to justify their regimes for social control. Indeed Patrick Joyce concludes that 'organised religion was in the main a principal support of employer hegemony'.[129] At Port Sunlight it has been suggested that Lever 'resorted to religious and pseudo-religious devices to buttress his ambitious experiment in community-based entrepreneurship'.[130] But despite the extraordinary religious devotion of the Poles, the complex and volatile socio-political climate in Russian Poland made this particular device difficult to implement at Marki.

Under the Tsarist program of Russification, mass gatherings and expressions of Polish culture were banned. As the Catholic Church was perceived to promote Polish traditions and language its activities were aggressively curtailed.[131] The same reasons that Western paternalists constructed churches – to influence the behaviour of their employees positively and provide a 'centre of a whole range of social, educational and cultural activities'[132] – led the Russian government to prevent their greater proliferation in Poland. Although it is arguable that national subjugation and state support of capitalist employers rendered this particular social-overhead unnecessary at Marki, when state restrictions were relaxed after industrial unrest in the 1890s, the Briggs-Posselt partnership quickly applied for planning permission for a church.

By the early twentieth century the religious aspect of industrial employers' strategies had become less successful in Britain. Increased education and political articulacy in the working classes, combined with revolutionary ideas such as Darwinism or Socialism, undermined the authority of the church and workplace paternalism in equal measure. Lever's attempts to impose 'his liturgical preferences on the new congregation' at Port Sunlight proved ineffective.[133] But in Marki the addition of the church harmonised with the socio-political views of the inhabitants and the denominational difference between the Briggs brothers and their employees only heightened the workers' sense of obligation towards their employers. Lobbying for planning permission to build the church was perceived as a gesture of great respect to their workforce which favourably contrasted the British entrepreneurs with the oppressive Tsarist state which had attempted

127 Jowitt, *Model Industrial Communities*, p. 80.

128 Chadwick, *Church and People in Bradford and District*, p. 237.

129 Patrick Joyce, *Work, Society, Politics; the Culture of the Factory in Later Victorian England* (New Brunswick, New Jersey: Rutgers University Press, 1980), p. 178.

130 Jeremy, 'The Enlightened Paternalist', p. 59.

131 Żarnowska, 'Religion and Politics', p. 303.

132 Jowitt, *Model Industrial Communities*, p. 111.

133 Jeremy, 'The Enlightened Paternalist', p. 69.

to coerce them into Russian Orthodoxy for generations. It was a prime public-relations coup and following lengthy prevarication by the authorities, planning permission for the St Izydor church at Marki was granted in 1899. Without bearing the whole cost of construction, the Briggs brothers made symbolic donations such as the oak doors and church bells and, like Lever and his wife at Port Sunlight, John and Flora Briggs laid the foundation stone.[134]

In conclusion, this chapter has shown that a paternalistic-management framework and highly selective employment policy were as crucial to the Bradford partners' success at Marki as modern-machine technology. The enterprise was promoted as the epitome of foreign philanthropy and based on a proscribed formula for model industrial communities which had become largely outdated in the contemporary British context. Conversely, the socio-economic environment of Russian Poland made this form of investment appropriate and dictated the quality of the firm's social-overhead provision. It is worth mentioning here that in 1875 Edward Briggs attended the Bradford Albion Cricket Club annual dinner where the chairman, J.H. Mitchell, toasted the club's success and alluded to 'the opportunities now presented to the working classes, by shorter hours of labour, for recreative purposes as compared with the time when he was a youth, at which time he had to commence work soon after five a.m., and keep on until half-past seven o'clock in the evening'.[135] Whereas many examples of British best practice were instituted by the Marki firm which never employed children, housed and provided medical assistance to workers, it is also evident that the working hours instigated had been long outlawed in England and other facets of the investment program, most notably the school, constituted little more than window dressing to promote the British paternalists' reputation locally.[136]

Although the Marki work environment was undoubtedly harsh, the Bradford men were considered good employers: they laid out their terms clearly, made every effort to ensure safety and compensated for industrial accidents. Whether under state pressure, or by their own volition, a continual improvement to their employment practices and welfare provision is in evidence in the factory inspectors' reports and the Polish press. The methods of the Briggs-Posselt partnership were closely monitored by the Russian government and certainly influenced many contemporary Russian-Polish employers locally, as a recipe for political as well as economic success. However, it is important to note that the Marki community did not reflect a microcosm of general society, but a carefully engineered sample, selected for compliance.

---

[134] Wartalska, 'Fabryka i osada fabryczna', p. 666, shows that the Briggs brothers paid 15,000 rubles towards the construction of the church.

[135] 'Cricket', *Bradford Observer*, 16 November 1875, p. 4.

[136] Jeremy, 'The Enlightened Paternalist', p. 58.

Chapter 9
'English foremen, English machinery and English business methods':[1] International technology transfer and the Yorkshire community of Marki

International trade has always been deeply rooted in British culture, but the rapid technological development of the Industrial Revolution created a new class of economic migrant. Distinct from the merchants and colonialists who traded internationally for the profit of British-based businesses, an increasing group of practically trained independent working men sought their fortunes abroad. This chapter will examine the roots of this trade in skill, its gradual development from espionage into legitimacy and its role in the worldwide diffusion of industrial technology. It is evident that the strict adherence of this émigré group to their national cultural traditions contrasted strongly with the assimilation tactics of their cosmopolitan employers. The reasons for this characteristic behaviour and its socio-political implication in Russian Poland will be considered. By the early twentieth century, despite almost universal dissemination of technology, high-quality foreign education and an increasingly cost-conscious commercial climate, this chapter will offer some explanations for enduring British domination of key technical and managerial roles in industries worldwide.

Early International Technology Transfer

By the late eighteenth century, foreign engineers, posing as tourists or academics, flocked to England's industrial cities to glean scientific data for their developing national industries and British manufacturers bemoaned a patent system which failed to protect their valuable ideas.[2] Britain's ambitious industrial competitors sought not simply new machine technology, but the results of time-consuming experiments in manufacturing processes which facilitated price competitiveness in mass production. They needed methods to prepare large quantities of raw wool and techniques to smelt iron with coke instead of charcoal which was prohibitively

---

1 'Edward Briggs Obituary', *Yorkshire Weekly Post*, 12 March 1898.

2 Eric H. Robinson, 'The Early Diffusion of Steam Power', *Journal of Economic History*, 34: 1, (1974), p. 91.

expensive for factory-scale production in order to compete effectively.[3] But although a proliferation of scientific journals satisfied the growing international hunger for the specifications of British industrial innovations, the empirical nature of technology made it hard to transfer by written description.[4] Thus it proved possible to emulate British machinery abroad perfectly, but variations in construction materials, the quality of fuel used or failure to make other adjustments appropriate to local conditions led foreign industrial experiments to fail consistently.[5] It was quickly ascertained that British skill and experience, rather than detailed plans, were the key to success and, consequently, practically trained British labour was increasingly lured abroad.

In the first two decades of the eighteenth century the French government pursued British industrial expertise keenly, but the King of Sweden and Catherine the Great also proffered special privileges to attract the necessary skills to their infant industries in this period.[6] In 1719 the British state's concerns particularly for the loss of iron founders and watchmakers led to legislation against acts of enticement and allowed for the prosecution of the mercenary artisans when they returned to England. However, when groundbreaking developments in textile manufacture became the chief objective of foreign industry, successive British governments sought to outlaw the export of skilled men, tools and machinery entirely.[7] But rather than preventing the further diffusion of British industrial developments, this reactive legislation instigated a steady flow of human capital abroad. As English engineering firms were prevented from exploiting the growing export market for machinery and tools, with which they would have supplied expert fitters for short-term work, foreign machine manufacturers flourished to fill the void and employed British engineers permanently. Numerous entrepreneurs and skilled workers were encouraged to abandon the increasingly competitive domestic trade to profit in less-saturated continental markets. By 1824 this brain drain was of sufficient concern for the British government to appoint a select committee to determine the effectiveness of the existing export bans on men and

---

3 A. Gerschenkron, *Economic Backwardness in Historical Perspective* (Cambridge, MA: Harvard University Press, 1962), p. 15.

4 David Jeremy, 'The International Diffusion of Cotton Manufacturing Technology, 1750–1990s', in *The Fibre that Changed the World: The Cotton Industry in International Perspective, 1600–1990s*, eds Douglas Farnie and David Jeremy (Oxford, New York: Oxford University Press, 2004), p. 93.

5 Stuart Thompstone, 'The Russian Technical Society and British Machinery Imports', in *The Fibre that Changed the World: The Cotton Industry in International Perspective, 1600–1990s*, eds Douglas Farnie and David Jeremy (Oxford, New York: Oxford University Press, 2004), pp. 350–54.

6 John Harris, *Industrial Espionage and Technology Transfer: Britain and France in the Eighteenth Century* (Aldershot: Ashgate, 1998), Gavin Weightman, *The Industrial Revolutionaries: creators of the Modern World 1776–1914* (London: Atlantic Books, 2007), pp. 10–21 and pp. 31–3.

7 Weightman, *Industrial Revolutionaries*, p. 11.

machines.[8] Its findings were an already well-developed global field of industrial exploitation, heavily populated with both émigré British industrialists and skilled working men.

The 1824 report highlighted the failure of the existing embargo with numerous rags-to-riches stories of bold men undeterred by the law. For example, Charles Albert, a Strasbourg industrialist, was jailed at Lancaster for five years in 1792 for attempting to entice British labour. He returned to France to establish a successful spinning mill, run by expatriate-English artisans and was awarded a gold medal for his products at the 1806 Paris Industrial Exhibition.[9] Mr Manby, the English manager of one of the largest French iron factories, was also prosecuted for the 'seduction of English artizans abroad' but continued to work in Paris undeterred, with numerous Englishmen in his employ.[10] In 1839 the American *Journal of the Franklin Institute* described the huge factory of John Cockerill at Seraing in Belgium which employed a workforce of 3,000 under the supervision of seven English engineers: 'combining English skill with the advantages of cheap labour'.[11] This article drew particular attention to the humble beginnings of the flourishing enterprise which had been established by Cockerill's father 'a common blacksmith, [who] could neither read nor write, I believe, till the day of his death'.[12] Similarly Mr Dixon from Manchester was reported to have had 'no money when he came to France',[13] nevertheless, he established a thriving machine factory in the Alsace. 'Peter Kennedy, late of Manchester',[14] in partnership with the Swiss industrialist Hans Escher, ran several paper mills, weaving and spinning factories in Switzerland, Piedmont, Savoy, the Tyrol and Wirtemberg. Meanwhile Escher's son Albert trained as an engineer with Fairbairn and Lillie of Manchester.[15] The very concerns voiced by the government committee and press reports served to publicise broadly that daring men, without wealth or education, could achieve financial and social preferment abroad.

In the eighteenth century, enterprising intermediaries such as John Holker, who was credited with disseminating British textile technology to France under the sponsorship of the French Bureau of Commerce, were branded as spies, thieves and traitors. In 1785 Holker's offences were described as having 'entailed more ruin and mischief on this kingdom [England] than perhaps even the loss of

[8] *HC Report from Committees*, Vol. V, 'Artizans and Machinery', 3 February to 25 June 1824.

[9] Weightman, *Industrial Revolutionaries*, p. 16.

[10] 'Artizans and Machinery', p. 8.

[11] Thomas P. Jones, *Journal of the Franklin Institute of the State of Pennsylvania and Mechanic's Register* (Philadelphia: Franklin Institute, 1839), p. 257.

[12] Jones, *Journal of the Franklin Institute*, p. 257.

[13] 'Artizans and Machinery', p. 101.

[14] Jones, *Journal of the Franklin Institute*, p. 259.

[15] Jeremy, 'International Diffusion of Cotton Manufacturing Technology', p. 99.

America'.[16] But following the 1824 report the law was revised and some notable merchants broadened the scope of their dealership to encompass both men and machinery. Most notably for this case study, Ludwig Knoop, dubbed the 'father of the Russian cotton industry',[17] founded his own vast cotton manufacturing dynasty in Russia with the profits of his dealership in Lancashire textile machinery as well as 'English managers, technicians and supervisory staff'.[18]

By the nineteenth century, in addition to the wave of artisans and industrialists who sought their fortunes abroad, British engineers dominated the market for foreign-government tenders.[19] Thus they furnished nations abroad with the vital infrastructure to enable their industrial development and resource exploitation. For example, in 1839 two Edinburgh men played a vital role in Poland's first steps towards industrialisation: Mr Blackie was 'employed by the government to build Polish canals and public roads', while Mr Pritchard was 'engineer to the government zinc mines'.[20] Despite a comprehensive survey of German and Russian talents, much to the disgruntlement of the Warsaw's city engineer Orotowski, the British Lindley family were employed by General Starynkiewicz to construct the city's celebrated water works and sewage system in 1881.[21] This prolific engineering family designed similar systems for Hamburg, Frankfurt, Düsseldorf, Budapest, Moscow and St Petersburg.[22]

The enduring cachet of British industrial and commercial skill meant that the traffic in businessmen was by no means one way and the curriculum vitae of most well-known Russian businessmen included periods in England or Germany. Men seeking experience in trade might spend time in Liverpool or Hamburg and the sons of influential industrialists were sent to London, Dresden or Berlin for apprenticeships in banking, or to Switzerland as the growing centre of expertise in dyeing. In this way, the skill base of family firms was diversified, relatives could be deployed in related areas of commerce and contact networks were expanded to capitalise on increasing international opportunities.

By the time of the Marki venture the British press routinely advertised posts as far afield as Japan, Africa, India and Australia. The early government attempts to curb the outflow of technical expertise had given way to a general acceptance. Press reports even betrayed a note of national pride when describing, for example,

---

16 Weightman, *Industrial Revolutionaries*, p. 17.

17 Luigi Villari, *Russia Under the Great Shadow* (London: T. Fisher Unwin, 1905), p. 215.

18 Thompstone, 'Russian Technical Society', p. 348.

19 Weightman, *Industrial Revolutionaries*, p. 44.

20 Jones, *Journal of the Franklin Institute*, p. 260.

21 Feliks Kucharzewski, 'Wodociąg i kanalizacya w Warszawie' ['Waterworks and sewerage system in Warsaw'], *Przegląd Techniczny*, Warsaw, 1879, p. 102.

22 Robin de la Motte, *D44: Water Time Case Study – Warsaw, Poland: Research Project supported by the European Commission* (London: University of Greenwich, 2005), p. 4.

a Russian-owned mill at Narva where 'the manager is an Englishman, and has four English assistant managers, four English carders, four English spinning masters, one English mechanic, one gas master, two Swiss over the turbines and strapping, and two English weaving masters'.[23] In international partnerships the supply of British skilled staff constituted a tangible asset, equal to the investment capital or local commercial intelligence provided by a foreign cohort. Thus a proposal conveyed by Consul Maude to the potential London-based partner of a Warsaw industrialist described: 'he is prepared with £10,000 which he thinks will suffice for the greater part of the undertaking, and the gentleman who joins him would have to furnish the remainder, and bring over with him enough English workmen to start the affair'.[24] Despite a popular perception that Russian industry was cash poor, it is interesting to note that, in this case at least, the Polish investor had both capital and local intelligence but sought international partnership as a way to acquire skills and innovation.

Human Capital in Foreign Direct Investment

Human capital was naturally a key component to ensure the success of foreign direct investment. Although there was no financial interdependence between the Briggs-Posselt partnership's British and Polish interests – they were separate companies with distinct strategies tailored to the local commercial environments – the provision of experienced managers was a fundamental way in which the parent did support the satellite enterprise. Indeed Jones suggests it was the 'managerial and technical competences [developed] at home before investing abroad which enabled them to sustain their investments'.[25] In a well-supplied British labour market, particularly during a persistent economic downturn, opportunities for promotion were limited. But rather than losing ambitious young managers to other Bradford factories, suitably qualified men could be redeployed to Marki where relevant experience was in short supply. Although it has been emphasised that foreign factories were generally equipped with machinery appropriate to a lack of operative skills, its effectiveness still relied on practiced engineers and tuners. At the same time the vast first-generation industrial workforces of the Russia empire needed expert supervision to ensure maximum productivity and order.

Throughout the duration of the Marki venture, men from the same families were employed both in Bradford and Poland for short-term experience and long-term, lucrative postings. This mutually advantageous arrangement offered greater career prospects to ambitious employees and secured the loyalty of family groups

23 'Foreign and Colonial: from our own correspondent, Moscow, 14 January 1884', *Textile Recorder*, Manchester, 15 February 1884, p. 233.

24 FO393/16, Maude to Robert J. Johnstone, Leadenhall Street, London, 20 September 1882, p. 74.

25 Jones, *Merchants to Multinationals*, p. 9.

to the Briggs' extended interests. But it is also evident that the shared language and cultural understanding between the owners and their senior staff played a significant role in the firm's business strategy. The founders intended to create an elite British, even Yorkshire enclave around their foreign factory and use the cultural distinctiveness of their 'English foremen, English machinery and English business methods'[26] to reinforce the impression of British industrial superiority to their workforce, competitors and local government.

Greater Affluence and Improved Social Status

Increased income would have been the central motivation for British men to emigrate. Accurate comparisons between British-management salaries at home and abroad are problematic, as market demand determined the value of each skill and regional fluctuations, as well as changes over time, were usual. But in the early years of industrialisation, the British in France earned two and a half to three times the salary of their French counterparts.[27] In the early twentieth century the French consul at Warsaw noted with a trace of envy that French directors and engineers in Polish textile mills earned salaries equivalent to high-ranking army officers.[28] During the interwar period, despite an expected international levelling of pay and serious economic depression in Poland, Bradford factory overlookers earned £5, 10s, 5d per week while the same role in Marki merited seven guineas.[29] In addition the émigrés were rewarded with extended paid holidays, housing, healthcare and the loyalty or bonus schemes that were described in the last chapter. But the Secretary of State's admonishment to the British consul, that 'Warsaw must be one of the cheapest places in the world!',[30] highlights the low cost of living in Poland which rendered a considerably higher value, in real terms, to the employment packages of the Marki staff.[31]

The letters and memoirs of the Briggs-Posselt partnership's employees suggest that two distinct groups of British managers lived in the factory community. Men who relocated their families to Poland were rewarded with detached houses and gardens on the 'English Row';[32] a terrace of family homes in a separate road to the workers' accommodation and close to the Briggs' villa. They were able to employ

---

26 'Edward Briggs Obituary', *Yorkshire Weekly Post*, 12 March 1898.

27 'Artizans and Machinery', p. 8.

28 McKay, *Pioneers for Profit*, p. 169.

29 Hinchcliffe, 19 May 1921.

30 FO65/1633, Sir Villiers Lister in London to Murray at Warsaw, 16 October 1901, p. 41.

31 McKay, *Pioneers for Profit*, p. 169.

32 This label was in common usage in English communities across the industrialising world. Blewett, *Yankee Yorkshireman*, p. 71 mentions the 'English Row' at Lowell, Massachusetts.

Figure 9.1 John Hinchcliffe and family in Bradford circa 1908 (left) and in more affluent circumstances in Marki (right) 1910
Source: By kind permission of Ralph Haigh

servants and a governess, or send their children to boarding school in England, whereas the single men shared flats in the worker-housing complex. However, it is evident that the demarcation related less to their level of income or favoured status. Men who fully committed to life in Poland enjoyed substantially improved circumstances, whereas those who supported a second household in England by their 'Polish exile'[33] squandered the real economic advantage of their posting.

Although greater earning power and job security were important, a significant attraction to move abroad for many of these essentially working-class men, and for their wives, was the prospect of increased social status. Electrical engineer and long-term employee of the Marki firm, John Hinchcliffe, proudly highlighted in a letter to his mother that the 'Briggs treat me as though I were one of them'.[34] Defined by their superior housing, foreign dress, language and attitude, the British in towns like Marki enjoyed a standing more commensurate with employers than employees. Hinchcliffe noted the respect that was conferred on him when he went shopping in the factory town: 'rough English was spoken, and I was much struck by the courtesy shown to me'.[35] A benchmark of his newfound affluence is suggested in the usual subject of his letters: 'I have had a good four days eating turkey, pork, ham and everything one could mention'.[36] The family's photographs

33 Hinchcliffe, Summer 1911.
34 Ibid., 5 May 1924.
35 Hinchcliffe's memoir.
36 Hinchcliffe, Easter 1910.

reveal their significantly improved circumstances as the cloth-capped factory worker of 1908 Bradford wore a bowler hat and three-piece suit in Marki by 1910 and his children had fur-collared overcoats. Nevertheless, it is worth noting that beyond a superficial improvement in the family's status, the living conditions in Marki were challenging and Hinchcliffe's wife Isabel returned to Bradford with her children within a year.

Hinchcliffe's letters and unpublished memoir provide a fascinating insight into life in Marki and particularly the social interactions, sense of community and petty infighting amongst the expatriate foremen. His evidence often implies the distinctly Yorkshire character of the Polish town, for example he described the welcoming Sunday dinner with Yorkshire pudding that the mill's general manager Thackray provided on his arrival from Bradford. The Bradford engineer's observations of Poland invariably drew comparison to Yorkshire. He wrote to his daughter that 'the road from Warsaw to Marki is something like the avenue of trees in Esholt springs' and Warsaw 'is I believe much bigger than Leeds and Bradford put together'.[37] But rather than revealing any transnational integration marking the cultural tone of the settlement, Hinchcliffe tends to show the staunch preservation of British culture and traditions which differentiated Marki's foreign contingent from its Polish inhabitants.

The majority of the Briggs-Posselt partnership's imported staff was unlikely to have experienced national, let alone international, travel before. They relished tales of murder and injustice concerning life under the 'Czar', but in stark contrast to their cosmopolitan employers, few knew more than the smattering of Russian, Polish or German necessary to berate an employee or buy groceries. In fact, despite the long settlement of many Yorkshire families in Marki, there is little evidence of any engagement with the local community and culture. Their lack of linguistic proficiency and the general availability of English newspapers meant that British news was very much more accessible than any active interest in the current affairs of their adopted homeland. Mary Blewett suggests that a powerful sense of Yorkshire identity in the Bradfordians of Greystone, Rhode Island, kept them 'culturally rooted'[38] in their homeland, but in Marki it seems evident that more pragmatic and class factors were the key.

A parochial outlook and single-minded focus on their hierarchical importance within the expatriate community seems evident in Marki's managers. In this environment Britishness was closely associated with social class, and departing from accepted cultural conventions, even developing a fondness for foreign food, was frowned upon. Claiming Anglican faith rather than non-conformism, that is, church rather than chapel attendance, ideologically aligned them with their wealthy employers rather than the workers. Similarly, voicing Conservative views on, for example, the Irish question or the escalating trade unionism in Bradford was considered educated, whereas the local persecution of Jewish minorities,

37 Ibid., February and March 1910.

38 Blewett, *Yankee Yorkshireman*, p. 14.

Polish nationalism or the Russo-Japanese War had little relevance to their insular existence. This emulation of the perceived beliefs and behaviour of their employers reflected a prudent conformity as well as the social aspirations of this expatriate group. Thus whereas Priestley illustrated the cosmopolitanism of his Yorkshire home town by suggesting that its 'suburbs reached as far as Frankfurt and Leipzig',[39] Marki more strongly resembled a suburb of Bradford than of neighbouring Warsaw. Indeed, at the outbreak of the First World War, even after five years in Poland, Hinchcliffe still relied on English newspapers and the British consul for information about the nearby political situation.

The Yorkshiremen of Marki and Poland's British Community

Analysis of Marki's expatriate community naturally reveals many typically Yorkshire surnames including Bottomley,[40] Firth,[41] Kellet,[42] Haigh,[43] Holroyd,[44] Illingworth,[45] Shackleton[46] and Thackray,[47] along with other less regionally distinct names such as Grey,[48] Hay (sometimes seen as Hey),[49] Hopkinson,[50] Lambert[51] and Wilson.[52] The brothers, uncles, cousins or fathers of almost all these men worked at

39 Priestley, *English Journey*, p. 160.

40 FO394/10, Register of Passports 1876–1914, 19 July 1913, No. 322, George Bottomley is likely to have been a relative of the Briggs as the founder's uncle was the Bradford worsted spinner Moses Bottomley.

41 APW, 72/1151, *Starszy Inspektor Fabryczny GubernieWarszawskiej*, signature 1180, 28 May 1913, p. 6.

42 Ibid.

43 FO640/12, Consular log of correspondence, 17 September 1890, No. 103 shows that Ernest and Catherine Haigh lived in Marki in the 1890s.

44 FO394/10, 22 July 1884, No. 277 shows that Harry and Ruth Holroyd settled in Marki in 1884 with their children Ethel and Florence.

45 FO394/10, 6 July 1883, No. 239 and 242 shows John A. Illingworth and his wife Ruth (nee Hey) settled in Marki in 1883, by 1899 they had four children.

46 FO394/10, 22 October 1911, No. 232, Shackleton, his wife Mary and their daughter Elyza lived in Marki in the early twentieth century.

47 FO394/10, 28 February 1913, No. 295, George Thackray and his wife Edna lived in Marki in the early twentieth century and Victor Thackray is mentioned in the same source 5 May 1913, No. 305.

48 FO394/10, 30 September 1896, No. 29 shows Richard Gray (or Grey) lived in Marki with his sons John and Richard, *Bradford Daily Telegraph*, 23 October 1911, shows his brother Charles also worked in Poland.

49 Hinchcliffe letters show James Hey (or Hay) worked in Marki in 1910.

50 Richard and Emma Hopkinson went to Marki in 1900, this information kindly supplied by their grand-daughter Nancy Peel.

51 FO640/12, 7 January 1889, p. 92, shows Charles Lambert a mechanic from Horton in Bradford died at Marki.

52 Hinchcliffe's letters show Oscar Wilson and his wife Maud came to Marki in 1910.

Briggella Mills in Bradford which created a strong bond of loyalty and obligation to the Briggs. When the security of broader family groups was vested in this way, individuals tended to tow the company line and, it was doubtless hoped, would resist local temptations to freelance their skills in the adopted country. However, technical exchange amongst the British managers of various Russian-Polish mills was commonplace and soon after his arrival in Marki, Hinchcliffe was dispatched to Łódź to review a cotton mill managed by a Mr Miller. Such commercial cooperation and the resultant close social links between the expatriates of the region inevitably led to head-hunting. Indeed, by the early twentieth century, the Bradford press reveals that many émigrés were becoming more opportunist; flitting between international industrial centres depending on economic conditions. For example, in 1911 a Bradford wool sorter in Boston reported that 'trade here is very quiet, and no one can tell when it will brighten up. There are quite a lot of sorters here going home to Bradford, as trade is much better there'.[53]

A distinct pattern of local intermarriage illustrates the tightly embedded British community which developed in the Polish lands during the nineteenth century. A typical example is the Hay (or Hey) family: John Illingworth, a founder employee of the Briggs-Posselt partnership, was married to Ruth Hay.[54] In 1891 Peter Garvie, a manager at Żyrardów, announced the marriage of his daughter Lucy to Albert Hay of the same town.[55] Then in 1910 James Hay relocated from Żyrardów to Marki. It is also evident that the bereaved of this extended community swiftly remarried within their adopted homeland rather than retreating to England. For example, when George Thackray's wife died he married Mrs Miller, the widow of the previously mentioned Łódź factory manager.[56] Another case of surprisingly quick remarriage, and perhaps an illustration of the precarious existence of the Bradford men at Marki, is revealed when in January 1913 Hinchcliffe wrote: 'Oscar Wilson fell on the ice on Sunday and injured his arm. The doctor and the barber have been pulling it into joint for 3/4 hour, and today Oscar has been to infirmary in Warsaw where it was found it was a fracture'.[57] It would appear that the demise of Wilson came soon after as in July Hinchcliffe reported: 'I saw Mrs Maudie Wilson in Warsaw yesterday. She is not Mrs Wilson now as she was with her new husband'.[58]

It is worth noting here that the management at Marki was not exclusively English. In 1887 the factory inspector highlighted that of 24 foremen employed by the Briggs-Posselt partnership, seven were Prussian and five were Russian subjects. The firm's office contained three Russians including one Jew, four

53 *Wool Record*, Bradford, Vol. 2, No. 120, 31 August, 1911, p. 2.

54 FO394/10, 6 July 1883, Nos 239 and 242.

55 *Glasgow Herald*, 30 September 1891, p. 1.

56 Hinchcliffe, 1 October 1912, wrote that 'Mrs Miller will be here next Sat, and on Sunday G.T. and her will be spliced at Warsaw'.

57 Ibid., 13 January 1913.

58 Ibid., 24 July 1913.

Prussians and surprisingly an American.[59] Hinchcliffe's memoir describes the friendly integration of these nationalities who used the Marki schoolhouse as a social club at night. When the electrical engineer performed a drinking song: 'I was quickly followed by others in different languages. The manager of the colour department presented us with a rendering in German, while Nikorov, a sturdy Russian, surprised us with a version in his own tongue'.[60]

State Expectations for International Technology Transfer

The primary reason for foreign governments to encourage transnational industrial investment was undoubtedly the potential for business-tax revenue but it also represented an expedient shortcut to advanced technology. With the fast-track state authorisation of foreign industrialists' business plans came the expectation that (for example British) specialists would convey their industrial knowhow to the local population. Indeed the Polish press suggests that foreign investors were required to prove that necessary industrial skills did not exist locally, as justification for the importation of workers and many used the promise of training as a bargaining chip to gain local cooperation.[61] Whether the reputation of English expertise was still merited by the early twentieth century, the perception persisted in Russia that 'the prosperity of mills is largely bound up with the employment of foreigners, and that when the latter are dismissed by chauvinistic Russian owners who wish to employ natives in their place, the undertaking in question becomes less flourishing'.[62] Highly paid British professionals were considered a necessary expense to build modern-manufacturing businesses and the symbol of industrial advancement used to bolster the image of a new company. Thus the Polish *Gazeta Rzemieślnicza* betrays a resigned attitude that 'to ensure the success of their business when setting up factories, people often with the best intentions must bring … foreign workers'.[63]

Nevertheless, following the traditions long associated with the skill trap of British industry, the expatriate managers tended to minimise diffusion of their expertise to keep their skills scarce and valuable. This approach, combined with deeply entrenched attitudes of national superiority, for example that 'no foreign johnnies can ever be bred that can spin and weave like Lancashire lasses and lads',[64] increased their sense of invulnerability in Russian industry. The British press even qualified evaluations of rapid industrialisation abroad with slurs on

59 APW, Ref.1, 159/1887, No. 125, pp. 2–3.
60 Hinchcliffe's memoir.
61 *Gazeta Rzemieślnicza*, No. 2, 1884, p. 10.
62 Villari, *Russia under the Great Shadow*, p. 215.
63 'Rzemieślnik nasz i obcy' ['Our artisans and foreigners'], *Gazeta Rzemieślnicza*, No. 11, 13 December 1884, p. 2.
64 Coleman, 'Gentlemen and Players', p. 105.

their competitors' capabilities: 'it must not be supposed … that Russia is making machinery anything like equal to the machinery that is sent from this country; neither have they at present, but in very rare instances, the talent to work such machinery to advantage'.[65] British staff believed they could ensure their indispensability by aligning themselves socially and culturally to their powerful employers and by minimising the dissemination of their skills. But whereas the cosmopolitan industrialists understood the importance of nurturing local political and commercial relationships and keeping an expert entrepreneurial eye on a changing climate which might threaten their economic interests, the narrow-minded approach of the managerial class and scant regard to local sensibilities made them increasingly unpopular. Their eagerness to impress their employers frequently translated into the 'contemptuous treatment of local workers'[66] and the routine fist violence that was described in Chapter 8.

The Foreignness of Polish Industry

Nineteenth-century Polish industry was characteristically different from the rest of the Russian empire – dominated by an ethnically German ownership and management, as compared to the largely British supervision of Russian industry – but the outcome was much the same: a business class defined as foreign held power over a predominantly peasant Polish- or Russian-speaking workforce. In 1889 the factory inspectorate's statistics showed that only 10 per cent of foremen in the Kingdom of Poland were Polish.[67] Thus ethnicity, religion and language formed the demarcation between a prosperous owner-manager class and the workers.[68] During the 1890s, the importation of skills which rendered 'local artisans unable to compete with foreign arrivals'[69] caused mounting political tension and, in an attempt to pacify the natives of industrial Łódź, the state pressed for Poles to be admitted to the exclusively German technical-training schemes offered by industrialists and stipulated that overseers must be able to speak the Russian and Polish languages.[70]

In the face of growing industrial and nationalist unrest the apparent foreignness of Polish industry became a convenient scapegoat for the Tsarist administration. However, the reality of the situation was far more complex than the state edicts suggested. Many of Poland's so-called German middle classes were Polish-speaking Russian nationals, but German remained the language of business. The long-term deprivation of education for Poles, even the insistence under

65 'Technical education in Russia', *Textile World*, December 1882, p. 460.

66 Żarnowska, *Workers, Women and Social Change*, p. 300.

67 Crago, 'The "Polishness" of Production', p. 22.

68 Ibid., pp. 16–41.

69 'Rzemieślnik nasz i obcy', p. 2.

70 'Brutal German Overseers', *New York Times*, 16 November 1892.

Russification that their limited schooling be conducted in Russian, impeded the development of a sufficiently qualified local group to aspire to managerial roles. Thus the 1892 state directive, as with most factory legislation, was only arbitrarily enforced and most industrialists maintained their successful ethnically defined management hierarchy until 1905 when the issue became a tangible threat to their economic interests.

The circumstances surrounding the 1892 Łódź Rebellion and leading up to the 1905 revolution will be explored in more detail in Chapter 11, but it is clear that the perceived foreignness of Polish industry became the focus of increasingly xenophobic rhetoric at that time. In the context of greater political tension, the often tyrannical management style and arrogance of the British made them as unpopular as their German contemporaries. However, a particular facet of their behaviour compounded their problems in the Russian empire. High wages and freedom from the restrictive social conventions of their homeland led to widespread alcohol abuse among the imported management of industrial centres worldwide. The 'excessive drinking of expatriate English artisans clashed with American industrial values at the beginning of the nineteenth century',[71] while the supervisors imported to Russia by Knoop were frequently characterised as 'semi-literate and hard drinking English skilled workmen'.[72] Hinchcliffe regularly commented on his compatriots' insobriety and vividly described his companion on the business trip to Łódź as 'drunk the whole time from the wine and whisky'.[73] Although their reputation as uncouth, uneducated drunkards may well have been merited, this unfavourable characterisation was heavily exploited by a range of political opponents in the early twentieth century. The Russian Technical Society proliferated the adverse stereotype when academically trained local engineers consistently failed to break into the managerial ranks.[74] Socialist groups publicised the foreign foremen's supposed misdemeanours to whip up worker protest and, as has been described, they were an expedient target of blame for the state, in the face of unprecedented political mobilisation of the masses.

At the beginning of the twentieth century informal acts of resistance and petty threats against individual foremen escalated to violent retaliation. One unpopular English director of a Russian factory 'met a tragic end, axed to death by one of his employees'.[75] Across the Russian empire, 'recurring waves of revolutionary

[71] D. Jeremy, *Transatlantic industrial revolution: the diffusion of textile technologies between Britain and America, 1790–1830s* (Cambridge, MA: MIT Press, 1981), pp. 22–37.

[72] M.I. Tugan-Baranovsky, *The Russian Factory in the Nineteenth Century* (Georgetown Ontario: R.D. Irwin, 1970), p. 297.

[73] Hinchcliffe, Easter 1910.

[74] Thompstone, 'The Russian Technical Society', pp. 360–61, the Russian Technical Society was a scientific body founded in 1866 in St Petersburg to promote technology and industry in Russia.

[75] S.A. Smith, *Workers and Supervisors: St Petersburg 1905–1917 and Shanghai 1895–1927* (Oxford: Oxford University Press, 1993), p. 16.

terrorism killed, maimed, and threatened top foreigners repeatedly', which caused some to flee and others to demand 'hardship premiums':[76] beyond political pressure or xenophobic violence, several factors contributed to a reduction in foreign management of Russian-empire factories at that time. Although the general diffusion of industrial technology should have reduced the value of British expertise, it is evident that the salaries of foreign staff remained appreciably higher than those of native managers and exceeded pay scales in British industry well into the twentieth century. But whereas 'English foremen, English machinery and English business methods'[77] might have represented a winning formula in the nineteenth century, venture capitalists were shrewd in judging the real worth of their employees in a changing commercial or political climate. Pressure from all social strata in the host nation as well as pragmatic business considerations led many firms to take on more high-level Russian or Polish staff.

The honeymoon period when foreign cash and entrepreneurship cut through Russian officialdom soon gave way to the stultifying bureaucracy imposed on native businesses. At the same time the requirements of established foreign direct investments began to change. Foreign technicians were undoubtedly invaluable for founding enterprises and even their overbearing management style generally served the factory owner's purposes. But their effectiveness in commerce abroad: appraising and securing raw materials, managing sales and negotiating government contracts, or social and legal disputes, was generally found wanting. All corporations, foreign or domestic, required authorisation from the Tsar for a range of capital investments, buildings permissions and changes to employment practice, thus the skills of local men often proved more valuable in the longer term. At Marki it is evident that a large proportion of Russians or Poles had always held relatively senior management positions in the firm, particularly for the effective administration of sales to the Russian empire. However, in the early twentieth century the status of a new Polish mill manager, Walerian Zawiszewski, increased. His marriage to Emily Thackray, the daughter of Marki's longstanding mill manager, undoubtedly sealed his position in the extended family of the firm. By the first decade of the twentieth century Zawiszewski signed most correspondence to the Russian state on behalf of the Briggs brothers. His apparently cooperative relationship with the factory inspector Goncharov arguably attests to the prudence of the British ownership's strategy to promote him.

Rising Competition and Industrial Espionage at Marki

By the early twentieth century the commercial environment in Russian Poland was subject to increasingly complex state legislatures, internal market forces and economic depression. The success of pioneer foreign direct investment such as

[76] McKay, *Pioneers for Profit*, p. 196.

[77] 'Edward Briggs Obituary', *Yorkshire Weekly Post*, 12 March 1898.

the Marki venture arguably inspired Russian finance minister Witte's incentive program for greater foreign investment, which in turn increased competition and saturation of market opportunities. In Russian Poland the trade secrets of competitors, and particularly the methods of successful foreign-owned factories, became the natural preoccupation of local rivals scrapping for diminishing returns while industrialists became more guarded about their methods. A British journalist advised from Moscow: 'I must tell you it is very difficult to obtain trustworthy statistics ... manufacturers do not like to give information respecting their operations for fear it may be used against them by foreign competitors'.[78] Under such conditions the desire for profit outweighed gentlemanly notions of loyalty and the field of industry degenerated into a battleground in which industrial espionage became as commonplace as it had been in the earliest years of the Industrial Revolution. Many long-serving foreign specialists, having forged networks of contacts amongst other émigrés, continued to trade on their expertise and, in some cases, on the trade secrets of their employers. The market for technical progress no longer pitted nation against nation, but firm against firm as competing companies hoped to secure the smallest commercial advantage.

The roots of this type of sharp practice can be seen in the company archives of the worsted manufacturer, John Foster of Queensbury, who in the 1840s sent two of his brothers-in-law and another employee to work for one of his key customers, *Machinen Wollen Weberei* [Mechanical Wool Weaving Mill] at Wuste Giersdorf, in Germany. It was common for influential men to seek employment for relatives with business associates, if their own business could not sustain more high-level personnel. However, these men reported regularly to Foster on the commercial dealings and plant improvements of their German employer and on several occasions warned the Bradford manufacturer about the manoeuvres of his British competitors. When Foster began to supply the Łódź industrialist Ludwik Geyer, Thomas Jowett made the strategic move from Wuste Giersdorf to perform similar 'reporting duties' from Poland.[79]

In 1904 Warsaw's *Gazeta Sądowa* reported that a former clerk at the Marki factory, Kirsz, had brought a case against his employers for non-payment of salary when his contract was prematurely terminated. It emerged that the complainant had given notice under the pretext that he would start his own business, but then gathered sensitive technical information and commercial intelligence from Marki for Markus Kohn of Łódź, by whom he had actually been employed. It is evident that the Briggs were not inclined to prosecute the espionage, perhaps because it was a common occurrence or considered too costly, but Kirsz still felt he was entitled to his full pay despite his dismissal. The judgement astutely describes the cost of such crimes to industry:

---

[78] 'Foreign and Colonial, from our own correspondent, Moscow January 14th 1884', *Textile Recorder*, Manchester, 15 February 1884, p. 233.

[79] Sigsworth, *Black Dyke Mills*, p. 293.

> There is no doubt that every factory while aiming to improve their goods, are trying to create a product at the lowest price. Because the experiments made to this end take much work, time and money, communicating the results of such experimentation to a competitor must result in a severe loss for the factory.[80]

When his case was rejected by Warsaw's Commercial Court, Kirsz appealed but was told in no uncertain terms that his dismissal was his own fault, yet so firm was his sense of entitlement that he pursued two months' salary for more than six years.

In conclusion, the Yorkshire men who moved to Marki followed a historic legacy which had begun more than a century earlier and had played a large part in diffusing industrial technology across the world. Burgeoning foreign industry was perceived to offer skilled members of the working class both an increased income and an opportunity to rise up the social hierarchy. A characteristic preservation of British identity which initially served to entrench these practically skilled foreman and managers in the foreign-owned industry of Russian Poland eventually made them vulnerable to political criticism and even physical attack. But despite often forbidding political conditions they proved reluctant to forgo the preferential social status and earnings abroad. During the 1890s many realised their ambitions to join the factory-owning classes, cementing their positions with investment in their employer's business while the most ambitious 'ploughed back part of their large salaries'[81] into new ventures. Although there was an undoubted international levelling of industrial expertise by the twentieth century and despite the distinctly higher cost of employing British men abroad, there remained a 'remarkable persistence of English managerial and technical personnel in virtually every industry in which the British were active'[82] until the First World War.

---

80 'Zwolnienie oficjalny fabrycznego od obowiązków służbowych' ['Clerk fired from factory duties'], *Gazeta Sądowa Warszawa*, 27 March 1904, pp. 236–7.

81 McKay, *Pioneers for Profit*, p. 207.

82 Carstensen, 'Foreign Participation in Russian Economic Life', p. 157.

Chapter 10
'Glowing accounts are being received from Warsaw':[1] Evaluating the firm's mode of operation and performance from 1883 to 1914

Each facet of the Briggs-Posselt partnership's strategy – their commercial networking, modern plant, importation of British management and policy to recruit a workforce of women and girls – was intended to deliver one end: a profitable and sustainable business. This chapter will consider the mode of operation, products and diversified commercial activities which formed the heart of the Marki enterprise. It will continue to examine the influence of the entrepreneurs' Bradford-trade experience on their foreign enterprise and show how local environmental factors impacted on their evolving strategy. It will evaluate the entrepreneurs' success in developing the Russian-empire wool trade and achieving a monopoly for Bradford-style worsteds.

The Central Importance of Raw-materials Supply

There are three fundamentals which determine the viability of manufacturing enterprises: 1) the availability of suitable and sufficient raw materials, 2) the ability to manufacture saleable goods, and 3) existing product demand and market potential. Although each of these factors is heavily reliant on the others, product is arguably the most flexible of these essentials as it can be tailored to suit both customer tastes and obtainable resources. Indeed innovation and continuous modification are central to the success of all manufacturing trades. Seeking out new components such as Titus Salt's so-called discovery of alpaca at Liverpool docks, immortalised by Charles Dickens in *The Great Yorkshire Llama*,[2] dyeing or finishing trials using chemical developments, even adjusting types of fuel could increase a company's competitive edge. Such experiments arguably contributed as much to the advancement of industrialisation as improvements to machinery or process.

---

1 *Textile World*, Bradford, December 1882, p. 475.

2 Charles Dickens, 'The Great Yorkshire Llama', *Household Words*, Vol. VI (1853).

A prospective market is always crucial to a new venture, but demand can be stimulated by skilful promotion or by increasing the scope of goods and services offered as local requirements become apparent. For example, manufacturing plants in heavily industrialised areas might offer a speciality product but also provide commission services to competitors. Many nineteenth-century factories processed industrial bi-products to create auxiliary income. But whereas types of manufacture and sales outlets might be shaped to some extent by an astute industrialist, the availability of raw materials was an immovable prerequisite: with quantity, quality and proximity being the determinants of a workable price. The instant accessibility and development potential of resources ascertained both the immediate viability of a new company and its longer-term expansion possibilities.

Shortfalls in necessary fuel, water or raw materials could thwart the plans even of a well-capitalised entrepreneur with a strong market demand for a speciality product. This point is well-illustrated by the case of Władysław Kronenberg, the entrepreneurial son of the famous Polish banker Leopold Kronenberg, who built a reputed million-ruble linen mill at Błeszno near Częstochowa in 1884. Kronenberg doubtless saw the potential of challenging the monopoly of Russian Poland's foremost linen manufacturer Hielle and Dietrich of Żyrardów by building a state-of-the-art plant which would surpass that of the market leader. However, the entrepreneur's neglect of the most basic consideration, raw-materials supply, proved his downfall as he belatedly discovered that all national and neighbouring countries' flax had been contracted to the Żyrardów firm.[3] Thus Kronenberg's vast factory was offered for sale even before production had started and was purchased by the only possible customer under the circumstances, his would-be competitor Hielle and Dietrich.

The founding of the Marki business coincided with rapidly improving worldwide transport networks which increased the speed and reduced the cost of transit. These advances, coupled with industrial-scale wool growing in the southern hemisphere, meant that the Bradford men could feasibly import sufficient raw wool to Warsaw to satisfy their requirements. But contrary to this, the *Yorkshire Post* reported that their plan was to 'utilise Russian, Polish and Austrian wools with the object of manufacturing a class of yarn suitable for the textile industries of continental markets'.[4] Starożyk similarly asserted that at Marki 'cloth and yarn will be made from the wool of our country, in the English method, but much more cheaply'.[5] Indeed, in June 1883 the Briggs-Posselt partnership qualified their petition to the Russian finance minister Bunge for import-duty concessions on British machinery with the economic argument that Russia exported raw wool for 50 kopeks per pound and imported wool yarn at 75 to 80 kopeks per pound, thus making a loss of '25–30 kopeks per pound of wool from a national economic point

---

3 *Gazeta Rzemieślnicza*, Warsaw, No. 11, 13 December 1884, p. 7.

4 'Mr Edward Briggs of Bradford', *Yorkshire Weekly Post*, 12 March 1898.

5 Starożyk, 'Nowa Fabryka sukna i kortów', p. 165.

of view'.[6] Nevertheless, in 1887 a government survey of Warsaw industry revealed that Briggs, Posselt and Co., Marki actually supplied a third of its raw materials from abroad and in 1896 Litten went as far as to describe the concern as 'reliant for the greater part of its raw material on foreign supplies' from Australia and New Zealand.[7] The emphasis of the 1887 Russian industrial survey – on the ratio of foreign to local workers that each Warsaw firm employed, the proportion of imported to local raw materials that they utilised and the percentage of their inland to export sales – certainly suggests that it would have been politically expedient to express the intention to develop a business based on national supplies. It would also have been to the advantage of the new firm to source and sell within the Russian empire, reducing transaction costs and circumventing the vagaries of the world commodity trade, but the practical difficulties of acquiring adequate appropriate wool locally forced the Bradford men to source internationally.

In the early 1880s worsted manufacture was largely new to Russia and Bradford-style long or hard-wool worsted yarns and cloth were entirely imported. Indeed, the technology to make these products in bulk was relatively modern even in the context of more-advanced British industry. Evidence presented to the state by the *Warszawskiego Komitetu Przemysłowego* [Warsaw Committee for Industry] by a Warsaw businessman, Salzman, in support of the Bradford partners' application for import concessions stated in no uncertain terms that:

> Cloth of this type has not been produced anywhere in our country and it is only imported from England, from the area of Bradford. Thus establishing such a textile factory would be, in my opinion, very much in demand and very beneficial for local industry. Moreover a combing facility to prepare the wool, which is used to make so-called worsted, *kammgarn*, *fils peigné*, does not exist in our country, therefore establishing such a facility could encourage industrialists to set up weaving factories to use the combed wool. Up until now few weavers have used worsted because they had to import it from abroad.[8]

Branches of Worsted Manufacture

In his statement, Salzman's clarification of the Polish term for worsted or combed wool *przędza czesana* with both the German *kammgarn* and French term *fils*

6 AGAD, *Akta Warszawskiego Komitetu Przemysłowego z 1883 r.*, transcript of a letter in French from the Bradford partners to finance minister Bunge in St Petersburg, signature 11/1883.

7 APW, 72/1416, *Rząd Gubernialny Warszawski Referat II* [The Government of Warsaw], signature 403, 'All Industry, Factory and Manufactory establishments that are located in Warsaw Governorate', p. 4, Litten, *Englische Wollspinnerei*, p. 5.

8 AGAD, *Akta Warszawskiego Komitetu Przemysłowego z 1883 r.*, letter from M. Salzman, signature 11/1883, 7 July 1883.

peigné highlights the unfamiliarity of the proposed branch of textiles. But despite his assertion that there was absolutely no worsted spinning in the Russian empire prior to the Marki venture, early twentieth-century commercial directories do reveal some pre-existing worsted plants in the region.[9] However, wool is not a generic product, its quality and fineness are determined by the climate, breed of sheep and the part of the body from which it is clipped and each type is used to make different yarns or cloths. For example, the wool used to create a soft sweater or fine suit is entirely different to the fibre used in carpets. Generally in Polish scholarship the three worsted pioneers of the Russian empire are identified as the German H. Dietel who invested at Sosnowiec in 1879 and employed 670 workers in 1885, the French-financed firm of Allart, Rousseau and Co., was founded at Łódź in 1880 with 451 workers and in 1883 Briggs, Posselt and Co., launched the Marki enterprise with 515 workers and by 1886 had a workforce of 930 strong.[10] Allart, Rousseau and Dietel both spun French-style worsted yarns which were suitable for hosiery or knitwear and, limited by their lack of tensile strength, for use as weft in woven cloth.[11] The unique selling point of the Marki company would be the manufacture of British-style components suitable for weaving fine worsted dress fabrics, heavy-duty furnishings and particularly uniform cloths within the Russian empire.

A second equally significant facet of the Briggs-Posselt partnership's plan is revealed by Salzman's assertion that no Russian factory had the capability to comb worsted fibre. The traditional woollen manufacturers of Białystok employed the old-fashioned carding method to process the coarsest wool into yarns suitable for blankets or thick coatings. Any Polish firms that did spin worsted had to import semi-processed wool known as *top* from abroad. Thus, the modern combing facility at Marki would process worsted top for its own use and for sale to other spinners. The strategy owed much to the successful course taken by John Briggs senior at Briggella Mills, and numerous other Bradford manufacturers, who built their businesses on short lead-time products which yielded the swiftest returns before they developed more labour-intensive, high-profit product lines.

Theoretically the vast population and rapidly increasing industrialisation of the Russian empire would have suggested huge potential demand for worsted to the British venture capitalists. But the high price and relative novelty of worsted inside the tariff-controlled zone meant that it had only achieved minimal market penetration. In the founding stages of the new enterprise the primary concern of

---

9 *Księga adresowa przemysłu fabrycznego w Królestwie Polskim za 1905 r.* [*Address Book of Industrial Companies in the Kingdom of Poland for 1905*] (Warsaw: L. Jeziorański, 1904) and *Przemysł i handel Królestwa Polskiego* [*Industry and Business of the Kingdom of Poland*], Stowarzyszene Techników w Warszawie (Warsaw: Antoni R. Sroka, 1912).

10 Tadeusz Manteuffel, *Historia Polski* [*Polish History*] Vol. 3, Part 1 (Warsaw: Państwowe Wydawn. Naukowe, 1955), p. 389, APW, 72/1416, *Rząd Gubernialny Warszawski Referat II*, signature 403, p. 4.

11 *Księga adresowa przemysłu fabrycznego w Królestwie Polskim za 1905 r.*, p. 360.

the Bradford men would have been to develop and consolidate a market for their speciality: persuading existing weavers to introduce worsted to their ranges and educating a wider Russian consumer about the merits of a product which had formerly been priced beyond their reach. Once established, the firm could seek out opportunities that were particular to the region, perhaps in the form of under-utilised raw materials or an unmet local requirement which could be fulfilled by their flexible manufacturing plant.

Wool Sourcing in the Russian Empire

By the second half of the nineteenth century, more-industrialised nations such as Germany, France and to some extent Britain had turned agricultural land over to more lucrative arable farming, to provide food for growing urban populations, and they imported wool from the southern hemisphere, as they did cotton from the colonies. By contrast, wool growing in Poland had changed little for centuries; aristocratic landowners produced small quantities of high-quality, soft merino as a cash crop intended to generate the highest export profits. On the eve of the Marki venture a British trade journal reported that 'glowing accounts are being received from Warsaw with regard to the state of the wool trade there, the demand from abroad having been very brisk since the commencement of the month' and the majority of Polish wool was destined for Austria and Germany.[12] Despite their declared intention to use local resources, the Bradford partners' extensive experience of the global wool trade suggests that they would have been well aware that only these small quantities of merino and some coarse Donskoi wool actually emerged from the Russian empire. Thus the underdeveloped raw-materials supply, particularly for fibre suitable to make Bradford-style worsteds, would be one of the first challenges the venture capitalists would face.

As the Marki plant was under construction the founders' attempts to secure sufficient raw materials featured prominently in the Polish press. They were noted at the Warsaw Wool Fair in June 1883 'amongst a number of foreign buyers and factory agents who have already arrived at Warsaw are two British manufacturers from Bradford, who aim to gain a better understanding of Polish wool'.[13] Beyond the aforementioned long wool, they sought a variety of fibres to create a broad range of products such as Persian, Russian Donskoi, Astrakhan, Gypsy Bessarabian as well as Turkish mohair and camel hair which were traded in Asian Russia.[14] Thus they braved the forbidding winter conditions of the Russian interior to visit the wool fair and horse market at Kharkov; picturesquely described

[12] *Textile World*, Bradford, December 1882, p. 475.

[13] *Gazeta Warszawska*, No. 129, 1 June 1883, p. 2.

[14] APW, *Starszy Inspektor Fabryczny Guberni Warszawskiej*, signature 375, price list for E. Briggs Brothers of Marki, 1911, pp. 025–026v.

as where '80,000 sledges come over the snow'.[15] But in January 1884 the Łódź press announced that Messers Briggs and Posselt were still 'looking for a thicker wool yarn, worsted long wool, because stocks bought by them at a fair in Kharkov have proved insufficient'.[16]

Although many elements of the Briggs-Posselt partnership's strategy in Russian Poland were naturally influenced by their experience of Yorkshire's West-Riding worsted trade, some notably responded to local market conditions. In Bradford, a surplus of wool and the concentration of manufacturers making similar products created a price-competitive market for both goods and resources: keen competition and oversupply, in combination with changes in fashion and global-trade unpredictabilities, caused cyclical fluctuations in wool prices which transformed business behaviour in the world's worsted capital. By the late nineteenth century, Yorkshire manufacturers could no longer afford to tie up working capital in wool stocks, as lengthy time lags between raw-material acquisition and product sale increased the likelihood of their being adversely affected by falling prices. Plentiful wool reserves meant there was little danger that an industrialist would not be able to buy the necessary stock to satisfy an order. Therefore a prudent 'just in time' policy was increasingly adopted in which wool was bought only to fulfil definite contracts.[17] By contrast, in Russian Poland, the comparative scarcity of wool and 'steady demand for yarn from factories in the interior of Russia'[18] made stock-piling more appropriate. Monopolising wool stocks could even increase their value, that is to say, reducing circulation could drive up the local price. Raw materials were, moreover, a useful liquid asset which provided the flexibility to manufacture a range of products according to demand, but could be traded locally to raise cash or exported as a form of currency in times of hardship or war.

The case of Kronenberg's Błeszno factory suggests that failure to secure plentiful and diverse wool supplies would have constituted the greatest risk to the Bradford partners' Polish enterprise. But with minimal pre-existing worsted manufacture in the Russian empire it is unsurprising that they struggled to obtain suitable resources and importation provided a vital safety net at the outset of their venture. While a dependence on foreign stocks exposed the company to the unpredictabilities of the global trade and inevitably higher transit costs, exchange rate fluctuations could also create opportunity. In 1889 the consul particularly remarked that 'the high value of the rouble during the past year has made it profitable for local consumers to obtain their wool from abroad and they got a great deal of it from Australia'.[19] However, the contrast between England's well-

[15] Matthew Fontaine Maury and Mytton Maury, *Manual of Geography* (Michigan: University Publishing Company, 1880), p. 92.

[16] *Dziennik Łódzki*, Łódź, 9 January 1884, p. 1.

[17] Sigsworth, *Black Dyke Mills*, p. 124.

[18] 'Industrial Progress in Russia', *Textile World*, February 1884, p. 919.

[19] J.C. Winzer, 'Annual Wool Fair Held at Warsaw June 1889', No. 580, Annual Series 391.

developed mercantile environment which was finely attuned to international trade and Russia's inexperienced, import-resistant, commercial culture are also highlighted in contemporary consular correspondence, which described 'the delay, during three months and seven months respectively, of two samples of wool, sent by Messrs Daniel and Rudolph Delius of Bradford to Białystok. These gentlemen complain that similar delays are constantly occurring'.[20] Investigations revealed that parcels received by the Russian post office had to be forwarded to the customs office before dispatch to the addressee. If this was not achieved within a fixed period, the customs officials returned the item to the sender abroad. At the end of the century complaints still abounded regarding 'the great disadvantages to British trade caused by the want of a parcel post between Russia and Great Britain'.[21]

Marki's Domination of the Polish Wool Trade

Analysis of nineteenth-century Polish wool-trade reports is problematic because of their interchangeable use of weights, measures and currencies. The pud, hundredweight, centner, bale and *kamień* (stone) might appear in a single article, priced in rubles, talers and even occasionally marks.[22] Wool grades ranged from Inferior to Extra Fine in both washed and raw state. But, from its inauguration, the significance of the Marki venture in the scale of the Polish wool industry was evident. Whereas the press generally quoted wool-purchase figures for whole cities or regions such as Łódź, Białystok, Tomaszów or Łużyce, Briggs, Posselt and Co. were invariably mentioned by name. For example, in the first quarter of 1887 'the spinning mill at Marki of Briggs and Posselt purchased 151 bales of *mojka* washed in Odessa ... and 2,400 puds unwashed ... Łódź purchased approximately 1,200 puds of *mojka*'.[23] The reason the press singled out Marki is clear as their total acquisition at Odessa equivalent to 5,500 puds dwarfed the 1,200 puds bought for the whole Łódź industry and rendered negligible the 430 pud purchase by merchants from the Polish wool capital, Białystok.[24] This report also highlights a major advantage that the Bradford men held over their competitors. Few Polish wool manufacturers had facilities to clean wool and thus bought washed fleece known as *mojka*, while the high-capacity scouring plant at Marki was 'able to

20 FO65/1227, Maude to the Secretary of State, 13 December 1885, p. 112.

21 FO65/1542, Murray to the Secretary of State, 28 May 1897, p. 108.

22 A pud (or poud) equalled 36 lbs, a hundredweight (cwt) equalled 3.11 pud or 112 lbs, a centner equalled 3.3 pud or 120 lbs, a bale was 20 pud or 720 lbs. However, a Russian pound or funt was less than an English pound at 14.445 oz, *Gazeta Warszawska*, No. 52, 22 February 1885, p. 5.

23 'Wełna' ['Wool'], *Gazeta Warszawska*, No. 76, 22 March 1887, p. 4, *mojka* is washed wool.

24 Ibid.

deliver up to 130,000 lbs of washed wool per week', that is over 3,600 puds.[25] Thus the Briggs-Posselt partnership made the only purchase of entirely unprocessed wool at Odessa at a considerable cost saving, as greasy wool cost only 9 rubles 25 kopeks compared with the 26 rubles per pud for clean fleece.[26]

In the 1880s Warsaw's importance as a national and international trading hub grew. The city's central location between Western Europe and Russia was enhanced by increased investment in the rail network which connected it with Moscow, Vienna and Odessa. There was easy access to the Baltic via 'the Vistula, which is navigable above Warsaw, and traverses the whole breadth of the Kingdom of Poland'.[27] Improvements to Warsaw's commercial infrastructure and growing industrialisation became as much a stimulus as a response to the explosive population growth and burgeoning market for manufactured goods. British consular correspondence particularly noted a 'great development in the woollen industry':[28] 12,000 cwt of wool, imported mainly from 'Australia, Buenos Ayres, and la Plata',[29] was consumed annually by factories throughout Poland in the mid-1880s and there was a steady upward trajectory in the quantities of home-grown wool sold at the annual Warsaw Wool Fair from roughly 16,000 cwt in 1888, to in excess of 21,000 cwt by the late 1890s.[30] In 1896 Litten reported that the warehouses at Marki often stocked 200,000 puds of wool,[31] that is 64,000 cwt, or over three times the average total quantity traded annually at Warsaw. With a purchasing power that outstripped the combined national consumption and export sales, it seems evident that the Marki enterprise made a significant contribution to the rising economic importance of the Kingdom of Poland in this period. Indeed, as Chapter 6 highlighted, a member of the firm was invited to join the Warsaw Wool Fair's select committee throughout the late 1880s and 1890s, usually under the chairmanship of the city's president General Starynkiewicz.[32]

---

25 Litten, *Englische Wollspinnerei*, p. 5.

26 'Wełna', p. 4.

27 Francis Maude, *Reports from Her Majesty's Consuls on the Manufactures, Commerce*, Vol. 28, 1880.

28 Winzer, 'Annual Wool Fair Held at Warsaw June 1889', note that the word 'woollen' is often used as a term for the wool trade generally and encompasses both woollen and worsted product.

29 *Diplomatic and Consular Reports on Trade and Finance: Russia*, Report for the year 1886 on the trade of the district of the consulate-general at Warsaw, Foreign Office Annual Series, No. 128, 1887, p. 4.

30 *Sydney Morning Herald*, New South Wales, 1 October 1889, p. 5.

31 Litten, *Englische Wollspinnerei*, p. 5.

32 'Kronika ekonomiczna' ['Economic bulletin'], *Gazeta Warszawska*, No. 146, 7 June 1890, p. 3 and *Gazeta Warszawska*, No. 155, 1889, p. 4 and 'Jarmark na wełnę' ['Market for wool'], *Gazeta Warszawska*, No. 151, 1889, p. 4.

The Warsaw Wool Fair

Nineteenth-century Polish press reports provide a fascinating insight into the operations of the annual Warsaw Wool Fair. As soon as shearing was complete across the region, the fleece was delivered to the city's wool bank, a temporary-storage facility, where state-regulated agents accurately weighed and insured it. Government control 'as to the conduct of the fair, and the wool sold thereat being very strict'[33] meant that wool growers had to provide certification from the head of their district, assuring that their sheep were in good health and did not share pasture with any diseased animals. The largest clips considered worthy of note in 1889, for example 80 puds from Kronenberg in Łękińsko and 90 puds from Michalski in Borowno, provide fresh perspective for the scale of stock holdings at Marki.[34] These growers were not specialists but traded wool as one of a number of agricultural products at local fairs as well as the annual event in Warsaw.

By the end of the nineteenth century intercontinental-cable communications began to create a global price convergence in commodity trades and southern-hemisphere wool growers increasingly gauged future demand by observing European consumption figures.[35] In 1885 a surge in Polish wool dealing totally exhausted the holdings of Warsaw's merchants and it was reported that 'the stocks of Russian wool acquired at the last fair in Kharkov by local warehouses had been disposed at profit even before its arrival in Warsaw'.[36] Once again only Briggs, Posselt and Co. was mentioned by name, reputedly clearing Białystok's warehouses of wool. The Australian press noted that 'Poland is making great strides in wool growing … the whole of this year's growth was cleared, so that prospects are favourable for next season's sale'.[37]

Building Partnerships with Suppliers and Trading at Source

In the last decade of the nineteenth century a change in commercial practice became evident in Warsaw which strongly resonated with earlier transformations to Bradford's trade. In 1898 consul Alex Murray remarked that although production had not diminished to any great extent, the total quantity of wool sold at Warsaw was significantly less than the previous year. He concluded that 'considerable transactions between buyers and sheep-farmers must have taken place before the fair commenced'.[38] That is to say that wool was being sold at source rather than at the annual fair. Several factors might account for this change in business

33 Murray, 'Report on the Warsaw Wool Fair of 1898'.
34 'Jarmark na wełnę', p. 4.
35 Brearley, *International Wool Market 1840–1913*, p. 146.
36 *Gazeta Warszawska*, No. 52, 22 February 1885, p. 5.
37 *Morning Bulletin*, Queensland, 16 September 1898, p. 3.
38 Murray, 'Report on the Warsaw Wool Fair of 1898'.

behaviour, beyond the likely influence of the Bradford men. In this period several new foreign-owned worsted plants were established in the Kingdom of Poland, all reliant on securing suitable raw materials. According to early twentieth-century commercial directories Dietel and Allart, Rousseaux prospered but faced fresh competition from French investors at Częstochowa such as Peltzer and Co., founded in 1887, which employed 1,800 workers by 1905 and Motte, Meillassoux, Caulliez and Delaoutre and Co., with a workforce of 1,400, or the German company of C.G. Schön established at Sosnowiec in 1887 who employed 2,500 workers at the beginning of the twentieth century.[39] These French-style worsted manufacturers did not necessarily compete with the Briggs-Posselt partnership in product sales, but their wool requirements undoubtedly overlapped. Therefore increased competition between manufacturers, all desperate for a foothold in the raw-materials market, almost certainly encouraged the conspicuous pattern of direct dealing.

Cooperation between wool growers and industrialists provided distinct advantages to both the manufacturer, who guaranteed supply of a predetermined quality and quantity of wool at a fixed price and to the farmer, who perhaps only secured an average price for his clip, but circumvented the onerous state-imposed bureaucracy of the trade fairs and transportation costs. In principle both parties could proceed with confidence: greater investment in livestock could be made on the land and the factory could confidently tender for large orders without reference to fluctuations in the value or supply of raw materials.

Edward Briggs' 1898 obituary suggests that collaboration with local growers was always part of the Bradford men's strategy in the Russian empire. It described how 'the wool had to be bought from the farmers and growers, washed, combed and spun'.[40] The volatility of the commodity market made it less attractive for Western manufacturers to contract supply, but in the Russian empire the scarcity of raw materials combined with the unpredictability of import tariffs and embargos led large manufacturers to frequently integrate back into raw-materials production. On his death in 1881, Scheibler owned one of the largest textile empires in the world, mainly supplied by his own cotton plantations in the Caucasus Mountains.[41] The Briggs-Posselt partnership soon identified a local man to facilitate their collaboration with Russian and Polish wool growers. Sypniewski, who in partnership with Leszczyński, was a 'well-known sorter' and classifier of wool at the Warsaw Wool Fair, is regularly mentioned in Hinchcliffe's letters.[42] His attendance at John Briggs' Bradford funeral in 1911 suggests that this was a longstanding and close alliance.[43]

---

[39] *Księga adresowa przemysłu fabrycznego w Królestwie Polskim za 1905 r.*

[40] 'Mr Edward Briggs of Bradford', *Yorkshire Weekly Post*, 12 March 1898.

[41] Popławska and Muthesius, 'Poland's Manchester', p. 153.

[42] *Gazeta Warszawska*, No. 151, 1887, p. 4 and No. 154, 1888, pp. 2–3 amongst many more.

[43] 'Funeral of Mr John Briggs', *Bradford Daily Telegraph*, 23 October 1911.

Types of Yarn Manufactured at Marki

This chapter has described the central importance of raw-materials supply to the viability of the Marki enterprise and the entrepreneurs' strategy to dominate national wool resources while supplementing their requirements with imported qualities. It has revealed the scale of the venture in the context of the Polish wool industry and its likely influence on changing buying practice in the host nation, both to circumvent the bureaucracy of state-managed wool fairs and as a result of growing competition for resources. The initial target market and gradual adaptations of the firm's strategy, product and plant in order to realise local opportunities will now be considered.

By the late nineteenth century, with rising foreign competition and escalating tariff control across Europe and the US, Bradford's industry increasingly focused on home and colonial markets. Although competition was fierce, these were the largest, most intelligible and accessible customer bases, both to distribute to and secure repayment from. There is no doubt that the Briggs-Posselt partnership brought the same approach to Marki, intending to develop a new *home* trade. They spun a range of yarn counts (thicknesses) that were standard to industry requirements and offered semi-processed worsted top, in both hard wool and merino qualities to the weavers and spinners of, for example, Łódź, Białystok and Moscow. At the 1888 Warsaw Weaving Exhibition these products were judged to be 'perfect specimens ... of single yarn, twisted examples of combed wool, alpaca and mohair, dyed and undyed, yarn'.[44] These were the exact products with which the Briggs and their Bradford contemporaries Lister, Salt and Foster had made their fortunes earlier in the century. In the first ten years the Marki venture made great strides in consolidating this industrial customer base. In 1886 the firm declared an annual value of production of 1.2 million rubles, approximately £120,000, which was almost two-fold the entrepreneurs' investment capital.[45] By the turn of the twentieth century this figure had almost doubled again to 2,383,200 rubles.[46]

Diversification to Meet Market Opportunities

Within a decade the Bradford men extended their plant and, in response to local market requirements and available resources, incorporated several new products to their repertoire. The Russian commercial environment strongly contrasted with that of contemporary England; predominantly rural and unsophisticated, it had one of the world's poorest and least concentrated populations where communications

[44] 'Dyplomy zasługi' ['Diplomas of merit'], *Gazeta Warszawska*, No. 71, 1888, p. 3.

[45] APW, 72/1416, *Rząd Gubernialny Warszawski Referat II*, signature 403, p. 4.

[46] Stanisław Koszutski, *Nasz przemysł wielki na początku XX stulecia* [*Our Great Industry at the Beginning of the Twentieth Century*] (Warsaw: Nakładem Księgarni Naukowej, 1905), p. 7.

and therefore distribution networks were patchy. Across the Russian empire the success of industry depended heavily on the harvest; in a good season manufactured goods or craft materials were bought, but in a bad year not just grain but livestock had to be sold. The Briggs-Posselt partnership identified the potential of the domestic customer – the typical Russian peasant who 'passed the long winter months making his own clothing, household utensils and farm implements'.[47] Thus, despite the establishment of several other merino manufacturers, the Marki plant used its French-system spinning machinery to make soft *zephir* yarns for hand knitting. By 1896 this branch of production accounted for 30,000 lbs of yarn per week compared with an overall weekly plant capacity of 100,000 lbs.[48] Chapter 7 described the providential acquisition of Meyerhoff's woollen plant in 1892, which allowed the Marki firm to produce industrial quantities of heavy woollen yarns, particularly for carpets.[49] A factory inspector's report of the year 1900–01 provides a useful indication of the relative importance of each branch of production for the Marki firm, in terms of both quantity and value. It shows that 14 per cent of the firm's output was combed wool, that is, semi-processed raw material sold to other spinners, 54 per cent was worsted yarn which included both weaving and hand-knitting qualities, 16 per cent was woollen yarn and 16 per cent was yarn using recycled fibres. The value in rubles for each product group, with the exception of the recycled yarn qualities, was given and shows that, despite their diversified manufacturing capability, worsted yarn sales produced 1,638,131 rubles in the period 1900–01 compared with only 622,140 rubles worth of woollen yarn and a 122,968 ruble return on combed top.[50]

The central reason to expand into these household markets – both hand-knitting and carpet yarns – was naturally profit, but it was also prudent for some more complex economic reasons. Kochanowicz suggests that Polish industry particularly suffered in the long term from its overdependence on the Russian industrial customer.[51] But fluctuations in core sales resulting from any number of unpredictable political, economic or environmental factors could impact on any company worldwide which overcommitted to a single market sector. By servicing a variety of customer bases affected by different market forces and seasonal requirements, manufacturers could spread risk, regulate production, retain their skilled employees and increase revenue. The same motivations, in combination with a practical necessity for self sufficiency, also account for the very broad scope of other product and service diversifications that the Marki firm developed.

---

47 Anne Lincoln Fitzpatrick, *The Great Russian Fair: Nizhnii Novgorod 1840–90* (Basingstoke: Macmillan in association with St Antony's College, 1990), p. 62.

48 Litten, *Englische Wollspinnerei*, p. 5.

49 *Prawda: Tygodnik Polityczny, Społeczny i Literacki*, Warsaw, No. 52, 24 December 1892, p. 10.

50 APW, signature 375, p. 043.

51 Kochanowicz, *Backwardness and Modernisation*, p. 134.

As was discussed in Chapter 7, the rudimentary infrastructure of most nineteenth-century industrialising cities fostered a surprisingly diverse skill-set in manufacturers. A partnership agreement drawn up in 1891 for the large Bradford worsted-manufacturing company John Foster illustrates the breadth of activities that the firm undertook as 'mechanical engineers, manufacturing chemists and druggists and colliery owners and mettalurgists, brick and tile manufacturers, farmers, builders and contractors'.[52] Logistically isolated factories such as Bradford Mills at Marki, John Foster's Black Dyke Mills at Queensbury or even Salt's Mill at Saltaire, in a period when horse-drawn transport was the standard, needed self-sufficiency in a range of industrial requirements to operate efficiently. Indeed Litten particularly remarks that because Marki was some distance from Warsaw the 'founders felt obliged to free the principal supplies from urban sources'.[53] Thus, a great iron foundry, machine shop, soap works, tannery and leather belt factory, joinery and brush-making workshop to create the clothing for combing machines were all established in support of the core business. Although many of these activities might appear incongruous for a worsted manufacturer in a modern context, in nineteenth-century industrial communities they were practical necessities which often developed into fully fledged auxiliary businesses. For example, Litten notes that asphalt was manufactured at Marki from bi-products of worsted manufacture and sold to other industrialists,[54] and the linen manufacturer Hielle and Dietrich was among a handful of firms who tendered to supply 5.1million bricks for construction of Lindley's Warsaw sewer system in 1883.[55]

Leather and Dairy Production

Beyond bi-product processing and textile-related service industries, the Marki enterprise also developed some significant sidelines which largely related to the intermarital relationships of the founders. The Marki tannery worked in close cooperation with Warsaw leather manufacturers Temler and Pfeiffer, whose founders were relations by marriage to John Briggs.[56] By the turn of the twentieth century the Marki estate also supplied dairy products to Charles Whitehead's brother-in-law's company, the Wedel chocolate factory at Praga. Unfortunately no data exists to reveal what proportion of the firm's income was attributable to these secondary enterprises, but it is evident that Bradford entrepreneurs' relationship with the chocolate manufacturer provided more than just an additional revenue stream. In times of particular hardship for the worsted manufacturer, most notably

52 Sigsworth, *Black Dyke Mills*, p. 187.

53 Litten, *Englische Wollspinnerei*, p. 4.

54 Ibid., p. 6.

55 'Kanalizacya i wodociągi' ['Sewer and water system'], *Gazeta Warszawska*, No. 134, 1883, p. 2.

56 Wartalska, 'Fabryka i osada fabryczna', p. 655.

in the 1920s, Wedel provided temporary employment to the women workers of Marki.[57] The Briggs' strategies to cope with the privations of the interwar period will be discussed in greater detail in Chapter 12 but it is pertinent to note here that in 1933, E. Briggs Brothers and Co., of Marki, as the firm became known after Posselt's retirement in 1897, applied for the concession to supply the municipality of Warsaw with electricity.[58] Although their tender was unsuccessful it does show the very flexible approach the entrepreneurs took towards local opportunities and their philosophy to maximise the productivity of every aspect of their plant.

Cloth Manufacturing at Marki

From the foundation of the Marki enterprise the partners' intention to become a fully integrated operation was apparent in press reports that they would build 'a factory for yarn and cloth'.[59] But it seems evident that the Bradford men opted to maximise their component-manufacturing capabilities and a range of commercial sidelines before they invested in looms which would complete the worsted-production cycle. Despite their acquisition of 120 power looms from Meyerhoff in 1892,[60] it was not until 1898 that reports emerged that 'a large percentage [of yarn] was, moreover, manufactured by the firm into cloth, woven, dyed and finished in the premises'.[61] Several factors might account for the delay in realising their aspiration. Despite excellent capitalisation and early success, it seems clear that the Marki entrepreneurs took a typically cautious approach to their foreign investment. They intended to establish their place in the market as a valuable supplier of components to existing industry, to assess the opportunities of the market and accumulate sufficient profits to reinvest. While weaving would appear to have been a natural progression for the firm – to utilise their own components and create a more profitable product – such an expansion would entail greater investment in machinery, skills and most significantly the development of a completely new sales market for the firm. The industrial weavers or domestic consumers who bought yarn were entirely different from the clothing factories, tailors and cloth merchants who would take fabric. In fact, there would have been a danger of alienating their longstanding clientele by appropriating their sales outlets. Fabric manufacture certainly afforded the firm greater profit potential but it was a very much more risky proposition than yarn. It required a much greater insight into the demands of the market from the point of view of both fashion and utility. Therefore, it seems

57 Ibid.

58 *Nowinny Codzienne*, Warsaw, 29 October 1933, p. 4.

59 Starożyk, 'Nowa fabryka sukna i kortów', p. 165.

60 *Diplomatic and Consular Reports on Trade and Finance: Russia*, 'Report for the year 1886 on the trade of the district of the consulate-general at Warsaw', Foreign Office Annual Series, No. 128, 1887, p. 5.

61 'Mr Edward Briggs of Bradford', *Yorkshire Weekly Post*, 12 March 1898.

most likely that when the Marki enterprise finally acquired looms, they focused on the safe and consistent state-contracted demand for uniform cloths. Evidence to support this theory is scarce, but Hinchcliffe certainly mentions that the Russian authorities placed large orders at Marki in 1914.[62]

Marketing and Trade Fairs

Whereas other aspects of the Briggs-Posselt partnership's operations – their prodigious wool purchasing and investment in plant – can be traced through the press and occasional Russian industrial surveys, the firm's sales strategy and distribution networks are harder to pinpoint. The company never advertised its products, although Chapters 7 and 8 showed how they used the press to promote their reputation as rich philanthropists. Such promotional reporting and the concerted social networking described in Chapter 6 undoubtedly created interest in the new firm, but the meticulous planning of the rest of the enterprise and the fact that the owners invariably attributed a measure of their success to their 'English business methods'[63] implies they imported an English sales style of sorts. Kirchner suggests that 'marketing was not a field in which the Russians were strong, but foreigners understood its importance and built up a network of efficient sales and service agencies'.[64] However, as has already been described, almost every aspect of the host market was characteristically different from the commercial arenas in which the Marki entrepreneurs had formerly operated.

In the Russian empire the state regulated commerce under an ancient guild system whereby merchants were taxed according to their income and assets, then rewarded with privileges. This rendered them cash poor with 'little enthusiasm for risky ventures, innovative business techniques, [or] open competition'.[65] Although the Bradford men launched an ostensibly new product rendering competition negligible compared to the UK, the poor commercial infrastructure and inflexible, bureaucratic approach to trade would have presented serious challenges to them. To sustain their foreign enterprise the Briggs-Posselt partnership needed to cultivate consistent sales and manage far-reaching distribution for a varied product range. It is likely that the internationally experienced merchant, Ernst Posselt, took a leading role in this aspect of the enterprise.

From the limited available evidence and based on the characteristic behaviour of the entrepreneurs, it seems probable that the Bradford men took as diversified an approach to sales in the Russian market as they did to sourcing raw materials or target markets. Just as they travelled to the Russian interior to buy raw wool,

62 Hinchcliffe's memoir.

63 'Mr Edward Briggs of Bradford', 12 March 1898 and Starożyk, 'Nowa fabryka sukna i kortów', p. 165.

64 Kirchner, *Russian Tariffs and Foreign Industries*, p. 370.

65 Lincoln Fitzpatrick, *Great Russian Fair*, p. 6.

acquired further stocks from the warehouses of Białystok and imported quantities from Australasia, so they would have exploited every possible outlet for their products. Fulfilling orders for industrial-scale quantities of yarn or spinning components for the direct sale to the manufacturers of Łódź, Białystok, Moscow and so forth would have been most lucrative, nevertheless, selling lesser quantities to middlemen such as merchants and warehouses would have provided a consistent outlet for standard yarn qualities.

The disposal of manufactured goods through warehouses was common in Russian Poland. A review of the 1888 Warsaw Weaving Exhibition describes that companies including Briggs, Posselt and Co., Hielle and Dietrich, Scheibler and Poznański showcased their wares in impressive salons on Ujazdowski Square in Warsaw. The displays were not priced because 'the warehouses have requested that the manufacturers keep the costs to themselves, so that the public would be kept in ignorance as to the wholesale price of the goods'.[66] The Marki firm also maintained a Warsaw warehouse at Trębacka 4 but it remains unclear whether a dedicated sales team operated from this satellite, or if it was a simple storage facility.[67] Hand-knitting yarn was undoubtedly traded in the Russian interior via independent travelling salesmen, specialists in this type of commerce, who might relay the requirements of the dispersed domestic customer back to the mill and thus influence the quality or colour of future collections.

The introduction of carpet yarn to the Marki firm's repertoire in 1892 almost certainly resulted from Posselt's commercial connections. Meyerhoff's factory was close to his own cotton factory in Zgierz and shortly after the Marki firm was equipped to make carpet yarns Posselt established the Warsaw Carpet Company.[68] The wartime correspondence of Posselt's nephew and director of the carpet firm, Arnold Korff, and various German carpet manufacturers such as the Persian Carpet Co., Berlin and Wilhelm Röper of Leipzig shows the extensive circle of customers that Posselt opened up for the Marki firm and might indicate this was one of the few products that they exported.[69] In 1902, the Briggs applied to the British consul for contacts with wool suppliers in Persia. Alex Murray appealed to the Secretary of State in London for permission to assist 'a large British firm of wool spinners in this district have asked me to put them in direct communication with producers of Khorassan [sic: Khorasan] wool in Persia'[70] because the Briggs brothers were eager to 'buy direct instead of as at present through middlemen'.[71]

66 'Wystawa tkacka' ['Weaving exhibition'], *Gazeta Warszawska*, 4 February, 1888, p. 2.

67 Wartalska, 'Fabryka i osada fabryczna', p. 654.

68 *Kurjer Kolejowy*, Warsaw, No. 30, 1898, p. 2.

69 APW, 'Firma Arnold Korff w Warszawie', signature 2818–21, Group 3 includes many of these letters.

70 FO65/1652, Murray to Secretary of State, 1 September, 1902, p. 103.

71 Ibid.

Figure 10.1 Invoice header showing medals from trade fairs
Source: By kind permission of Urząd Miasta Marki

Indications of the Growth and Success of the Marki Enterprise

By the early twentieth century textiles was the dominant industry in the Kingdom of Poland, producing 207 million rubles per annum compared with nearest rivals food processing, which generated 52 million, or the engineering and mining industries which each produced approximately 57 million. More than 120,000 workers were employed in textile manufacture compared to 42,000 in mining and 24,000 in food processing.[72] In 1905 Stanisław Koszutski compiled an influential review entitled *Nasz przemysł wielki na początku XX stulecia* (*Our Great Industry at the Beginning of the Twentieth Century*) using a basic criteria of the number of factories, size of workforce, product and annual incomes for each industrial settlement in the Kingdom of Poland,[73] based on various pan-Russian censuses of the previous decade.[74] Koszutski perhaps surprisingly shows that although cotton manufacture is generally considered the mainstay of Polish industry, there were more than double the number of wool factories to cotton mills in the region, however the value of production for each of these branches of industry similarly generated close to 89 million rubles.[75] These findings reflect the greater modernisation of the cotton industry which was concentrated in fewer large plants, while more expensive wool products were still predominatly manufactured in smaller factories and workshops. Chapter 4 described the marked contrast between industrial expansion in the Polish lands and central Russia, but it is worth noting here the very particular success of the Kingdom's spinning industry encompassing both cotton and wool, which by 1890 had a value of 'over 18 million rubles a year surpassing the total Russian yarn production, which did not exceed 6 million rubles'.[76]

The state survey of Warsaw industry commissioned by the Ministry of Internal Affairs in December 1886 provides some rare insight into the operations at Marki. It stated that Briggs, Posselt and Co. had four steam engines and 285 machines although their accumulated power and type were unspecified. They made wool yarn worth 1,200,000 rubles annually, employed 38 foreigners and 892 local workers and paid an annual wage bill of 156,000 rubles. The firm's raw materials were stated to be wool and coal of which 205,000 rubles worth, or one-third, was imported and 410,000 rubles worth were described as locally purchased. The firm's fixed assets

[72] *Opis ziem zamieszkanych przez Polaków: Krolestwo Polskie* [*Description of the Lands Inhabited by the Poles: the Kingdom of Poland*], Tom II (Warsaw: J. Sikorski, 1905), Henryk Radziszewski, 'Przemysłu', p. 310.

[73] Koszutski, *Nasz przemysł.*

[74] P.A. Orlov and S.G. Budagov, *Ukazatel' fabrik i zavodov Evropeĭskoĭ Rossīi* [*List of Factories and Industrial Plants European Russia*] (St Peterburg: V. Kirshbaum, 1894), eds N. Langowoja and W. Michajlowski, *Wykazu fabryk i zakladow w 1897* [*List of Factories and Business in 1897*] (St Petersburg: Department of Business and Industry, 1897), Koszutski also used the *Spis fabryk* [*Table of Factories*] compiled in St Petersburg by the Department of Industry in the Ministry of Finance between 1900–01.

[75] Koszutski, *Nasz przemysł*, pp. 8–9.

[76] *Opis ziem zamieszkanych przez Polaków*, p. 307.

were valued at 300,000 rubles (roughly £30,000) and they exported nothing beyond the Russian empire.[77] The roundness of many of the figures would suggest them to be approximations, whereas the very specific totals presented for the wage bill and employee numbers suggests they are likley to have been derived from factory inspectors' reports. The following year, however, the factory inspector Swiatłowski recorded an 8 per cent larger workforce which shows that any statistical snapshot of industry can only be considered loosely representative.[78] As would be expected from an appraisal of the Warsaw area, the only other wool processers mentioned were 12 artisan woollen manufacturers in Kaluszyn, none of whom used steam power, and their combined annual production amounted to a meagre 5,165 rubles.

Koszutski's 1905 analysis provides less-detailed information but does show that the Marki factory produced 2,383,200 rubles annually and then employed 1,348 workers.[79] Both British and Belgian consular accounts provide further testimony to the growing capacity of the Marki mill which was established with 30,000 spindles and 1,000 hp[80] and by the late 1890s operated 50,000 spindles with 3,000 hp.[81] In this context it is worth mentioning that in the post-war era the *Textile World* journal reported retrospectively that, in the year spanning 1913–14, Poland had approximately 337,400 spindles for French system combed wool and about 88,300 spindles producing English worsted, which suggests that Marki maintained its domination of this branch of industry.[82] In 1886 the Bradford press reported that 'the premises at Marki are even more extensive than those of Briggella Mills and provision has been left for still further extensions which the success of the enterprise will render necessary in the immediate future'.[83] That imminent huge expansion of building and plant was realised within a decade of the firm's foundation and, in addition to the acquisition of Meyerhoff's woollen plant and installation of another Hick Hargreaves 'giant steam engine',[84] included the Briggs brothers' investment in the Marki railway to improve their transport connections with Warsaw and the port of Praga.[85] Thus in 1903 Alex Murray informed the

77 APW, 72/1416, *Rząd Gubernialny Warszawski Referat II*, signature 403, pp. 1 and 4. The British consul consistently cited an exchange rate of 10 rubles to £1 in this period.

78 APW, Ref.1, 159/1887, pp. 2–3.

79 Koszutski, *Nasz przemysł*, p. 7.

80 *Diplomatic and Consular Reports*, Annual Series Issues 82–160 (London: Foreign Office, 1887), p. 37.

81 *Recueil Consulaire Contenant les Rapports Commerciaux des Agents Belges à L'Étranger* [*Consular Return Including the Commercial reports of Belgian Agents Abroad*], Vol. 95, 1897, p. 351 and Litten, *Englische Wollspinnerei*, p. 5.

82 'Polish Textile Needs', *Textile World*, New York, 6 September 1919, p. 91.

83 *Illustrated Weekly Telegraph*, Bradford, 19 March, 1886.

84 'Maszyna olbrzym', p. 4.

85 *Prawda: Tygodnik Polityczny, Społeczny i Literacki*, Warsaw, No. 52, 24 December 1892, p. 10 and in J. Braun, 'Warszawskie kolejki dojazdowe na przełomie XIX i XX wieku' ['Warsaw's rail communications at the turn of the nineteenth and twentieth centuries'], *Rocznik Mazowiecki*, p. 86.

Secretary of State in London that E. Briggs Brothers and Co., of Marki 'employ over 2,500 hands and is an unqualified success'.[86]

The accumulated evidence suggests strongly a meteoric rise for the Marki enterprise until the early part of the twentieth century. After 1905 the main source of industrial statistics is a series of commercial directories entitled *Księga adresowa przemysłu fabrycznego w Królestwie Polskim* [*Address Book of Factories in the Kingdom of Poland*] which consistently repeat the annual production [*roczna produkcja*], used interchangeably with the approximate annual turnover [*przybliż. obrót roczny*] of the Marki firm as 2,383,200 rubles until the First World War. By contrast, the French-style worsted manufacturers Dietel and particularly Allart, Rousseaux recorded steadily increasing returns. According to the 1905 directory Allart, Rousseaux had 1,660 workers and an annual production of 6,242,204 rubles. By 1911 they claimed a massive turnover of between 7 and 8 million rubles, however Henryk Radziszewski's contemporary examination of foreign investment in Poland records a production value of only 3,850,000 rubles and 1,500 labourers for the French-owned firm in 1905.[87] The figures for Dietel are even more inconsistent, for example in 1905 this firm reputedly had 1,543 workers and an annual production of 5,088,415 rubles. By 1908 their workforce had reduced to 1,200 but their value of production had risen dramatically to 8,947,956 rubles. By 1911 the firm's employee numbers were stable but the annual value of production had reduced to 4,000,000 rubles.

The data provided by these early twentieth century Polish directories cannot be ignored but their limitations as a dependable source of industrial statistics must be acknowledged. The main drawback was their reliance on the industrialists' responses to a standard questionnaire. There was no official obligation to provide updated or necessarily accurate information and there are many reasons for company directors to provide either vague approximations or exaggerated valuations for their operations. The consistent repetition of exactly the same financial summary for Marki suggests that the Briggs declined to update their entry, although the 1911 publication does show an increase in the size of workforce to 1,750 which may have been obtained from factory inspectors' reports.[88] In general the accounts of joint-stock companies were more transparent, or even exaggerated, than those of privately owned firms and their directory entries often included additional details such as the names of board members, the firm's capital, their accumlated steam power and so forth. For example, in 1905 Poland's premier engineering firm Lilpop, Rau and Loewenstein *Akcyjne Towarzystwo Przemysłowe Zakładów Mechanicznych* [Joint Stock Company of Mechanical Industries] declared a work force numbering a 1,000, capital of 2 million rubles and an annual turnover of 4 million rubles under the directorship of Henryk Marconi.[89]

86 FO65/1671, Murray to Secretary of State, 2 July 1903, p. 269.

87 *Opis ziem zamieszkanych przez Polaków*, pp. 288–313.

88 *Przemysł i handel Królestwa Polskiego*, No. 10155.

89 *Księga adresowa przemysłu fabrycznego w Królestwie Polskim za 1905 r.*, p. 351.

The few surviving factory inspectors' reports for Marki reveal the firm's steadily increasing workforce from its inauguration to the First World War. A workforce of 1,115 was recorded in 1887 rising to 1,630 in 1894. By 1896 the employees numbered between 1,708 and 1,800 and although a slight fluctuation was noted in 1901 the firm's workforce had increased to 1,990 workers by 1902. Even in a period of dire economic depression for the Russian empire after the 1905 Revolution, Bradford Mills at Marki maintained a workforce of between 1,420 and 2,092 in the year spanning 1908–09. The only report that the firm significantly reduced its production hours came in August 1907 when a four-day week was introduced which was further reduced in February 1908 to a three-day week. At that time the British consul noted that 'the trade in worsteds in 1908 was worse than in the two preceding years'.[90] Nevertheless, by 1909 Bradford Mills at Marki was working at full capacity once again[91] and in August of that year a two-shift system was introduced to support production from 4 am until 10 pm.[92]

In conclusion, this chapter has revealed that while foreign direct investment in the Russian empire was largely made in pursuit of market opportunities, its viability rested heavily on the availability of sufficient and suitable raw materials. The underdevelopment of the Russian wool trade, the import-resistant political culture and poor international communications in the host nation presented serious challenges to the Briggs-Posselt partnership. On the other hand, recent improvements to the international trading arena, many of which had been pioneered by Bradford's Chamber of Commerce, helped to facilitate their foreign enterprise. The development of southern-hemisphere wool growing, steam shipping, the invention of the wool press and opening of the Suez Canal all made feasible the importation of raw wool to Warsaw which would supplement Russian-empire resources.

In June 1883 the Tsarist Governor of Warsaw, Pyotr Albedynski, visited the building site at Marki and reported to the Ministry of Internal Affairs in St Petersburg that the Bradford men intended, even at the outset of their venture, to 'expand the factory by four times'.[93] The venture capitalists boasted of their ambition to achieve the scale of Poland's foremost linen manufacturer Hielle and Dietrich and of Scheibler, the Łódź cotton king. In their applications to the state and in the Polish press, the partnership presented their foreign enterprise as an enhancement to Russian-empire industry. They would reliably provide reasonably priced 'British' components to both the spinners and weavers. Contrary to

[90] *Diplomatic and Consular Reports on Trade and Finance: Russia*, Report for the year 1908 on the trade and agriculture of Poland and Grodno, Foreign Office Annual Series, No. 3988, 1909.

[91] APW, *Starszy Inspektor Fabryczny Guberni Warszawskiej*, signature 375, p. 012.

[92] Ibid., p. 014v.

[93] AGAD, *Akta Warszawskiego Komitetu Przemyłowego z 1883*, the Head of the Warsaw District (the highest ranking representative of the Russian Foreign Office in Warsaw), to the Ministry of Internal Affairs in St Petersburg, signature 11/83, 24 June 1883.

contemporary best practice in Bradford, where the wealthiest industrialists favoured fully vertical processing to maximise profits, the Marki entrepreneurs concentrated on raw-materials domination and specialised in component manufacture as the most appropriate and risk-averse strategy for the less familiar and underdeveloped markets of the Russian empire. It remains debatable whether the venture capitalists' projections of Russian demand for Bradford-style worsted failed to materialise and they resorted to more locally understandable woollen and French-style worsted manufacture as a defensive strategy. However, there is no indication to suggest these additions to the firm's repertoire were anything other than a proactive response to market opportunities in the host nation and a prudent form of diversification.

The Briggs-Posselt partnership allocated considerable resources to build a state-of-the-art plant, to train and retain a skilled workforce under a largely British management team. In the last two decades of the nineteenth century a diverse body of evidence suggests they enjoyed tremendous success and within a decade the firm had accumulated sufficient profits to extend both buildings and plant. It is worth noting that this was accomplished against a backdrop of rising industrial unrest in Poland which will be discussed in the next chapter. Thus in 1896 Litten applauded the 'efficiency of the prevailing forces here, to have created so much in a relatively short time'.[94] Nevertheless, after 1905, Polish commercial directories do suggest stagnant returns and that the Marki enterprise lagged far behind the region's French-worsted makers. But beyond promotional reporting of their own philanthropy, the size of their mill's engines, the height of the chimneys and so forth, Yorkshire's industrialists were habitually secretive to evade their competitors and deter state interference. This individualistic approach was characteristic for family firms like the Briggs, which retained absolute control of both finance and management of their businesses. Thus, it seems likely that the Bradford men only revealed the vaguest statistics about their operations when compelled by the Russian state surveys of the late nineteenth century. Incidents such as the industrial espionage which was described in the last chapter undoubtedly entrenched the owners' determination to conceal their interests and decline to update their entries in the aforementioned factory address books. In 1921 the *Gazeta Bankowa* explored the changing face of foreign investment in the Polish textile industry as a result of the First World War, and highlighted the withdrawal of German capital in favour of French and Belgian interests. The article detailed the value of every firm to survive the war in either rubles or francs, including Allart, Rousseau, Motte, Meillasoux and Caulliez, Posselt's Russian-Italian Silk Company alongside a few newly formed joint-stock operations. Even the Nottingham lace manufacturer Birkin, who had established a branch in Warsaw in 1903, declared a value of two

94 Litten, *Englische Wollspinnerei*, p. 8.

million rubles but E. Briggs Brothers and Co., Marki was the only firm included in the report without a declared value.[95]

The absence of surviving business records for the Marki enterprise has been an undoubted drawback to a thorough analysis of the firm's performance over time. But it has certainly been possible to outline the key facets and execution of the entrepreneurs' original plan, to reveal the firm's growing success and its ability to take advantage of host-market opportunities. Excellent capitalisation allowed the owners to maintain a typically British proprietorial approach to their foreign enterprise, retaining control of both finance and management, while most of their competitors had taken on joint-stock status by the end of the nineteenth century and only fragmentary evidence suggests that the Marki firm failed to maintain the upward trajectory that its early performance promised into the twentieth century. The following chapters will explore the many unforeseen political factors which undoubtedly challenged the firm's operations and profitability in the lead up to the First World War.

---

95 'Obcy kapitał w polskim przemyśle włókienniczym' ['Foreign capital in the Polish textile industry'], *Gazeta Bankowa*, Lwów, 10 October 1921, p. 18.

Chapter 11

'Under Threats and at the Revolver's Point':[1] Political instability and its impact on business behaviour after 1905

For the duration of the Marki venture, from 1883 to 1939, it is evident that the British owners operated in a climate of perpetual political volatility which would culminate in a series of very significant social, political and national transformations at the beginning of the twentieth century. This chapter will consider whether the Briggs-Posselt partnership's comprehensive strategy for worker control – their social-overhead investment and largely female workforce – successfully insulated the firm from the unrest which consumed Russian Poland at the turn of the nineteenth and twentieth centuries. It will show how the rising politicisation of the working class fundamentally altered relations between leading industrialists and the state, forcing adjustments to their business behaviour in order to survive.

Russian Rule of the Polish Lands

Following the Congress of Vienna, the Russian sector of the Polish lands became not only the most industrialised area of the empire but also its most 'nationally charged'.[2] The campaign of Russification, which has already been mentioned, included the suppression of the Polish language and culture to stamp out resistance to Tsarist rule.[3] Had the scheme incorporated some general incentives for the Polish people such as local infrastructural investment and secure employment it might have enjoyed greater success, but the heavy-handed implementation of political domination, in combination with reduced educational and economic opportunities for natives of the region, stoked rather than quelled Polish discontent. In 1883 the appointment of General Gurko as Warsaw's Governor General began one of the most concerted periods of denationalisation for the Polish lands.[4]

---

1 Dawson, *It Might Have Happened To You*, p. 111.

2 Weeks, 'Defending Our Own', p. 541.

3 Robert E. Blobaum, *Rewolucja: Russian Poland 1904–1907* (Ithaca and London: Cornell University Press, 1995), p. 4, Weeks, 'Defending Our Own', p. 540 and Słoniowa, *Sokrates Starynkiewicz*.

4 Blobaum, *Rewolucja*, p. 6.

Traditional perceptions of social hierarchy informed Russia's approach in Poland. The aristocracy were considered the greatest threat to the Tsar's sovereignty and subjected to numerous petty edicts. For example, Polish nobles were barred from using traditional Russian costume as a livery for their servants.[5] Exploitative taxation 'more than five times as great as many other of the governments into which the Russian empire is divided'[6] forced Polish landowners to mortgage their property to meet their dues.[7] Periodic changes to the system of taxation were used to extract the maximum revenue from the region. Thus the taxable value of Polish land which was originally calculated by its wheat productivity, perhaps in consideration of land-use changes to circumvent the levies, was graded 'upon the distance of the property from good roads, railways and markets' after 1869.[8]

Imperial Russia's concerns about future rebellion in the Polish lands were matched by a preoccupation with potential international hostilities. The strategic importance of Poland as the empire's frontier to Western Europe and Russia's longstanding antagonisms with neighbouring Prussia and Austria Hungary had a significant impact on the region. Military requirements dictated local investment in bridges, roads and rail links and a large proportion of the Russian population in the region were itinerant soldiers. Throughout the second half of the nineteenth century the British consul reported and repudiated numerous rumours of Russian military manoeuvres in the Polish territories.[9] In 1886 Henry Grant described that fortifications around Warsaw were being built with 'increased activity' and a military telephone line had been established between Warsaw and Zegrze on the River Narew.[10] By December heavy artillery was being installed in the fortresses around Warsaw.[11] In May 1888 the consul reported that the 'Vistula Railway has suspended goods traffic for a fortnight. As far as can be ascertained at present it is owing to retention of the 500 vans for conveyance of troops'.[12]

It is evident that the political energies of the Tsarist regime were largely preoccupied with international political tensions in the late nineteenth century. Policies for economic growth were not instigated to improve the conditions for business or standards of living but to finance military supremacy and the autocracy's engagement in regional political discourse was virtually non-existent. However, that is not to suggest that the state neglected any united nationalist threat from the Poles in this period. Chapter 4 described how the Polish political landscape was characterised by diversity and division: indeed the British consul suggested that 'the reason of the gradual fall of the Poles as a nation has been their

5 FO65/1193, Maude to the Secretary State, 13 June 1885, p. 10.

6 Ibid., 11 June 1884, p. 5.

7 FO65/1478, Grant to Secretary of State, 4 July 1894, p. 208.

8 FO65/1193, Maude to Secretary State, 11 June 1884, p. 5.

9 FO65/1146, Maude to Secretary of State, 31 December 1882, p. 103.

10 FO65/1277, Grant to the Secretary of State, 16 October 1886, p. 13.

11 Ibid., 24 December 1886, p. 20.

12 FO65/1340, Grant to the Secretary of State, 10 March 1888, p. 8.

inability to act in accord even against a common enemy'.[13] While open rhetoric against the Russian regime was rare, there was 'a certain freedom of speech and of the press'[14] where the deep factionalism of the Polish political arena is revealed.

The Factionalism of the Polish Political Arena

Under heavy Russian oppression after 1863, many of the dispossessed Polish nobility moved to Warsaw to join an outspoken intelligentsia. While some subscribed to a Loyalist-Conservative approach to Russian rule and promoted conciliation, they struggled to gain ground as no reciprocal goodwill was extended by the Russian regime. Bent on Russification and suspicious of even moderate Polish political activism as separatism, the ruling administration arguably overlooked this opportunity to strengthen relations with this troublesome region of the empire. Needless to say some quarters advocated armed conflict and radical terrorism while a large group nurtured the Romantic-nationalistic ideals of an earlier period. The heroic 'achievements of the insurgents ... their boldness, sacrifice, tactical skills, immense courage'[15] continued to inspire a sense of patriotic mission in many. Positivist activist Prus caricatured this nostalgic outlook through the medium of the character Rzecki in his classic novel *The Doll*.[16] By contrast, the outspoken newspaper editor Świętochowski roundly rejected such sentimentality, claiming: 'we ought not expect anything from political revolutions, wars, international agreements, changeable favours from strangers; but let us trust our own vitality'.[17]

In the place of risky nationalist polemic, economic and social issues formed a safe platform for all political groups to increase their public profile and expound their philosophies. Polish commentators and campaigners honed their ideas by studying industrialisation and the resultant social transformations in Western Europe. Darwin, Mill, Tyndall, Gladstone and Bismarck were regularly quoted and extracts from the British press were expounded to give weight to their views.[18] In response to greater foreign direct investment in the region in 1883, for example, the *Kurjer Warszawski* noted 'currently we have at hand the *Bradford Daily Chronicle and Mail* in which the introductory article ... shows that the evacuation of the island [England] by the wealthy is disastrous for the country'.[19] The author

[13] FO65/1631, Murray to Secretary of State, 23 December 1901, p. 201.

[14] Stepniak, *Russian Storm Cloud*, p. 149, and Blobaum, *Rewolucja*, p. 28.

[15] Magdalena Micinska, *Inteligencja na rozdrożach 1864–1918* [*Intelligentsia at the Crossroads*] (Warsaw: Instytut Historii PAN, 2008), p. 8.

[16] Prus, *The Doll*.

[17] Blobaum, *Rewolucja*, p. 33 and Blit, *Origins of Polish Socialism*, p. 12.

[18] Jedlicki, *Suburb of Europe*, Bonnell, *Russian Worker*, p. 150, Blit, *Origins of Polish Socialism*, p. 22.

[19] 'Anglicy w Polsce', p. 2.

welcomed the British capitalists who would reportedly be 'moving their smoking chimneys to the Vistula',[20] mentioning the Briggs of Bradford in the vanguard. In 1896 Ernest Williams' political diatribe *Made in Germany* was cited to lend weight to fears about a growing German domination of world trade: 'A certain Mr E. Williams announced a detailed set of statistical data on English trade and industry – and shows clearly that Germany has pushed England from the position, that she held until recently in the commercial-industrial world, and that Germany threatens the complete destruction of England's remaining commercial viability'.[21] Numerous similar examples can be found to support diverse political beliefs from Liberalism to, all too regularly, anti-Semitism.

Polish intellectuals also expounded their economic theories with arguments for and against a growing capitalist culture over which they had absolutely no influence. The lawyer and university professor, Adolf Suligowski, reasoned that capital growth was in the interests of the working classes, as investment would lead to mass production, reducing prices and therefore increasing consumption to ultimately improve the national wealth.[22] Ludwik Krzywicki, one of the leading exponents of Polish Marxism, conceded in 1889 that 'mutual harmony ... exists on the bedrock of contradictory interests',[23] therefore the wellbeing of workers did depend on the success of the factory owners. Nevertheless, in the early 1880s the Polish Socialist movement denounced such ideology as 'bastardly liberalism'.[24] They argued that accumulating national wealth in capitalist hands would not eradicate poverty but make it more widespread. They proposed 'the most equal division of wealth, power, rights and obligations possible'[25] and questioned both the ethics of competition and the dehumanising effects of factory labour, which reduced the worker 'to the level of a commodity'.[26]

Industrial Employers' Social-overhead Investment

In contrast to the political arena of Victorian England, the business elite of Russian Poland were largely precluded from political office. All their energies were devoted

20 Ibid.

21 Ernest Edwin Williams, *Made in Germany* (Brighton: Harvester Press, 1973 originally published in 1896) was quoted in *Gazeta Rzemieślnicza*, Warsaw, 26 September 1896.

22 Jedlicki, *Suburb of Europe*, p. 242.

23 Ludwik Krzywicki, *Dzieła* [*Works*] Vol. 4 (Warsaw: Państwowe Wydawn Naukowe, 1958), p. 289.

24 Jedlicki, *Suburb of Europe*, p. 245.

25 Alina Molska, *Pierwsze pokolenie marksistów polskich: Wybór pism i materiałów źrodłowych z lat 1878–1886* [*The First Generation of Polish Marxists: Selected Writings and Source Materials from 1878–1886*] Vol. 2 (Warsaw: Ksiażka i Wiedza, 1962), p. 631.

26 F. Tych, *Polskie programy socjalistyczne 1878–1918* [*The Polish Socialist Program 1878–1918*] (Warsaw: Ksiąka i Wiedza, 1975), p. 65.

to commerce and a few permitted charitable or trade-related committees. Although their political attitudes, largely cultivated in Western Europe, were inevitably influential due to their extraordinary wealth and ability to circumvent Russian bureaucracy, there is little evidence that they played any part in the regional discourse. Nevertheless, while Poland's numerous disenfranchised political groups debated philosophies to alleviate local poverty, many large employers such as the Briggs-Posselt partnership, Granzow, Natanson, Hielle and Dietrich, Scheibler and later Poznański routinely addressed the problems without debate. Showing a consummate practical understanding of social and industrial infrastructure, they successfully established their business empires and supplied their localities with water, energy, housing, sanitation, transport networks and, in the short term at least, secured the loyalty of their working-class employees.

Studies of late nineteenth-century Poland characteristically focus on how industrialisation and capitalism in the age of empire spawned working-class revolutionary movements, national self-determination and the rise of Socialism in the early twentieth century. However, the typically Marxist suggestion of a class war in which the interests of the workers were diametrically opposed to those of the employers and revolution constituted a wrangle for power in the workplace and society provide a less than complete picture of early twentieth-century Poland. In reality, while the various political groups theorised over the best interests of the poor and visualised a new social order, many industrialists built modern communities with all necessary amenities. As impotent political campaigners considered the collective needs of society and how to pay for them, the employers had already formulated an effective taxation system, in the form of deductions from gross income, to pay for incapacity benefit and fund healthcare. Although utopianism was bandied in the press, the most successful business leaders already marketed their enterprises under the banner of philanthropy. It is clear that in the politics of poverty there were few differences in the fundamentals of the debate, but only the industrialists had the wealth and motivation to make meaningful provision for the working-class masses in the Kingdom of Poland.

The shrewdest employers' strategy to gain total control of their workforces has already been described. The Briggs-Posselt partnership's highly selective employment policy, provision of housing, food supply, education and medical assistance was unusually comprehensive and created an entirely dependent and therefore malleable workforce. Many industrialists in Russian Poland introduced lesser measures to achieve similar ends and combined with the illegality of trade unions, under the protection of the Russian regime, they remained invulnerable to the zealous rhetoric in the press. Although many groups resented the large-scale employers and the Socialists particularly despised paternalism, no viable alternative emerged. Left-wing activists conceded that 'even if society were to rid itself of all the Dittrichs [sic: Dietrichs] and Scheiblers whom they heartily disliked, no one will be any better off'.[27]

---

[27] Jedlicki, *Suburb of Europe*, p. 242.

The Rise of Polish Socialism

This period of employer control under the protection of the state might be described as an interlude of relative calm. Anna Żarnowska describes the tradition of obedience among Polish peasants towards the church and employers which created a 'lack of democratic aspirations' in the first-generation industrial labourforce.[28] The workers were, in general, much better off than they had been prior to industrialisation, thus the intelligentsia's impotent theorising failed to engage their political interests. But in the 1880s Poland's political underground increasingly viewed working-class support as critical to bring about meaningful change and the first clumsy attempts to rally the masses began to appear in Polish factories. In 1883 the British consul highlighted the crude form of these incitements which, perhaps predictably, did not attack the state, but the employers: 'Will you allow the miserable agents of the government to harass the weaker part of your class? Will you tender them a spoil for the utmost utilisation and debauchery by the owners of factories, who feed on your blood'.[29] This exhortation by an organisation claiming to be the Committee of Workmen belonging to the Socialist and Revolutionary Party Proletariat was typical, but despite the distinctly working-class titles applied, such groups rarely included a membership of labourers. In 1886 the Russian political activist Stepniak described the difficulty Warsaw's Socialists had in recruiting workmen to their cause and the scope of the local movement which comprised a mere 150–200 recruits which were 'the result of the work of only three agitators of the educated classes'.[30]

While most scholars agree that workers and intellectuals had little common ground, it is worth noting that the delineation between them was not clear-cut. Many disinherited nobles and members of the Polish intelligentsia who attended Russian universities and technical institutes went on to pursue careers in Polish industry. Some were radicalised by Russian Socialist ideas and returned to form a powerful contingent of the Polish revolutionaries.[31] Such young men, despite their assertions that they worked in industry in order to understand the 'real proletarians',[32] and regardless of the government's frequent conclusion that the troublemakers had infiltrated companies such as 'Lilpop, Handtke, Orthwein and Schulze',[33] in reality needed an income like any other workers and followed the only career path open to them. The same might be said of notables who perfected their radical ideas in Britain's industrial cities such as Engels in Manchester, or Weerth in Bradford.

---

28 Żarnowska, *Workers, Women and Social Change*, p. 299.

29 FO65/1167, Maude to the Secretary of State, 21 February 1883, p. 9.

30 Stepniak, *Russian Storm Cloud*, p. 146.

31 Blit, *Origins of Polish Socialism*, p. 17.

32 Ibid., Blit quotes Ludwik Waryński, a member of a Polish Socialist underground.

33 Ibid., p. 51.

Although the Polish working classes were reluctant to join the political polemic, protests and spontaneous outpourings of anger in retaliation for grievances were not uncommon. A typical incident was described by Maude in 1884 when 'a *strażnik* [rural policeman] in the neighbourhood of Biala ... was hanged by some exasperated peasants ... driven to desperation by constant terrible persecution'.[34] Such incidents, typically unorganised and articulating few demands, were routinely and brutally quashed by the Russian authorities. In 1894 the consul described the harrowing state response to a local protest against Catholic persecution in Kowno when Cossacks drove people into the frozen river where many drowned, 20 were 'cut down' and 80 were flogged.[35] Despite the paternalistic approach of many industrialists and apparent concern about the welfare of their employees, in cases of industrial unrest, they invariably called for state assistance, trusting violence rather than diplomacy to mediate dispute with their workforces. Indeed an eyewitness report of strike action at Łódź in 1892 suggested that 'the military have to be paid by all the manufacturers and Jews who wish to save their property'.[36]

Religion and Nationality

In the second half of the nineteenth century it is clear that even the most fundamental issues divided rather than united the Russian-Polish population and there were few truly unifying ideas or institutions. Most ethnic Poles were Catholic, thus the church as the 'only universal national institution'[37] was considered by the state to have great influence and was oppressed heavily following the 1863 Uprising.[38] In 1893 Henry Grant reported the 'painful impression among the Polish people'[39] caused by the decision to build a large Russian Orthodox cathedral in Warsaw's Saxon Square. Religion became the benchmark of nationality and was used to mete out preferential employment and educational opportunities to certain groups while restricting the activities of others. Adherents of the Orthodox faith were naturally favoured whereas Catholic Poles were periodically purged from state institutions. For example, in 1886 'all the Roman Catholic employees of the Warsaw law courts ... have been summarily dismissed by order of a high official and the same fate has befallen female Roman Catholic teachers attached to the different educational establishments of this city'.[40]

---

34 FO65/1193, Maude to the Secretary of State, 30 December 1884, p. 19.

35 FO65/1478, Grant to the Secretary of State, 31 March 1894, p. 160.

36 'The Labour Riots at Łódź', *Daily News*, London, 11 May 1892, p. 6 quotes the *Breslauer General Anzeiger*.

37 Żarnowska, 'Religion and Politics', p. 303.

38 Blobaum, *Rewolucja*, p. 3.

39 FO65/1452, Grant to the Secretary of State, 4 April 1893, p. 130.

40 FO65/1277, Grant to the Secretary of State, 28 October 1886, p. 18.

In the melting pot of the Polish lands, however, where the diversity of the population resulted from centuries of free as well as enforced migration, intermarriage and assimilation, generalisations about religious and national identities were largely impossible. Davies highlights the unreliability of Russian definitions of ethnicity, noting that 'bilingual and bi-religious families were not uncommon. People subjected to official questionnaires notoriously gave different answers to different investigators'.[41] Despite the shortcomings of the data the 1897 Russian census showed that rural Poland remained essentially Catholic, while only 48.2 per cent of the urban population were categorised as Polish at the end of the century: Jews constituted 38.6 per cent, Germans 6 per cent (18 per cent in Łódź) and 4 per cent were Russian.[42] The census made no distinction between Protestants or Jews that had been born in Poland and recent immigrants; all three groups were categorised as foreign based on their religion. In addition to the state-imposed classification, society had its own entrenched hierarchical order in which religion, wealth or social standing influenced where people lived, the parks or salons they were admitted to and only the highest echelons of the bourgeoisie socialised without segregation.[43]

In the late nineteenth century, two essentially foreign groups held power in the Kingdom of Poland; the Russian authorities and a wealthy bourgeoisie. Chapter 6 showed that Poland's so-called German business elite mainly comprised second- and third-generation Polish families. Many had taken a leading role in the 1863 uprising and participated in pro-Polish cultural and quasi-political organisations, but at the end of the nineteenth century the rapid infusion of capital from abroad produced a 'defensive nationalist reaction'[44] which pervaded all social strata. The long-established Warsaw bankers and landowners of Protestant faith with German surnames and a new wave of foreign venture capitalists were all understood to enjoy the protection of the Russian government. Middle-class Poles saw their employment prospects eroded not just by Russian administrators but also by foreign engineers and managers who dominated the region's growing industry. As the British consul noted in 1891, 'the difficulty of the situation is increased by the number of young men, students, and others who finding most careers closed against them in Poland [feel] much exasperation'.[45] Thus, Polish nationalists concentrated their energies on anti-German campaigning rather than the taboo subjects of Russian occupation and the much-hated policies of Russification. The longstanding antagonism was fuelled by reports of invasive German settlement of Polish agricultural land to the west and Bismarck's anti-Catholic policies in Prussia. In 1901 Alex Murray highlighted that 'the whole Polish nation, if one may use that expression, is up in arms at the methods employed by the Germans for the

41 Davies, *God's Playground*, p. 181.

42 Blobaum, *Rewolucja*, p. 22.

43 Słoniowa, *Sokrates Starynkiewicz*, p. 27.

44 Jedlicki, *Suburb of Europe*, p. 275.

45 FO65/1404, Grant to the Secretary of State, 14 April 1891, p. 184.

Germanisation of the Polish province of Posen'.[46] The xenophobic sentiment that increasingly unified Polish attitudes did not escape the notice of the government, indeed it provided some prime public-relations opportunities for the Russian administration to show pan-Slavic solidarity with the Poles. A typical incident was described by the British consul in 1884 when:

> A quarrel took place, between German and Polish workmen employed at a factory, and they proceeded to blows. Two Police interfered and were themselves beaten. General Tcherkassoff, the governor of the district, instantly proceeded to the spot, and after a brief enquiry, ordered the immediate expulsion of the whole of the German workmen, ten in number, from Poland.[47]

Thus the Tsarist regime, which had traditionally championed the foreign ownership of business and enjoyed the profits of the Kingdom of Poland's thriving economy, simultaneously encouraged negative, often racist, stereotypes of the ethnically German or Jewish industrial bourgeoisie. As a tactic to preserve the delicate *status quo*, they intended to make the wealthiest and most powerful segment of the population a target of hatred for the majority; to create in them a scapegoat for social discontent rather than an alternative leadership. In the last quarter of the nineteenth century the harassment of foreign elements and particularly Jews in the Kingdom of Poland became a significant facet of the Russian state's armoury to create compliance in the Polish population. Indeed Murray testifies that agitation of the Poles against Germanisation 'would not, of itself be of much importance, were it not that they are being more or less openly egged on and encouraged by the Russian government'.[48]

The Łódź Rebellion

During the late 1880s and early 1890s there was a significant rise in mass political mobilisation in Poland. But the formulaic response of the Tsarist administration to brutally quash unrest, examine 'the causes of worker dissatisfaction'[49] and make scant gestures towards worker pacification, while seeking out conspiracies amongst the intelligentsia, began to fail them. In May 1892 the Łódź Rebellion presented the Russian police with an unprecedented challenge to their authority. Opinion is naturally divided about the complex causes of the unrest: some suggest it arose from a demand for 'an increase in their wages',[50] others insist that 'the

46 FO65/1631, Murray to Secretary of State, 23 December 1901, p. 201.

47 FO65/1227, Maude to the Secretary of State, 9 October 1885, p. 21.

48 FO65/1631, Murray to Secretary of State, 23 December, 1901, p. 201.

49 Giffin, 'Formative Years of the Russian Factory Inspectorate', p. 644.

50 'Horrible Massacre in Poland', *Sheffield and Rotherham Independent*, 3 October 1892, p. 5.

ethnic apportionment of jobs' was the root.[51] Naturally any implication that the protests were an expression of anti-Russian feeling was banned and local press reports were heavily censored. Thus, many political groups subsequently claimed the insurrection for their cause and attributed their own ideals to the strikers. But although some scholars suggest the rebellion was the result of better regional cooperation between political activists, both Franaszek and Blobaum conclude that the sudden explosion of violent disorder in Poland's city of industry was not orchestrated by any political organisation and caught the Polish Socialists by surprise.[52]

The general chaos at Łódź was widely reported in the foreign press as 'thirty thousand suspended work until Thursday, and paraded the town in disorderly crowds, attacking the Jewish inhabitants, and committing other excesses'.[53] The London *Daily News* described 'manufacturers, factory bookkeepers, and Jews are knocked down and stabbed'.[54] Anti-Semitic rhetoric was rife in approved press reports of the events and one eyewitness suggested that the Cossacks seemed 'to rejoice at the fate of the poor Jews'.[55] A state of emergency ensued in which General Gurko reputedly telegraphed: 'kill without mercy. Do not spare the powder'.[56] Although the action was largely unsuccessful with more than 200 protesters reportedly killed in the disorder, many imprisoned and 300 foreign workers expelled from the city,[57] the Łódź Rebellion is generally accepted as a defining moment for the Polish labour movement as the first collective action with clearly articulated demands. However, it is clear that it also marked another significant turning point as thereafter the Russian state appeared to modify its campaign to subjugate Polish culture and its customary support of capital over labour.

In the aftermath of the 1892 disturbances, in a complete *volte-face* on Russification, the government demanded that factory rules were posted in both the Polish and Russian languages. The predominantly German-speaking factory supervisors received notice that they must be proficient in one of these tongues to retain their position. Although the concessions might have been superficial and as poorly administered as previous factory legislation, they reveal the ruling regime's growing fear of the working masses. In 1892 all commentators concur that the manufacturers received government orders to 'make no concession to the strikers'.[58] Whereas in 1903 when a strike occurred at the Odessa Tramway Company, the Russian chief of police reputedly instructed the firm's Belgium owner to 'accept all the strikers' conditions. 'If you do not I shall have you led to

---

51 Crago, 'The "Polishness" of Production', p. 23.

52 Blobaum, *Rewolucja*, p. 37. Franaszek, 'Poland', p. 405.

53 *Leeds Mercury*, 9 May 1892, p. 2.

54 'The Labour Riots at Łódź', p. 6.

55 Ibid.

56 'Horrible Massacre in Poland', p. 5.

57 *Birmingham Daily Post*, 12 May 1892, p. 8.

58 *Sheffield and Rotherham Independent*, 18 May 1892, p. 5.

the border by two gendarmes and we will seize the company'.[59] Whether this was fact or propaganda, the state's outward stance against notably foreign industrialists on behalf of the workers was increasingly promoted.

The Łódź Rebellion may have inspired greater organisation of Polish Socialist parties but it did not create political unity in Poland.[60] The following decade saw the establishment of numerous illegal political groups including the *Polska Partia Socjalistyczna* or PPS [Polish Socialist Party] and various splinter groups such as the *PPS-Lewica* [Left], *PPS-Rewolucja* [Revolution], *PPS-Proletariat*, *Socjaldemokracja Królestwa Polskiego i Litwy or SDKPiL* [Social Democrats of the Kingdom of Poland and Lithuania], the National League which became *Stronnictwo Narodowo-Demokratyczne* or *Endecja* (National Democratic Party), *Towarzystwo Oświaty Narodowe* or TON [Society for National Education], a nationalist workers' union the *Narodowy Zwiazek Robotniczny* or NZR [National Union of Workers],[61] also known as *Jednośc* [Unity],[62] an influential Jewish Union known as the *Bund* emerged later to be challenged by a Zionist Socialist movement active in Warsaw and Łódź amongst many more.[63] Despite their number, these organisations still failed to enlist significant worker support and remained the preserve of the intelligentsia in the post-1892 period.

May Day Protests at Marki

Workforce compliance was central to the Briggs-Posselt partnerships' strategy at Marki. It was intended to deliver maximum flexibility, productivity and profitability for the firm and protect their interests from external economic and political influences. Therefore, in the context of rising industrial unrest in Łódź, a decade after the isolated worsted plant was founded, it is possible to assess the success of the Bradford men's plans to immunise their workers from the general disorder. Indeed, in 1892 only the enlargement of the Marki plant and the British industrialists' investment in the local railway were reported in the press and the first indications of any political activity in the factory settlement were not recorded until May 1894.

Each May following the 1892 rebellion the Russian police prepared for orchestrated protests in industrial centres across the Russian empire. In 1894 the head of the district of Warsaw, Von Brinken, wrote to city's governor that there had been no trace of 'any Socialist movement or May Day celebrations at Briggs and Posselt's factory in Marki which have caused serious unrest amongst the workers

59 McKay, *Pioneers for Profit*, p. 281.

60 Crago, 'The "Polishness" of Production', p. 16 and Blobaum, *Rewolucja*, p. 35.

61 Davies, *God's Playground*, p. 200.

62 Crago, 'The "Polishness" of Production', p. 31.

63 Blobaum, *Rewolucja*, p. 38.

in other factories'.[64] However, a few days later he was forced to admit some signs of dissent as 'about 20 young people aged 16 to 20 surrounded the gates … and started to dissuade and block the female workers from entering the factory'.[65] It emerged that 1,000 employees of Briggs, Posselt and Co. stayed at home on that day which clearly constituted a protest of some significance. Nevertheless, the police chief congratulated himself on his successful management of potential conflict, stating that 'this was undoubtedly because I called fifty Cossacks to the village of Marki'.[66]

In the typical manner of Russian officialdom, Von Brinken was charged with seeking out the cause of the protest and particularly ascertaining whether the 'factory was entirely without guilt'.[67] His enquiries revealed an expected reticence among Marki's women workers to engage actively in the strike and many claimed to just be 'following the suit of others',[68] while only a few expressed their dissatisfaction with the factory and their wages. Some PPS brochures calling for an eight-hour workday and the right to form a workers' assembly were discovered in the homes of three Marki residents. But the ultimate arrest of a man who was not employed in the factory led blame for the troubles to be attributed to outside agitators.

In May 1895, SDKPiL proclamations which included anti-government slogans were scattered through the corridors of the factory housing at Marki.[69] In 1896 Von Brinken again reported that guards had found booklets and leaflets in the factory houses of Marki, this time issued by the Central Workers' Committee with instructions to 'stick' the leaflets to the factory walls.[70] These police reports show that, rather than forming a hotbed of political activity for radical groups, Marki was periodically bombarded with propaganda originating outside the town. Although the attempts of various political groups to coordinate strike action across the region are evident, the active involvement of Marki's workforce is not. Moreover, the Russian police record of one Marki arrest does reveal a key problem for the Socialist agitators. The interrogation of a man caught in possession of inflammatory material found in Marki revealed that he had pocketed the leaflet so that he could ask the landlord of a Praga pub to read it to him, because he was illiterate.[71]

---

[64] APW Ref. I, 26/1894, No. 212, Report by the head of Warsaw district A. Von Brinken to the Governor of Warsaw J. Adrejev, 20 April/2 May 1894, pp. 10–11.

[65] Ibid.

[66] Ibid.

[67] Ibid.

[68] Ibid.

[69] APW Ref. I, 28/1895, No. 230, report of the chief country guard of Warsaw I. Azbukin to the governor of Warsaw J. Andrejev, 20 February/5 March 1895, p. 7.

[70] Ibid.

[71] APW, Ref. I, No. 238, Report of the land guard of Radzymin W. Rosinski to the chief of the county of Radzymin, P. Macedonski about the May Day agitation at Marki, 20 April/2 May 1895, pp. 18–19.

In Chapter 8 it was argued that the Bradford entrepreneur's strategy to employ a largely female workforce was not principally to save money but to ensure compliance. As so-called workers' organisations proliferated illegally in the early twentieth century it is evident that, rather than representing their interests, women workers found themselves under increasing pressure from feuding PPS and SDKPiL agitators on factory floors across the country. The SDKPiL-sponsored *Gazeta Robotnicza* accused PPS delegates of collecting 'premiums from workers under duress, without invoice and without receipt'[72] and circulating the PPS newspaper *Czerwony Sztandar* in factories. The character of the beleaguered female workers who were pawns in the battle between the two parties is well-illustrated by the following description: 'some female workers place sacred images on their machines, and the [PPS] delegates began to incite our male comrades to strip them down. When this was done, the PPS delegates accused the SDKPiL of being hooligans who do not believe in God and go hand in hand with Russians'.[73]

The Briggs-Posselt partnership's employment policy and accepted wisdom that women were less likely to incite unrest seem to be confirmed by this contemporary repartee. The partisan press invariably represented men as the heroes of the workers' movements. For example, the *Gazeta Robotnicza* described a dispute at the gasworks on Ludna Street in Warsaw, when 40 men were allegedly about to lose their jobs: 'then in walked our comrade [SDKPiL], he highlighted the significance of the matter and put forward a resolution'.[74] This blatant propaganda suggested that the SDKPiL delegate negotiated not only to save the men's jobs but managed to secure an eight-hour day and free medical assistance for all the employees. He was said to have highlighted to the gas workers the swindling of their PPS representatives, but the strength of feeling and volatility of the situation is clear, as their opponents retaliated by brandishing Browning guns.[75]

The 1905 Revolution

Although the machinations of the numerous Socialist organisations were largely powerless in the nineteenth century, growing social and particularly economic pressures increasingly unified Polish political thought in the early twentieth century. An economic downturn led many foreign investors to withdraw their money from the region while the cost-saving measures instituted by other industrialists led unemployment to rise sharply. By the summer of 1904 the factory inspectorate

72 'Z fabryk i warsztatów' ['From the factories and workshops'], *Gazeta Robotnicza*, Warsaw, No. 4, 27 May 1906, p. 3.

73 Ibid.

74 'Wydalenie robotnikow czy 8-godzinny dzień roboczy?' ['The dismissal of workers or the eight hour day?'] *Gazeta Robotnicza*, No. 4, 27 May 1906, p. 2.

75 Ibid.

reported that 350 Łódź factories only worked a three-day week.[76] The advent of the Russo-Japanese War in 1904 created further privations as wealthy landowners were subject to war taxes and the rural *gminas* [regional government areas] were required to set aside 10 per cent of their community funds for the war effort. The Kingdom of Poland was reputedly required to provide a disproportionately high number of conscripts in comparison with other regions of the empire and the requisition of horses was hugely unpopular.[77] Inflated taxes, rents and prices for basic goods impacted on all sections of Russian-Polish society who united against the existing order for the first time.

Russian-language education, although it might be perceived a minor hardship in the context of appalling poverty and national subjugation, became the focus of the first demonstrations. During 1904, 'numerous walk-outs, closings and mass expulsions of students'[78] took place in Warsaw schools until a nationwide school strike broke out in January 1905. The protest embodied the unified rejection of both the Russification and Germanisation of Poland, the inadequate education of children, the commandeering of the best-paid jobs by foreign workers, the oppression of Polish culture and the Catholic religion and soon led to a general rebellion.

British consular correspondence provides rare uncensored accounts of the increasingly chaotic situation as a general strike took hold in early January which affected 'public works and services as well as factories at Warsaw'.[79] Alex Murray's initial reports registered the action as a series of minor aggravations: there was a shortage of coal and 'inconvenient stoppage of telephones' and no newspapers or bread were available.[80] The apparently measured response of the authorities seemed evident as the police took charge of the gas and water works. Murray played down the significance of unfolding events, announcing that the 'strikes are "merely" a workers disturbance to show sympathy with strikers at St. Petersburg not part of the Polish national movement although the Polish Party of Socialists are trying to make capital out of it, as are the Jewish Revolutionary Society "Bund"'.[81]

By the end of the month, unrest at Vilna, Korno and at Radom brought troops and strikers into collision.[82] A stronger anti-government or nationalist drive and greater organisation were apparent as processions of working men and students carrying the red flag or Polish national symbols demonstrated on the streets of

---

76 Blobaum, *Rewolucja*, pp. 43–57.

77 Ibid., p. 44 and FO393/16, Maude to Secretary of State, 31 December 1882, p. 103, mentioned 'the registration of horses (strictly administered) and manoeuvres of the Russian Army'.

78 Blobaum, *Rewolucja*, p. 65.

79 FO65/1714, Murray to the Secretary of State, 25 January1905, p. 11.

80 Ibid.

81 Ibid.

82 FO65/1714, Murray to the Secretary of State, 26 January 1905, p. 10.

Warsaw and there was no mob violence against the Jews.[83] Indeed the consul remarked on a palpable air of cooperation as 'the movement is being directed by the Russo-Jewish Revolutionary Party, the Polish Party of Socialists PPS and Social Democrats of the Kingdom of Poland and Lithuania'.[84] However, scholars tend to agree that despite greater unity, the Socialist parties still 'exercised only a slight influence on the industrial workers'[85] who were the principal instigators of the actions. The consul's reports of minor inconvenience and sympathy strikes were soon replaced by accounts of uncontrolled and vicious sorties by Cossack brigades in Warsaw. On 30 January Murray telegraphed London that 'Warsaw has today been proclaimed in a state of siege'.[86]

In contrast to the 1892 revolt, in 1905 the strikers' demands were clearly articulated, although the emphasis undoubtedly depended on which political group articulated them. The fundamentals were an eight-hour day, free medical treatment for families, removal of foreign overseers, old-age pensions, a 25 per cent pay rise and a minimum daily wage of 1.5 rubles for a man and 1.2 rubles for women. According to Murray the employers conceded a ten-hour day and a 10 per cent pay increase to no avail and he added 'both manufacturers and the authorities are afraid of the men'.[87] During February he offered three explanations for the strike's endurance, surprisingly suggesting that 'the strikers have no difficulty in holding out as the manufacturers are continuing their full pay during the strike'.[88] Later he speculated, 'I believe I am rightly informed that the International Socialist Committee is allowing 10 copeks a day a head to the strikers and their families'[89] and also that many received financial support from emigrated relations in the USA. The mayhem continued throughout 1905; at the beginning of the year Murray's assessment was that 'the authorities have just grasped that the real power in Russia is in the hands of the lower classes',[90] and in December he confirmed 'it is almost a mockery to speak of Russian rule in Poland'.[91]

Strike Action at Marki

Whereas Polish scholars provide great detail about strike action in numerous named factories across Russian Poland, no violent disorder is recorded in Marki. The employees of E. Briggs Brothers and Co. were undoubtedly better off than

83 Ibid., 10 January 1905, p. 4.
84 Ibid., 30 January 1905, p. 30.
85 Blobaum, *Rewolucja*, p. 98.
86 FO65/1714, Murray to the Secretary of State, 30 January 1905, p. 30.
87 Ibid., 11 February 1905, p. 34.
88 Ibid.
89 FO65/1714, Murray to the Secretary of State, 27 February 1905, p. 49.
90 Ibid., 11 February 1905, p. 34.
91 Ibid., 23 December 1905, p. 132.

many of their contemporaries: with housing and allotments which provided subsistence even if their income was reduced by short-time working. But in contrast to the cotton companies of Łódź, the specialist worsted manufacturer would have received government contracts for uniform cloth and thus maintained employment throughout the privations of the Russo-Japanese war. In 1905 the general strike that reputedly began in the Warsaw district of Wola escalated as 'crowds of workers roamed the streets spreading the unrest from factory to factory'.[92] It is likely that reluctance of the Briggs' female workers to jeopardise their jobs and Marki's isolation from more populated industrial areas held back the progress of worker revolt in the town. Indeed Żarnowska suggests that industrial workers in suburban communities 'frequently broke away from the strikers'.[93] However, although the British industrialists may have secured the loyalty of their employees, some evidence does suggest that the violent coercion of their workforce into strike action was unavoidable in 1905. Dawson later described that 'when the great strike occurred in 1905 and 1906 [the Marki employees] refused to leave their work, and only joined at length under threats and at the revolver's point'.[94] Further confirmation is suggested by a New Zealand press report that:

> The working people, of whom there are nearly four thousand, at the mills of Messrs Briggs Bros., at Warsaw, have joined in the Russian disturbances, and last week large numbers of them were shot as they were marching to join another body of strikers. Messrs Briggs, of course, are on the most friendly terms with their employees, for whom they have built houses and a church. No such bad news has yet come with regard to the mills of Messrs Posselt, at Riga, or of Messrs Thornton, at St. Petersburg.[95]

Whereas British, French or Italian minorities in the Kingdom of Poland had generally escaped the animosity that had been directed at its German and Jewish elements, in 1905 assaults were no longer confined to German or Jewish employers. In April 'Mr James Radcliffe of Łódź advises: a prominent British resident of Łódź ... stabbed this morning at nine o'clock ... would-be assassin not captured'.[96] Reports of the violent expulsion of foreign factory owners and management were widespread as a director and two foremen were thrown out of one of Scheibler's factories and numerous 'managers all of whom are foreigners and among them several Englishmen' were ousted from Żyrardów.[97] An apparent vigilante justice

[92] Blobaum, *Rewolucja*, p. 76.
[93] Żarnowska, *Workers, Women and Social Change in Poland*, p. 299.
[94] Dawson, *It Might Have Happened To You*, p. 111.
[95] *Wanganui Chronicle*, New Zealand, 25 March 1905, p. 2, a similar report appeared in the *Yorkshire Telegraph and Star*, 2 February 1905, p. 3.
[96] FO65/1714, Murray to the Secretary of State, 10 April 1905, p. 62.
[97] Ibid., 9 December 1905, p. 125.

was rife and in the spring 'many of Łódź's wealthier inhabitants together with subjects of foreign states left the city from fear of "terrorist acts"'.[98]

Terrorism at Marki

During the 1905 strike actions the Marki factory owners suffered nothing worse than brief loss of workforce control and some income, but there was a considerable difference between the retributions meted out to unpopular employers during the mob violence of their workers and planned acts of terrorism by political activists. The economic value of the foreign contingent in the Kingdom of Poland to the much-hated Russian regime made them a useful lever for Polish political groups and few were untouched by terrorism in the revolutionary period. Thus in October 1905 Alfred Briggs wrote to his family in Bradford that 'ten men came out to Marki to do mischief'[99] and he went on to describe the course of events which began with the murder of three Russian policemen in the mill's front office and culminated in the bombing of the factory owners' residence. Considering the state of national unrest, the presence of a small number of police inside the factory was not extraordinary and even suggests that Marki's workforce presented little cause for greater precautions.

Failing to find John Briggs inside the mill, the murderers went to the industrialist's home where Briggs' wife, Flora, reportedly confronted them on the doorstep. An account of the incident entitled 'Mrs Briggs' Cool Courage' appeared in the *Yorkshire Daily Observer*.[100] It suggests that despite the careful planning of the attack which 'commenced by the cutting of all telephone and telegraph wires leading out of Marki',[101] and although the men acted without hesitation in killing the Russian policemen, they stood patiently on the industrialist's doorstep expecting the factory owner to present himself. Briggs and his nephew Charles Whitehead fled upstairs and when 'the fellows got tired of waiting'[102] they threw bombs into Mrs Briggs' conservatory, causing only superficial damage before they ran away.

In the aftermath of the attack Alfred Briggs alluded to a possible motive for the attack that 'people say it is out of revenge for having those delegates arrested during the night a few weeks back at the time of the strike'.[103] But the industrialist denied the provocation, insisting that any arrests had been a police matter.

98 Blobaum, *Rewolucja*, p. 89.

99 'The Attack on a Gentleman's Villa: Mrs Briggs Cool Courage', *Yorkshire Daily Observer*, 20 October 1905.

100 Ibid.

101 Ibid.

102 Ibid.

103 Ibid.

The industrialist's frayed nerves after almost a year of uncertainty were evident in his emotional conclusion that:

> This shows how we are protected. People come in broad daylight to commit a crime and carry it out with all ease in the presence of hundreds, and nothing happens to them as everybody is afraid, and the murderers get away. Why this dastardly act should have been enacted in Marki I do not know.[104]

Terrorist attacks on isolated settlements were an effective form of intimidation due to the practical difficulties of calling for reinforcements. After the attack at Marki 'a policeman managed to secure a bicycle and rode to a neighbouring village and secured the presence of some Cossacks who searched the woods but the murderers escaped'.[105] From this report it seems evident that although employers still hoped for police protection, in 1905 state resources were stretched to control the mob violence of the cities.

Despite the disappointment of most of the agitators' demands in 1905 and continuing Russian rule, many concessions were made to appease the Polish population after the revolution. The state 'inclined towards compromise in the linguistic, cultural, and religious spheres',[106] and the British consul noted that 'Polish emblems are to be seen everywhere ... in the streets, the Russian text inscriptions, on notices, shop signs etc. is in most cases defaced or removed'.[107] The Polish workforce had suffered years of hardship from the economic downturn culminating in the strike action and were ready for the most part to tow the line and get back to work. Despite some disruption, the Bradford entrepreneurs could congratulate themselves on escaping the worst of the violence. Nevertheless the revolt had polarised a change of political climate and the Russian state's eagerness to find a scapegoat for the troubles caused most industrial employers to prudently adjust their business style in the coming years.

Polonising the Image of Industry

During the 1905 troubles, the press and political agitators had frequently drawn attention to a number of the industrial employers' characteristic failings. They had roundly criticised the absenteeism of foreign factory owners in the Kingdom of Poland as well as the standard employment of foreign skilled staff to oversee Polish workers. Although the Briggs brothers' permanent residence in Marki and their local intermarriage would have stood in their favour, there is some evidence to suggest that they took steps to reduce the number of British managers that they

---

104 Ibid.

105 Ibid.

106 Blobaum, *Rewolucja*, p. 260.

107 FO65/1714, Murray to the Secretary of State, 23 December 1905, p. 132.

employed. For example, in the early years of the business 'thirty-eight employees were specialists imported from abroad, mainly from England'.[108] By 1887 the factory inspector recorded that, of 24 factory foremen: 12 were English, 7 Prussian and 5 were 'Russian subjects'.[109] However, when John Hinchcliffe arrived in 1910 he wrote 'there are only about nine Englishmen here besides myself, not 15 nor 20'.[110] As was described in Chapter 9, Walerian Zawiszewski, took on a higher profile in the firm's dealings with the state in this period.[111]

It has been shown that the majority of industrialists in Russian Poland were of German origin. Despite a growing reticence of the Russian state to back them in conflicts with their workers, their long establishment in the region, huge fixed-asset investments, the continuing economic advantage of the Russian market and protectionism meant that few who survived the Revolution of 1905 retreated afterwards. Nevertheless these industrialists had witnessed how religious affiliations and ethnicity had been used by the Tsarist state to periodically purge the commercial arena of their Jewish colleagues, skilled employees and clients. Thus in the post-Revolution period it became politic for all foreign industrialists to attempt greater Polish assimilation. As 'intellectual activists ceaselessly attacked the textile elite for their lack of Polish surnames',[112] many Polonised their names: Carls became Karols, and typical German surnames such as Scheibler and Schulze increasingly used the Polonised spellings of Szeibler and Szulze.[113] When the state demanded joint-stock-company directors must declare their nationality, Łódź's manufacturers all pronounced themselves Polish.[114] The Briggs-Posselt partnership appears to have carefully disassociated itself from the heavily German culture of Łódź, John Briggs took Russian nationality to smooth his dealings with the state, safeguard the firm's assets and undoubtedly improve his tax position. But during the interwar period the chameleon quality of the ownership's national allegiances is suggested by Dawson's testimony that 'the owners of the mill were originally British, though circumstances have made it wise for them to become Polish citizens'.[115]

In the early years of the Marki factory, the British nationality of the owners and their products had been advanced as the symbol of modernity and product excellence. The Bradford men promoted their foreign enterprise unashamedly

[108] Wartalska, 'Fabryka i osada fabryczna', p. 653.

[109] APW, Ref.1, 159/1887, pp. 2–3.

[110] Hinchcliffe, January 1910.

[111] APW, 72/1151, *Starszy Inspektor Fabryczny Guberni Warszawskiej*, signatures 1180/1913, pp. 1–17.

[112] Crago, 'The "Polishness" of Production', p. 38.

[113] Given the Polish proclivity for translating all names into a Polish form, it cannot be categorically proven that this was to suit the industrialists' or the journalists' preferences.

[114] Dr Piotr Jaworski mentioned this in an interview with the author in April 2010.

[115] Dawson, *It Might Have Happened To You*, p. 111.

Figure 11.1 Early twentieth-century label for the Marki firm
Source: By kind permission of Urząd Miasta Marki

as using 'English business methods'.[116] However, in the twentieth century the imperialistic banners and medals depicted on the firm's stationery were replaced by the simple image of a Polish peasant girl knitting amongst sheep, beside a modern illustration of the factory. The remarketing of the Marki businesses with a much stronger Polish identity was a superficial change rather than a deep-seated transformation in business practice, but it arguably represented a new form of assimilation for the foreign factory owners, whose previous allegiances to the German-Evangelical Church or Russian state now took a back seat to retaining the loyalty of their employees as external influences threatened the *status quo*. In Łódź there was another conspicuous change in business behaviour as the factory owners, determined to safeguard their assets against future rebellion, increased the proportion of women in their workforces.[117] This strategy had been employed in Bradford several decades earlier to reduce trade union activity. It would not have escaped their Polish peers' notice that it had also allowed the Marki entrepreneurs to navigate the years of unrest successfully and emerge relatively unscathed.

[116] 'Mr Edward Briggs of Bradford', *Yorkshire Weekly Post*, 12 March 1898.

[117] Crago, 'The "Polishness" of Production', p. 39.

Democracy in the Workplace

Another government concession made as a result of the 1905 protests was the limited right for workers to elect representatives. This was not a dispensation to form unions but introduced some controlled democratisation of the management of, for example, factory sick funds. The ballots to elect these representatives at Marki provide a fascinating insight into the departmental divisions of the factory, the numbers employed in each area and the nationality of the managers. The exchange of correspondence between the factory owners and government regarding these elections suggest heavy-state scrutiny of a carefully regulated procedure. In 1913, the position of the ballot boxes, available voting hours and reckoning all had to be detailed by the Marki management, confirmed by the signatures of workers' representatives and forwarded to the factory inspectorate.[118] This meticulous observance of workers' rights contrasted dramatically with the nineteenth-century collaboration between industrialists and the state to condone infringements to labour legislation.

The increased state scrutiny and accompanying bureaucracy of the post-1905 era would have been undoubted irritations to the British industrialists for whom autocratic control had been an important pillar of their foreign enterprise. However, the Briggs of Marki were, by Russian standards, model employers who had arguably set the standard for factory legislation in the nineteenth century. They needed to make few material changes to working conditions to satisfy the increasingly vigilant factory inspectorate. The modifications to their outward image were arguably superficial and intended to make them a less obvious target for political criticism or terrorist attack. But in the emerging political climate Poland's industrial employers found a new ally to share responsibility for their workers' behaviour and wellbeing. The 1905 Revolution had created a crisis for the Catholic Church in Poland which, in the aftermath, enjoyed a more relaxed relationship with the state. Following the anarchy, religious leaders were less inclined to goad the workers with traditional arguments about the moral degradation of industry. They took a more conciliatory approach in their sermons and began to enjoy a freedom that had been denied since the 1863 Uprising. The strikes ideologically united employers and religious leaders for the first time and the loss of state support led industrialists such as the Briggs brothers to look to the Church for social control of their employees in a new alliance that impacted very little on their core moneymaking activities.[119]

In conclusion, it is evident that the basic paternalistic principles established by the Briggs-Posselt partnership at Marki in 1883 and their highly selective employment policy enabled them to negotiate safely the crises of political instability which began in the early 1890s and gathered strength in the first decade

[118] APW, 72/1151, *Starszy Inspektor Fabryczny Guberni Warszawskiej*, signature 1180/1913, pp. 1–17.

[119] Blobaum, *Rewolucja*, p. 249 and in Żarnowska, 'Religion and Politics', p. 311.

of the nineteenth century to reach revolutionary proportions in 1905. This chapter has shown that, as social and government attitudes were transformed after 1905, industrialists generally modified their public image and business behaviour. Foreign-owned firms in particular made a concerted effort to rebrand themselves as Polish as a survival strategy. The next chapter will consider the international factors which, in the following decade, would challenge the resilience of the Marki industrialists to the utmost and, in a new era of Polish independence, entirely transform the economic, social and political arena in which E. Briggs Brothers and Co. continued to operate.

Chapter 12

'The immensity of the calamity and the want of financial and material means':[1] The history of Bradford Mills at Marki from 1914–39

The later years of Bradford Mills at Marki reflect a complex period in both Polish and European history generally. In August 1914 the eastern front of the Great War surged across the Polish lands, Łódź was captured by the Germans in October but the Russian occupation of Warsaw held out for a year under increasing bombardment from the West. This chapter will contrast the success of Bradford's industry and the Marki firm to capitalise on unprecedented military investment in 1914. It will consider the general chaos and devastation caused first by the retreating Russian army and then by the occupying German regime to both Warsaw's municipal infrastructure and to private industries. Using the previously unexplored correspondence of the Warsaw merchant Arnold Korff, this chapter will describe the precarious situation the hostilities created for Warsaw's cosmopolitan elite and their tactics to protect their Polish assets. It will consider the logistical and economic challenges of re-establishing the Marki business in the post-war period against a back drop of continuing international hostilities, internal political chaos and hyperinflation, considering the loss of the Russian market and protection. It will describe the Marki partners' resourceful approach to recouping their war-time losses: through legal action in Poland and Germany, by using the 'free-standing company' model to raise funds in Bradford and their eventual participation in the cartel system, to restore their firm's profitability in an entirely transformed Polish commercial arena.

The Commercial Opportunity of War

Throughout this book it has been clear that the Bradford partners operated in a climate of extreme social and political tension in Poland. Indeed many of their strategies were designed either to counteract or gain advantage from the very particular socio-political circumstances of the region. The autocratic style of government and general poverty of the Polish lands led to periodic rebellions

[1] Bornstein-Łychowska, *Ten Years Social Policy in Poland*, p. 72.

Figure 12.1 Cartoon of 'Mars, the God of War, Bottling up Transport' in 1915
Source: Wool Record, Bradford, 18 February 1915, supplement

but, up to 1905 at least, the industrialists enjoyed the whole-hearted support of the Tsarist state to quash worker insubordination. At the same time the Russian empire's international relations were persistently strained by both trade wars and military actions. Although this high-pressure political environment was entirely at odds with Bradford, it represented a considerable opportunity rather than a deterrent to the British worsted manufacturers. The first foreign weavers had settled in the Polish lands in the 1820s solely to tender for the supply of 'broadcloth to the Polish army'.[2] As was described in Chapter 4, the pursuit of military contracts was the main reason that woollen manufacturers relocated to Białystok in 1830. Indeed, the Russo-Turkish war of 1877–78 and the wealth of the foreign militia based in Poland are considered the main catalysts for the Kingdom's spectacular industrial development in the last quarter of the nineteenth century.[3]

Although safe from the threat of direct conflict, Bradford's commercial community was familiar with the economic potential of war. Chapter 1 described how the city's industry increased exports by 50 per cent during the Franco-Prussian war.[4] Indeed the company history of the Bradford merchant Heydemann reveals no qualms about its single-minded pursuit of profit during that conflict when 'the firm saw the possibility in selling to both sides and flourished accordingly'.[5] Thus, in the first days of the Great War Bradford's *Wool Record* tentatively predicted 'this district stands to enjoy at least a temporary gain because of what was experienced during … the late South African and Russo-Japanese wars'.[6] Thereafter, increasingly bullish reports in the trade journal presented the war purely in terms of its economic potential for local industry: 'Khaki! Throughout the textile trade, as far as wool is concerned, khaki is about the chief subject of thought and talk'.[7] The extraordinary opportunity was emphasised by rallying declarations that 'Lord Kitchener's half a million and more recruits must be dressed in the usual soldier's uniform'.[8] Conscription in embattled European nations was discussed pragmatically for its local economic implications; as 'French and also Russian and Austrian manufacturers are badly provided for meeting the requirements of their own governments', an export surge was predicted.[9]

Bradford's industry experienced its greatest boom during the Great War, indeed many allied nations established procurement offices in the world's worsted capital. In early 1915 'the head of the Russian Supply Commission based in Bradford requisitioned 3.2 million yards of fabric specifically for the country's military

2 Davies, *God's Playground*, p. 172.
3 'Industrial Progress in Russia', *Textile World*, February 1884, p. 919.
4 Chadwick, *Church and People in Bradford*, p. 22.
5 *N. Heydemann and Co.*, p. 13.
6 *Wool Record*, Bradford, Vol. 6, No. 273, 6 August 1914, p. 129.
7 Ibid., No. 275, 20 August 1914, p. 179.
8 Ibid., No. 279, 17 September 1914, p. 264.
9 Ibid., No. 274, 13 August 1914, p. 162.

use'.[10] But the logistical difficulties of increasing the supply of raw materials to match the unprecedented demand were ever-present. In February 1915 'one of the Bradford stations has been so congested with wool that the railway company has been obliged to stop further consignments coming forward'.[11] But in the longer term it was the course of the war, the changing focal points of hostilities and territorial gains, which began to dictate international demand, the ability to acquire raw materials and supply cloth. Shipments of wool from South America and Australasia were increasingly delayed and vital transport corridors into the war zones were blocked. In the summer of 1915 it was reported that 'we are expecting good business from the Russian market once the Dardanelles are forced, but until then shipments are totally held up'.[12]

The KRA

Given the globally integrated trade arena that had developed in the nineteenth century, German industry had become heavily reliant on imported raw materials. Over £6,000,000 worth of yarn and semi-processed worsted top was bought from Britain and, like Bradford's industry, Germany imported large quantities of colonial as well as Russian-empire wool.[13] At the advent of the war, with trade embargos and transport blockades, the Jewish business magnate Walther Rathenau, of the electronics firm *Allgemeine-Elektrizitäts-Gellellschaft* – AEG, voiced his concerns that 'the war would last longer than Germany's existing supplies'.[14] On 8 August 1914 Rathenau was sanctioned to establish the *Kriegsrohstoffabteilung* or KRA [War Raw Materials Department] to keep German industries supplied with raw materials for the war effort. The British press took a keen interest in the activities of this agency which began to requisition 'stocks of wool in enemy countries, especially Luttich [Liege], Verviers, Roubaix, Tourcoing, Łódź ... to distribute them pro rata to the Army's orders and the individual manufacturers of military cloths'.[15] In December, quite specific figures were circulated that the fall of Antwerp had provided the enemy with 10 million marks worth of wool.[16] At Rheims, it was reported that the 'wool combing factory of Messrs. Jonathan

[10] Mark Keighley, *Woven with Wisdom and Skill, the History of Bradford Textile Society 1893 to 1993* (Bradford: Wool Record, 1993), p. 14 and in *Wool Record*, Bradford, 8 July 1915, p. 39.

[11] *Wool Record*, Bradford, 11 February 1915, p. 135.

[12] Ibid., 1 July 1915, p. 15.

[13] Ibid., Vol. 6, No. 277, 3 September 1914, p. 226.

[14] A.D. Harvey, *Collision of Empires: Britain in Three World Wars, 1793–1945* (London: Hambledon Press, 1992), p. 298. See also D.G.Williamson, 'Walther Rathenau and the KRA August 1914–March 1915', *Zeitschrift für Unternehmensgeschichte/Journal of Business History*, 23. Jahrg., H. 2 (1978), pp. 118–36.

[15] 'How Germany is Buying Wool', *Wool Record*, Bradford, 8 October 1914, p. 330.

[16] *Wool Record*, Bradford, 3 December 1914, p. 512.

Figure 12.2 Polish postcard of the Kaiser dropping bombs on Warsaw, October 1914

Source: By kind permission of Ralph Haigh

Holden has been practically ruined, and the works of Isaac Holden and Sons damaged'.[17] The apparently gratuitous destruction of factories in occupied France and Belgium was naturally disdained by the allied nations, but when German industry was hungry for supplies and access to their former resources was cut off, commandeering stocks was the only available course of action. The scope

[17] Ibid., 29 October 1914, p. 395.

of the theft soon increased to include 'thousands of machine tools ... for use in German armaments and munitions plants, and a few factories were even entirely dismantled for shipment to Germany'.[18]

German aggression in the Polish lands produced a predictably unifying effect on the Kingdom of Poland's divided society. Decades of anti-German propaganda that had been proliferated by the Tsarist regime undoubtedly encouraged the pan-Slavic cooperation. 'Local newspapers heartily endorsed the Russian cause, and there were no strikes, anti-war demonstrations, or any other obstructionist activities to impede the war effort'.[19] As refugees flooded into Warsaw with the German advance, the authorities approved the formation of a citizens' committee to maintain public order, food supplies and generally cope with the influx.[20] Stephen Graham reported for the *Times* on the 'spirit of buoyant optimism which pervades the place, and the life of restaurant and cafe, theatre and concert, has gone on as usual'.[21] Despite the capture of Łódź in October 1914 it was triumphantly reported that 'the efforts of Marshal Von Hindenburg's troops to present Warsaw as a Christmas gift to an expectant nation have been brought to nought'.[22]

Marki from August 1914 to August 1915

Although the advent of war was a greater threat to the Briggs' foreign investment than it was to Bradford's manufacturers, it similarly represented huge profit potential for the Polish firm. Marki's location to the east of Warsaw, beyond the natural defence of the Vistula, may have given the owners confidence and Russia's urgent demand for uniform cloth, blankets and so forth certainly focused their energies on the opportunity rather than the approaching menace. Indeed, Hinchcliffe's memoir particularly recalls Alfred Briggs' steely determination and exhortation to 'stick to the sod'[23] and keep the factory running. In the first weeks of the war the male population of Marki and its surrounds was conscripted into the Russian army and a few German managers certainly fled, but the firm's female-strong workforce meant that it was well-placed to continue production with minimal disruption.

Bradford Mills at Marki, like its Yorkshire contemporaries, received large state orders for cloth and its vast stock holdings of raw wool should have enabled it to capitalise on the spectacular military investment as it had during the Russo-

---

18 Peter Liberman, *Does Conquest Pay? The Exploitation of Occupied Industrial Societies* (Princeton: Princeton University Press, 1998), p. 77.

19 Edward D. Wynot, *Warsaw between the World Wars Profile of the Capital City in a Developing Land, 1918–1939* (New York: East European Monographs, 1983), p. 36.

20 Wynot, *Warsaw between the World Wars*, p. 36.

21 'The Story of Warsaw – A Great Cosmopolitan City', *The Times*, 6 August 1915.

22 'London and Warsaw', *The Times*, December 1914.

23 Hinchcliffe's memoir.

Japanese war a decade earlier. But with fighting on all sides of the town, the local transport infrastructure was quickly and thoroughly appropriated for troop and armaments movements, preventing the acquisition of coal. At the end of 1914, after a failed attempt to run the Marki boilers on wood from the vicinity, the firm appealed to the Russian state to supply the necessary fuel 'in order to hasten the supply of material' that they had ordered.[24] At the same time international transport difficulties compounded the problems for Russia's manufacturers, who like their German counterparts were 'very hungry for supplies, and wanted wool very badly in order to get out big khaki orders for the Government, but with the port of Archangel being closed along with the Baltic and the Dardanelles, there was no chance of getting wool into Russia except from Vladivostok in Siberia, and sending the wool forward through the heart of that province'.[25]

The first English families left Marki before Christmas 1914 on the advice of the British consul, but the firm persisted into the following year with a skeleton staff. Although Warsaw remained in Russian control, burning settlements could be seen on the horizons to the north and south of the industrial town and 'the noise from the guns was horrifying'.[26] Nevertheless, Hinchcliffe's description of the local conditions suggests inconvenience rather than real hardship: 'some food commodities were scarce, but supplies of butter, cheese and eggs, were fairly adequate. Sugar was not difficult to obtain, and meat did not go off the market. Tradesmen liked to be paid in silver, and paper money was not easy to negotiate'.[27] Fuel shortages led the resourceful women of Marki to gather pine needles and take up peat from the nearby fields but eventually the Briggs established a 'tea shop' in the town 'enabling the public to obtain … boiled water cheaply'.[28] During the winter the first Russian troops arrived in the settlement and a 'number of starved soldiers asked to be allowed to enter the factory's sorting room in order to treat their semi-frozen feet'.[29] By the spring Russian soldiers were regularly billeted in the factory housing.

By 1915, Warsaw's economy was in disarray, conscription had 'decreased the industrial workforce by nearly fifty per cent',[30] disruptions to raw-materials supplies and continual bombardment led many foreign direct investors to abandon the area. When the German advance on Warsaw seemed imminent, the remaining factory owners took precautionary measures to protect their assets. In the spring of 1915 the Marki firm resigned hope of safely negotiating the war with its works intact and began to liquidate stock, selling its vital wool reserves to the merchants of Białystok. The logistical difficulties of managing this were clear, as 'three bales

24 Ibid.

25 *Wool Record*, Bradford, 3 December 1914, p. 517.

26 Hinchcliffe, 16 April 1915.

27 Hinchcliffe's memoir.

28 Hinchcliffe, 16 May 1915.

29 Hinchcliffe's memoir.

30 Wynot, *Warsaw between the World Wars*, p. 37.

usually constituted one horse load ... the roads were nearly all in most wretched condition' and it was 120 miles from Warsaw to Białystok.[31]

Russian Asset Stripping and Sabotage

At the outset of the Great War the Polish population had been largely united with Russia against the common German enemy. But, in 1915 as the empire prepared to concede its western borders to the German aggressor, in a style which resonated strongly with pre-factory era eastward migrations of artisans, the Tsarist state urged Poland's industrialists to relocate their businesses into the Russian heartlands. 'The owners of plants were granted free transport to the eastward for what they could save'.[32] The sheer scale of many factories and the congestion of internal transport facilities made this largely unfeasible. But once the capture of Warsaw became inevitable, the state's entreaties gave way to a campaign of asset stripping and sabotage in the city. 'Day and night one heard the periodical roar of dynamited factory plant that was embedded in concrete or was too cumbersome to dismantle and transport. Each fragment of this dynamited metal was taken eastward on the railway'.[33] 'Gangs of soldiers were briskly stripping league after league of copper telegraph wires from the poles ... while aloft in the towers huge bronze bells were unslung lest they became food for Krupp cannon'.[34]

Whereas the Poles had stoically endured food and fuel shortages, even conscription, the wilful destruction of Warsaw's infrastructure and factories by retreating Russian armies finally alienated any lingering Polish sympathy for Russia.[35] At the end of the month the *New York Times* dramatically described the state of the city as it awaited German capture: 'emptied of population ... the churches stripped, factories blown up, every scrap of metal removed, standing crops destroyed'.[36] Warsaw fell on 4 August 1915 and remained under German occupation until 13 November 1918. However, 'from the outset, the Germans permitted the Poles a freedom and discretion in organising and managing local affairs not witnessed since 1830'.[37]

---

31 Hinchcliffe's memoir.

32 'Forsaken City', *The Times*, 9 August 1915.

33 Ibid.

34 Ibid.

35 Davies, *God's Playground*, p. 389.

36 'Warsaw Emptied of Population', *New York Times*, 31 July 1915.

37 Wynot, *Warsaw between the World Wars*, p. 39.

The Network of Trust during the War Years

In July 1915 the Marki mill was abandoned and the movements of Alfred Briggs and his German wife Augusta Schulz or Charles Whitehead and his Polish wife Eleonora Wedel remain unclear. It is most likely that, like their other remaining British staff, the industrialists fled into Russia and banked their liquidated assets there, although the recently widowed, courageous Flora Briggs undoubtedly remained in Marki. Certainly many of the Briggs' British employees sought work in Russian factories rather than return to Bradford at that time. Hinchcliffe wrote home in August 1915: 'I am still alive and well in Petrograd, although I have had rather a rough life since leaving Warsaw'.[38] One of the firm's foremen, Richard Hopkinson, worked in Moscow until the Russian Revolution in 1917.

The outbreak of the war created a particularly precarious situation for Warsaw's commercial elite. The traditional intermarriage between business partners had united German, Russian, Polish and other European nationalities in extended clans. Many had assumed Russian nationality in order to operate their businesses effectively in Poland but the German names and origins of many cosmopolitan bourgeois families made them the object of suspicion for the Russian authorities. Some were interned and many fled either into Germany or to surrounding countries such as Denmark where they hoped to continue their trade and await the outcome of the conflict. However, their national allegiances were by no means naturally inclined towards German collaboration and their position was little better once Germany had the upper hand in the war.

All Ernst Posselt's sons had been born in England and although they had spent only a brief period of their lives in Bradford, they staunchly maintained their British nationality throughout their residence in Russia. Thus, in 1914 the family scattered across Europe and their Polish assets – the Zgierz Cotton Company, the Russo-Italian Silk Company and the Warsaw Carpet Company – were all transferred into the guardianship of their cousin, Arnold Korff, a German national who had lived in Warsaw since the turn of the century.[39] During the Second World War, perhaps as a result of lessons learnt in the Great War, the family employed the same tactic to protect their interests with greater organisation. They thoroughly documented their Polish business and residential properties with comprehensive inventories, photographs and even positive testimonials written by their Polish employees, before transferring ownership to Anna Marie Ostermeyer, the German grand-daughter of Ernst Posselt 'to protect property from seizure by the Germans'.[40] This worked very successfully during the Nazi occupation of Poland but ultimately everything was lost to the Soviet nationalisation process after the war.

---

38 Hinchcliffe, 23 August 1915.

39 Arnold Korff was the son of Ernst Posselt's sister Christina.

40 FO 1004/245, the Posselt family, to Controller General, Trading with the Enemy Dept, Treasury Board of Trade, 24, Kensington Way, London, 18 December 1947.

Korff's war-time correspondence has provided invaluable insight into the fate of Warsaw's business elite and their assets after 1915. The merchant waited out the first few months of the war in Berlin but was bold in his appeals to the German state on behalf of his Warsaw circle, many of whom had sought sanctuary in Germany only to find themselves either stranded without means or even imprisoned. Most notably he wrote to the General of the Infantry and Chief of Staff, appealing on behalf of his bankers, the Natanson family, who had been detained in Berlin. The relationship with his uncle's former neighbours at Królewska 10 had endured from the earliest days of the Briggs-Posselt partnership and Korff insisted to the German authorities that the Natansons were 'not in any way sympathetic to the Russian regime' and should be allowed to return to Warsaw.[41] In the disarray of the war, Korff's dispersed family relied on him to keep them informed and in contact with each other. He wrote to Otto Stuck in Waldkirch, his cousin Ernest Posselt's father-in-law and shareholder in the Russian-Italian Silk Company, that 'Willy Posselt is in Moscow, Gustaw is in Riga, it looks as though Buckley of Zgierz has fled to Moscow and will go to England'.[42] He mentioned that Thomas Whitehead, the British manager of a local lace factory, was detained for a while in the Ruhleben prisoner of war camp but had since gone into Russia.[43]

When the abandonment of their factory became unavoidable, the Briggs similarly used their long-embedded familial connections with Warsaw's German community to their best advantage and entrusted their Marki factory to Arnold Korff.[44] It is extremely difficult to illustrate simply the complex pattern of intermarriage and business connections that still united the Briggs and Posselt families long after the deaths of both Edward Briggs in 1898 and Ernst Posselt in 1907. But it is evident that the original Bradford partnership still exerted a strong influence and the sense of obligation between its descendants superseded national differences in the twentieth century. The first generation of cooperative partners and brothers-in-law, whose interests were spread across Europe but particularly between Bradford, Elberfeld and Warsaw – Posselt, Briggs, Peters, Korff, Quitmann, Granzow, Whitehead and Wedel – had intermarried and employed each other's sons to create a powerful dynasty of business skills, wealth and trust. Thus Willy Posselt's wife was the cousin of John Briggs junior's wife, Flora Granzow, and Arnold Korff's brother Karl worked for the Peters family who had continued the firm of E. Posselt and Co. at Bradford. Korff's letters also suggest he might

[41] APW, Zespół 87, 'Firma Arnold Korff w Warszawie', Group 3, Korff in Berlin to Herr Freiherr V. Manteuffel, General of the Infantry and Chief of Staff in Berlin, 17 November 1914, p. 63.

[42] Ibid., Korff in Charlottenberg to Otto Stuck at Ringwald et Cie at Waldkirch, 9 November 1914, p. 116.

[43] FO394/10 describes Tom Whitehead (unrelated to the Briggs) as the manager of a local lace manufactory, probably T.I. Birkin, but his release from Ruhleben was negotiated on the basis that he was a consular official.

[44] *Gazeta Sądowa*, Warsaw, 30 September 1916, p. 7.

have been the cousin of Alfred Briggs' wife Augusta Schulz.[45] For this extended family the war placed an inconvenient restriction on their free association and the management of their commercial operations, in which nationality or national allegiances had previously played little part. But from the point of view of both the German and Russian authorities in the 1914–18 period, the Posselts were as British as the Briggs and Whitehead families and their German relative, Arnold Korff, was their best hope to protect all their Polish assets.

Arnold Korff: Official Receiver of the Firm 'E. Briggs Brueder und Co.'

Korff could not return to the Kingdom of Poland until January 1915 when he travelled as far as Łódź, only returning to Warsaw when the former Polish capital was captured in August.[46] Once re-established at his Warsaw offices on Wierzbowa Street, Korff was able to provide firsthand information to business associates and relatives abroad about the local situation. On 20 December 1915 he wrote to Gustaw Schultz 'I was at the factory this morning and found everything in order',[47] although it is unclear whether he referred to his own family's Warsaw Carpet Company or the Marki plant. In February 1916 he wrote to Lieutenant Waldemar Bernhoff, a prisoner of war at Schloss Hirschberg, explaining that the spinning department of the Posselt's Riga factory had been 'ordered by the Russian regime to be transported to Moscow whereas the weaving mill and dyehouse are back in Riga'.[48]

Despite Korff's best efforts to cooperate with the German authorities, to recommend trustworthy translators of the German-Evangelical faith and to source raw materials from Hungary for the wool purchasing department of the KRA: *Kriegswollbedarf-Aktiengesellschaft* [War Wool-Requirements Company],[49] his German credentials did not prevent the equal plunder of his own family's Polish assets alongside those British-owned factories under his guardianship. In fact it is clear from his correspondence of 1916–17 that the beleaguered merchant was expected to supply the requisitioning agency with the metal and raw materials from the factories himself. In March 1916 he reported to Max Baender of the

---

45 APW, Zespół 87, 'Firma Arnold Korff w Warszawie', Group 4, Korff to Gustaw Grams, 23 November 1915, p. 151. The name Schulz or Schultz is fairly common and it has not been possible to identify if a familial connection existed, although it is highly likely.

46 Ibid., Group 3, Georg Oelsner at Hannover to Korff, 23 January 1915, p. 130.

47 Ibid., Group 4, Korff to Gustaw Schultz, 20 December 1915, p. 120.

48 Ibid., Group 4, Korff to prisoner of war Herr Waldemar Bernhoff at Schloss Hirschberg, 3 February 1916, p. 73, Bernhoff was the brother-in-law of his cousin Ernest Posselt junior.

49 APW, Zespół 87, 'Firma Arnold Korff w Warszawie', Group 9, Korff to the *Kriegswollbedarf-Aktiengesellschaft* [War Wool-Requirements Company] in Berlin, 25 October 1917, p. 93.

Warsaw Carpet Company, that 'the KRA have paid me 50% yesterday. A further 20% will be paid in the course of the next week and the rest will follow soon after'.[50] His correspondence with the *Kriegsrohstoffstelle Abteilung Metalle in Warschau* [War Raw Materials Metal Department in Warsaw] in August 1916 reveals the thoroughness of the depredation of industry, as Korff begged for more time to deliver the metal fittings from the factories in his care:

> Here I ask you very humbly to prolong the deadline for delivery of the door handles, window knobs etc. etc. for the following companies: for my factory Warsaw Carpet Company and those factories standing under my receivership: T. Birkin and Co., Russian-Italian Silk Mill, Belgian Hat Factory, E. Briggs Brother & Co., I note that you have ordered the parts, but the delivery will take some time yet.[51]

In 1917 the *Kaiserlich Deutsches Bezirksgericht* [Imperial German District Court] in Łuków, south-west of Warsaw, enquired after the proceeds of the sale of Marki assets. It officiously demanded 'whether the pharmacy and drugstore goods mentioned are now sold and what was the revenue? You may be reminded to submit a report on this matter'.[52] The serious plunder of Bradford Mills at Marki took place in 1917 when 'all boilers, motors, piping, belting, brass and copper parts, [were] torn out. Even cork that insulated roofs [had] been removed'.[53] Wartalska suggests that 70 tons of metal was requisitioned which comprised two-thirds of the plant's machinery, but thanks to the efforts of the management and factory workers, some equipment and fittings made of non-ferrous metals were saved.[54]

Although the occupying-German regime are generally charged with the destruction of Polish industry and transporting the assets westward to feed the German war machine, this chapter has shown that Warsaw's infrastructure and industry had already been seriously sabotaged by retreating Russian armies before August 1915. In fact evidence suggests that during the German occupation appropriation proved the most efficient means to restore Warsaw's devastated municipal infrastructure. In May 1917 the Polish press reported that 'four boilers are being brought to power the tram from the factory of Briggs and Company in Marki',[55] indeed it was clearly stated that the Briggs' boilers would be used to

---

[50] Ibid., Group 5, Korff to Max Baender at Hotel Hessler Berlin, 6 March 1916, p. 252.

[51] Ibid., Group 7, Korff to War Metal Commodities Department in Warsaw, 28 August 1916, p. 78.

[52] Ibid., Group 6, *Kaiserlich Deutsches Bezirksgericht* [Imperial German District Court] in Lukow to Korff as the *Zwangsverwalter der Firma E. Briggs Brueder und Co.* [The official receiver of the firm E. Briggs Brothers and Co.], 30 April 1917, p. 5.

[53] Dawson, *It Might Have Happened To You*, p. 114.

[54] Wartalska, 'Fabryka i osada fabryczna', pp. 658–9.

[55] *Głos: dziennik polityczny*, 23 May 1917, No. 91, p. 2.

extend the city's electric tram system. There is a strong sense in the contemporary Polish press that, despite German occupation, the municipality of Warsaw was rebuilding the city actively and preparing for future independence in this period.

The Polish Landscape in the Aftermath of War

The Germans withdrew from Warsaw on 13 November 1918 and on the 22 November Poland declared independence. But 'her frontiers were virtually non-existent and her shape was undetermined',[56] as the new Republic remained at war on almost every front. There were wrangles with Czechoslovakia for control of formerly Austro-Hungarian Galicia and the coal-rich region of Cieszyn in the south and continued hostilities with Germany over Silesia and Poznań in the west. In February 1919 the Polish-Soviet War began and Poland's newly conscripted army made swift territorial gains in Belarus, Ukraine and Lithuania to the east. But the internal politics of the newly united state remained characterised by earlier political, cultural and philosophical divisions as various factions vied for power. Between 1918 and 1939 Poland had 28 changes of prime minister, none of whom held the post for more than a year until after 1935, there were two coup d'états and numerous ministers were assassinated. However, Zbigniew Landau suggests that the economic unification of the Polish state 'was a more difficult and time-consuming task than the political unification'.[57] In the first years of the Republic's existence the entire legislative, economic, judicial and taxation systems had to be reconstructed as each region had different customs and laws while there were five different currencies in circulation 'all inflating wildly'.[58] Rail transport networks were poorly integrated and no Polish sea port existed before the opening of Gdynia in 1927.

The Polish industrial landscape had also changed beyond all recognition. The destruction of the national plant has already been described leaving 'the textile factories of Łódź and Białystok … denuded of machinery and equipment; stocks of raw materials and semi-finished goods'.[59] It was estimated that millions of acres of agricultural land had been ruined by military operations and 1,800,000 buildings had been lost to fire.[60] The economic devastation was compounded by foreign investors' liquidation of assets and removal of cash and securities from the region.

[56] Piotr Wandycz, 'Poland on the Map of Europe in 1918', *Polish Review*, 35: 1(1990), p. 20.

[57] Zbigniew Landau, 'The Economic Integration of Poland, 1918–23', in *The Reconstruction of Poland, 1914–23*, ed. Paul Latawski (Basingstoke: Macmillan in association with the School of Slavonic and East European Studies, 1992), p. 145.

[58] Davies, *God's Playground*, p. 415.

[59] Ferdynand Zweig, *Poland between Two Wars: A Critical Study of Social and Economic Change* (London: Secker and Warburg, 1944), p. 31.

[60] Ibid.

The conflicts at Cieszyn, 'which contains some of the best coal in that part of the world', prevented vital mining activities.[61] But the role of the desperate population in the destruction should not be underestimated as six million acres of forest had been destroyed for fuel and 1,500,000 sheep had been slaughtered.[62] This practical solution to famine would have predictable consequences for the reconstruction of the wool industry. In 1930 Poland's national flock had only recovered 42 per cent of its pre-war size.[63]

Factory Legislation in Poland's Second Republic

Despite the appalling economic circumstances, the newly formed Polish administration's primary focus was factory legislation. One by one the demands first articulated during the strikes of 1892, and increasingly in the revolutionary period of 1905–08, were introduced by the Republic's administration. The day after the Republic was declared, reforms to include an eight-hour working day with rates of pay fixed higher for overtime were announced. In January 1919 a bill on compulsory health and maternity insurance was passed. In February the regulations concerning the formation of trade unions were liberalised. In May a directive concerning workers' holidays was introduced (only after one year's continuous employment). In December 1919 a Sunday Rest Law was introduced as an important social reform.[64]

Polish scholars have tended to stress the new regime's determination to 'improve the conditions of the working masses',[65] to contrast positively with the period of Tsarist oppression, when capital was seen to take precedence over the interests of labour. However, the image of the exploitative capitalist employer was largely a construct; an expedient stereotype used by various political parties to rally worker support. As was described in Chapter 11, it was a particularly convenient scapegoat advanced by the state for social problems caused by a lack of municipal investment or other Tsarist oppressions. Whereas the poverty-stricken Polish worker 'regarded the chance of employment in industry as an extra bonus, as a stroke of good fortune … Industrial wages, which to modern eyes look derisory, ensured an income that was twice as high as that of the average peasant family'.[66] Chapter 8 described how nineteenth-century industrial employers replaced the landowners of the old system of serfdom, providing a significant proportion of the Polish population with the security of employment and often housing, healthcare

61 *HC Debate*, 'World Going to Pieces', 16 April 1919, Vol. 114, cc. 2967.

62 Zweig, *Poland between Two Wars*, p. 31.

63 *Gazeta Bankowa*, Warsaw, 25 July 1930, p. 25.

64 Peter D. Stachura, *Poland between the Wars, 1918–1939* (Basingstoke: Macmillan, 1998), p. 139.

65 Bornstein-Łychowska, *Ten Years Social Policy in Poland*, p. 72.

66 Davies, *God's Playground*, p. 414.

and other basic necessities. Indeed many of the twentieth-century social-welfare policies across the industrialised world had their foundation in paternalism.

The focus of the new Polish administration on employment law certainly defined its intentions to represent and protect the ordinary people rather than the wealthy industrial employers. But its idealistic and politically palatable policies such as paid workers' holidays or the unemployment insurance act[67] were somewhat out of touch with the real conditions on the ground where industry lay in ruins, unemployment was rife and people were starving. While many of the vilified German foreign direct investors had cut their losses in Poland, those more embedded industrialists were faced with almost insurmountable difficulties of reconstruction as military actions continued and hyperinflation reduced their reinvestment capital. In this context, reforms to employment law constituted little more than positive public-relations propaganda, rather than a genuine strike at the heart of any so-called exploitative bourgeoisie of the Tsarist era.

The American Relief Administration at Marki

The new Polish administration's urgent introduction of pro-worker reforms was undoubtedly influenced by a factor that preoccupied much post-war European politics. The Russian Revolution had been a salutary example for many governments who developed an obsessive fear of the further spread of Bolshevism. In August 1919 the British Member of Parliament Josiah Wedgwood ascribed the revolutionary state of affairs in Budapest to various post-war privations but primarily to hunger. He attributed the containment of worker revolt in industrial cities such as Łódź and Warsaw to the establishment of feeding stations by the American Relief Administration – ARA – instituted by Herbert Hoover. He reported that 'in those towns, fortunately, I think we are feeding the inhabitants, or rather, Mr Hoover is feeding them'.[68] In 1919 an ARA feeding station was established in the Marki schoolhouse and in 1921 Dawson, commissioned by Hoover, provided one of the first accounts of the desperate conditions in the post-war industrial town:

> It was Mr Whitehead, part-owner of the pillaged mill, who led me to it. 'If you have any ability', he said, 'to make conditions known, I wish you would tell the World what Marki owes to America. Six hundred children died of hunger in our village the year before the Americans came. Whatever happens to us older fellows, they have saved our rising generation. I am getting money to patch up any machinery; if I live long enough, I shall have all of it running again. But shall I be able to patch up the machinery of human bodies? My people are no

[67] Bornstein-Łychowska, *Ten Years Social Policy in Poland*, p. 72.

[68] *HC Debate*, Consolidated Fund (No. 2) Bill, Colonel Wedgwood, 7 August 1919, Vol. 119, cc. 690.

> more capable of working than my machinery is of running at present. Their strength has been looted. They must be repaired, just the same as the machinery in my mill.[69]

It is difficult to determine if this impassioned report was an accurate account or a well-intentioned exaggeration, but the interwar memoir of Marki school teacher Władysław Rydel does provide some corroborative evidence. He describes how the workers lived rent-free in the company housing, though in dire poverty: 'everyone took what one could to survive. By night, even in the daytime, the Markians went out into the fields, cut down the ripening corn, lifted the potatoes, pulled out the vegetables – because they had to eat – whilst the nearby forest was devastated as they felled the timber to secure fuel'.[70]

Reconstruction of Marki in the Interwar Period

It is clear that in 1919 the aging Alfred Briggs and his heir Charles Whitehead had returned to Marki determined to repair their factory and get production underway again as soon as possible. An article in the New York *Textile World* journal suggests that the British industrialists had both capital and ambitious plans to rebuild Marki:

> J. Briggs & Co., Briggella Ltd., of Garden [sic: Gordon] Street Mills, Bradford, England, are desirous of receiving from American firms quotations for textile machinery and other equipment for their plant at Marki, near Warsaw, Poland. This machinery they are unable to get from British firms in less than six to seven months. Briggs & Co have large woollen and worsted mills near Warsaw, where before the war they employed about 3000 operatives. The enemy removed a large part of the machinery to Germany and destroyed everything they could not take away or did not want. Consequently the mills will have to be completely re-equipped. Everything will have to be replaced – boilers, engines, shafting, wool washing and drying machines, combs and carding machinery, spinning frames, looms and dyeing and finishing apparatus; also electric lighting installation, which will cost to replace approximately £65,000.[71]

For Briggs and Whitehead the Polish factory had been their lives' work and both were tightly embedded through marriage to Warsaw's commercial elite. But beyond their personal commitment to the enterprise, there were many positive

---

[69] Dawson, *It Might Have Happened To You*, pp. 117–18, first sent in a letter to Mr Burnett at the ARA in New York 6 January 1920, pp. 6–7.

[70] Władysław Rydel, *Little Man's Story*, trans. by Adam Truscoe (Melbourne, 1966), p. 285.

[71] *Textile World*, New York, 22 November 1919, p. 137.

commercial reasons to rebuild the Marki business: the 1919 call for tenders in the American press suggests that the supply of machinery rather than investment capital was a greater problem for the company in the immediate post-war period. Indeed although their declared restoration fund appears remarkably similar to their original investment capital of £68,000, by 1919, £65,000 was worth approximately two-thirds less than in 1883. The Bradford men owned the land and housing at Marki which had allowed them to retain their skilled staff throughout the hostilities. Whitehead's close relationship with his brother-in-law Jan Wedel provided some temporary employment for the Marki women in the nearby Praga chocolate factory. The firm's self-sufficiency and diversified interests all worked in their favour and the new state's heavy emphasis on military investment would have undoubtedly encouraged the worsted manufacturers in the task of reconstruction.[72] But the devastation of the First World War and the immediate supply difficulties only marked the onset of the Bradford entrepreneurs' difficulties.

Marki and the Polish-Soviet War

In August 1919 Marki found itself 'in direct path of Russian advance' as five Soviet armies approached the suburbs of Warsaw.[73] Lord D'Abernon, the British ambassador to Berlin, reported on 7 August that 'a treble entanglement of barbed wire is being put around Warsaw at a radius of 20 km, and a certain number of trenches have been built'.[74] Local historian Zbigniew Paciorek provides a detailed account of Marki's role during the Polish-Soviet War when Bradford Mills became an important military headquarters.[75] The town's strategic position to the east of Warsaw, the excellent communications established by the Briggs, including telephone lines and rail-link to Warsaw, made it an ideal army base. Soldiers and provisions could be transported easily from Warsaw to the front line and the wounded could be carried back efficiently. On 10 August 1920 General Tadeusz Jordan-Rozwadowski, Chief of Staff for the Polish Army, and the 11th division of infantry took up positions at Marki. They organised reservists from Modlin, Zegrze, Marki and Rembertów to fix telegraph lines along the main road to Radzymin. On 13 August 1920 Jordan-Rozwadowski telephoned the commander and future Chief of State, Józef Piłsudski, from the Briggs' residence that 'Radzymin is once again in our hands'.[76]

Although the Battle of Warsaw naturally delayed the reconstruction, in May 1921 Juljan Dąbrowski, Warsaw's regional engineer, reported that despite the

---

72 Davies, *God's Playground*, p. 415.

73 Coningsby Dawson in Warsaw to Burnett at the ARA in New York, 6 January 1920, p. 1.

74 Davies, *God's Playground*, p. 397.

75 Paciorek and Dudzika, *Mareckie zeszyty historyczne*, p. 20.

76 Ibid.

wartime devastation of 'the Żyrardow company in the region of Błoński, and the wool spinning mill Briggs Brothers and Co., in Marki near Warsaw ... under very difficult conditions the Briggs have started to rebuild, possibly even enlarge their production'.[77] That same month Hinchcliffe escorted replacement turbines and an electricity generator by boat to Warsaw via the Kiel canal which he cheerfully commented, 'is through some lovely country'.[78] The electrical engineer's letters home in 1921 reflect none of the horrors which Dawson suggested were apparent in Marki the year before: 'the stillness of death is in the streets. The chimneys are breathless. The people are lean, famine-fevered shadows. There is no laughter. No stir. Funerals are too common to cause excitement'.[79] By contrast, Hinchcliffe recalled that he was 'not very hard worked' and even suffered 'a small overdose of tarts' in the Café Bristol in Warsaw.[80] His wage was still negotiated on the basis of 'what the English overlookers draw when they come out here'.[81] He installed American Babcock boilers which would run efficiently with cheap coal dust rather than coal,[82] and 'electric motors ... boiler feed pumps and fittings and Westinghouse Morse Rocker Joint chain drives'.[83]

Hyperinflation and Economic Depression

Physical reconstruction was only one aspect of the challenge facing Polish industrialists in the post-war period. The independence of the new state removed all the economic advantages of annexation: the demands of Eastern markets, Russian raw-materials resources and protection. Russia's planned economy meant her 'share of world trade was only one per cent, and her principal requirements were tools and machinery' during the interwar period.[84] Without the traditional outlets for their cloth, Polish manufacturers had less demand for the yarn and components made by firms like the E. Briggs Brothers and Co., and the economy remained stagnant. The internal market was extremely small and substantially diminished by the impoverishment of the post-war population. These combined circumstances meant that Polish industrialists had to entirely rethink their strategies; to identify new resources and outlets whilst exposed to the pressures of world trade for the first time.

77 *Przęglad Techniczny*, Warsaw, No. 19, 12 May 1921, p. 131.

78 Hinchcliffe, 19 May 1921.

79 Dawson, *It Might Have Happened to You*, p. 116.

80 Hinchcliffe, 7 August 1921.

81 Ibid., 19 May 21.

82 Wartalska, 'Fabryka i osada fabryczna', p. 659.

83 Letter of recommendation of J. Hinchcliffe, from J Briggs & Co., Briggella Ltd., 'to whom it may concern', 28 March 1925.

84 Zweig, *Poland between Two Wars*, p. 11.

For the Marki firm all the preliminary indications were positive, their already diversified approach to products, markets and commercial activities should have allowed the firm to readjust to the new environment. They were better-acquainted with international commerce than many of their Polish peers but in 1921 Dawson first drew attention to the firm's growing financial difficulties when he wrote that 'to replace those parts is no easy task when six hundred Polish marks is only worth a dollar and most of civilised Europe is in disrepair'.[85] Between 1919 and 1923 hyperinflation dangerously undermined the value of the industrialists' capital and wage requirements rose to meet a dramatically increased cost of living.[86] At the end of 1923 Hinchcliffe's bitter complaints to his wife that he had not been paid reveal that production was not yet underway at Marki, although Alfred Briggs reassured him that 'they will do better for me when the mill runs'.[87]

Hinchcliffe provides a fascinating insight into the difficulties caused by local inflation and particularly reveals that, rather than sending money home, his wife in Bradford was posting money to Marki. He wrote that the 'fare to Warsaw formerly 3d, today 9d. Cheapest books over here £1 in England 10/–. Suits – out of reach of my pocket … Butter, which ought to be a cheap commodity in Poland, I paid for yesterday 1/3d per lb. You can send me less money for a week or two'.[88] Despite their financial difficulties it is evident that the factory owners at Marki used the doldrums to make improvements and the electrical engineer was kept busy installing an 'electric light machine for Briggs' and Whitehead's houses'.[89] While the firm continued optimistically to recruit British staff, as Hinchcliffe reported in May 1924: 'we have another Englishman coming out here; he is to do the carding and also the combing'.[90]

In the interwar period Poland's economy was in an almost perpetual state of crisis; political instability, economic depression and hyperinflation made the reconstruction of a profitable commercial environment extremely difficult. These circumstances, combined with war-time losses, fostered a general reluctance towards long-term investments which compounded the national economic difficulties. Internal legislative changes announced in 1924, including diverting the taxation system from wealth to income and turnover, the introduction of the Polish *złoty* currency, establishment of the Bank Polski, the funding of public works and rural improvements 'all contributed to the emergence of a viable system'.[91] However, the effectiveness of each economic reform was offset considerably by a range of uncontrollable external factors. With their traditional

85 Herbert Hoover Presidential Library, Coningsby Dawson to Burnett at the ARA in New York, 6 January 1920, p. 3.

86 Landau, 'The Economic Integration of Poland, 1918–23', p. 152.

87 Hinchcliffe, 16 December 1923.

88 Ibid.

89 Ibid., 1 October 1924.

90 Ibid., 5 May 1924.

91 Davies, *God's Playground*, p. 415.

Eastern markets closed, export to the West was the only course of action open to Poland's recovering industry and in the immediate post-war era, 'Germany absorbed nearly 50 per cent of Polish exports and supplied about 40 per cent of the imports'.[92] But the export strategy propelled Polish businessmen into the same competitive world-trade arena that nineteenth-century foreign direct investors into the Kingdom had sought to escape. Their transaction costs increased and predictably progressive protectionism soon thwarted their ambitions. After June 1925 Germany refused to take Polish coal, shortly thereafter the import of Polish timber and agricultural products was prohibited which resulted in a tariff war until March 1930. As Polish industrialists explored outlets further afield, in the British empire and the USA, their ambitions were systematically forestalled by rising tariff barriers and particularly the Hawley-Smoot tariff of 1930. By the time of the Great Depression when 'numerous plants ceased operations … in 1932 Warsaw industry operated at only 40% of its productive capacity'.[93]

Compensation and Refinance

In these circumstances the Marki entrepreneurs had to use all their resourcefulness to keep their interests afloat. In 1883, in a period of dynamism for Warsaw's economy, potential investors and collaborators rallied round the Bradford partners' establishment of the Marki venture and production was underway within a year. In the post-war period, the commercial network was significantly diminished, the moneys the Bradford men had or expected to receive in 1919 proved insufficient to the task of reconstruction and after four years the firm was still inactive. But it is evident that the owners had not given up hope of receiving reparations for their war-time losses. In 1922 Briggs and Whitehead brought a case against the municipality of Warsaw to release the boilers which had been expropriated to power the tramways in 1917.[94] In January 1923 the district court dismissed the case but suggested that 'the firm did have the right to demand fair compensation. This case was brought to a satisfactory conclusion for the municipality in 1924'.[95] Then in 1927 the *Gazeta Sądowa* reveals that E. Briggs Brothers of Marki were among a number of complainants who joined in a suit against Germany for recompense at market price plus interest for goods and money seized during the

92 Zweig, *Poland between Two Wars*, p. 11.

93 Wynot, *Warsaw between the World Wars*, p. 59.

94 'Tramwaje i autobusy' ['Trams and buses'], *Sprawozdania Komisji Rewizyjnej M. St. Warszawy* [Report of the audit committee for the city of Warsaw] Warsaw, 1939, p. 12.

95 *Sprawozdanie z Działalnosci Zarządu M. St. Warszawy za lata 1918–1923*, Vol. 1 [Report on the activities of the municipality of the city of Warsaw in the years 1918–1923] (Warsaw: Skład Główny w Wydz. Stat. Magistratu, 1925), p. 170.

war.[96] The German state perversely argued that as Poland was not a member of the Allied nations during the war, it was not an enemy state and thus not entitled to war reparations. Further to this it was argued that all requisitions had been paid for, leaving no satisfactory conclusion for Whitehead, who continued the firm alone following the death of his uncle in 1925.

Either the characteristic independence of the Yorkshire industrialists, or perhaps the dearth of Polish investors willing to risk money in the devastated worsted plant, discouraged Whitehead from contemplating joint-stock status for the Marki firm. However, the Warsaw-based businessman was able to exploit his Bradford connections to support his endeavours in Poland. After the war neither Alfred Briggs nor Charles Whitehead had a stake in Briggella Mills, Bradford. By 1907 Arthur 'Harry' Briggs owned the family firm in a new partnership called Briggs, Pollitt Co. Ltd. After John Briggs junior's death in 1911 no interlocking directorship between the British and Polish branches existed.[97] Nevertheless, it seems evident that Alfred Briggs did retain an element of the old family firm: Messrs Alfred Briggs and Co., Gordon Street Mills, in Bradford. Using this address his nephew set up a company called J. Briggs Briggella Ltd., Bank of Liverpool Chambers, Bradford (Private Company), [98] which he held in partnership with his brother-in-law Isaac Smith[99] and another partner H. Rhodes. By attaching a recognisable and reputable company name to the Bradford premises Whitehead was able to secure replacement machinery for the Polish mill, privately pool the cash of closely related parties without risk to the partners' personal assets and, perhaps most importantly, obtain a British mortgage. This private share enterprise was almost certainly an example of a 'free-standing company',[100] prevalent for raising capital to fund foreign investment in the period. It was registered in England with a nominal address: Gordon Street Mills, but had no domestic commercial activities and a restricted, rather than open market, subscribership. In 1925 the firm's capital was £100,000, divided into £50,000 preferential shares and £50,000 ordinary shares worth £1 each. £85,432 had been subscribed and paid up and from 18 August 1925 the company had a mortgage of £96,306.[101]

---

96 J. Namitkiewicz, *Gazeta Sądowa Warszawska*, No. 41, 10 October 1927, p. 7.

97 *London Gazette*, 19 September 1911, p. 6909.

98 *The World's Wool* (London, New York: T. Skinner & Company, 1927), p. 592.

99 Isaac Smith had married Charles Whitehead's sister, Annie Mildred Whitehead in 1900. He was son of the Bradford mayor who latterly owned Salt's Mill in a consortium with John Rhodes and James Roberts.

100 Wilkins, 'The Free-Standing Company'.

101 *The World's Wool*, p. 427.

Polishness and the Cartel System

In post-war Poland huge structural changes to industry emerged. Smaller firms flourished while the largest firms, that had been finely tuned to produce high-volume orders and maintained their profitability through continuous activity, struggled to adjust to the new commercial reality. Poland's foremost metal and engineering firms such as Rudzki, which had worked on the original Marki plant in 1883, August Rephan, Orthwein and Karasiński all 'suffered a substantial reduction'.[102] In general, the textile, mineral, clothing, leather and wood industries never attained their 1913 employment levels.[103] On the other hand, electricity generation, publishing, paper and construction industries boomed.[104] Diversification proved a very successful course for some large firms such as Lilpop, Rau and Loewenstein who bought a motor-car manufacturing plant in Lublin.[105] In 1933 E. Briggs Brothers and Co., of Marki saw the opportunity to employ their prodigious power plant as a subsidiary source of revenue. It was one of only six electricity plants in Poland whose generative capacity exceeded one MW.[106] Indeed the Marki power plant could generate 1.5 MW and applied to the municipality of Warsaw for the concession to supply electricity to Marki and to the surrounding communities of Wawer, Bródno, Radzymin and Okuniew. However, the tender was not welcomed by the authorities as it would 'only be of use for villages situated on the right bank of the Vistula. But if powers are to be granted, the government is asking for the shortest possible period in which the city will have the right to purchase or expropriate the electrical equipment from these areas, to connect them to the capital in the future'.[107]

Despite the growing success of smaller Polish-owned businesses and the withdrawal of many German foreign direct investors, the foreign ownership of factories, mines, shipping and insurance companies remained a bone of contention in the interwar period. Poles only formed 68.9 per cent of the population according to the 1931 census and 'the fires of Polish nationalism were fuelled by the fact that the ethnic minorities were so large'.[108] The stereotype of foreign exploitation, which both the Tsarist regime and various Socialist factions had cultivated, persisted in the interwar period. 'When the workers asked for an increase of wages or for more social benefits there was always a conscious or unconscious interpretation that their own people were struggling against foreign overlords or colonial exploitation'.[109]

---

102 Zweig, *Poland between Two Wars*, p. 91.

103 Wynot, *Warsaw between the World Wars*, p. 62.

104 Ibid.

105 Zweig, *Poland between Two Wars*, p. 90.

106 Wartalska, 'Fabryka i osada fabryczna', p. 660. MW is the abbreviation for a megawatt.

107 *Nowinny Codzienne*, Warsaw, 29 October 1933, p. 4.

108 Davies, *God's Playground*, p. 404.

109 Zweig, *Poland between Two Wars*, p. 123.

Chapter 11 outlined how the Marki firm began to subtly rebrand its image as a result of the 1905 Revolution. They promoted a Polish mill manager, reduced their foreign staff and toned down their outward Britishness. After independence it is evident that many industrial firms, including the Briggs of Marki, proclaimed their Polish patriotism by entrusting their insurance to the newly formed 'Polonia' insurance company.[110] Nevertheless, in Poland's Second Republic they faced continuing pressure as 'the political stance of the leading circles was unashamedly nationalist. "Polishness" became the touchstone of respectability'.[111]

With the re-establishment of industry, Polish industrialists enthusiastically embraced the right of association that had been denied under the Tsarist regime. Each industry formed cooperative alliances, akin to the British Chambers of Commerce, which represented and defended the rights of its members, particularly in their dealings with the state, and there was a strong 'drive towards cartelisation'.[112] Cartels were agreements between the proponents of each branch of manufacture to fix the market price and were increasingly instituted in interwar Poland in an attempt to simulate the advantages of protectionism. Although the Briggs were one of very few English worsted manufacturers in Poland, in March 1931 the *Gazeta Handlowa* recorded that they entered into a cartel with the Łódź companies of Karol Kröning and Co., Stephan and Werner, *Łódzka Czesalnia i Przędzalnia Wełny, S. A.* [Łódź Worsted and Wool Spinners and Co.], and perhaps most notably with the firm of Markus Kohn who had commissioned industrial espionage against the Briggs brothers before the war. The five participant businesses made English-style worsted yarn on a combined total of 50,000 spindles, producing 50,000 kg of yarn per week in 1931. The newly established convention immediately agreed to raise the price of worsted yarn by 10 cents in line with Britain and ideas were discussed for the 'rationalisation of production, which should be adapted to market needs'.[113] The partners even considered opening a central sales office for their products. Although it might appear entirely uncharacteristic for the Marki company to join such a coalition it is likely that, in the nationalistic political climate, Charles Whitehead could not afford to ostracise his company. Indeed the press announcement of the cartel particularly highlighted that the Marki firm was the only member 'owned by the English'.[114] He needed to monitor the activities of his competitors and enjoy the benefits of group membership, just as competing Bradford firms had joined forces in the nineteenth-century Chamber of Commerce to improve the trading environment.

The absolute destruction of Warsaw during the Second World War has meant that few records have survived to provide more substantive evidence about the firm's performance in the interwar period. Perhaps ironically, many earlier records

110 *Kurjer Asekuracyjny*, Warsaw, No. 11, 1918, p. 4.
111 Davies, *God's Playground*, p. 404.
112 Zweig, *Poland between Two Wars*, p. 103.
113 *Gazeta Handlowa*, Warsaw, No. 57, 11 March 1931, p. 1.
114 Ibid.

Figure 12.3 Remains of the Marki factory
Source: Author's photograph

about Marki were only preserved because under a system of unfathomable Russian bureaucracy they were stored in administrative outposts, rather than in Warsaw and the 'British, French, Belgian, and Serbian Consuls and their Consular archives' were safely evacuated to Moscow in August 1915 by a specially commissioned train.[115] But Wartalska's interviews with Karol Whitehead, son of Charles, in the

[115] 'Forsaken City', *The Times*, 9 August 1915.

1980s suggest that the firm's fortunes followed a general pattern for Polish industry in this period. The worsted mill worked intermittently until the second half of the 1930s 'when it began to experience the clear symptoms of a recovery'.[116] In 1938 the factory at Marki was running without a break and 'local industry appeared to have unlimited opportunities for development, only to be halted by World War II'.[117] On 14 September 1939 the first bombardment of Marki took place which ultimately destroyed the factory buildings.[118]

This chapter has outlined an extraordinarily complicated period in both Polish history and the story of the Marki firm. Although the available evidence from this period is rather fragmented and anecdotal it has been possible to provide a plausible impression of this phase of the company's existence. It has shown the enormity of the calamity that the First World War constituted for the company and how, in the interwar, it was not simply the challenges of reconstruction but those of an entirely transformed trading environment which the resourceful industrialists had to negotiate. But there was no question of retreat and the Bradford men typically adapted to cope with the extreme situation and capitalise on the opportunities of the period. They used their Bradford connections to raise further investment capital in England and sought war reparations, they diversified into electricity supply and united with their competitors under the cartel system. The family's firm commitment to Marki is perhaps best illustrated by the careers of Charles Whitehead's six sons whose educations were dedicated to furthering the potential of the worsted business and their extended family interests in the interwar period.

Francis or Franciszek (1907–77) studied textiles at the University of Leeds. He managed the Marki factory in the 1930s and was also a director of his uncle's chocolate company E. Wedel S.A. During the Second World War he was awarded the *Złotym Krzyżem Zasługi* [Gold Cross of Merit] for his service in the Polish army. George or Jerzy (1908–86), an Oxford graduate, was awarded the British Military Cross, the France and Germany Star Defence medal and the *Croix de Guerre* [Military Cross] for his heroic work with the French Resistance.[119] Thereafter he became Wedel's New York representative. Richard or Ryszard (1910–1943) went to agricultural college and directed Marki's milk production business during the interwar period. He died fighting for the British army in North Africa in 1943. Karol (1913–93) attended Grenoble Business School and became production director for the Wedel factory.[120] He was a member of the Polish *Armia Krajowa* [Home Army] during the Second World War and was wounded in the Warsaw Uprising. After the war he worked at the British Embassy to negotiate compensation for foreign-owned businesses that had been appropriated under the

116 Wartalska, 'Fabryka i osada fabryczna', p. 650.

117 Wynot, *Warsaw between the World Wars*, p. 59.

118 Paciorek and Dudzika, *Mareckie zeszyty historyczne*, p. 25.

119 Miliszkiewicz, *Polskie gniazda rodzinne*, p. 45.

120 Marie Barbasiewicz, *Ludzie interesu w przedwojennej Polsce* [*People's Interests in Interwar Poland*] (Warsaw: PWN, 2013), p. 226.

Soviet nationalisation process. He was arrested in 1947 and became the subject of a notorious Warsaw show trial in 1948 when his case was championed in the British Parliament by Ernest Bevin.[121] Nevertheless, he spent several years in the Polish mines before he was 'cleared of all charges and fully rehabilitated' in the 1950s. He then took up a post at the Polish Academy of Sciences in Warsaw.[122] Karol Whitehead is famous for being the largest private landlord in the Soviet Union. He retained nominal ownership and responsibility for the estate and housing at Marki until the 1980s.[123] Little is known about the pre-war careers of the youngest brothers Alfred (1912–84) and Jan (1918–2001) or their sister Małgorzata (1919–2011) but her husband, the Polish pianist and close friend of Arthur Rubinstein and Władysław Szpilman, Roman Jasiński, emphasises in his memoir that 'despite these cosmopolitan appearances, a sense of belonging to Poland, clearly dominated in the younger generation of the family'.[124] Alfred is particularly revered in Poland as member of the elite *Cichociemni* [the silent and unseen] brigade with the code-name *Dolina 2* [Valley 2]. He was arrested by the NKVD in August 1944 and sent to a labour camp at Ryazan in Russia. He escaped to England in 1949 where he lived for the next 35 years. But it is evident that he always considered himself Polish and retired to his homeland in 1981 where he died in the mountain resort of Zakopane in 1984.

121 *HC Debate*, Poland (Mr Charles Whitehead, arrest), 5 November 1947, Vol. 443, cc. 1818–20.

122 'Polish Court Clears Mr C. Whitehead', *The Times*, 6 April 1958.

123 Miliszkiewicz, *Polskie gniazda rodzinne*, p. 44.

124 Roman Jasiński, *Zmierzch starego świata: wspomniena, 1900–1945* [Twilight of the Old World: Memoirs, 1900–1945] (Krakow: Wydawnictwo Literackie, 2006), p. 653.

Conclusion

This book has explored the Marki enterprise from its roots in nineteenth-century British industry to its demise with Poland's Second Republic in 1939. The final chapter will summarise some of the case study's central findings, such as the contemporary incentives to undertake foreign direct investment, the influence of British industrial experience on the venture capitalists' strategy, indications of the firm's performance and particularly the vital importance of local cooperation to establish and operate an enterprise abroad effectively. However, as this was primarily an exploration of individual entrepreneurship rather than British or Polish trade legislatures and industrial histories, it seems appropriate in this concluding chapter to consider in greater detail the personalities, motivations and methods of the men who built the Marki venture.

This case study has revealed that many aspects of Briggs, Posselt and Co., Marki reflected contemporary British industrial culture: first and foremost, the partnership form of the company, privately financed to provide optimum control, was absolutely characteristic of British manufacturing tradition. It differed markedly from the majority of large companies in the Polish lands where a shortage of cash or expertise and risk aversion led most to adopt joint-stock status in this period. Although swift construction of an instant factory contrasted starkly with the cautious reinvestment that typified British-manufacturing culture, two proven aspects of British-industrial prudence certainly applied at Marki: firstly the Briggs-Posselt partnership, like their Bradford forefathers, limited their activities to component manufacture until they understood Russian-empire market requirements and had accumulated sufficient profits to increase their plant's capabilities to achieve the fully vertical model. Secondly, harking back to the earliest days of the Industrial Revolution, the foreign plant was equipped to manufacture machine parts, building materials, soap and to generate power. This economical and self-sufficient approach led to some significant commercial diversifications for the firm.

The Bradford partners' determination to redress the shortcomings of British industry is evident in many of their actions: fundamentally, they by-passed overwhelming domestic competition for Bradford staples by choosing a nation with no rivalry in their field of expertise. In Russian Poland, as opposed to tariff-protected France, Germany or the US, the undercapitalised commercial environment allowed them to monopolise and develop both resource and sales markets. Secondly, they rejected the conglomerations of Łódź, Białystok or Moscow, which resembled Bradford, in favour of an undeveloped site with unbounded-expansion potential and a plentiful water supply. Thirdly, their highly selective employment policy, favouring 'widows with children',[1] evaded the skills trap and growing unionisation of British industry. In commercial terms, circumventing these institutional failings of their home trade was more valuable than cheap wages or protectionism which were additional benefits in Poland. Finally, they equipped the foreign plant to manufacture the widest possible range of products, appropriate to several different market sectors, instead of restricting their capabilities to the mass production of generic goods which had spelled disaster for many of their compatriots in the light of recent changes to fashion and particularly French competition.

A very broad definition of international technology transfer has been identified in this case study which encompassed British experiments in machinery, resource management and workforce control; nevertheless it is evident that the Bradford men did not seek to emulate a British industrial plant at Marki. The design and layout of the factory buildings, the fuel-efficient engines, modern belt-drive transmission and groundbreaking novelties, such as electric lighting and modern fire precautions, were intended to exceed contemporary British standards and create the optimum manufactory. Nevertheless, despite the growing failure of paternalism to control England's second- and third-generation industrial workforces at the end of the nineteenth century, the Briggs-Posselt partnership deduced its particular appropriateness to Polish social conditions and to promulgate a positive reputation for themselves as foreign employers in the Russian empire. Although social overhead investment and charitable patronage by Russian-Polish industrialists was commonplace, it is clear that the Briggs-Posselt partnership's program, in which 'a worker is taken care of by his employer',[2] was viewed as peculiarly British in the region and laudable; its influence on the founders' close circle at Warsaw has been shown.

The viability of this foreign enterprise depended on some very recent global-trade developments: for example, although domination of Russian-empire wool supplies was central the Bradford partners' strategy in Poland, to preclude following competition and forge trade relationships with both weavers and spinners in the host nation, the firm still relied on colonial resources. Thus steam shipping, rapidly improving Russian rail networks and international communications generally – factors which simultaneously challenged the primacy of British industry and the merchant's role in Bradford – facilitated operations at the remote worsted factory in a way that would have been unfeasible any earlier in the century. Similarly, inventions such as the ring spindle, developed by Lancashire engineering firms to increase their export trade, enabled unskilled foreign workers to replicate the quality and quantity output of Britain's experienced labour as never before.

1 *Kurjer Warszawski*, 28 September 1884, p. 11.

2 'Gazetka' ['Newsletter'], *Gazeta Warszawska*, No. 147, 1892, p. 3.

Protectionism and the British Free-trade Debate

This case study has dispelled many myths regarding foreign direct investment; for example that it was intended to deliver cheap offshore processing, that low-cost land and wages or a lack of foreign factory legislation were primary catalysts. Centrally the common conclusion that building factories abroad was entirely a response to protectionism has been challenged. Although the impact of progressive international tariff control to change the emphasis of British manufacturing output has been highlighted, it also clearly forced some positive adjustments on industrialists to cut costs, specialise and seek out new markets at the end of the nineteenth century. Contemporary ballots of Bradford Chamber of Commerce members show that the city's woolmen remained overwhelmingly in favour of the British government's liberal trade policies. Moreover, the generally disadvantageous social and commercial infrastructure which characterised nineteenth-century protectionist states such as Russia and the unreliability of national trade legislatures as a basis for fixed-asset investment have been highlighted. Nevertheless, venture capitalists' usual tactic to justify their capital export as a desperate measure to counteract implied losses caused by foreign protectionism has been exposed. Therefore reportage of the Marki venture falls into two distinct categories: an abundance of positive Polish promotion contrasts dramatically with the limited British accounts made largely in the context of the anti-Free-trade debate.

Monopoly of Market Opportunity

This case study has emphasised that nineteenth-century foreign investment was invariably a response to the *pull* factor of rising opportunity abroad, rather than the *push* factor of domestic hardship. The most successful businessmen were adept at devising strategies to gain advantage from the increasingly complex commercial environment rather than lobbying the state for legislative protection of their industries. Although the British press described Edward Briggs as a 'fair trader',[3] it is evident that he devoted his professional energies to devising profitable solutions to commercial challenges rather than to political action. He directed Briggella's production into difficult-to-manufacture specialities such as umbrella cloths and fancy yarns and simultaneously spread his assets into a burgeoning foreign economy.

The exclusion of international competitors, local tax exemptions and poorly enforced labour laws were undoubtedly welcome benefits in tariff-protected Poland, but the Bradford partners' 1883 letter to Russian finance minister Bunge shows that their first thoughts were not for Tsarist protectionism but for monopoly in the Russian empire:

---

[3] 'Emigration of Capital', *Sheffield Daily Telegraph*, 1 March 1883, p. 3.

> The spinning mill that we are establishing at Marki is the first in Russia of this type in which the English system will be used to produce long wools, mohair, alpaca and English lustre wools. These wools are used to make cloth and equally for making shawls and upholstery fabrics. All these wool yarns presently come exclusively from England, they have tried in France and Germany to produce them, but nothing has been forthcoming because it requires great experience and the machines are rather complicated … We are in the process of constructing a quality spinning mill using workers who are indigenous to Warsaw and Praga. Over the past few months we have sent these workers to our establishment in Bradford (England) to teach them the necessary skills. But we have had significant problems with our English workers who threatened to strike and refused to instruct these workers knowing that the monopoly that Bradford has in this industry would be spread to Russia.[4]

Tsarist Support for Foreign Direct Investment

Although the driving force of the Marki enterprise was foreign opportunity rather than international trade legislature, this case study has revealed many subtle ways that Tsarist politics directly and indirectly supported foreign investors in the Polish lands. The punitive taxation and bureaucratic control, intended to curtail the activities of any potential Polish leadership class, simultaneously suppressed native entrepreneurship and contrasted strongly with the fast-track authorisation of foreigners' investment plans. This favouritism is evident in the Bradford partners' earliest dealings with Warsaw's Tsarist administrators. In 1883 the head of the district implored Warsaw Governor, Pyotr Albedynski, to authorise swiftly the tax-free import of machinery and raw materials to Marki: 'I humbly ask if you can address this in a short period of time, to allow the factory owners to bring the equipment they need into the country'.[5] Within two days the Governor had visited the construction site and hastened to assure the Ministry of Internal Affairs in St Petersburg:

> That Messrs Briggs and Posselt have already made a large financial investment and it seems that they have a huge capital at their disposal. Undoubtedly the factory is going to bring benefit to the whole country not just to the Warsaw district. With time they intend to expand the factory by four times and they are already preparing to increase their production four-fold.[6]

4 AGAD, *Akta Warszawskiego Komitetu Przemyłowego z 1883*, signature 11/1883.

5 Ibid., head of the Warsaw district to the Governor of Warsaw, Pyotr Albedynski, signature 11/1883, 22 June 1883.

6 Ibid., Albedynski to the Ministry of Internal Affairs in St Petersburg, 24 June 1883.

This case study has highlighted that the Bradford men made every effort to present a philanthropic image in Poland and were in many ways excellent employers by Russian-empire standards. But the host state's continuing collusion with these wealthy foreign investors is evident in the factory inspector's mention of a 'special decree of the finance minister',[7] which allowed minors at Marki to work very much longer shifts than Russian labour laws stipulated in 1887.

The Entrepreneurs

International economic and political factors undoubtedly had a role in the form and long-term fortunes of the Marki enterprise, but it is important to remember that it was primarily product of the ambition, vision and entrepreneurship of its founders. The Briggs-Posselt partnership was in many ways a remarkable international alliance of skills and capital, but characteristic differences in the customary business behaviour of the associates have been identified: the Yorkshire industrialists concentrated their assets in one family firm, whereas their German partner spread his interests among numerous companies, nations, products and services throughout his career. Nevertheless, they united to realise a vision which was unusually radical for all participants and swam against the tide of contemporary manufacturing practice. The Briggs introduced a non-family member into partnership for the first time and similarly for the first time Posselt joined a commercial undertaking without the controlling interest. Against an industrial trend to reduce costs, the partners built the most capital-intensive business model to achieve their goals in Poland. While English manufacturers sought to minimise stock holdings in favour of cautious just-in-time resourcing, huge quantities of raw wool were accumulated in the vast warehouses of Marki. When most British capital export was concentrated in arm's length speculations and a few Bradford industrialists attempted foreign direct investment, mainly in the US, the Briggs-Posselt partnership took their cash east.

In this case study the founders and the firm have been described generally as a single entity – the Briggs-Posselt partnership however, it is evident that each partner had markedly different motivations and vested interests in the venture. Their individual characters and contributions, and those of the company's inheritors, Alfred Briggs and his nephew Charles Whitehead, arguably influenced the course of the business as strongly as any of the international economic or socio-political factors that have been explored in this case study. Thus it seems relevant in this final chapter to consider the individuals who brought this unique commercial experiment to fruition.

---

7 APW, Ref.1, 159/1887, pp. 2–3.

Edward Briggs

Edward Briggs has been identified as the originator and strategist of the project. The entrepreneurial second son of John Briggs of Briggella Mills in Bradford, whose practical education in his father's factory and at Joseph Wright's school had developed in him some formidable qualities as a businessman. Ambitious, hardworking and meticulous, he was unable to relax his control even when on holiday and kept 'the mills alive with telegrams' from the Riviera.[8] Although the financial success of the Marki venture was undoubtedly intended, Edward Briggs' motivations to launch the enterprise were not primarily financial. Before the death of his father and elder brother, he had risen to become the wealthy managing director of the family firm. He was deeply embedded in Bradford society where he later became a JP. His connection with Bradford Cricket, Athletic and Football Club was not just a hobby but a close involvement in the business of sport. Briggs was the principal benefactor and guarantor of loans for the club which, by the 1890s, was one of the highest-profile sporting organisations in the north and among the richest in England. John Dewhirst describes Edward Briggs' single-minded pursuit of sporting success and prestige as he employed professional footballers at Briggella Mills to maintain their amateur status and took a leading role in the purchase of the stadium freehold at Park Avenue.[9] Indeed one obituary summed up his life, without even mentioning his *magnum opus* at Marki, as 'best known for three things – his strong support of the Bradford Cricket, Athletic and Football Club; his private unostentatious charities, in which unfortunate and aged workpeople had a full share; and his close attention to business'.[10]

Edward Briggs' social aspirations are evident in his conversion from Wesleyan-Liberal roots to become known as an Anglican and a Conservative. The British press described him as the 'Mr Tate of the Midlands',[11] in allusion to his prodigious art collection and in 1886 compared him with industrial heavy-weight Titus Salt by referring to Marki as 'a second edition of Saltaire'.[12] This combined evidence suggests Edward Briggs' desire to increase his reputation as a businessman in his own right, rather than under the auspices of his father's company. But another incentive for the foreign project is suggested by his political machinations within the family firm. Despite the founder's egalitarian bequest of Briggella equally to his five sons and one son-in-law in 1886, by the early twentieth century the Briggs' British assets were controlled entirely by Edward's only son, Harry. The eldest Briggs brother Moses died in 1885, Charles Briggs bowed out of the firm

[8] 'Observatory', *Bradford Observer*, 12 March 1898, p. 4.

[9] John Dewhirst provided these insights in an interview with the author in October 2014, his research will be published in John Dewhirst, *Room at the Top: The Origins of Bradford City AFC & Bradford (Park Avenue) AFC* (Bradford: Bantamspast, 2015).

[10] 'Observatory', *Bradford Observer*, 12 March 1898, p. 4.

[11] *Pall Mall Gazette*, London, 21 December 1892, p. 1.

[12] *Illustrated Weekly Telegraph*, Bradford, 19 March 1886, p. 1.

in 1893 and none of their sons inherited a stake in the family firm. Thus it seems credible that diverting the professional interests of his youngest brothers, John and Alfred, away from the company which he intended his own son to inherit was a central facet of Edward's agenda. In this context it is unsurprising that his brother-in-law's only son, Charles Whitehead, was also dispatched to Marki in the 1890s. Although Edward Briggs never intended to live in Poland, it seems clear that the success of the foreign enterprise was vital to smooth the progress of his personal ambitions for the Bradford firm, therefore he needed a trustworthy and well-qualified collaborator to guide the project locally.

Ernst Posselt

Marki was not an isolated example of British colonialism; much of the enterprise's success has been attributed to its integration with Warsaw commerce and the adjustment of its products and services to meet local demands. Although Edward Briggs undoubtedly drove the project, it was the charm offensive orchestrated by Ernst Posselt which facilitated the vital cooperation of Warsaw's cosmopolitan business community, engendered the support of the Tsarist administration and counteracted the widely held negative Polish views towards foreign investment particularly and industrial development generally.

Posselt's motive for involvement in the Marki venture was not dissimilar to that of Edward Briggs but he used the prestige of association in a more pragmatic way; as a useful currency to forge broader commercial connections in the Russian empire. The swift establishment of the Marki factory is a tribute to the practiced efficiency with which the German businessman could engender trust to mediate business as an outsider. His work on behalf of the Briggs was naturally a matter of mutual advantage when his public-relations efforts among the Evangelical press barons of Warsaw aggrandised all the partners' reputations in equal measure. But whereas the Briggs took a typically long-term view to their fixed-asset investment, it is evident that Marki was only one element of Posselt's considerable portfolio. The duration of his participation was not planned but rested on whether the worsted business could sustain his interest and finance his other projects.

Chapter 6 suggested that, *in loco parentis*, Ernst Posselt brokered prestigious marriages in Warsaw for both John and Alfred Briggs, as he did for his own sons. The scope of his Russia-empire business interests has been outlined already, but the prolific entrepreneur's character and methods are described most effectively in the memoir of his eldest son William and in Louis Lochner's biography of the violinist Fritz Kreisler. These accounts relate the gregarious entrepreneur's relish for his role as a mentor, indeed his 'hobby was that of helping struggling young talents'.[13] William Posselt recalled that, despite his numerous business activities, his father always 'found time to take a warm interest in his colleagues. Many

[13] Lochner, *Fritz Kreisler*, p. 44.

young businessmen benefitted from his advice and owed the existence of their companies to his assistance'.[14]

In the case of the young violinist, Posselt lent him a Stradivarius from his own collection and guaranteed the sale of 500 tickets for his Berlin debut in 1899. Kreisler performed at the industrialist's lavish silver wedding anniversary celebrations at Heidelberg Castle in 1894 and frequently gave private recitals in his Berlin home on fashionable Klopstockstrasse in the Tiergarten. There Posselt advised him to visit J.C. Schaarwächter, the royal court photographer, to pose for 'a picture which made him look like a wealthy young man about town to whom money was an object of utmost indifference'.[15] William described that his father loaned Kreisler a winter paletot (loose-fitting coat) and advised him to roll back one side to impress people with the fur lining. The amusing anecdote is an indication of the considerable attention to detail with which the cosmopolitan businessman cultivated his apprentices. Similarly, the young John and Alfred Briggs, and Posselt's own nephew Arnold Korff, would have been coached on how to present themselves in the best light in order to achieve their potential in the Russian empire.

John and Alfred Briggs

John Briggs junior, or Ivan Ivanovich Briggs as he was named in most Russian documents, and his younger brother Alfred had much lower public profiles in Warsaw but were undoubtedly the workhorses of the Marki firm. After Posselt's withdrawal from the partnership in 1897 and despite John's founder status, the company became known as E. Briggs Brothers and Co., never *Braci Briggsów* [Briggs brothers] as it was frequently dubbed in Poland. Although this chapter has suggested that Marki was partly intended to compensate John and Alfred for the loss of a leading role at Briggella Mills, it was nevertheless a rare opportunity for these younger sons to gain proprietorship of a large manufactory. In the style of their father they were the face-to-face paternalists of the Polish industrial settlement. The desire for financial success certainly would have motivated them and John Briggs' aspiration to achieve the status of his older brother is certainly suggested in his donations to the Praga hospital and Warsaw's first motorised ambulance in 1909.[16]

In the context of the Marki firm's history John Briggs enjoyed the heyday of its establishment and early success. He thrived in the reflected glory of the Posselt and Granzow families and their extended connections in Warsaw. Apart from the revolutionary years of 1905–08 he did not suffer any hardship through his

14 Posselt, *Gottfried Posselt 1693–1768*, p. 203.

15 Lochner, *Fritz Kreisler*, p. 54.

16 'Podziękowanie', *Gazeta Warszawska*, No. 330, 1890, p. 3 and Majewski, 'Do wypadku co koń wyskoczy!'

Figure C.1 The Briggs' family grave, Evangelical-Augsburg cemetery, Warsaw

Source: Author's photograph

endeavours and retired in 1911 to a substantial estate in the fashionable spa town of Ilkley in Yorkshire, almost as wealthy as his older brother had been.[17] Alfred Briggs, on the other hand, lived through the privations of the First World War and appears to have sunk his entire wealth into the reconstruction of the Polish plant during the interwar years. From the age of 25, Alfred devoted his career to Marki, but only inherited an ownership stake at the age of 40 following Edward's death in 1898. He married at Warsaw and is the only partner to be buried there; in the German-Evangelical Cemetery. A reference to the company Messrs Alfred Briggs and Co., of Gordon Street Mills, Bradford in his uncle Francis Whitehead's 1907 obituary might imply that he cultivated a personal enterprise in tandem with his work in Poland. However, as the Gordon Street premises had been part of J. Briggs and Co., it is likely that Alfred received it in the division of family assets after Edward's death. Chapter 12 revealed the use of this company as a fund-raising vehicle to bolster Marki in the interwar period.[18]

Charles Whitehead

A chameleon quality in the Marki ownership, and many Russian-Polish industrialists, has been revealed in this case study. The enterprise was launched in 1883, with a bold British identity and the support of the Tsarist state, into an increasingly nationally charged nineteenth-century Polish society. But a gradual adaptation to the evolving socio-political environment was required after 1905 and particularly during the Second Republic to ensure the company's survival. Charles Whitehead's introduction to the firm in the 1890s, his propitious marriage to Eleonora Wedel and something of his six sons' careers have already been described. But it is worth noting a paragraph from the recently published memoir of his son-in-law, Roman Jasiński, who wrote:

> Whitehead senior was one-hundred per cent English. He inherited a large spinning factory in Marki outside Warsaw from his uncle Briggs and married the daughter of Emil Wedel; he settled permanently in Poland. One should particularly say that his life was spent in almost total isolation from local society, its affairs and problems. He never learned to speak Polish over the several decades that he lived in Poland … He was moreover not an easy man to be with; dry and closed in. Slight, blond with a closely-clipped moustache and an English-type ruddy complexion, he was always extremely neatly dressed. He

[17] Edward Briggs died in 1898 leaving £37,251 and John Briggs junior had an estate worth £31,989 in 1911. It is worth noting here that the estate of their father only amounted to £1,311 in 1886.

[18] 'Mr Francis Whitehead of Bradford', *Yorkshire Daily Observer*, 14 March, 1907.

> abided to English standards and customs in his home within an inch of pedantry and he did not care for broader society so it was rare ever to see him at a party.[19]

This case study has credited the early success of Briggs, Posselt and Co., Marki to the business acuity of Edward Briggs and the socio-commercial talents of Ernst Posselt. In basic terms these partners devised profitable solutions to a complex of practical, economic and political challenges which impacted on global trade in the last quarter of the nineteenth century. It must be acknowledged that under Charles Whitehead's direction, the firm faced some major setbacks, including economic depression, war-time asset stripping and loss of the Russian market. To his credit Whitehead showed immense resilience and determination to rebuild his factory in the interwar period after his uncle Alfred's death in 1925. Nevertheless, Jasiński's testimony raises the question of whether the inheritor of Marki ran operations in rather more isolation than his predecessors to its severe detriment? It seems arguable that, whether through his linguistic shortcomings or a lack of the sociable bonhomie that characterised the founders' mediation of business, the enterprise lost some of its original dynamism in the twentieth century.

Indicators of the Firm's Performance

No business records from Marki or the Briggs' Bradford firm are known to have survived the destruction of the Second World War and the sale of Briggella Mills after the untimely death of Edward Brigg's grandson, Arthur, in 1928. Nevertheless, comparing and contrasting diverse evidence such as consular correspondence, the records of the *Warszawskiego Komitetu Przemysłowego* [Warsaw Committee for Industry] and, for example, tempering effusive promotional press reports with the factory inspectors' more pragmatic testimony, it has been possible to provide a balanced view of the industrialists' strategy, *modus operandi* and fortunes in Poland. British Foreign Office archives have provided some rare firsthand accounts of the entrepreneurs' activities and a useful barometer of the firm's local profile. For example, Murray's 1903 survey of British-owned companies in his jurisdiction, which was one of the most industrialised regions of the Russian empire, shows the scale and local perception of the venture:

> The only two factories established in this Consular District since 1880 by British Manufacturers are the wool spinning factory of Messrs E. Briggs Bros at Marki ... and the lace curtain factory started at Warsaw by Messrs Birkin and Co., Nottingham. The former employ over 2,500 hands and is an unqualified success, the latter employs at present only about 50 hands it is not yet in full work. The only other British works in this district are the machinery works of

19 Jasiński, *Zmierzch starego świata*, p. 651.

> Mr Greenwood at Łódź which were started in 1873, are doing well and employ some 150 hands.[20]

Chapter 10 drew conclusions about the Marki enterprise's performance over time from the available statistical sources which, in its first two decades at least, describe rapidly increasing productive capacity and turnover, plus a consistently employed and growing workforce. Many self-evidential gauges of success have been advanced in this case study, such as the plant's great expansion of 1892, the unwillingness of the workforce to participate in strike actions and Marki's survival beyond the Briggs' longer-established Bradford firm. That Posselt's involvement exceeded the minimum contractual period specified in the partnership agreement suggests the benefits of continuing association. In the context of Western fears over growing Bolshevism among industrial workforces after the First World War, the establishment of the ARA feeding station at Marki in 1919 perversely shows the perceived importance of the industrial settlement. As does the fact that writers such as Edward Litten or Coningsby Dawson singled out the venture for special attention in English, Russian and German publications.[21] It is also worth considering that a third of the company's value will have been withdrawn on Posselt's retirement from the partnership in 1897. Although Edward Briggs left his Russian assets to his Warsaw-based brothers the following year, in 1911 John Briggs similarly removed his share of the firm's capital. That the company withstood these disbursements and devastating losses during the First World War seems a substantial indicator of its financial robustness.

The importance of this case study, however, transcends assessments of financial success or failure. Bradford Mills at Marki was not the only foreign direct investment of the period, indeed comparisons with several other British undertakings have been made throughout this book and a contemporary Polish industrial landscape characterised by German, French, Belgian and even Italian investment has been shown. Nevertheless, this is a uniquely comprehensive cross-cultural record of one of the largest and most enduring privately owned foreign enterprises of the period.

This book has examined the Briggs-Posselt partnership's Marki venture from many angles, exploring the entrepreneurs' practical steps to establish a foreign factory and their fortunes from the late nineteenth into the twentieth centuries: it has described the British socio-economic conditions which led to growing capital export in this period and how experience accrued in the industrial north of England informed the style and implementation of the enterprise. Poland's complex historiography was outlined, revealing a Russian tradition of enticing foreign capital and industrial skills which long-predated Witte's program of the 1890s. Although the ethno-religious social profile, created by historic eastward

20 FO65/1671, Murray to Secretary of State, 2 July 1903, p. 269.

21 Litten, *Promyslennost Rossii* and *Englische Wollspinnerei*, Dawson, *It Might Have Happened to You*.

economic migrations, clearly assisted the Bradford partners' integration among Warsaw's commercial elite, the need for a diplomatic *tour de force* to counteract an influential perception of foreign exploitation in Polish society has been explained. The role of the British consul and other intermediaries such as Ludwig Knoop and Wilhelm Rau, to provide local commercial intelligence, negotiate Tsarist bureaucracy, gain the credit and cooperation of a variety of contractors, suppliers and the Warsaw press revealed the venture capitalists' *modus operandi* in remarkable detail. Although prodigious capital was undoubtedly vital, accessing a circle of trust to mediate business abroad has emerged as one of the primary building blocks of this foreign enterprise. Thus the Bradford men socialised and married among the Varsovian families most able to further their endeavours in Poland – the architects, brick makers, newspaper magnates and financiers – rather than British expatriates. In this context, the Briggs brothers' surprising affiliation with the German-Evangelical Church, rather than the Anglican Ministry at Warsaw, was explained. Moreover, the enduring sense of obligation that the original international partnership exerted on its descendants, which superseded national allegiances during the First World War, was a revelation in the last chapter. This book details the technology that was installed at Marki in comparison with contemporary British and Russian-empire standards and shows how the firm progressively developed its strategy and capabilities in line with Polish conditions, resources and opportunities to achieve long-term sustainability. The experiences of Marki's complete hierarchy of staff have been considered: through three generations of the family-capitalist owners, their skilled Yorkshire managers and the first-generation industrial workforce of woman. Ultimately this case study of the Briggs-Posselt partnership and their Marki venture is worthy of historians' interest as a rare account of individual entrepreneurship, which provides fresh perspective on the larger political, economic and social histories of England and Poland through one of Europe's most dynamic and turbulent periods of history.

Bibliography

Archival Sources

AGAD – *Archiwum Główne Akt Dawnych w Warszawie* for *Akta Warszawskiego Komitetu Przemysłowego z 1883*, *Starszy Inspektor Fabryczny Guberni Warszawskiej* signatures 1180, 403, 3028, *Rząd Gubernialny Warszawski Referat II and XVII.*

APW – *Archiwum Panstwowe w Warszawie* for *Firma Arnold Korff w Warszawie, Starszy Inspektor Fabryczny Guberni Warszawskiej*, signature 375, *Rząd GuburniaWarszawski.*

Biblioteka Cyfrowa Politechniki Warszawskiej [Digital Library of Warsaw University of Technology], *Biblioteka Cyfrowa Politechniki Ziemi Łódzkiej* [Digital Library of the Polytechnic of Łódź] and *Biblioteka Uniwersytetu Warszawskiego* [University of Warsaw Library] for nineteenth-century Polish press.

British Library Newspaper Collection for the nineteenth-century trade journals and newspapers.

Family collections including the Hinchcliffe memoir and letters, the Hopkinson family letters, Grey, Lilpop and Ringstedt family histories.

Hansard archive of the House of Commons debates.

Heidelberg Stadtarchiv.

Herbert Hoover Presidential Library for the Coningsby Dawson Archive.

Historical Business and Patent Information Services provided by Leeds and Sheffield libraries and archives.

Leeds Russian Archive at the University of Leeds.

National Archives, Foreign and Consular Documents, refs: FO1004, FO181, FO366, FO393, FO394, FO396, FO397, FO399, FO400, FO417, FO566, FO65, FO640 and Diplomatic and Consular Reports on Trade and Finance from 1886 to 1910.

PBN – *Państwowe Biuro Notarialne w Warszawie Archiwum.*

West Yorkshire Archive Services at Bradford and Wakefield for the Bradford Chamber of Commerce and Posselt archives.

Interviews

Dr Annette Frese, curator of the Posselt art collection at the Heidelberg *Kurpfälzische Museum*.
Dr Piotr Jaworski, senior curator of the *Centralne Muzeum Włókiennictwa*, Łódź.
Zbigniew Paciorek, local historian of Marki.

Books

Akroyd, E., *The Yorkshire Penny Bank*, Leeds: Longmans, Green, 1872.
Aldcroft, Derek, *The Development of British Industry and Foreign Competition 1875–1914*, London: George Allen and Unwin, 1968.
Aldcroft, Derek H. and Steven Morewood, *Economic Change in Eastern Europe since 1918*, Cheltenham: Edward Elgar, 1995.
Anan'ich, Boris V., 'The economic policy of the tsarist government and enterprise in Russia from the end of the 19th through the beginning of 20th century', in *Entrepreneurship in Imperial Russia and the Soviet Union*, edited by Gregory Guroff and Fred V. Carstensen, pp. 125–39, Princeton: Princeton University Press, 1983.
Ashton, Rosemary, *Little Germany: exile and asylum in Victorian England*, Oxford: Oxford University Press, 1986.
Ausubel, Herman, *In Hard Times, Reformers Among the Late Victorians*, New York: Columbia University Press, 1960.
Baker, James, *Our Foreign Competitors, their Life and Labour*, London: Sampson Low, Marston and Company, 1892.
Barbasiewicz, Marie, *Ludzie interesu w przedwojennej Polsce*, Warsaw: PWN, 2013.
Behrens, J. and H., *Memoir of Jacob Behrens 1806–1889*, Bradford: Percy, Lund, Humphreys and Co., 1925.
Biernacki, Richard, *The Fabrication of Labor, Germany and Great Britain, 1640–1914*, Berkeley: University of California Press, 1995.
Blackwell, W., 'The Russian entrepreneur and the Tsarist period' in *Entrepreneurship in Imperial Russia and the Soviet Union*, edited by Gregory Guroff and Fred V. Carstensen, pp. 13–26, Princeton: Princeton University Press, 1983.
Blewett, Mary H., *The Yankee Yorkshireman: Migration Lived and Imagined*, Urbana and Chicago: University of Illinois Press, 2009.
Blit, Lucjan, *The Origins of Polish Socialism: The History and Ideas of the First Polish Socialist Party*, Cambridge: Cambridge University Press, 1971.
Blobaum, Robert E., *Rewolucja: Russian Poland 1904–1907*, Ithaca and London: Cornell University Press, 1995.
Bolz, Walter, *Krupps-Siemens: Nebenerwerbssiedlung fur Kurz- und Vollarbeiter*, Berlin: J. Springer, 1934.

Bonnell, Victoria E., *The Russian Worker: Life and Labour under the Tsarist Regime*, Berkeley, Los Angeles and London: University of California Press, 1983.

Bornstein Łychowska, M., *Ten Years Social Policy in Poland, 1918–1928*, Warsaw: Ministry of Labour and Social Welfare, 1928.

Bowers, Brian, *A History of Electric Light and Power*, Stevenage: Peter Peregrinus, 1982.

Brodzicki, Czesław, *Marki koło Warszawy*, Marki: Urząd Miasto Marki, 2002.

Bromke, Adam, *Poland's Politics: Idealism versus Realism*, Cambridge, MA: Harvard University Press, 1967.

Burnley, J., *West Riding Sketches*, Bradford: Hodder and Stoughton, 1875.

Caffyn, L., *Workers' Housing in West Yorkshire 1750–1920*, Royal Commission on the Historical Monuments of England, London: Her Majesty's Stationery Office, 1986.

Cairncross, A., *Home and Foreign Investment, 1870–1913*, Cambridge: Cambridge University Press, 1953.

Carstensen, Fred V., 'Foreign Participation in Russian Economic Life: Notes on British Enterprise, 1865 to 1914', in *Entrepreneurship in Imperial Russia and the Soviet Union*, edited by Gregory Guroff and Fred V. Carstensen, pp. 140–158, Princeton: Princeton University Press, 1983.

Casson, M., 'Entrepreneurship and Business Culture', in *Entrepreneurship, Networks and Modern Business*, edited by J. Brown and M.B. Rose, pp. 30–54, Manchester: Manchester University Press, 1993.

Chapman, Stanley, *Merchant Enterprise in Britain: From the Industrial Revolution to World War I*, New York and Cambridge: Cambridge University Press, 1992.

Clapham, J.H., *The Woollen and Worsted Industries*, London: Methuen and Co, 1907.

Clapham, J.H., *Economic History of Modern Britain*, Vol. 2, Cambridge: Cambridge University Press, 1932.

Clegg, H.A., *The System of Industrial Relations in Great Britain*, Oxford: Basil Blackwell, 1970.

Corrsin, Stephen D., *Warsaw Before the First World War: Poles and Jews in the Third City of the Russian Empire 1880–1914*, New York: Columbia University Press, 1989.

Cottrell, P.L., *British Overseas Investment in the Nineteenth Century*, London: Macmillan, 1975.

Court, W.H.B., *British Economic History 1870–1914*, Cambridge: Cambridge University Press, 1965.

Cudworth, W., *Worstedopolis: a Sketch History of the Town and Trade of Bradford*, Bradford: The Old Bradford Press (originally W. Byles and Sons, 1888) 1997.

Davies, Norman, *God's Playground, A History of Poland Volume II 1795 to the Present*, New York: Columbia University Press, 1982.

Dawson, Coningsby, *It Might Have Happened to You*, London: John Lane The Bodley Head Ltd, 1921.

Dejung, Christof, 'Bridges to the East: European Merchants and Business Practices in India and China', in *Commerce and Culture: Nineteenth-century Business Elites*, edited by Robert Lee, pp. 93–116, Farnham: Ashgate, 2011.

Dewhirst, John, *Room at the Top: The Origins of Bradford City AFC & Bradford (Park Avenue) AFC*, Bradford: Bantamspast, 2015.

Dickie, John, *The British Consul: Heir to the Great Tradition*, London: Hurst and Company, 2007.

Dintenfass, M., *The Decline of Industrial Britain 1870–1980*, London: Routledge, 1992.

Dunin-Wąsowicz, Krzysztof, *Warszawa 1914–1918*, Warsaw: Państwowe Naukowe, 1989.

Dunning, J.H., *Studies in International Investment*, London: Allen and Unwin, 1970.

Dunning, J.H., 'Changes in the Level and Structure of International Production: the Last One Hundred Years', in *The Growth of International Business*, edited by M. Casson, pp. 84–139, Boston: Allen and Unwin, 1983.

Dunning, John H., *The Globalisation of Business: the Challenge of the 1990s*, London: Routledge, 1993.

Dziewulski, Stefan, Henryk Radziszewski, *Warszawa 1913–1915*, Vol. II, Warsaw: Gebethner and Wolff, 1913.

Edelstein, M., *Overseas Investment in the Age of High Imperialism: the United Kingdom, 1850–1914*, New York: Columbia University Press, 1982.

Ellis, Norman, *Towards Little Germany*, Bradford: Low Moor Local History Group, 1997.

Feldman, Wilhelm, *Dzieje polskiej myśli politycznej 1864–1914*, Warsaw: Instytut Badania Najnowszej Historji Polski, 1933.

Firth, Gary, 'Bradford Trade in the Nineteenth Century', in *Victorian Bradford*, edited by D.G. Wright and J.A. Jowitt, pp. 7–33, Bradford: City of Bradford Metropolitan Council, 1982.

Fontaine Maury, Matthew and Mytton Maury, *Manual of Geography: Complete Treatise on Mathematical, Physical, and Political Geography*, Michigan: University Publishing Company, 1880.

Foreman-Peck, James, *A History of the World Economy, International Economic Relations Since 1850*, London: Harvester Wheatsheaf, 1983.

Franaszek, Piotr, 'Poland', in *The Ashgate Companion to the History of Textile Workers, 1650–2000*, edited by Heerma Van Voss, L. Hiemstra-Kuperus and E. Van Nederveen Meerkerk, pp. 397–420, Farnham: Ashgate, 2010.

Friedgut, Theodore H., *Iuzovka and Revolution: Vol. 1, Life and work in Russia's Donbass, 1869–1924*, Princeton: Princeton University Press, 1994.

Gaskell, Elizabeth, *North and South*, London: Chapman and Hall, 1855.

Gerschenkron, A., *Economic Backwardness in Historical Perspective*, Cambridge, MA: Harvard University Press, 1962.

Giles, *Colum and* Ian Goodall, *Yorkshire Textile Mills 1770–1930*, London: H.M.S.O Royal Commission on the Historical Monuments of England, 1992.

Glickman, Rose L., *Russian Factory Women: Workplace and Society 1880–1914*, Berkeley, Los Angeles, London: University of California Press, 1984.

Grzonkowski, Jacek, Wojciech Adalbert Maślarz and Barbara Rzeczycka, *Żyrardów miasto wielu narodów*, Żyrardów: Muzeum Mazowsza Zachodniego, 2006.

Harris, John, *Industrial Espionage and Technology Transfer: Britain and France in the Eighteenth Century*, Aldershot: Ashgate, 1998.

Harvey, A.D., *Collision of Empires: Britain in Three World Wars, 1793–1945*, London: Hambledon Press, 1992.

Holroyd, Abraham, *Saltaire and its Founder*, Bradford: Piroisms Press and Falcon, 1873.

Hulka-Laskowski, Paweł, *Mój Żyrardów: z dziejów polskiego miasta i z życia pisarza*, Warsaw: Czytelnik, 1958.

Ianzhul, Ivan Ivanovic, *Przemysł fabryczny w Krolestwie Polskiem: Studyum ekonomiczne*, Petersburg: Trenke and Fusnot,1887.

Illingworth, T., *A Sixty Years Retrospective of the Bradford Trade Indicative of the Some of the Causes of the Present Depression*, Bradford: privately published, 1882.

James, J., *History of the Worsted Manufacture in England*, London: Longman, Brown, Green, Longmans, and Roberts, 1857.

Jaroszewski, Tadeusz S., *The Book of Warsaw Palaces*, Warsaw: Polish Interpress Agency, 1984.

Jasiński, Roman, *Zmierzch starego świata: wspomniena, 1900–1945*, Krakow, Wydawnictwo Literackie, 2006.

Jedlicki, Jerzy, *Jakiej cywilizacji Polacy potrzebują: studia z dziejów idei i wyobraźni XIX wieku*, Warsaw: Państwowe Wydawn. Nauk, 1988.

Jedlicki, Jerzy, *A Suburb of Europe: Nineteenth-Century Polish Approaches to Western Civilization*, Budapest, New York: Central European University Press, 1999.

Jeremy, D., *Transatlantic industrial revolution: the diffusion of textile technologies between Britain and America, 1790–1830s*, Cambridge, Mass: MIT Press, 1981.

Jeremy, David, 'The International Diffusion of Cotton Manufacturing Technology, 1750–1990s', in *The Fibre that Changed the World, The Cotton Industry in International Perspective, 1600–1990s*, edited by Douglas Farnie and David Jeremy, pp. 85–125, Oxford, New York: Oxford University Press, 2004.

Jones, Geoffrey, *Merchants to Multinationals; British Trading Companies in the Nineteenth and Twentieth Centuries*, Oxford: Oxford University Press, 2000.

Jones, Thomas P., *Journal of the Franklin Institute of the State of Pennsylvania and Mechanic's Register*, Philadelphia: The Franklin Institute, 1839.

Jowitt, J.A., *Model Industrial Communities in Mid-Nineteenth Century Yorkshire*, Bradford: University of Bradford, 1988.

Joyce, Patrick, *Work, Society, Politics; the Culture of the Factory in Later Victorian England*, New Brunswick, New Jersey: Rutgers University Press, 1980.

Keighley, Mark, *Woven with Wisdom and Skill, the History of Bradford Textile Society 1893 to 1993*, Bradford: Wool Record, 1993.

Keighley, M., *Wool City*, Bradford: Wool Publishing, 2007.

Kochanowicz, Jacek, *Backwardness and Modernisation: Poland and Eastern Europe in the 16th–20th Centuries*, Aldershot: Ashgate Publishing Limited, 2006.

Koszutski, Stanisław, *Rozwój przemysł wielkiego w Królestwie Polskiem*, Warsaw: Nakładem Redakcji Gazety Handlowej, 1901.

Koszutski, Stanisław, *Nasz przemysł wielki na początku XX stulecia*, Warsaw: Nakładem Księgarni Naukowej, 1905.

Krąpiec, Mieczysław Albert, *Studia polonijne*, Vol. 21, Lublin: Towarzystwo Naukowe Katolickiego Uniwesytetu Lubelskiego, 2000.

Krzywicki, Ludwik, *Wspomnienia*, Vol. 2, Warsaw: Czytelnik, 1958.

Krzywicki, Ludwik, *Dzieła*, Vol. 4, Warsaw: Państwowe Wydawn. Naukowe, 1958.

Księga adresowa przemysłu fabrycznego w Królestwie Polskim za 1905 r., Warsaw: L. Jeziorański, 1904.

Księga adresowa przemysłu fabrycznego w Królestwie Polskim za 1908 r., Warsaw: L. Jeziorański, 1908.

Kusiński, J., R. Bonisławski and M. Janik, *Księga fabryk Łodzi*, Łódź: Wydawn Jacek Kusiński, 2010.

Landau, Zbigniew, 'The Economic Integration of Poland, 1918–23', in *The Reconstruction of Poland, 1914–23*, edited by Paul Latawski, pp. 144–57, Basingstoke: Macmillan in association with the School of Slavonic and East European Studies, 1992.

Langan, Mary, Bill Schwarz, *Crises in the British State 1880–1930*, London: Hutchinson, 1985.

Lee, Robert, 'Commerce and Culture: A Critical Assessment of the Role of Cultural Factors in Commerce and Trade from c.1750 to the Early Twentieth Century', in *Commerce and Culture: Nineteenth-century Business Elites*, edited by Robert Lee, pp. 1–34, Farnham: Ashgate, 2011.

Le Guillou, Michael, 'Technical Education 1850–1914', in *Where Did we Go Wrong? Industry, Education and Economy of Victorian Britain*, edited by Gordon Roderick and Michael Stephens, pp. 173–84, Lewes: Falmer Press, 1981.

Liberman, Peter, *Does Conquest Pay? The Exploitation of Occupied Industrial Societies*, Princeton: Princeton University Press, 1998.

Lincoln Fitzpatrick, Anne, *The Great Russian Fair: Nizhnii Novgorod 1840–90*, Basingstoke: Macmillan in association with St Antony's College, 1990.

Litten, E., *Promyslennost Rossii w słowach i kartinach*, Łódź, 1897.

Litten, J. Edward, *Die Englische Wollspinnerei der Firma Briggs, Posselt and Co. in Marki bei Warschau*, Warsaw: Alexander Ging, 1896.

Lochner, L.P., *Fritz Kreisler*, London: Rockcliffe, 1950.

Łukasiewicz, J., *Przewrót techniczny w przemyśle Królestwa Polskiego, 1852–1886*, Warsaw: Państwowe Wydawn Naukowe, 1963.

Luxemburg, Rosa, *The Industrial Development of Poland* [*Die Industrielle Entwicklung Polens*, 1898] New York: Campaigner Publications Inc, 1977.

Madouvalos, Ikaros, 'The Entrepreneurial Activity of Dimitrios and Stephanos Manos in Central Europe in the Nineteenth Century', in *Commerce and Culture: Nineteenth-century Business Elites*, edited by Robert Lee, pp. 145–65, Farnham: Ashgate, 2011.

Manteuffel, Tadeusz, *Historia Polski*, Vol. 3, Part 1, Warsaw: Państwowe Wydawn. Naukowe, 1955.

Markiewicz, Tomasz, Tadeusz Władysław Świątek and Krzysztof Wittels, *Polacy z wyboru, rodziny pochodzenia niemieckiego w Warszawie w XIX i XX wieku*, Warsaw: Wydawnictwo Dom Spotkań z Historią 2012.

Mathew, W.M., *Keiller's of Dundee: The Rise of the Marmalade Dynasty 1800–1879*, Dundee: Abertay Historical Society Publication, 1999.

Mathias, Peter, *The First Industrial Nation, An Economic History of Britain 1700–1914*, London: Methuen and Co., 1969.

Maude, Francis Cornwallis, John Walter Sherer, *Memories of the Mutiny*, London: Remington, 1894.

McKay, John P., *Pioneers for Profit Foreign Entrepreneurship and Russian Industrialisation 1880–1914*, London and Chicago: University of Chicago Press, 1970.

McKay, J.P., 'The house of Rothschild (Paris) as a multinational industrial enterprise, 1875–1914', in *Multinational Enterprise in Historical Perspective*, edited by A. Teichova, pp. 74–86, Cambridge: Cambridge University Press, 1986.

Men of the Period: The Records of a Great Country, London: The Biographical Publishing Company, 1897.

Micinska, Magdalena, *Inteligencja na rozdrożach 1864–1918*, Warsaw: Instytut Historii PAN, Wydawnictwo Neriton, 2008.

Miliszkiewicz, Janusz, *Polskie gniazda rodzinne*, Warsaw: ISKRY, 2003.

Missalowa, G., 'Przemysł włókienniczy do 1918 roku', in *Uprzemysłowienie ziem polskich w XIX i XX wieku*, edited by I. Pietrzak-Pawłowska, pp. 219–76, Wrocław: Studia i materialy, 1970.

Molska, Alina, *Pierwsze pokolenie marksistów polskich: Wybór pism i materiałów źrodłowych z lat 1878–1886*, Vol. 2, Warsaw: Ksiażka i Wiedza, 1962.

Morgan, E.V. and W.A. Thomas, *The Stock Exchange: Its History and Functions*, London: Elek Books, 1962.

Morton, C.W., *A History of Rolls-Royce Motor Cars: Volume 1*, London: G.T. Foulis, 1964.

Mosse, W.E., *An Economic History of Russia 1856–1914*, London: I.B. Tauris, 1992.

N. Heydemann and Co, Bradford 1852–1952, Bradford: Company History, 1952.

Owen, Thomas C., *Russian Corporate Capitalism from Peter the Great to Perestroika*, New York: Oxford University Press, 1995.

Oxford Dictionary of National Biography.

Paciorek, Zbigniew, *Marki, dzieja, tradycja, kultura*, Marki: Urząd Miasta, 2004.

Paciorek, Zbigniew, *Rocznik Marecki Tom 1*, Marki: Urząd Miasta Marki, 2014.

Paciorek, Zbigniew and Grzegorza P. Dudzika, *Mareckie zeszyty historyczne*, Marki: Urząd Miasta Marki, 2007.

Parker, James, *Illustrated History of Wibsey, Low Moor*, Bradford: Matthews and Brooks, 1902.

Perkin, Harold, *The Origins of Modern English Society 1780–1880*, London: Routledge and Kegan, Paul, 1969.

Pietrzak-Pawłowska, Irena, *Żyrardów, 1829–1945: praca zbiorowa*, Warsaw: Państwowe Wydawn Nauk, 1980.

Pipes, R., *Russia under the Old Regime*, London: Scribner Book Company, 1974.

Polski Słownik Biograficzny.

Portal, Roger, 'Muscovite Industrialists: the Cotton Sector 1861–1914', in *Russian Economic Development from Peter the Great to Stalin*, edited by W.L. Blackwell, pp. 161–96, New York: New Viewpoints, 1974.

Posselt, William, *Gottfried Posselt 1693–1768, sein Leben, seine Vorfahren und seine Nachkommen*, Munich: privately published, 1926.

Powell, Ellis T., *The Mechanism of the City*, London: King and Son, 1910.

Prestwich, Menna, *Cranfield: Politics and Profits under the Early Stuarts*, Oxford: Clarendon Press, 1966.

Pretty, Dave, 'The Cotton Textile Industry in Russia and the Soviet Union', in *The Ashgate Companion to the History of Textile Workers, 1650–2000*, edited by L. Heerma Van Voss, E. Hiemstra-Kuperus and E. Van Nederveen Meerkerk, pp. 421–48, Farnham: Ashgate, 2010.

Priestley, J.B., *English Journey*, London: William Heinemann, 1934.

Priestley, J.B., *Margin Released*, London: William Heinemann, 1962.

Prus, Bolesław, *The Doll* [*Lalka*, 1887], trans. by David Welsh, Budapest: Central European Classics, 1996.

Przemysł i handel Królestwa Polskiego, Stowarzyszene Techników w Warszawie, Warsaw: Antoni R. Sroka, 1912.

Puś, Wiesław, *Przemysł włókienniczy w Królestwie Polskim w latach 1870–1900*, Łódź: Zeszyty Naukowe Uniwersytetu Łódzkiego, 1976.

Radziszewski, Henryk, 'Przemysłu', in *Opis ziem zamieszkanych przez Polaków: Królestwo Polskie Tom II*, pp. 288–313, Warsaw: J. Sikorski, 1905.

Reymont, Władysław, *The Promised Land* [*Ziemia obiecana*, 1898], trans. by M.H. Dziewicki, New York: Alfred A. Knopf, 1927.

Roberts, Andrew, *Salisbury: Victorian Titan*, London: Phoenix, 2000.

Roberts, John S., *Little Germany*, Scarborough: Bradford Art Galleries and Museums, 1977.

Rocke, Alan J., 'The Theory of Chemical Structure and its Applications', in *The Cambridge History of Science: Volume 5, The Modern Physical and Mathematical Sciences*, edited by Mary Jo Nye, pp. 255–71, Cambridge: Cambridge University Press, 2002.

Rocznik adresowy firm handlowych, przemysłowych i rękodzielniczych, Warsaw: Alexandra Ginsa, 1884.

Rojahn, Jürgen, 'Poland', in *The Formation of Labour Movements, 1870–1914: An International Perspective*, edited by Marcel Van Der Linden and Jürgen Rojahn, pp. 487–521, New York: E.J. Brill, 1990.

Rose, William John, *Poland Old and New*, London: G. Bell and Sons, 1948.

Ruskin, J., *The Crown of Wild Olive: Four lectures of Industry and War (1866)*, London: George Allen, 1900.

Ruuskanen, Leena, *Der Heidelberger Bergfriedhof im Wandel der Zeit*, Heidelberg: Stadtarchivs Heidelberg, 2008.

Rydel, Władysław, *Little Man's Story*, trans. by Adam Truscoe, Melbourne, 1966.

Saul, S.B., *The Myth of the Great Depression, 1873 –1896*, London: Macmillan, 1969.

Sigsworth, E.M., *Black Dyke Mills A History*, Liverpool: Liverpool University Press, 1958.

Sigsworth, E.M. and J.M Blackman, 'The Woollen and Worsted Industries', *The Development of British Industry and Foreign Competition 1875–1914*, edited by Derek Aldcroft, pp. 128–57, London: George Allen and Unwin, 1968.

Słoniowa, Anna, *Sokrates Starynkiewicz*, Warsaw: Państwowe Wydawnictwo Naukowe, 1981.

Smiles, Samuel, *Thrift*, New York: Harper & Bros, 1875.

Smith, S.A., *Workers and Supervisors: St Petersburg 1905–1917 and Shanghai 1895–1927*, Oxford: Oxford University Press, 1993.

Stachura, Peter, *Poland between the Wars, 1918–1939*, Basingstoke: Macmillan, 1998.

Stegner, Tadeusz, *Ewangelicy warszawscy 1815–1918*, Warsaw: Semper, 1993.

Stepniak, S., *The Russian Storm Cloud*, London: Swan Sonnenschein and Co, 1886.

Sunderland, David, *Social Capital, Trust and the Industrial Revolution 1780–1880*, London and New York: Routledge, 2007.

The History of E. Posselt and Co 1858–1958, Bradford: Company History, 1958.

The World's Wool, London, New York: T. Skinner & Company, 1927.

Thomas, Colin, *Dreaming a City – From Wales to the Ukraine*, Ceredigion: Welsh Books Council, 2009.

Thompson, E.P., *The Making of the English Working Class*, New York: Pantheon Books, 1964.

Thompstone, Stuart, 'The Russian Technical Society and British Machinery Imports', in *The Fibre that Changed the World: The Cotton Industry in International Perspective, 1600–1990s*, edited by Douglas Farnie and David Jeremy, pp. 337–64, Oxford: New York, Oxford University Press, 2004.

Tugan-Baranovsky, M.I., *The Russian Factory in the Nineteenth Century*, George Town, Ontario: Richard D. Irwin, 1970.

Tych, F., *Polskie programy socjalistyczne 1878–1918*, Warsaw: Książka i Wiedza, 1975.

Villari, Luigi, *Russia Under the Great Shadow*, London: T. Fisher Unwin, 1905.

Von Schultze-Gävernitz, G., *Volkswirtschaftliche Studien aus Russland*, Leipzig: Duncker & Humblot, 1899.

Weightman, Gavin, *The Industrial Revolutionaries: creators of the Modern World 1776–1914*, London: Atlantic Books, 2007.

Wilkins, Mira, 'Defining a Firm: History and Theory', in *Multinationals: Theory and History*, edited by Peter Hertner and Geoffrey Jones, pp. 80–96, Aldershot: Gower, 1986.

Williams, Ernest Edwin, *Made in Germany*, Brighton: Harvester Press (1896) 1973.

Wilson, John F., *British business history, 1720–1994*, Manchester and New York: Manchester University Press, 1995.

Wilson, John F. and Andrew Thomson, *The Making of Modern Management, British Management in Historical Perspective*, Oxford: Oxford University Press, 2006.

Wojtkowski, Ryszard, *Wykonywa się fotografie*, Warsaw: Miasto Stołeczne Warszawa, 2008.

Wolfe, Humbert, *Now a Stranger*, London: Cassell and Company, 1933.

Wynot, Edward, D., *Warsaw between the World Wars Profile of the Capital City in a Developing Land, 1918–1939*, New York: East European Monographs, 1983.

Yorkshire Textile Directory, and Engineers and Machine Makers' Advertiser, Oldham: John Worrall, 1891.

Żarnowska, Anna, 'Working Family in the Kingdom of Poland at the end of the C19th', in *Polish Population Review 10, Household and Family on the Polish Territories in Historical Perspective*, edited by C Kuklo, pp. 51–75, Warsaw: Polish Demographic Society, 1997.

Żarnowska, Anna, *Workers, Women and Social Change in Poland, 1870–1939*, Aldershot: Ashgate Variorum, 2004.

Zweig, Ferdynand, *Poland between Two Wars: A Critical Study of Social and Economic Change*, London: Secker and Warburg, 1944.

Zwolinski, Krzysztof, *Zakłady Żyrardowskie w latach 1885–1915*, Warsaw: Książka i Wiedza, 1979.

Articles

Abercrombie, Nicholas and Stephen Hill, 'Paternalism and Patronage', *British Journal of Sociology*, 27: 4 (December 1976), pp. 413–29.

Aldcroft, D.H., 'The Entrepreneur and the British Economy, 1870–1914', *Economic History Review*, 17: 1(1964), pp. 113–34.

Brittain, James E., 'The Early Diffusion of Electrical Power Technology, 1870–1920', *Journal of Economic History*, 34 (1974), pp. 108–21.

Busfield, Deirdre, 'Job Definitions and Inequality: the 'unskilled' women workers of the West Riding textile industry 1850 to 1914', *Textile History*, 19 (Spring 1988), pp. 61–82.

Cain, P.J. and A.G. Hopkins, 'Gentlemanly Capitalism and British Expansion Overseas II: New Imperialism, 1850–1945', *Economic History Review*, New Series, 40: 1 (February 1987), pp. 1–26.

Casson, Mark, 'The Organisation and Evolution of Multinational Enterprise: An Information Cost Approach', *Management International Review*, 39 (1999), pp. 77–121.

Chapman, S.D., 'British-Based Investment Groups before 1914', *Economic History Review*, New Series, 38: 2 (May 1985), pp. 230–251.

Coleman, D.C., 'Gentlemen and Players', *Economic History Review*, Series 2, 26 (1973), pp. 92–116.

Cookson, Gillian, 'Family Firms and Business Networks: Textile Engineering in Yorkshire, 1780–1830', *Business History*, 39: 1 (1997), pp. 1–20.

Crago, Laura A., 'The 'Polishness' of Production: Factory Politics and the Reinvention of Working-Class National and Political Identities in Russian Poland's Textile Industry, 1880–1910', *Slavic Review*, 59: 1 (2000), pp. 16–41.

Giffin, Frederick C., 'The Formative Years of the Russian Factory Inspectorate, 1882–1885', *Slavic Review*, 25: 4 (1966), pp. 641–50.

Grosse, Robert, 'International Technology Transfer in Services', *Journal of International Business Studies*, 27: 4 (1996), pp. 781–800.

Haiko, Peter, 'The Industrial City of Berndorf in Lower Austria', *Kwartalnik Architektury i Urbanistyki* (1984), pp. 83–93.

Hobson, J.A., 'The General Election', *Sociological Review* (1910), pp. 105–17.

Jeremy, David J., 'The Enlightened Paternalist in Action: William Hesketh Lever at Port Sunlight before 1914', *Business History*, 1 (1991), pp. 58–81.

Jones, C., 'Great Capitalists and the Direction of British Overseas Investment in the Late-nineteenth Century: the Case of Argentina', *Business History*, 32 (1980), pp. 152–69.

Jones, Geoffrey, 'The Growth and Performance of British Multinational Firms before 1939: The Case of Dunlop', *Economic History Review*, New Series, 37: 1 (February 1984), pp. 35–53.

Jowitt, J.A., 'Textiles and Society in Bradford and Lawrence, USA, 1880–1920', *Bradford Antiquary*, 5 (1991), pp. 3–24.

Kininmonth, Kirsten W., 'The Growth, Development and Management of J. & P. Coats Ltd, c.1890–1960: An Analysis of Strategy and Structure', *Business History*, 48: 4 (October 2006), pp. 551–79.

Kirchner, W., 'Russian Tariffs and Foreign Industries before 1914: The German Entrepreneur's Perspective', *Journal of Economic History*, 41: 2 (June 1981), pp. 361–79.

Kubiak, Janusz and Teresa Szyburska, 'Urbanystka i architektura Żyrardowa – Jej wartosci i problemy konserwatorskie', *Kwartalnik Architektury i Urbanistyki* (1984), pp. 95–111.

Lee, C.H., 'The Service Sector, regional specialisation and economic growth in the Victorian economy', *Journal of Historical Geography*, x (1984), pp. 139–55.

Lillibridge, Robert M., 'Pullman: Town Development in the Era of Eclecticism', *Journal of the Society of Architectural Historians*, 12: 3 (October 1953), pp. 17–22.

Lisle-Williams, M., 'Beyond the market: the survival of family capitalism in English merchant banks', *British Journal of Sociology*, xx (1984), pp. 241–71.

Lougheed, A.L., 'British company formation and the Queensland mining industry, 1886–1890', *Business History*, 25 (1983), pp. 76–82.

Markiewicz-Kozańska, Ewa, 'Rozwój przestrzenny wielkich i dużych zespołów fabryczno-mieszkalnych na terenie Łodzi w drugiej połowie XIX wieku', *Kwartalnik Architektury i Urbanistyki*, (1984), pp. 137–44.

McFarlane, L.A., 'British Investment in Midwestern Farm Mortgages and Land, 1875–1900: a comparison of Iowa and Kansas', *Agricultural History*, 47 (1974), pp. 179–98.

Nenadic, Stana, 'Businessmen, the Urban Middle Classes, and the 'Dominance' of Manufacturers in Nineteenth-Century Britain', *Economic History Review*, New Series, 44: 1 (February 1991), pp. 66–85.

Nicholas, Stephen, 'Agency Contracts, Institutional Modes, and the Transition to Foreign Direct Investment by British Manufacturing Multinationals before 1939', *Journal of Economic History*, 43: 3 (September 1983), pp. 675–86.

Nye, John Vincent, 'The Myth of Free-Trade Britain and Fortress France: Tariffs and Trade in the Nineteenth Century', *Journal of Economic History*, 51: 1 (March 1991), pp. 23–46.

Platt, D.C.M., 'The Role of the British Consular Service in Overseas Trade, 1825–1914', *Economic History Review* (1963), pp. 494–512.

Popławska, I. and S. Muthesius, 'Poland's Manchester: 19th–Century Industrial and Domestic Architecture in Łódź', *Journal of the Society of Architectural Historians*, 45: 2 (1986), pp. 148–60.

Pustoła-Kozłowska E. and E. Wartalska, 'Historia papierni w Jeziornie', *Kwartalnik historii kultury materilnej*, XXXIV, 1 (1986), pp. 61–89.

Robinson, Eric H., 'The Early Diffusion of Steam Power', *Journal of Economic History*, 34: 1, Cambridge University Press (1974), pp. 91–107.

Rollin, A.A., 'Builders of Bradford', *Jewish Historical Society of England*, XVII (1950/51), pp. 45–51.

Schofer, Lawrence, Reviewed work, Irena Pietrzak-Pawlowska, edited, 'Uprzemyslowienie ziem polskich w XIX i XX Wieku', *Journal of Economic History*, 31: 4 (December 1971), pp. 986–8.

Shannon, H.A., 'The Limited Companies of 1866–1883', *Economic History Review*, 4: 3 (October 1933), pp. 290–316.

Szram, Antoni, 'The impact of the investor on the work of the architect taking as examples the activities of factory owners in Łódź – J.K. Poznański and K. Scheibler', *Kwartalnik Architektury i Urbanistyki*, 29 (1984), pp. 281–7.

Thompstone, Stuart, 'Ludwig Knoop the Arkwright of Russia', *Textile History*, 15 (1984), pp. 45–73.

Varley, Martin, 'The Thornton Woollen Mill, St. Petersburg', *History Today*, 44 (December 1994).

Von Laue, Theodore H., 'Factory Inspection under the "Witte System": 1892–1903', *American Slavic and East European Review*, 19: 3 (1960), pp. 347–62.

Wandycz, Piotr, 'Poland on the Map of Europe in 1918', *Polish Review*, 35: 1 (1990), pp. 19–25.

Wartalska, E., 'Fabryka i osada fabryczna w Markach w latach 1883–1945', *Kwartalnik historii kultury materilnej* (1987), pp. 647–71.

Weeks, Theodore R., 'Defending Our Own: Government and the Russian Minority in the Kingdom of Poland, 1905–1914', *Russian Review*, 54 (1995), pp. 539–51.

Wilkins, Mira, 'The Free-Standing Company, 1870–1914: An Important Type of British Foreign Direct Investment', *Economic History Review*, New Series, 41: 2 (May 1988), pp. 259–82.

Williamson, D.G., 'Walther Rathenau and the KRA August 1914–March 1915', *Zeitschrift für Unternehmensgeschichte/Journal of Business History*, 23. Jahrg., H. 2 (1978), pp. 118–36.

Wilson, C., 'The Entrepreneur in the Industrial Revolution', *History*, XLII (1957), pp. 101–17.

Winder, Gordon M., 'Webs of Enterprise 1850–1914: Applying a Broad Definition of FDI', *Annals of the Association of American Geographers*, 96: 4 (December 2006), pp. 788–806.

Wójcicki, A., 'Instytucje fabryczne i społeczne w przemyśle Królestwa Polskiego', *Ekonomista*, XIV (1914).

Żarnowska, Anna, 'Religion and Politics: Polish Workers c. 1900', *Social History*, 16: 3, London (1991), pp. 299–316.

Żarnowska, Anna, 'Education of Working Class Women in the Polish Kingdom (the 19th Century – Beginning of the 20th Century)', *Acta Poloniae Historica*, 74 (1996), pp. 137–59.

Theses

Brearley, Stephen, *The International Wool Market 1840–1913* (PhD thesis, University of Leicester, 2004).

Chadwick, Rosemary E., *Church and People in Bradford and District 1880–1914: The Protestant Churches in an Urban Industrial Environment* (DPhil St Hilda's College, Oxford, 1986).

De la Motte, Robin, *D44: Water Time Case Study – Warsaw, Poland: Research Project supported by the European Commission* (London: University of Greenwich, 2005).

Hutchinson Dawson, A., *The Industrial Geography of Woollen Textile Manufacturing in Poland after 1870* (PhD thesis, University College London, 1966).

Pratt, Michael, *The Influence of the Germans on Bradford* (MA thesis, Margaret MacMillan College, 1971).

Web-published Material

'Cm.Ewangelicko-Augsburski – Szlenkierowie', *Gazeta.pl*, 14 April 2008, accessed at http://fotoforum.gazeta.pl.

Hübner, Piotr, Jan Piskurewicz and Leszek Zasztowt, *The History of the Józef Mianowski Fund* (Warsaw, 1992), accessed at http://www.mianowski.waw.pl/history.htm.

Kawęczyń Brick Company 'K.Granzow' SA, 12–18 Chełmżyńska Street, accessed at http://madein.waw.pl.

Majewski, Jerzy S., 'Dyskretny urok burżuazji przy Królewskiej', *Gazeta.pl*, 11 June 2010, accessed at http://warszawa.gazeta.pl.

Majewski, Jerzy S., 'Do wypadku co koń wyskoczy!', *Warszawa Gazeta.pl*, 28 January 2011, accessed at http://warszawa.gazeta.pl.

Index

Modern Economic and Social History Series

General Editor
Derek H. Aldcroft, University Fellow, Department of Economic and Social History, University of Leicester, UK

Derek H. Aldcroft
Studies in the Interwar European Economy
1 85928 360 8 (1997)

Michael J. Oliver
Whatever Happened to Monetarism?
Economic Policy Making and Social Learning in the United Kingdom Since 1979
1 85928 433 7 (1997)

R. Guerriero Wilson
Disillusionment or New Opportunities?
The Changing Nature of Work in Offices, Glasgow 1880–1914
1 84014 276 6 (1998)

Roger Lloyd-Jones and M.J. Lewis with the assistance of M. Eason
Raleigh and the British Bicycle Industry
An Economic and Business History, 1870–1960
1 85928 457 4 (2000)

Barry Stapleton and James H. Thomas
Gales
A Study in Brewing, Business and Family History
0 7546 0146 3 (2000)

Derek H. Aldcroft and Michael J. Oliver
Trade Unions and the Economy: 1870–2000
1 85928 370 5 (2000)

Ted Wilson
Battles for the Standard
Bimetallism and the Spread of the Gold Standard in the Nineteenth Century
1 85928 436 1 (2000)

Patrick Duffy
The Skilled Compositor, 1850–1914
An Aristocrat Among Working Men
0 7546 0255 9 (2000)

Robert Conlon and John Perkins
Wheels and Deals
The Automotive Industry in Twentieth-Century Australia
0 7546 0405 5 (2001)

Sam Mustafa
Merchants and Migrations
Germans and Americans in Connection, 1776–1835
0 7546 0590 6 (2001)

Bernard Cronin
Technology, Industrial Conflict and the Development of Technical Education in 19th-Century England
0 7546 0313 X (2001)

Andrew Popp
Business Structure, Business Culture and the Industrial District
The Potteries, c. 1850–1914
0 7546 0176 5 (2001)

Scott Kelly
The Myth of Mr Butskell
The Politics of British Economic Policy, 1950–55
0 7546 0604 X (2002)

Michael Ferguson
The Rise of Management Consulting in Britain
0 7546 0561 2 (2002)

Alan Fowler
Lancashire Cotton Operatives and Work, 1900–1950
A Social History of Lancashire Cotton Operatives in the Twentieth Century
0 7546 0116 1 (2003)

John F. Wilson and Andrew Popp (eds)
Industrial Clusters and Regional Business Networks in England, 1750–1970
0 7546 0761 5 (2003)

John Hassan
The Seaside, Health and the Environment in England and Wales since 1800
1 84014 265 0 (2003)

Marshall J. Bastable
Arms and the State
Sir William Armstrong and the Remaking of British Naval Power, 1854–1914
0 7546 3404 3 (2004)

Robin Pearson
Insuring the Industrial Revolution
Fire Insurance in Great Britain, 1700–1850
0 7546 3363 2 (2004)

Andrew Dawson
Lives of the Philadelphia Engineers
Capital, Class and Revolution, 1830–1890
0 7546 3396 9 (2004)

Lawrence Black and Hugh Pemberton (eds)
An Affluent Society?
Britain's Post-War 'Golden Age' Revisited
0 7546 3528 7 (2004)

Joseph Harrison and David Corkill
Spain
A Modern European Economy
0 7546 0145 5 (2004)

Ross E. Catterall and Derek H. Aldcroft (eds)
Exchange Rates and Economic Policy in the 20th Century
1 84014 264 2 (2004)

Armin Grünbacher
Reconstruction and Cold War in Germany
The Kreditanstalt für Wiederaufbau (1948–1961)
0 7546 3806 5 (2004)

Till Geiger
Britain and the Economic Problem of the Cold War
The Political Economy and the Economic Impact of the
British Defence Effort, 1945–1955
0 7546 0287 7 (2004)

Anne Clendinning
Demons of Domesticity
Women and the English Gas Industry, 1889–1939
0 7546 0692 9 (2004)

Timothy Cuff
The Hidden Cost of Economic Development
The Biological Standard of Living in Antebellum Pennsylvania
0 7546 4119 8 (2005)

Julian Greaves
Industrial Reorganization and Government Policy in Interwar Britain
0 7546 0355 5 (2005)

Derek H. Aldcroft
Europe's Third World
The European Periphery in the Interwar Years
0 7546 0599 X (2006)

James P. Huzel
The Popularization of Malthus in Early Nineteenth-Century England
Martineau, Cobbett and the Pauper Press
0 7546 5427 3 (2006)

Richard Perren
Taste, Trade and Technology
The Development of the International Meat Industry since 1840
978 0 7546 3648 9 (2006)

Roger Lloyd-Jones and M.J. Lewis
Alfred Herbert Ltd and the British Machine Tool Industry, 1887–1983
978 0 7546 0523 2 (2006)

Anthony Howe and Simon Morgan (eds)
Rethinking Nineteenth-Century Liberalism
Richard Cobden Bicentenary Essays
978 0 7546 5572 5 (2006)

Espen Moe
Governance, Growth and Global Leadership
The Role of the State in Technological Progress, 1750–2000
978 0 7546 5743 9 (2007)

Peter Scott
Triumph of the South
A Regional Economic History of Early Twentieth Century Britain
978 1 84014 613 4 (2007)

David Turnock
Aspects of Independent Romania's Economic History with Particular Reference to Transition for EU Accession
978 0 7546 5892 4 (2007)

David Oldroyd
Estates, Enterprise and Investment at the Dawn of the Industrial Revolution
Estate Management and Accounting in the North-East of England, c.1700–1780
978 0 7546 3455 3 (2007)

Ralf Roth and Günter Dinhobl (eds)
Across the Borders
Financing the World's Railways in the Nineteenth and Twentieth Centuries
978 0 7546 6029 3 (2008)

Vincent Barnett and Joachim Zweynert (eds)
Economics in Russia
Studies in Intellectual History
978 0 7546 6149 8 (2008)

Raymond E. Dumett (ed.)
Mining Tycoons in the Age of Empire, 1870–1945
Entrepreneurship, High Finance, Politics and Territorial Expansion
978 0 7546 6303 4 (2009)

Peter Dorey
British Conservatism and Trade Unionism, 1945–1964
978 0 7546 6659 2 (2009)

Shigeru Akita and Nicholas J. White (eds)
The International Order of Asia in the 1930s and 1950s
978 0 7546 5341 7 (2010)

Myrddin John Lewis, Roger Lloyd-Jones, Josephine Maltby and Mark David Matthews
Personal Capitalism and Corporate Governance
British Manufacturing in the First Half of the Twentieth Century
978 0 7546 5587 9 (2010)

John Murphy
A Decent Provision
Australian Welfare Policy, 1870 to 1949
978 1 4094 0759 1 (2011)

Robert Lee (ed.)
Commerce and Culture
Nineteenth-Century Business Elites
978 0 7546 6398 0 (2011)

Martin Cohen
The Eclipse of 'Elegant Economy'
The Impact of the Second World War on Attitudes to Personal Finance in Britain
978 1 4094 3972 1 (2012)

Gordon M. Winder
The American Reaper
Harvesting Networks and Technology, 1830–1910
978 1 4094 2461 1 (2012)

Julie Marfany
Land, Proto-Industry and Population in Catalonia, c. 1680–1829
An Alternative Transition to Capitalism?
978 1 4094 4465 7 (2012)

Lucia Coppolaro
The Making of a World Trading Power
The European Economic Community (EEC) in the GATT Kennedy Round Negotiations (1963–67)
978 1 4094 3375 0 (2013)

Ralf Roth and Henry Jacolin (eds)
Eastern European Railways in Transition
Nineteenth to Twenty-first Centuries
978 1 4094 2782 7 (2013)

Manuel Pérez-García
Vicarious Consumers
Trans-National Meetings between the West and East in the Mediterranean World (1730–1808)
978 1 4094 5685 8 (2013)

Manuela Albertone
National Identity and the Agrarian Republic
The Transatlantic Commerce of Ideas between America and France (1750-1830)
978 1 4724 2136 4 (2014)

Leslie Rosenthal
The River Pollution Dilemma in Victorian England
Nuisance Law versus Economic Efficiency
978 1 4094 4182 3 (2014)

Robert E. Forrester
British Mail Steamers to South America, 1851-1965
A History of the Royal Mail Steam Packet Company and Royal Mail Lines
978 1 4724 1661 2 (2014)

John Woodland
Money Pits: British Mining Companies in the Californian and Australian Gold Rushes of the 1850s
978 1 4724 4279 6 (2014)

Ralf Roth and Colin Divall (eds)
From Rail to Road and Back Again?
A Century of Transport Competition and Interdependency
978 1 4094 4046 8 (2015)